Living Atlanta

Living Atlanta

By Clifford M. Kuhn, Harlon E. Joye,

An Oral History

and E. Bernard West

of the City

Foreword by Michael L. Lomax

1914-1948

The Atlanta Historical Society   Atlanta

The University of Georgia Press   Athens and London

© 1990 by the University of Georgia Press Athens, Georgia 30602
Published in conjunction with the Atlanta Historical Society, Atlanta,
Georgia 30305

Designed by Sandra Strother Hudson
Set in 10½ on 14 Century Old Style

The paper in this book meets the guidelines for permanence and durability of
the Committee on Production Guidelines for Book Longevity of the Council on
Library Resources.

Printed in the United States of America

94   93   92   91   90   5   4   3   2   1

Library of Congress
Cataloging in Publication Data

Kuhn, Cliff.
    Living Atlanta : an oral history of the city, 1914–1948 / by Clifford M. Kuhn,
Harlon E. Joye, and E. Bernard West ; foreword by Michael L. Lomax.
        p.   cm.
    "A project of Radio Free Georgia Broadcasting Foundation, Inc."
    Bibliography: p.
    Includes index.
    ISBN 0-8203-1161-8 (alk. paper)
    1. Atlanta (Ga.)—History.   2. Atlanta (Ga.)—Social life and customs.
3. Atlanta (Ga.)—Race relations.   4. Oral history.   I. Joye, Harlon.   II. West,
Bernard.   III. Radio Free Georgia Broadcasting Foundation.   IV. Title.
F294.A857K84   1990
975.8'231—dc20
89-4903
CIP

British Library Cataloging in Publication Data available

Frontispiece: Street scene, 1945. (Atlanta Journal-Constitution)

Contents

Foreword

Atlanta's most notable tradition is that we have no traditions, or at least that we are not bound by traditions and a reverence for the past in the way that some other communities, especially in the South, have been. Like Rhett and Scarlett, we don't look back. Instead, we look forward to the future with courage and confidence and one eye on the cash register. We'll try anything once, and if it works, we'll keep it until something better comes along.

For the most part this attitude has served us well. Much of the social strife that has occurred, and continues to occur, in American cities is a result of an inability to escape the dead hand of the past. We deserve the reputation we enjoy as a progressive, enlightened community, "the city too busy to hate." This reputation has been a key ingredient in the successful promotion of Atlanta to America and the world. In recent periods when other cities struggled just to maintain their ground economically, we have prospered. Is it only because we have an airport and some well-run financial institutions? It's also because we represent an idea, a quintessentially American idea, the pioneer dream that because people are basically good the New Jerusalem will descend if we can only free ourselves from our history. Implicit in this idea is the suggestion that maybe the New Jerusalem is us.

This is why people who call New York the Big Apple call us the Big Hustle. There are some difficulties with this idea we have of ourselves and that we have sold so successfully to the world, like Coca-Cola. No one and no community can altogether escape its history. A simpleminded indifference to the past can be foolish. It can blind us to the real nature of the problems we face, as well as to the solutions. As *Living Atlanta* shows so well, the past is with us today in every part of our common life. Atlanta's unique past is the wellspring from which our future flows.

This book is an effort to capture the spirit and the substance of that history during a time of tremendous growth and change—a time when Atlanta was transformed from a small, regional capital into a giant center of industry, education, finance, commerce and travel. The statistics and the narrative highlights of this period are detailed in other works. In *Living Atlanta*, we listen to the voices of the people who made the history of our city.

These voices speak to us with immediacy and force. They convey the experience of another Atlanta, yet one recognizably related to us. We see ourselves in them.

For black Atlantans in particular the story is a triumph of a people in the face of overwhelming obstacles. For Atlanta was a place where, as in few other places, black Americans were able to build a stable and strong community with strong educational, commercial and religious institutions.

Our legacy of segregation and racial injustice is felt today, and the legacy of racial cooperation as well. Black leaders and white leaders make an effort to maintain a dialogue. They have done so for decades, including the period chronicled in this useful volume.

Atlanta is the home of the civil rights movement, the birthplace of Martin Luther King, Jr. Living in Atlanta is something like living in Athens in the Age of Pericles. One of the great pleasures of living in Atlanta is that we inhabit the same space as historic giants like Andy Young and John Lewis. On the other hand, we give example of the adage that no prophet is without honor except in his own country. Our human nature dictates that we must treat these giants as ordinary human beings when we meet them in the supermarket. Often we forget to pay them the honor we owe them. One of the surprising pleasures of *Living Atlanta* is that it communicates this sense of historic excitement. It communicates with a special conviction and freshness because the homage is paid freely by ordinary citizens of Atlanta who marked the days and doings of the King family when Dr. King was a child.

For decades the black community in Atlanta has been politically active, and, what is more, compared to its counterpart in other cities, the black community has been politically successful. As a result, black political candidates receive white votes and vice versa to a degree that is unusual. This would not happen if Atlanta's black community had not developed a considerable degree of political experience and sophistication during the period described in this volume.

Today our shared political experience and the bonds that unite us as a multiracial community are being tested as never before. We have a decaying infrastructure and apparently lack the resources to repair it. Owing to the power of drugs, the housing projects that began as a noble experiment during the period under consideration now seem almost ungovernable.

We attract huge corporations and the jobs they bring, but we also attract the poor. Today, over 40 percent of the black population that lives in my city lives below the poverty line.

Today in Atlanta, when I see a young black girl in a low-income area, I am probably looking at someone who will be a mother before she is an adult. Badly prepared for pregnancy and motherhood, she will give birth at a public hospital. She will likely give birth to a baby that will be weighed not in pounds but in ounces, a baby that will cost us as a community a thousand dollars a day to keep in an incubator until it is big enough and healthy enough to take home. The baby will go home to an apartment in a housing project where Mother is twelve years old and Grandmother is twenty-five and Great-Grandmother is under fifty. Every likelihood indicates that twelve years later we will pay for this child to start another generation, and the cycle of self-destruction will continue.

When I pass by an inner city playground, I see a young black male full of excitement and energy at five or six. He may likely end his life before he's twenty-five, from homicide or some other misadventure common to the streets of the inner city. If he lives he may very likely spend time in jail. There are more black males behind the bars of our prisons today than there are in our colleges. For the $31,000 it costs to incarcerate them each year, we could send them to the finest schools in the country.

The housing projects that were pioneered in Atlanta in the period chronicled here have been transformed from a brave and noble experiment into a battleground. Local officials are fighting to maintain a measure of control in these places, which, because of the drug trade, have become more alien to many of us than most foreign countries.

To deal with these problems, we must face the future with courage and imagination. Our innovativeness and self-confidence will come to our aid. We must also scrutinize our past, searching it for every vestige of a *useful history* which we can employ in our effort to imagine a humane future for ourselves and our children. *Living Atlanta* will be an enormous asset in that enterprise.

The symbol of Atlanta is the Phoenix. It is not merely hype, hustle and rhetoric. It is a deeply held, shared myth that binds us together as a community. It guides us in our search through our past and as we pioneer the uncharted territory of the future. It assures us our faith will prevail. *Living Atlanta* is a product of that faith.

Michael L. Lomax

Acknowledgments

Many individuals contributed to the completion of this book through its various incarnations. First, of course, are the people who were interviewed for the Living Atlanta radio series, who generously and graciously allowed interviewers equipped with rather foreboding gear into their homes and offices. Needless to say, without their contribution none of this would have been possible. The two grants from the National Endowment for the Humanities provided the funding for the series.

This project has been a typical venture of WRFG Radio, involving board members, staff and volunteers throughout. The WRFG Board of Directors has overseen implementation of both the Living Atlanta radio series and the book. Chris Carroll worked closely with project staff as station manager throughout the original radio series; Melanie Collins served in a similar capacity during most of the book's evolution. Literally hundreds of WRFG volunteers assisted in the production of the series, performing tasks ranging from tape duplication to final mixing. Student interns Steve Pierce, Torgunn Blix, Adina Back and Mark Reynolds also worked long, productive hours on the radio programs.

Once plans for the book got under way, the EMSA Fund and the late Phoebe Franklin Lundeen supplied critical seed money for the project. In the fall of 1985, Marcia Klenbort organized a benefit for the book and kept sagging spirits up. Later that year the University of Georgia Press, through an arrangement with the Atlanta Historical Society, provided an advance that allowed transcribing to get going. The support of the Society and its director, John Ott, has been most appreciated.

With the assistance of Denny Betts and Leslie Graitcer of Southern Bell, in June of 1986 Fulton County Commissioner Michael Lomax hosted a breakfast on behalf of the book with various corporate representatives. The response to that breakfast in fact enabled the *Living Atlanta* book to be completed. Corporate donors included AT&T, the Atlanta *Journal-Constitution*, C&S Bank, Citizens Trust Bank, First Atlanta Bank, Georgia-Pacific, the Georgia Power Company, Rich's and Southern Bell. To their credit, at no time did any of these donors attempt to influence the book's content. One hopes that Atlanta's corporate community will be as generous toward future ventures of this sort.

In addition, the Fulton County Arts Council, the Metropolitan Atlanta Community Foundation, the Lubo Fund, Sandra Heartfield, and numerous other private individuals provided support for the project, as did the Atlanta Historical Society's Franklin Fellowship. The Society, the Martin Luther King Center for Nonviolent Social Change, and the Atlanta-Fulton Public Library also supplied transcribing services.

Tom Gray, Robert Reeves and Linda Carlson proved to be transcribers *extraordinaires,* converting hour upon hour of tape recordings to the printed page. Chris Carroll, Julia Parker, Fay Bellamy and Judy Tedards also transcribed interviews, as did Louise Cook, then with the Martin Luther King Center for Nonviolent Social Change, and Lil Salter of the Atlanta Historical Society. Kent Raymond of TDK Associates was invaluable as a guide through the shoals of microcomputers and word processing. The Atlanta Writers Collective supervised the production of the manuscript, from tape to text.

Historians Tim Crimmins, Franklin Garrett, Lawrence Goodwyn, Alton Hornsby and Dana White served as consultants to the radio series, helping select topics and hone interpretation. Jacquelyn Dowd Hall, Leon Fink and Allen Tullos reviewed individual chapters, while Tim Crimmins and Bob McMath read the entire manuscript, lending their customary insights to the final work.

Special thanks go to Kathie Klein, who for over three years has lived with *Living Atlanta.*

Introduction

This book represents a lot of work by a lot of people over a long period of time. It began in 1977 as the Living Atlanta radio series, a direct outgrowth of the mission of noncommercial community radio station WRFG in Atlanta. On the air since 1973, WRFG—or "Radio Free Georgia"—was founded to highlight the culture and heritage of the Southeast, to provide a broadcast voice for those traditionally denied access to the media, and to offer alternative programming to that carried over the local airwaves.

More specifically, the developers of the Living Atlanta series felt that while the history of prominent local individuals and events—the Coca-Cola story, the *Gone With the Wind* premiere, Martin Luther King, Jr.—was generally well known, much of Atlanta's past was rapidly fading from public consciousness. The tremendous influx of newcomers to the metropolitan area since World War II had contributed to this collective amnesia, as had the wholesale demolition of local historical landmarks. In addition, the sweeping racial transformations of the 1950s and 1960s had tended to blur memories of the era of segregation.

In 1977, WRFG received a grant from the National Endowment for the Humanities to produce a pilot series of five half-hour programs on Atlanta history, under the direction of sociologist and WRFG veteran Harlon Joye. It was Harlon who really was the architect of the Living Atlanta series. George Mitchell, Bernard West and Marcellus Barksdale conducted oral history interviews for the pilot programs, which included two shows on Atlanta's historically black colleges and three depicting work on the railroads, the city's dominant industry of the interwar era.

Combining interviews with narration and topical music from the period, the programs showed that radio was a highly effective medium for presenting history in a substantive and accessible manner, and that oral history—and *aural* history—could make good radio. In fact, one of the programs on railroad workers received an award from the National Federation of Community Broadcasters (NFCB) as one of the top ten community radio programs of 1978.

Along with project staff, several Atlanta historians helped develop program topics for a longer series. A number of considerations informed their choices. It was felt that the period between the world wars constituted a coherent period for the series. The early twentieth century marked the hardening of the system of segregation, as well as the outer reaches of memory for those living in the late 1970s. The World War II years were seen as something of a watershed for Atlanta, in terms of economic development, politics and race relations. The interwar era offered at once a critical historical distance from the subject matter and an opportunity to interview large numbers of people who lived through the period.

Project staff and consultants tried to select subjects that had not by and large been treated in the popular historical literature (though often they had been written about by professional historians) and that had an impact on Atlantans from all walks of life. They sought topics for which the staff could find informants, and ones that would make interesting radio. While focusing, of course, on Atlanta events, developments and individuals, they chose program themes which for the most part extended beyond the city's boundaries. Particular attention was paid to the complexities of life in a segregated city.

In the spring of 1978, the NEH awarded WRFG a major grant to produce forty-five additional programs, again under the direction of Harlon Joye. The front room of Harlon and Barbara Joye's home was soon converted into a production room, historians Bernard West and Cliff Kuhn joined the staff, and administrative procedures and interview questions were developed. For each program, the staff received an outline prepared by a local historian or someone else with expertise in the subject matter. These outlines sketched the key individuals, events and developments of the topic in question, listed potential interviewees, and described "gray" historical areas not fully addressed in the literature.

Equipped with reel-to-reel tape recorders, mike stands, microphones and headphones, interviewers West and Kuhn soon found that conducting oral history interviews for radio was quite different from academic efforts. Attention had to be paid to background noise and mike placement. Interviewers could not cut in as quickly as they might in normal conversation, and had to draw out stories rather than short bits of information. With radio in mind rather than television or film, they could not rely on body language or facial expressions to get a point across, but rather had to get the respondents to paint an audio "picture" for the listeners.

The interviewers located respondents in a variety of ways, relying on a combination of contacts, diligence and sometimes luck. Well-known individuals like educator Benjamin Mays and former police chief Herbert Jenkins were of course easy to track down. For others, the task was more complicated. Original residents of University Homes, one of the nation's first public housing projects, were located through the project tenants association. The City Hall payroll department supplied the name of Hugh McDonald, one of the last surviving firemen who fought the Great Fire of 1917. Workers at the Exposition Cotton Mill—long since torn down—were found through newspaper clippings, city directories and the former barber for the community. Often one person would open the door to a network of people—streetcar men and maids, baseball players, social workers and jazz musicians.

In all, close to two hundred people were interviewed for the series, resulting in some four hundred hours of recordings. Ranging in age from under sixty to one hundred and six, and averaging in their late seventies, the Living Atlanta respondents represented a broad cross section of Atlanta society. They included the famous and the obscure, those who had been interviewed on numerous occasions and those who had never before seen a tape recorder.

The scope and nature of the project meant that most of the respondents were interviewed only once, and by someone of their own race, with West interviewing blacks primarily and Kuhn interviewing whites. Same-race interviews helped the narrators feel a bit more relaxed and comfortable. They also yielded information about "niggers" and "crackers" that might never have been forthcoming had the interviewer been of a different race than the respondent. Given the central series theme of life in a segregated city, same-race interviewing thus proved to be of critical importance.

The interviews pointed out what historian Scott Ellsworth has called "the segregation of memory."[1] On the whole, black respondents—along with some white liberals—tended to be more forthright, open and specific than whites concerning racially sensitive matters. Whites in turn often deflected questions concerning personal responsibility, maintained that race relations during the period were generally harmonious, and displayed a tremendous ignorance of the black community. In other ways, too, the interviews revealed a great deal about how people remembered as well as what they recalled.

Once the interviews were completed, Harlon Joye reviewed and logged all the tapes, marking those sections that might be included in a given program. With the help of numerous WRFG volunteers, these possible interview segments were then dubbed off onto new reels of tape, each reel containing all the material in a given subject area. Thus, one reel for a program on the Ku

Klux Klan might have included material on Klan membership and recruitment; another reel, memories of Klan activities; and so forth.

Harlon Joye then took this dubbed material and—using razor-blade technology—created a "mock-up," a draft version of the interview portions of a proposed program. Given the amount of material available and the considerations of what would make good radio—timing, pacing, sound quality—this task involved a tremendous amount of effort. The mock-up was then submitted to the other staff members for review. Again, the importance of a biracial staff was underscored, as Bernard West in particular often brought to these review sessions a perspective that revealed omissions and oversights, and that thus enhanced both the breadth and the depth of the series.

Once a mock-up had been reviewed, staff members went over program narrations, for the most part written by Harlon Joye, and musical selections. Narrators then recorded the script, copies were made of the original tapes, and mixing and production took place, in the Joyes' home and at the WRFG studios. Throughout it all reverberated the series theme song, "Atlanta Moan" by "Barbecue Bob" Hicks: "Oh, nobody knows Atlanta like I do, nobody knows Atlanta like I do."

A pioneer in the genre of radio oral history, the Living Atlanta series opened in November 1979. One of the two programs on the Atlanta Black Crackers baseball team won an NFCB "Top 10" award in 1981, while other programs were featured over National Public Radio, at history conferences, and in articles and dissertations. Author Studs Terkel hailed Living Atlanta as "an important, exciting project—a truly human portrait of a city of people." Some thirty educational organizations across the country acquired programs, ranging from major universities to the Atlanta Public Schools. The series also spawned WRFG documentaries on the 1906 race riot, the Leo Frank case and other subjects.

From the outset of the radio series, the producers of Living Atlanta had considered a book drawn from the interviews. The reasons for such a work were numerous. Fully 95 percent of the original interview material was never made public, including much as rich as that actually aired, but never broadcast due to time and technical considerations. For the radio series, each program had to stand more or less on its own; it was felt that a book would treat the subject matter in a more comprehensive, systematic fashion, as well as in a more permanent medium, without losing the flavor of the radio series. The age—and subsequent death—of many of those interviewed lent added significance to a Living Atlanta book.

In 1979 and again in 1981, members of the project staff contacted various university press representatives about the book possibility. Despite interest in the project, time and financial considerations precluded any further activity at these times. In the summer of 1984, Cliff Kuhn renewed contact with the University of Georgia Press. A proposal for a Living Atlanta book was developed that fall, and approved by the Press in early 1985.

Funding for the book effort was a major obstacle. None of the three principals in the radio series had an academic job that would allow time for writing. In addition, the original NEH grant did not include funds for transcribing interviews, a prerequisite for completion of the book. A grant from the EMSA Fund, a benefit organized by Marcia Klenbort, and an advance made possible through an arrangement with the Atlanta Historical Society got the project rolling. Corporate, government, foundation and private contributions all played a role in bringing the book to fruition.

Cliff Kuhn spearheaded fund-raising efforts and oversaw the dubbing of tapes onto cassettes and the transcription of nearly six thousand pages of transcripts. He also was the principal author of the book—reviewing, arranging and editing transcripts, conducting historical research, locating photographs, and writing the drafts of the chapters. Harlon Joye and Bernard West reviewed the manuscript and the photographs, in a manner not unlike the review sessions for the radio series. Again, the presence of a biracial team proved critical in sharpening analysis and overcoming historical myopia.

Drawing substantially from the organization of the radio series, the book provides a narrative history of life in Atlanta between the world wars. The first and last of the book's eleven chapters provide snapshots of Atlanta during World War I and World War II respectively, while the other chapters are arranged topically, treating neighborhoods, transportation, commerce, education, the city's underside, the Depression and the New Deal, health and religion, leisure, and politics. Oral history excerpts are woven into, rather than separated from, the narrative text.

Photographs reflecting and complementing the themes developed in the book accompany the text. In addition, scattered throughout the book are thirteen "profiles," longer excerpts of interviews with people that the staff found especially informative and interesting. The individuals profiled serve to illuminate and personalize the broader themes discussed nearby in the text.

The staff made a number of decisions concerning *how* the oral history interview excerpts appeared in the book. For instance, the quick cuts often used in radio as a rule did not work in print; consequently, the oral history extracts in the book tended to be longer. In order to convey the flavor of the respondents' speech (something which radio of course did extremely well), transcribers were instructed to replicate the spoken word as accurately as possible, using punctuation creatively but not editing syntax or grammar. The only exceptions were verbal tics (such as "you know"), which transcribers left out after noting a few times, and the dropped endings of words. Because of the way dialect has often been misrepresented, all word endings ("doing," for instance, instead of "doin'") were maintained. To further capture the immediacy of the spoken word, the present tense is used with interview excerpts throughout the book ("Mr. Brown relates," for example).

Similar concerns informed the editing of transcripts. Transcripts were only amended to make the text flow easier, not to correct grammar or syntax. From time to time, two different segments of a respondent's interview were combined, when it was decided that the combination read better or more thoroughly covered a subject than the individual segments alone. As much as could be determined, at no time was the meaning of what was originally said altered or taken out of context. As there were so many voices included in the text, individual quotes were not footnoted. Anyone who wishes to personally inspect the interviews may consult the Living Atlanta tapes, logs, cassettes, transcripts and disks deposited at the Atlanta Historical Society.

An attempt was made to check conflicting oral accounts with other sources, to make sure everything mentioned fell within the time framework of the book, and to eliminate hyperbolic remarks or obvious misstatements of fact from the text. In so doing, the authors paid attention to the specificity of what was said in any given interview as well as the degree to which other interviews confirmed and reiterated what was stated. For instance, oral interviews revealed the presence of an informal curfew whereby a black person stopped by the police on the street late at night had to produce a work card from his employer verifying that he or she had a "good reason" to be out. While this practice does not appear in the historical literature, it was described again and again by police officers, blues musicians, hotel workers and others, and is included in the book.

There no doubt are occasions in *Living Atlanta* where the memory of the respondents is subject to question, a reflection of the authors' belief that *how* as well as *what* people remember has a significance of its own. *Living Atlanta* is at once something of a folk history and a history of the folk.

Concerning content, the book was intended to be a corrective to much of the historical literature on Atlanta, reflecting as much as possible all walks of life, not primarily the white elite. As with the radio series, its central subtheme is the complexity of life in a segregated city—how segregation affected and in many ways crippled both black and white Atlantans, the interlocking community institutions developed amidst segregation, the losses as well as the gains accompanying the end of segregation, and the changes taking place in both the white and black communities during the seemingly static era of segregation, changes which would anticipate and inform the great transformations of the 1950s and 1960s. The book tends to focus on public life rather than the private sphere, and in general provides an overall impression of the period rather than detailing specific decisions, individuals and events.

Accordingly, *Living Atlanta* tells more about the housing in working-class sections of the city than in Buckhead or Ansley Park, more about the view from the bandstand at the Piedmont Driving Club than at the dinner tables, more about work on the railroads and streetcars than in the corporate boardrooms, more about grass-roots politics than Atlanta's community power structure. There are other things that the book does not really address: the life of children or older people during the period, consumer culture, the building trades, fraternal orders, or sexuality, to name a few. *Living Atlanta* is but one effort to document and present Atlanta's unwritten past; we encourage others to get in there and dig, before it's too late.

The voices heard in this book bring to life a time when the foundations of today's Atlanta were being laid, a period rapidly disappearing from public consciousness. Through *Living Atlanta*'s democratic emphasis on Atlanta's diverse heritage, we hope to help bring together groups that historically have been splintered. Only through an exploration of our past in all of its dimensions can we mature psychologically as a people.

Clifford M. Kuhn

Living Atlanta

Chapter One

World War I

"You're going back a long way when you go back to 1918," states Atlanta University professor E. A. Jones. And, indeed, the Atlanta of the World War I era is barely recognizable today. "It was a small city," nostalgically recalls Coca-Cola executive Hunter Bell. "All the department stores were locally owned at the time. Banks had presidents who knew all the customers. They were the days when they kind of looked you in the eye and decided whether you were worth the loan. It was a nice place to live in, a delight. I'm glad I lived in that era."

By today's standards, Atlanta was quite a small place. The city limits extended only to Morningside on the north and the Federal Penitentiary on the south. Buckhead, Buford Highway and much of Cascade Heights did not become part of Atlanta until 1952. As teacher Evelyn Witherspoon states, at the beginning of the period "there was almost no housing beyond Tenth Street." "Virtually all the area south of Oglethorpe Avenue and west of Ashby Street was woods and fields," adds Georgia Power Company engineer Roy Harwell. "It's not like it is now," exclaims chauffeur L. D. Keith, "northwest, southwest, northeast and the like, and the distance we have to travel now. I mean, the districts were close together. Everybody was living together."

At the turn of the century, the city's population was only 89,000, about 40 percent black. By 1910, the number of Atlantans had soared to 150,000, climbing to 200,000 in 1920. Many of these newcomers hailed from the hardscrabble farms of the rural South, fleeing falling crop prices, sharecropping and tenant farming, washed-out land, and the boll weevil. Typical of those who left the country was domestic worker Lula Daugherty, who came to town in 1920: "We was farmers and the boll weevils got there and you couldn't make anything. So my husband come up here and went to work at the Atlanta Paper Company. And he sent back for me and I come up here."

The same refrain was echoed time and again: "My aunt wanted me to come up here and live with her and work, because we wasn't making anything on the

Street scene, ca. 1917. (Courtesy Atlanta Historical Society)

farm. My father raised food for us to eat but at the end of the year you had nothing." "We farmed. We couldn't get along. I just quit and came to Atlanta." "I didn't think I could stay down there and work, and I decided I'd come to Atlanta." "I was like any other country boy, I wanted to go to the big town."

Despite Atlanta's efforts to become the foremost metropolis of the South, its size, surroundings and the country roots of many of its people gave the city a decidedly rural flavor throughout the period. "My grandfather had horses," remembers teacher Estelle Clemmons, who grew up near the present site of Morris Brown College, "and as a little girl you could just hear the hooves of the horses clopping down the street. And to me as a little girl they made sort of a musical sound."

"Back in those young days it was country in Atlanta," recounts musician Rosa Lee Carson of the Cabbagetown neighborhood. "It sure was. Why, you could even raise a cow out there in your yard, and we did have chickens for a long time. And Mama, she'd have her a big garden out there in the backyard and we'd raise okra and corn and Irish potatoes, tomatoes, onions—good old eats, you know, good old eats."

Even after people migrated to town, they often lived in a setting that was "really very primitive," in the words of schoolteacher Evelyn Witherspoon. "There was outdoor plumbing. We used oil lamps and most people had a wash-basin and pitcher and maybe a nice big washtub to take your bath in Saturday night. We cooked with a wood stove. I doubt you would find that in the back-woods these days."

"We didn't have electricity," recalls factory worker and faith healer Ardell Henry. "We didn't have gas. We didn't have nothing like that. We used fire-places, wood heaters and stuff like that. Some of the houses they lived in back in them days you could look through the cracks in the floor. You could look through the floors in the house and see the chickens walking around under the house, find hens' nests full of eggs laying up under the pillars of the house under there. I've slept in houses myself that—now, this sounds like a false story but it's true—I laid in the bed at night and you could see the stars at night through those old wood shingles. And the walls, most of them wasn't sealed. Some of them was plastered, some had old sealing, and some of them wasn't even sealed at all—just old two-by-fours running along the walls."

"Of course, there were some who had nice bathrooms and good toilets," relates teacher Ruth Reese, "but where we lived, on Fraser Street [in the Summerhill neighborhood], they didn't have that. You had to go out to the out-house, had a big old tub that the effusions from your body ran [into], and about once a week the citizens would get a big old tub to empty the slop in. And sometimes when they come down, the place would stink so bad." "The rest room was on the outside and the water was on the outside," adds Lula Daugherty. "Wasn't any running water in the kitchen. You had to go outdoors and get it, in the yard. That's how we got water. And we washed our dishes and throwed the water out in the yard. That's just the way we would live."

"The streets wasn't all paved," relates Ardell Henry. "They had what they called Belgian block in most of them, and brick and stuff like that. That's the way the street was. About the only way they had to travel most of the time, back in the real old days, was mules and wagons."

To meet the demand of people in the city as well as farmers throughout the region, itinerant horse and mule traders came to town every year. Textile worker and city employee Alec Dennis recalls: "They was Irish horse traders, not gypsies, but they traveled like gypsies. And they camped on both sides of Bankhead. They'd winter right there at Bankhead and Ashby, and they'd trade. There'd be, I guess, two hundred tents there. Of course, there was a lot of horses and mules sold back then, and anybody that wanted a horse, they'd get them."

Draymen, transfer truck drivers, and other Atlantans all used horses or mules in their work. "Once a week," remembers Laura Belle Keith of the Summerhill neighborhood, "the men on the wagons would come and collect the material that had accumulated through the week—we had to use an outside toilet—and then we would have sanitary conditions." "At that time most all the homes was heated with coal," adds E. B. Baynes, "and they had what you call a soft coal and a hard coal. And they would peddle the coal off of a wagon. A mule-driven wagon would drive around, and they had usually a colored man driving, and he would sing out that he was the hard jelly coal man, and people would come and purchase the coal. But they had a world of those wagons."

"The iceman would come around with a horse and wagon," recalls Evelyn Witherspoon, "and he would cry out, 'Iceman!' And the mother would send the child to the door and the child would shout out, 'Iceman, Mama wants a nickel's worth of ice.' And Mama would get the dishpan. A little later we got iceboxes, not mechanical refrigerators. I got my first mechanical refrigerator about 1932, I think it was.

"The vegetable vendors came around with fruits and vegetables. And the chicken man would bring bunches of chickens with their legs tied together, and cry out, 'Chickens, chickens!' And there would be a man come around to pick up bottles, bones and rags. You had the scissor grinder come along and grind, sharpen anything, scissors or knives."

Horsedrawn delivery truck. (Special Collections, Georgia State University)

Horsedrawn wagons. (Courtesy Atlanta Historical Society)

"There was not a single automobile on the campus until the second year I was there," exclaims Hunter Bell, who came to Emory University's recently established Atlanta campus in 1919. "And then there was one. There were three dormitories. Before the days of pavement one of the chief accomplishments was to get up a steep muddy bank in order to get to the dining hall. We were really pioneers."

In 1916, there were barely six thousand automobiles registered in all of Fulton County.[1] Motor vehicles had only just started to be used for city services. "Right after I came they got the automobile ambulances," relates Durise Hanson, who entered Grady Hospital's nursing program in 1918. "And, oh my goodness, that was quite a thing for us, and we'd slip away and go for an ambulance drive."

For the most part the Police and Fire Departments were still not motorized either. "The police officers in the neighborhoods rode horses in the daytime and bicycles at night," recalls jeweler Irwin Shields. "When I went to work on January the eleventh, 19-and-28," adds policeman Sanders Ivey, "they had just recently done away with the bicycles."

Atlanta policemen of the period also used a network of "lock boxes" around town to detain suspected criminals. "Well, it kind of looked like a telephone booth in a hexagon shape," relates officer J. T. Bowen, "made out of ornamental iron. And you'd put your prisoner in it and lock him up until the patrol wagon come to pick them up. But those was out of existence somewhere in the early twenties."

"I very well recall," relates E. B. Baynes, "that Number Six Fire Station up there on Boulevard had horse-drawn fire-fighting vehicles then. I think in some locations they were beginning to use the ones that were motivated by gasoline engines. But I very well recall that when they used the horses it was quite a fascinating place for a young boy to go and see.

"Oh, it was interesting. When they received the alarm they had a big bell and it bonged. And when it did, it alerted those horses, and if they were lying down or munching hay or whatnot, right away they were eager to go. They stood still, and they had a contraption that dropped the harness down over their bodies. And the firemen then led the horses out of the stalls and backed them up to the wagon and fastened the harness to the wagon, and they were gone in, it looked like, a couple of minutes from the time that alarm come in."

"Yes, they had the horse-drawn wagons and horse-drawn engines," adds fire fighter Hugh McDonald. "They had steam engines drawn by horses. They had the engine loaded with the coal, and the kindling back in the back, and every

Horsedrawn fire wagon. (Courtesy Atlanta Historical Society)

time you'd go to a fire they'd have to set that off, you see, to get up steam before they could pump water. And when they pumped at a fire, they had to have a supply of wagons carrying coal."

Coal- and wood-burning stoves combined with the hundreds of steam engines that passed through Atlanta every day to create high level air pollution. "Atlanta was the dirtiest city," recalls Durise Hanson. "We used to see the trains coming up and spouting out all that smoke and dirt. And the chimneys were coal dust coming up and dirt coming out. Atlanta was a dirty, dirty city. And I was just dirty all the time. I just didn't seem to know how to keep myself clean, my face clean especially. I wanted to go back home so bad, where I could be clean."

Atlantans had a hard time keeping cool, too. "Well, nobody had air conditioning then," explains businessman Duncan Peek. "We suffered through the heat and all. But really not. We used to improvise air conditioning. You could build a box in front of a window and put excelsior in there, and take a pipe and punch little pinholes in it and let the water spray through there, and take a fan in back of it and push the air. And that was great air conditioning." It was only in the late 1920s, however, that mechanical air conditioning was introduced, first in Rich's and Davison's department stores, then in the leading movie theaters.

Department stores and movie theaters, like all aspects of life in Atlanta, were strictly segregated. "I passed through a period in Atlanta which might be rightfully labeled the dark days of bondage," declares Reverend William Holmes Borders, pastor of the Wheat Street Baptist Church. "Absolutely everything here was segregated—the schools, the busses, the trains, the courthouse, the City Hall, the cemetery, the . . . everything." "Everything was separate, of course," adds Warren Cochrane, director of the Butler Street YMCA, "separate but certainly not equal." And, indeed, the color line was the Great Divide in Atlanta throughout the period between the world wars.

The late nineteenth century saw an increase in lynchings and the rise of formal segregation laws known as "Jim Crow," laws upheld by the United States Supreme Court. A wave of racially linked violent episodes took place in the early twentieth century, culminating in the Atlanta Race Riot of 1906, which left dozens killed or wounded. By the World War I era, black Atlantans were thoroughly relegated to second-class citizenship.[2]

Black residents were legally excluded from voting in the city and state Democratic Party primaries, where it really counted. Black schoolchildren received only a fraction of the funds allocated to their white counterparts. Black doctors could not practice at Grady Hospital, the city's only charity institution. Until the 1920s, black Atlantans could not visit a single park in the city. Throughout the period between the world wars, there were no black judges or jurors, no black police or fire fighters. Access to other jobs was also extremely restricted. "They had to take substandard jobs," relates Warren Cochrane. "Even trained college graduates took jobs as porters and baggage handlers. And we couldn't do a whole lot about it."

On streetcars, in waiting rooms, at the train stations, in restaurants and at City Hall, the signs read "White" and "Colored." "In all the buildings downtown," relates physician Homer Nash, "one elevator was for Negroes, freight and baggage. The others—all of them—were for white people. If you had to go to the courthouse or had an appointment in one of those tall buildings you've got to stay down here and wait till that Negro elevator came down. When it did, those white patrons didn't pay no attention. They rushed in there and you could hardly get in. Whatever one come down, they grabbed it. But don't you go over there in those that they had."

Drinking fountains and bathrooms were symbols of intimate relationships, and therefore among the places where segregation customs and codes were the tightest. Other areas that suggested "social equality" were also strictly regulated. "Of course, eating downtown was out of the question," recounts nurse Ruby Baker.[3] "You had to either come back to Mitchell Street or go to Decatur Street or Auburn Avenue."

Extending eastward from downtown, Auburn Avenue was the social, commercial, and entertainment heart and soul of black Atlanta. Reportedly dubbed "Sweet Auburn" by black community leader John Wesley Dobbs, Auburn Avenue had a reputation that extended far beyond the city's boundaries. "It was one of the inspirations of Negroes who came to Atlanta," states Dr. Homer Nash, who opened his practice on Auburn in 1910. "And if you didn't come down Auburn Avenue, you hadn't been to Atlanta if you were black. You had not been to Atlanta." "Auburn Avenue was talked about town," echoes Horace Sinclair, who began barbering on Auburn after World War I. "Then, you could go to other cities and people would ask you, 'You live in Atlanta, what about Auburn Avenue? You ever been on Auburn?' And it was tagged as being the place to go."

Auburn Avenue's prominence as a black commercial district increased with the hardening of segregation at the turn of the century. In addition to modest shops and storefronts, larger structures began to mark the street—the Rucker Building, erected in 1904, the Odd Fellows Building, built in 1912, and the Herndon Building, constructed in 1924.

Union Station, 1940s. (Atlanta University Collection, Woodruff Library, Atlanta University Center)

The cluster of black businesses on Auburn provided a buffer as well as a change of pace from many of the hardships and humiliations of everyday life in a segregated society. For as much as the actual Jim Crow laws, it was the etiquette of race relations during the period, the "daily insults and high humiliations under the segregated system," in the words of E. A. Jones, that upset black Atlantans.[4] For instance, whites rarely used polite titles with reference to black citizens. "They could call him 'Doctor' and they could call him 'Reverend,'" states Morehouse College president Benjamin Mays, "but not 'Mr.' 'Mr.' and 'Mrs.' and 'Miss' were signs of social equality. They didn't call you that."

In other ways, too, whites showed disrespect for black Atlantans. "For years my husband was news editor for WSB radio," relates white liberal Eliza Paschall, "but before that he was a reporter for the *Journal*. I remember so well his description of the first time that he had ever really thought about race relations. When he went out on the police beat, as they all started out in those days, he phoned the paper and said, 'We've got three murders.' 'Wow, where are they?' So he gave the addresses, and all of a sudden the man said, 'They all niggers?' And Walter said, well, he really didn't know, but did that make any difference? They were all murders. And the man said, 'Look, anytime there's this address or this section of town, just don't bother us. That's not news.'"

One murder that *did* make news was the celebrated slaying of factory girl Mary Phagan in 1913. Her Jewish employer, Leo Frank, was accused of the murder.[5] Amid a highly charged atmosphere marked by a sensationalist press and virulent anti-Semitism, Frank was found guilty. "There was no possibility of him not being found guilty," declares salesman Clarence Feibelman, then a high school student. "There were mobs outside of the courthouse. It was hot, it was the summertime. And the mobs outside were hollering, 'Kill the Jew!' and 'Lynch the Jew!' and all that sort of stuff. And I'd be on the streetcar and sometimes I'd get off and walk past there, and it was just harrowing to hear those people. It made your blood run cold."

In 1915 vigilantes took Leo Frank from jail and lynched him. The Frank case had many far-reaching consequences. Country musician Fiddlin' John Carson's song "The Ballad of Mary Phagan" became a regional classic. Atlanta's Jewish community was profoundly affected for decades. The case helped bring about changes in the legal system concerning the right of a defendant to a fair trial. To this day, it is one of the episodes in the city's history most vividly remembered by older Atlantans. The Frank case also helped spawn two national organizations—the Anti-Defamation League of B'nai Brith and the revived Ku Klux Klan, headquartered in Atlanta.

Strikers from the Fulton Bag and Cotton Mills, 1914. (Special Collections, Georgia State University)

"Oh, there was people all over this city in the Ku Klux," states Alec Dennis, who did *not* belong. "County and state, too, but more in Atlanta than anywheres else that I knowed of." During the early 1920s the Ku Klux Klan became a major force in local, state and even national politics.[6] In Atlanta as elsewhere, the Klan targeted radicals, Jews, aliens, Roman Catholics, labor organizers and suspected violators of Victorian moral standards, as well as members of the black community.

Along with anti-Semitism, class tensions contributed to the uproar surrounding the Frank case. In the days before minimum-wage laws and effective child-labor legislation, work for many Atlantans was marked by "those long hours and that low pay," in the words of maid Alice Adams. "I was fourteen and a half when I went to work," recalls textile worker Katie Lovins, "and I went to work at night and I worked twelve hours at night. And of course the day hands got an hour for dinner, or forty-five minutes, you might say, but the night hands didn't. They had to work from six to six."

Much of the labor force remained unorganized, due in part to the tremendous influx of people into the city, as well as often intense employer resistance. As Alec Dennis remembers, the Exposition Cotton Mill once used an ingenious method to rebuff a union drive: "That was about 1917. They was trying to organize the mills here and down in Columbus, Georgia. A fellow come here and he just about had them all joining the union. But at that time, they put that moving picture show there in that boarding house. And they'd give them free tickets to go to that show. You'd go in that office. 'How many tickets do you want?' And they'd go in that moving picture show. Well, it would keep people from going to the union meetings at night."

Yet there did exist major pockets of trade union strength, in the printing trades, on the railroads and elsewhere. Atlanta's streetcar men staged two major strikes during the World War I era. "They had meetings at different homes," recalls conductor I. H. Mehaffey, "and talked about the union and how it would be favorable. Of course, the men that was trying to organize it had had experience in organizing other unions. We had one man here especially that was pretty well versed in labor movements and all, Mr. Hardy Teat [of the Brotherhood of Locomotive Firemen]. There had been a lot of discussion, and several men were fired for meeting." "The company would refuse to recognize them," adds motorman H. E. James, "and they went out on strike."

Seeking union recognition and improvements in working conditions, hundreds of streetcar men walked off their jobs in October 1916, triggering what was perhaps Atlanta's most tumultuous strike ever. Reflecting their visibility and position in Atlanta's working-class neighborhoods, the striking streetcar

*Union commissary established during Fulton Bag Strike. (Special
Collections, Georgia State University)*

Labor Day float, 1921. (Special Collections, Georgia State University)

men received considerable popular backing. "Well, they had a lot of support, they had right smart support," recalls conductor T. Ross Couch. "Other working people came forward, you know."

Some strikers and their supporters operated jitneys, private automobiles conveying passengers, along the regular streetcar routes during the strike. The bane of the street railway company, jitneys existed in Atlanta from 1915 until they were banned in 1925. E. B. Baynes explains the system: "They were usually Model T Ford touring cars and there were five passengers, three in the back and two in the front seat. And they had a top that could be let back. Anybody that had an automobile, if you wanted to put it into the jitney service you just let it out on the street and put you a sign on the front of it for Fort Gordon or West End or College Park or wherever you wanted to drive it. And you drove it up and down the street and picked up fares and took them to where you was going, and they gave you a nickel. There wasn't too many regulations and things like that back then."

"A lot of jitneys were running during the strike," recalls I. H. Mehaffey, who did *not* walk out. "They'd go out and try to get ahead of the streetcars. And all of them were pretty good automobiles, they could run faster than we could. It was quite confusing to us to have an automobile to run in front of you and pick up your passengers. When you had been used to having a good load, why it would make the trip pretty lean sometimes." Adds Alec Dennis, "They'd all crawl on the jitneys, in nearly every section of Atlanta. Now, you might get out in Druid Hills and it would be a few there that would ride the trolley to town, but people didn't want to ride the trolleys. Women and all would ride a jitney bus."

The strike was marked by violence, including a dynamiting wave. "There was some shenanigans from both sides," recalls motorman Lloyd Adair. "There was a school on English Avenue, a streetcar came up through there and they opened up and shot all the windows out of it and everything, and they jumped off and run and left it. But there wasn't nobody there when the police got there, so they couldn't find out who did it.

"There was funny things done. They accused the union men of dynamiting their streetcars, but sometimes they knowed there was something a-going on down there. At least I was told there was. One old streetcar man that didn't come out on the '16 strike told me, he said, 'I thought the union people was dynamiting. But,' he said, 'the supervisor told me, said, You wait right here, we think there's some dynamite down there and we're going to check. And they went down there and found it, brought it back, toting it out, and said, Yep,

we found it.' This old fellow told me, 'Now, the union didn't put that dynamite there.' He thought the company was doing their part of it, to try to get the public off the union."

Dozens of suspected union members were fired during the strike, including motorman A. L. Nelson: "I had just had a spell of typhoid fever and I didn't feel like I was ready to give up my job with me owing doctor's bills and nurse bills. I didn't strike. I was called to the office of Mr. Leach, my superintendent, and he fired me. And I went down to a fellow that run the little store there where a lot of them ate, asked him how much I owed him. He said, 'What do you want to pay now for?' I said, 'I was fired.' He said, 'No.' I said, 'Yessir.' He said, 'I'll see about it.' And he went up there and talked to Mr. Leach and come back and told me to go back up there and get my job.

"I went back and he said, 'Did you ever sign up to go in the union?' I said, 'I told you that a while ago, I have never signed up.' He said, 'Did any of them ever ask you?' I said, 'Well, they may have asked me, but I never signed up to go in no union.' He said, 'Well, go on back and get your job.'"

Union leaders like T. Ross Couch's brother, J. Allen—later an Atlanta city councilman—were singled out even more: "He was one of the organizers and they made it rough on him, they'd lock him up every opportunity they'd get. He was discharged from the company. Here in Atlanta they wouldn't give him a job, so he went to Akron, Ohio, worked up there in a rubber factory."

As I. H. Mehaffey notes, the availability of labor was a key factor in breaking the 1916 strike: "It was about half of the men, I guess, that come down, and the other half stayed on. And they immediately started hiring other men to fill in the vacancies. It wasn't long before we had a full schedule out on the routes." "They just went out here in these country towns," adds H. E. James, "and just got these people out of the country, from Gwinnett and Paulding and Clayton and all these surrounding counties, and brought them in here."

By the end of the year the system was practically back to normal. While the 1916 strike failed, there were some important consequences. In its aftermath, railroad engineer Arthur Corrie ran a strong mayoral campaign against Coca-Cola magnate Asa Candler, head of a citizens' law and order committee during the strike. James L. Key, later four-time mayor of Atlanta, gained considerable political mileage from his role as the strikers' attorney. And the momentum toward unionization continued, assisted by the outbreak of World War I, as Lloyd Adair explains: "In July 1918, living conditions was bad. The war drove prices of everything high but still wages hadn't gone up. Men began to talk union pretty heavy. And the superintendents was strictly opposed to it, so they

Streetcar men. (Courtesy Atlanta Historical Society)

undertook to organize a company union, meeting up in one of them old lofts
down there at Moore and Decatur streets. We went in the barn, and they'd left
orders for you to go there, going to organize a company union.

"Most of the men wasn't in favor of a company union. Somebody spoke up
and said, 'Well now, the charter, Local No. 732's charter of 1916, is still in
Atlanta,' and told who had it and who was secretary. And somebody suggested
to send and get him. And all of us joined the union at one time. And the next
day they sent the men that worked at night down, and they joined it.

"We had a strike. It was for an increase in wages, is all it was, we had to
have an increase in wages. And it was a safer bet to go out while the war was
still going on than it was after the men come back. And finally they agreed to
arbitrate it. I was making twenty-two cents an hour and it went to forty cents
an hour. Well, that was a pretty good raise, but the price of everything had
gone up."

After National War Labor Board hearings, on January 1, 1919, the company
signed a contract with Local No. 732, reinstating some of the men who had
been discharged and improving various working conditions. The agreement
also marked a turnaround in the attitude of company president Preston S. Arkwright. Prior to the 1916 strike, according to T. Ross Couch, "He was hard set
against it. And after recognizing it and seeing what it was, he was very, very
cordial."

"In 1921," recalls H. E. James, "the Amalgamated Association of Street and
Electric Employees of America had their International convention in Atlanta.
And when the delegation that came in here from headquarters got out of the
gate down there at the Terminal Station, the Georgia Power Company band
was there, had the biggest drum in the world at that time. And Brother Edward
McMurrah from Chicago said, 'Gee, begolly! Arkwright sent this band down
to greet us. Had a bunch of sheriffs and everything the last time I come here,
trying to run me out. Well, I never would have believed it.'"

Everybody knows about the fires that burned down San Francisco and
Chicago. Atlanta suffered *two* devastating fires, the more famous of course
when General Sherman leveled the city during the Civil War. The Great Fire of
May 21, 1917, was even more destructive. Starting around noon near Auburn
Avenue, the blaze continued up Boulevard and crossed Ponce de Leon before
it was finally stopped. It destroyed seventy-three square blocks, left some
10,000 people homeless and caused millions of dollars of damage.[7]

"Gosh, I'll never forget the fire in 1917," declares Ruth Reese, "never forget it. It was terrible, it was awful." "It was a horrible, horrible thing, that 19-and-17 fire," says I. H. Mehaffey. "All through there, there was just residents that had been there for years. It burned them out. It was looked on as just a great loss to the city of Atlanta, white and black." "I knew what they meant when they said Sherman set fire to Atlanta," declares Homer Nash. "1917 showed me what fire can do, and do it quickly."

May 17 was a windy day. Several other fires already ablaze in other sections of town drew the attention of many of the city's fire fighters. Hugh McDonald was one: "Soon as we reported down, they said, 'Go to the Woodward Avenue fire.' Well, we started down to that fire, going out Hunter Street [now Martin Luther King Jr. Drive] and I threw a tire—they had about four or five engines that was motorized. The tire went down Hunter Street and just kept rolling, and hit a store on the corner of Fraser and Hunter. And it knocked the stock of goods off the shelf. And we was out of service for quite a while. Then as soon as we reported in service there at Woodward Avenue, they said, 'Go to Old Wheat Street,' over off of Edgewood Avenue.

"And when they sent us over there, Old Wheat Street had already got away. The way I understood it, they didn't have the equipment to send. Woodward Avenue, that's where the fire apparatus were. They didn't have no water to put it out, because they didn't have a pumper or hose wagon. That's where it just spread."

As fireman McDonald relates, houses with wood shingles were crowded together in the surrounding black neighborhood: "Around Wheat Street over there was colored at the time. They was awful close together. And then the wind blowing that way, it was awful—the wind got pretty high. There'd be a big board on fire, and the wind would carry that board, and it'd hit another house and start right up on that one. And it just kept spreading."

After wreaking havoc near Auburn Avenue, the blaze swept north along Boulevard, then a white middle-class thoroughfare. "People were running down the sidewalk saying that the town was on fire and for everybody to get out," relates Stella Smith, who lived nearby. "And they had to force a lot of people out of their homes. They didn't want to leave their homes. And the streetcars loaded and moved and hauled people.

"Further on out, they began to move people's furniture, move their beddings and some of their belongings out. And they moved all the things plumb out to the edge, to the country I call it, way out to where there wasn't any houses. They just carried them out there and dumped them, don't you know. And when

The Great Fire of May 21, 1917. (Courtesy Atlanta Historical Society)

they got all that out there, they couldn't hardly separate the things. They were all piled out there together."

The family of William Culbreath joined others in guarding their belongings in a field a few blocks east of where Georgia Baptist Hospital now stands: "When the fire broke out, I was in school, Gate City School at Houston and Butler. They had double sessions at the time,[8] and they were letting the kids out early. When I got home, there was a field and every person in that section had a space on this particular field. They would bring their little personal belongings and get them a corner. My mother brought out a few things, a chair out there, and a mattress. And we just stood around.

"There were thirty-five or forty families out there, white and colored on the same field together. There was no segregation there. There was no incidents whatsoever. Everybody was thinking about the little personals that they had. In some corners, you'd believe there was a prayer meeting going on, because the people were praying. They were praying and praising God to stop this thing happening."

"The fire spread like the old saying, like wildfire," recounts Culbreath's wife, Mattie. "We seemed almost to have been almost in the dead center of it. Everything around us was burning. We could see nothing but flames and caving roofs all around us. And we finally realized that the house next door, the roof on it was almost collapsing.

"We got out, and my mother tried to save a few possessions, important papers and things like that. We got out safely, [then] realized my grandmother was inside. My mother became distressed and was trying to call her and get her attention to get out of the house, because the house next door was caving in flames. And a little white boy coming from the Boulevard Elementary School saw my mother's distress and said, 'You want me to go in there? I'll get your mother out.' And he went in. He was just a little fellow, I guess less than twelve years old. And he brought my grandmother out to safety. I never knew what happened to him. I don't know who he was. He just vanished there in all the confusion.

"We proceeded on, not knowing where we were going, because everything was in flames. There was nowhere *to* go. Everything was burning. By some means, we began to head toward the First Congregational Church, which is all we knew to go to. And we proceeded on up there, wandering aimlessly and distressed, to the First Congregational Church, where at that time Dr. Henry Hugh Proctor, who is now deceased, threw the doors of the church open to all the people who had not a place to go. And at that point the news had spread, and my family, they had gotten the news, or instinct, one, brought them to the church. And that is where our family found itself, reunited."

E. B. Baynes also attended the Boulevard Elementary School: "Prior to going to school that morning I'd asked my mother to let me go to a picture show that afternoon. There was a picture called *Twenty Thousand Leagues Under the Sea* based on Jules Verne's submarine story. I was very anxious to see it. And she didn't have any change and she gave me half a dollar. She told me to spend a nickel to get into the show and bring her the change. I put this half a dollar in the little watch pocket of the trousers I was wearing and went on off to school.

"Before school recessed that afternoon we heard fire wagons going down Boulevard, around 1:30. And when school was out, I happened to look back over toward West End, in kind of a southwest direction, and saw a tremendous amount of smoke. And the kids was kind of scared and I wasn't any exception, I was scared, too. I decided I wouldn't go to that picture show, I'd go home and get a clearance from Mother.

"I walked on over to the house and when I got there, the people all around the neighborhood were pretty excited. And some of them were taking some of their belongings and furnishings out of the house, dragging them in the yard so they wouldn't be destroyed in case the fire burned the house up. Mother had someone pull a trunk that had some of her belongings in it, and she wanted to try and save that if she could. It was pulled out, and she had her purse in a handbag, and she put it in the trunk and closed the lid of this trunk and was sitting there talking, until someone with authority—I don't remember whether it was a policeman or one of the members of the National Guard—they were coming through and notifying people that they had to leave, they just had to go.

"The streetcar line ran right up in front of the house, and we walked out of the yard and out to the streetcar line, and when the car came we got on the car. It was my mother and my sister and I, and I had a little Manchester terrier dog. I had picked up that little dog up in my arms and got on the streetcar with it. And went to pay the fare—Mother realized that her purse was in the trunk, and that upset her more than she already was. We couldn't get off the car and go back and get it. They wouldn't let anybody back in that area. You had to go one way and that was out.

"We were going downtown and transfer to another streetcar and go out to visit a relative of mine that lived near Brookwood Station. But first I wanted to pay the conductor the fare, and I reached into my pocket and got that half a dollar that Mother gave me to go to the show with, and offered it to him. He wouldn't accept it and said he wasn't accepting any fares from people that was leaving that area."

Pretty soon not even the streetcars were able to run, as I. H. Mehaffey relates: "They pulled us in. It burned the wires down, it burned the telephone poles down that supported the trolley wires. There was wires in the street. And I've seen it burn the Belgian blocks. Some of the pavement was wood held together with tar, and that Belgian block would burn."

The city was thrown into confusion. Power went out in many parts of town, and martial law was declared. Soldiers from Fort McPherson came into the fire area to assist residents and to prevent looting. And firemen like Hugh McDonald struggled gamely through the night to control the blaze: "We were just moving from place to place, trying to head it off, which we couldn't do. I was running the pumper, and the others was manning the hose and the nozzles. I was out there on Boulevard. The water pressure was bad. And I had a pump running. And I got up there in the attic, and I had two lines on the pumper and some men helping me. They wasn't firemen. Somebody come and says, 'You'd better come out. The houses on both sides are on fire.' I got out and unfastened the section from the hydrant and pulled those two lines of hose down for another block and connected up down there.

"And I had to leave there, couldn't stay. It was blowing, coming towards me. And the assistant chief made a remark, says, 'Well, the pumper's gone.' It enveloped . . . the fellows that was helping me, they got down in the body of the pumper, you know, where the hose went, and it didn't hit them, but it singed my arms and all. And that carburetor says, 'Blup, blup, blup, blup, blup.' I thought it was going to fade out. But I got through all right. And I disconnected the hose and went and got more hose, and went to Ponce de Leon Avenue. I run the pump out there till one o'clock in the morning, I believe it was."

Fire fighters from as far away as Birmingham and Columbus loaded their engines on special trains into Atlanta to help put out the blaze. But it continued to burn until finally houses were dynamited to keep it from spreading. "I imagine about ten o'clock that night," recalls Hugh McDonald, "they come out there and blowed up those houses up there on Ponce de Leon Avenue just before you get to Ponce de Leon Park [a major recreation area, across the street from the present Scars Building]. It kept it from jumping over. A man from DuPont came in there and put the charges in the fireplace.

"Those houses flattened just as soon as it hit. I had to dodge one of the boards coming over. I was running the pump, close to it, and one of the one-by-twelve's comes—I had to duck out behind the machine. And the last I remember, the soldiers was playing water on these houses to keep them wet down, keep it from jumping over there. So that's the way it ended."

The fire left some 1,900 families homeless, over 5 percent of the city's population. Churches and other public buildings provided refuge for many, while hundreds spent the night in Piedmont Park. "It was just a time," states I. H. Mehaffey, "that everybody seemed to try to help. And they was a lot of help, aid and assist that come to the people of Atlanta that lost their homes." "The Red Cross welcomed people to come, to try to aid them," recalls Mattie Culbreath. "We were given assistance, much needed assistance, by the Red Cross."

"The community responded," adds Homer Nash. "They had nothing. Nowhere to sleep, nothing to sleep on, nothing! They had, oh, I don't know how many hundreds of them in the City Auditorium over there, going to arrange somewhere for them to sleep. And the other large buildings, [too]." "They threw church buildings and school buildings and various different things open to people that didn't have any place to stay," seconds E. B. Baynes. "But we had relatives in Atlanta, and relatives kind of looked out for each other, and we spent the night with some of our relatives.

"The next day my brother located us. He had an old Model T Ford. He drove us back over to where our house was. The only thing left was ashes and chimneys. I distinctly remember I had a Daisy air rifle, and I used to keep it behind the bed in a corner of my room. I went right to where I kept that gun, and all that was left was the barrel. The stock had burned up.

"And it was kind of unhappy-making to see everything you had destroyed. You couldn't hardly help but crying and a boy, he'd be ashamed to be seen crying. You couldn't hardly hold the tears back just to see your home and whatever kind of little toys and things you had. You could see where your friends had lived and your neighbors had lived, and the only thing you could see was smoldering ashes and chimneys. It was kind of unhappy-making, to say the least. It just wiped out everything, left nothing but those brick chimneys standing."

"Just the chimneys," echoes Stella Smith, "just the chimneys. Best as I could refer to how it looked, was like a cemetery." "That was just like a ghost town," recalls Homer Nash. "At night, oooh, dark and no lights and all the houses down. Two or three days after the fire I was walking up the street with two or three friends. And a trunk had been set over there—the fire had burnt it down to ashes. And I looked down there, and said, 'That looks like something, let me see.' I scratched in there, it was a roll of bills. I carried that down to the *Georgian,* that was the evening paper here, and told them what happened. And they advertised and the people got their money. But they thought it was just all gone, that particular family, because everything else burned up."

Many other people visited the fire site, including maid Ruby Owens: "My husband carried me to walk where the fire had burned. We went and walked way out, all out on Boulevard and all out that way. The fire burned big fine houses all along the street down that way. We was coming back home and [there was] a colored folks' house on a hill, that little house sitting right there. That house didn't scorch. Didn't burn that house at all, that little house sitting up there."

Hugh McDonald and other firemen remained on duty for quite some time to make sure the fire was completely out. "The chief left instructions that we wasn't to be off till it was all over. They wouldn't even let us off. And we had to work over three weeks before we ever got an off day. It kindled back up. It's like coal, it's hard to put out. And maybe it'd leave a spark in there, and it'd smolder for a day or two before it started back up."

"It did what we had been fighting for years for the *people* to do," states Dr. Nash. "It didn't discriminate against anybody." Yet, in fact, many black and poor Atlantans could not rebuild after the fire. Nina King Miller, the daughter of Auburn Avenue businessman Cornelius King, explains: "I think we didn't ever rebuild. In fact, the most people who lost property in the fire were like my father. They didn't have funds to carry enough insurance to rebuild the house. They would take enough insurance, maybe, to replace a roof or part of a house, but no one thought of the house being burned completely, so some people just weren't able to rebuild. It was quite a struggle."

The fire worsened an already overcrowded housing situation on the city's east side, thereby contributing to the migration of black Atlantans to the west side of town. There were other consequences as well. "Right after the fire," states E. B. Baynes, "I understand that an ordinance was passed that no more houses could have in the city of Atlanta wood shingles. Houses would be covered with composition shingles, some kind of fire-resistant, pliable shingles." The fire also sped up the motorization of the Fire Department, although men like Hugh McDonald received no commendation or medal for their work: "Naah, got nothing. Didn't even get a good salary."

"I don't think it was ever determined how that fire started," relates E. B. Baynes. "There were various different rumors. It was right at the beginning of

World War I and some think that a German spy started it. It was quite a rumor going about that the fire was started by German spies that had been sent to this country to destroy things.

"When we got off the streetcar and went to the home of this relative of mine, she was a person that was pretty excitable, and she got pretty wrought up, screaming that it was the Germans. She'd seen the smoke and heard the fire wagons and various different rumors and things, and had no hesitation in blaming it on the German spies." "Everybody claimed that the Germans set it," adds Homer Nash, "but they didn't set it. It was set in some of that poor housing. All that's been rebuilt now, and you will go up in that area and never know that they had a terrific fire in 1917."

There were other disasters during the period, too. At a time when vaccinations and sulfa drugs were unknown, epidemics periodically swept the city. One of the worst was the infamous flu epidemic of November 1918. "They were dying just like leaves off of them trees," remembers midwife Mattie Varner. "Man, they sure did die," says textile worker Clifford Lovins, who hailed from the nearby city of Douglasville. "Not only there but all over the United States. My mom and my oldest sister had it, and there were five of us boys and all of us come down with the flu but one brother. Well, it got so bad that they had to stop the mill. This sister of mine died a week and four days before my mother did. Oh, there was a lot of them that way."

On November 11, 1918, the Armistice was signed, ending the war. "We were happy to see that day come," remembers Evelyn Witherspoon, "the end of World War I. The church bells rang. We all paraded. The whole school paraded from the English Avenue School to Marietta Street, to celebrate Armistice. It was a big day in Atlanta."

Two years later she marched again, after the Nineteenth Amendment established woman suffrage.[9] "I turned twenty-four before I could vote. I didn't take an interest in politics. That was for men to do. I remember seeing torchlight parades for candidates and they would march in downtown streets, but it was strictly for the men to vote.

"And when we got the franchise, suffrage, Miss Lula Kingsbery was my principal and she said, 'We are going to City Hall together and register to vote.' So we all went together in a body, and she was first in line. The clerk said, 'Your age?' and she said, 'Over twenty-one.' And he said, 'I have to know your age.' She said, 'Young man, write *over twenty-one*. And I guess he wrote *over twenty-one*."

The postwar era brought new situations and problems. "It was about forty

Flag-raising ceremony at Five Points during World War I (Atlanta Journal-Constitution)

Black recruits at Camp Gordon, outside Atlanta. (Courtesy Atlanta Historical Society)

days after the Armistice before they commenced putting them back in America," recalls barber Horace Sinclair. "They had that bonus and three hundred dollars, I think that was the amount of money they were giving them when they were turning them loose, to start life all over again. And all of them wanted to come to Atlanta and just drift out to these little cities and towns where they lived."

The South's leading liberal organization for a generation, the Commission on Interracial Cooperation, was founded in 1919 in Atlanta to address post–World War I racial tensions. "The government had drafted Negroes from all over the United States," explains Morehouse College president Benjamin Mays. "Drafted them and sent them to Europe to fight to 'make the world safe for democracy.' And those Negroes got more decent treatment in Europe, particularly in France, than they ever had before."

"Maybe they hadn't been treated as differently as some of the Southern whites said they had been treated," cautions Arthur Raper, research director of the Interracial Commission from 1926 to 1939. "[There was] wild talk about the escapades they had had with the French women and the acceptance they had had, and these folks just weren't going to behave themselves." "I think it was in 1919," adds Mays, "riots broke out all over the South. Even up in Chicago a great riot broke out. And out of that situation the Commission on Interracial Cooperation was born, to meet that emergency.

"The commission did a lot of good. But they were trying to get better treatment for the Negro within the segregated pattern. They didn't try to break down segregation. That was a sacred cow in the South."

Chapter Two

Neighborhoods

Atlanta's physical appearance during the period was considerably different than it is today. The city consisted of a downtown core surrounded by diverse residential neighborhoods whose character and location were shaped by natural topography, the railroads, race relations, real estate interests, streetcars and automobiles. Two major population shifts took place in the era between the world wars: a gradual movement of middle-class white Atlantans to the north side of town, and a migration of black Atlantans from east of downtown to the west side. While housing conditions improved during the period, most dwelling units within the city still were considered substandard as late as 1940.[1]

A number of elements helped determine where people lived in the city.[2] Atlanta's streetcar lines, for instance, provided a link between working-class communities and industrial districts like the Fifth Ward northwest of downtown, and enabled domestic workers to get to their places of employment on the north side. At the turn of the century they helped stimulate the growth of such prestigious neighborhoods as Inman Park, Ansley Park, and Druid Hills. In the 1920s they extended to new commuter suburbs like Boulevard Park, just east of Piedmont Park.[3]

Originally built along ridge lines and on top of overland Indian trails, the railroads also played a key role in shaping the patterns of local development from Atlanta's very outset. The city's earliest settlements were built on the comparatively level land adjacent to the first railroad tracks. Until the construction of the Courtland Street viaduct in 1906 and the Spring Street, Central Avenue and Pryor Street viaducts in the 1920s (spanning what is now Underground Atlanta and adjacent areas), the vast cluster of railroad tracks in the heart of town provided real and symbolic barriers to growth, separating the north and south sides, downtown from the west side.[4]

The railroads spawned working-class neighborhoods like Pittsburgh and Mechanicsville on the south side of town, as well as such outlying communities as Oakland City and Edgewood, annexed into Atlanta by the early twentieth century. As redcap porter Matthew Housch relates, they also provided the means for many Atlantans, black and white, to become homeowners: "Those were pretty good jobs for black people. And they were able to buy homes and that contributed to a lot of our sections in the city of Atlanta. The west side grown considerably, and not only the west side but other parts of town where blacks owned property by working with the railroad."

In other ways, too, employment influenced residential patterns. For instance, some of Atlanta's Jewish residents, especially newer immigrants from eastern Europe, lived adjacent to their places of business. "They were small establishments," recalls Ethel Meyers, who lived south of downtown, "and the family sometimes lived above the store, or in back of the store, or nearby the store. The immigrants lived in a business section and not a high-class section. They lived very near the colored section." "I remember a store run by a Jewish family, and they lived in the neighborhood," relates west side resident Estelle Clemmons, "because the daughter, Sarah, and I used to play together. And we were always visiting the homes of each other."

Some small Jewish shopkeepers also settled in white working-class areas, including the city's cotton mill districts. While company towns and mill villages were nowhere near as prevalent in Atlanta as around Birmingham, for instance, there did exist pockets of company-supplied housing within the city, especially adjacent to the Fulton Bag and Exposition Cotton Mills. "The mill village was a great big place," states Exposition Cotton Mill worker Nesbitt Spinks. "The company owned all the houses and they'd rent you the houses pretty cheap. I think I paid four dollars and something a month for a three-room house. Of course, all house rent was cheap back then, but that was cheaper than you could get it anywhere else, you know."

"There used to be a row of houses up there they called Chinch Row," recalls Cabbagetown resident Calvin Freeman of some of Fulton Bag's housing, "and everybody wanted to stay away from Chinch Row. Didn't nobody want to live in those houses over there because they were full of chinches. Then they had these other little homes that would handle a family of maybe five people. You had a hard time, you know, waiting on the list to get a good home to live in." It was only after World War II that Atlanta's textile mills, like their counterparts elsewhere in the region, finally began to sell their company housing.

There also existed black enclaves in otherwise white neighborhoods throughout the Atlanta area, where black residents doing domestic work had settled in order to be closer to their employers. One of these communities was Johnson-

Slum housing, 1936. (Photograph by Walker Evans. Courtesy Library of Congress)

town, located in the shadow of what is now Lenox Square and essentially wiped out with urban expansion and the coming of MARTA. "All those Negroes owned their homes," states Eloise Milton, whose grandfather, pioneer black undertaker David T. Howard, also owned property in the area. "But as the city grew, that property was condemned and they were forced to sell. As the white people encroached upon the area, the Negroes were forced to leave."

More common than such all-black settlements was a residential pattern dating back to the nineteenth century, when black servants often lived in alleys behind their white employers' houses. "The white folks' houses was on the street," explains Summerhill resident Lula Daugherty, "and in the back of the white folks' houses was the colored people. You would call that 'in the rear.' At that time, that's where we colored folks was living, in the rear, unless you had a good job, you know, what they call kind of well-off." "Yes, there were plenty of houses in the rear away back there," seconds Ruby Baker, who came to the city with her family in 1923. "When we first moved here, we moved in the rear of Merritts Avenue [in the Bedford-Pine section]. There was a row of houses for blacks right there behind a row of whites that lived on Merritts Avenue who really wasn't much better off than we were."

Class, ethnic and racial divisions not only helped define Atlanta's communities, but also contributed to a strong sense of neighborhood identity that on occasion shaded into territoriality and even violence. For example, Bankhead Highway was the dividing line between the Exposition Cotton Mill district to the north and the white working-class Fifth Ward to the south. "Out here at the Exposition," recalls textile worker Clifford Lovins, "used to be us cotton mill boys wasn't allowed to cross Bankhead. We could get up to Bankhead, but if we come on the other side, it was a fight. Now we could go to Marietta Street, they didn't bother us, but if you got up on Bankhead, that's when it started. Then finally some of those Bankhead boys came over there [to the cotton mill] and went to work, they all got together and there was no more trouble."

From time to time, members of Atlanta's small Jewish community, then centered on the south side right where the stadium is today, also faced hostility when they ventured into adjacent neighborhoods. "A Jew always had to live next to other Jews," relates Sol Beton, a member of the local Sephardic Jewish population, "and form their own little *shtetl* or *juderia* or little community. They had known this practice in the old country, and in order to maintain their closeness and identity, it was necessary to stay together. When people first came here, they were very clannish, they kept closely knit together.

"The area on Pryor Street and Central Avenue from Woodward Avenue to Georgia Avenue was basically like a ghetto of the Sephardic Jews. And everyone knew everyone else. The Ashkenazi [Jews from Germany and eastern Europe], they lived on Washington Street, Pulliam Street, Crew Street, Georgia Avenue, a little further south. But they were all in the same situation as we were. We had our synagogue on Central and Woodward. Two blocks up was 'the Big *Shul,*' the AA [Ahavath Achim] synagogue on Washington and Woodward. About two or three blocks further down was Shearith Israel."

"We all lived in a very small neighborhood," recalls Louis Geffen, whose father was rabbi at Shearith Israel, "because everyone in those days wanted to live next to the synagogue, and for that reason most of us went to the elementary school right there in the neighborhood. Once in a while, some of the non-Jewish boys would get up a little gang and they would try and frighten you and throw rocks at you, trying to dominate you or make you feel that you're trespassing on their territory, or something of that nature. But the Jewish boys were pretty well organized when a problem would arise of that nature, and they didn't let them run over them most of the time."

"As the Jews began to prosper," relates Sol Beton, "they felt it was necessary to migrate to the north side of town. Now, it started as a slow movement at the beginning. These families ventured out in this particular area, then over a period of years other families began to move close by. They moved, let's say, from Central Avenue to Parkway Drive or Boulevard. Or they moved on Highland Avenue. Then later, they began to move into Johnson Road and Lenox Road, then towards the Briarcliff and LaVista area. The ones who became prosperous started to go into the northwest part of town, in areas like Margaret Mitchell Drive, Sequoia Drive."

"[Originally] it was sort of a no-man's-land for Jews," recalls Clarence Feibelman of the affluent neighborhoods in the northwest, "almost off limits. I think the covenants or the leases included a clause that they shouldn't be sold to Jews. Now it's as many Jews live out here as Christians."

Neighborhood territoriality also often went hand in hand with racial antagonism. "Well, after dark a colored man wasn't allowed in Cabbagetown at all," remembers one resident. "We'd rock them out of there, you know. We used to have a time rocking the colored boys back across the railroad track towards Edgewood Avenue and over on Decatur Street." "You couldn't go to Kelly Street," recalls Laura Belle Keith of Summerhill. "Kelly Street was out-of-bounds. Whites lived over there. I mean, the colored couldn't move any further than Connally Street. If you were colored, you knew not to go over there and try to move in." "That was the unwritten law," adds her husband, L. D. Keith. "I think our color determined that."

There were written laws, too, that perpetuated and reinforced racially segregated housing patterns. In 1913 and 1917 City Council passed residential segregation ordinances, both of which were eventually ruled unconstitutional. Atlanta's first municipal zoning plan, developed in the early 1920s, continued to define residential districts according to race. And a state constitutional amendment permitting segregated zoning in Atlanta was passed in 1928.[5]

In addition to Jim Crow ordinances, other developments contributed to an actual increase in residential segregation after the turn of the century. Atlanta's rapid population growth and the commercialization of downtown intensified competition for space near the city's center and drove both blacks and whites into outlying neighborhoods. The rapidly deteriorating race relations of the era culminated in the infamous Atlanta Race Riot of 1906, when local whites launched several raids into the black community, murdering dozens of people in the process. In the riot's aftermath, black Atlantans retrenched, relocating both businesses and homes further away from whites. Increasingly, black residents tended to move to the area between downtown and Atlanta University, and to a growing black section on the east side of town, known today as the Old Fourth Ward.[6]

Atlanta's east side black neighborhoods were quite varied in character. Substandard housing and inadequate city services marked such rough-and-tumble communities as Darktown and Buttermilk Bottom, located near the present site of the Civic Center. A bustling and colorful thoroughfare that was home to the 81 Theatre and other nightspots, Decatur Street had an unsavory reputation for some black Atlantans. "Decatur Street used to be a really tough street," remembers musician Edwin Driskell. "The implication I got then was that you found prostitutes or lower-life elements there. And as youngsters, we would never be caught going down Decatur Street."

"It was just a rough place," echoes Fourth Ward resident Alice Adams, "and we just didn't hang out over there. Because my peoples told me when I came to Atlanta, 'Stay off Decatur Street.' And I did just that. It wasn't no place for me. I stayed on the safe side. I would go to Sweet Auburn Avenue. That was my street, Sweet Auburn Avenue. I just enjoyed Auburn Avenue. It was a beautiful street."

By the turn of the century, Auburn Avenue had already become a well-established street. "Now, our parents always called it 'The Avenue,'" states Kathleen Adams, born on Auburn in 1890. "And maybe that came because

*Black community housing, 1936. (Photograph by Walker Evans.
Courtesy Library of Congress)*

the first homes for Negroes not only in Atlanta but in other places were the streets or alleys, you might say, that ran up behind the Caucasian homes. And to be living on a front street and it being called Auburn Avenue, they simply said, 'The Avenue.' 'Where do you live?' 'I live on The Avenue.' It was the best-appointed street for Negroes in the city of Atlanta at that time."

In 1956 *Fortune* magazine called Auburn Avenue "the richest Negro street in the world." Such a comparative accumulation of wealth during the era of segregation was a source of enormous satisfaction to Atlanta's black community. "In those years," relates Auburn Avenue barber Dan Stephens, "Auburn really was a black man's pride and joy, I'll put it like that. You didn't find people coming to Auburn in their shirttails like they do now, and just kind of loosely dressed. They had a lot of pride and they'd come to Auburn Avenue, they would be dressed up." "That's where we dressed up, because we couldn't dress up during the day," adds Alice Adams. "We'd dress up and put on our good clothes and go to the show on Auburn Avenue. And you were going places. It was like white folks' Peachtree."

In addition to being a hub of black enterprise, Auburn Avenue was also a tremendous gathering place, at all hours of the day and night. "Used to be, as I observed it during the years," recalls Dr. Homer Nash, "at five o'clock in the evening one crowd of people would be coming out of all those offices down there, going home to their meal and everything. At six o'clock another crowd would be coming down here to hang around here until about eight or ten o'clock, then go home. Right along eight or ten o'clock, the all-night crowd would come down here. And they'd be out all night."

"It was where the action was," says church worker Phoebe Hart. "My office was on the fourth floor, which gave me a good sweep of Auburn Avenue. And daily I stood there and watched, particularly at lunch hour, to see the young women coming from the Atlanta Life Insurance Company down to the Yates and Milton drugstore, which was really a mecca for business, for social life, for all relationships between twelve and one.

"And then Sunday, many people came immediately from the churches— Wheat Street, Ebenezer, four or five churches on Auburn—to Yates and Milton, if for no more than a soda. And if they got there for a soda there wouldn't be any end to it, because you came there under the pretense of a soda, but you wanted to find out what was going on, see who you could see. And you could see most anybody. You saw the people you wanted to see, you made your engagements for the next week. On Sunday you did Monday, Tuesday, Wednesday, Thursday and Friday's business. Then you stepped across the street to the James Hotel for your eating, or you went up the street to Ma Sutton's."

"They called her Ma Sutton," remembers barber Horace Sinclair. "Everybody all over the country would come to Atlanta and go get a decent meal at Ma Sutton's. She would really set the table. You'd get everything on the table just like you would be at home, serve yourself. You'd have meats and vegetables of all kinds, light rolls, cornbread, coffee, milk or tea. She'd even put preserves on the table, all that stuff.

"Then you'd go down further and go in the Odd Fellows Building to the top floor, [where there] would be the Roof Garden. You had to go there for real decent social entertainment, don't you see, and if you didn't take your girl over there back in those days, why, you were a cheapskate, see." "That's where they would have dances," recalls Dan Stephens. "They'd have dances two or three times a week at the Roof Garden. Sometimes they would have dances at one minute after twelve on Sunday night and so forth, and the people would come in their tails, full dressed, you might say."

After the Roof Garden's demise, the Top Hat Club, opened in 1938, became Auburn Avenue's principal entertainment spot. "The opening night at the Top Hat," relates Horace Sinclair, "that was a great night in Atlanta because we hadn't had anything like that before. The Roof Garden had done its part, but this far exceeded anything in our society. So, everybody clamored to go to the Top Hat. And I was among the first persons who went to the first entertainment there, and it was quite a gala affair. It was a lot of glory."

Despite the glory of Sweet Auburn, however, black Atlantans and their businesses began a gradual movement to the west side of town after World War I. "That's when Negroes just took over the west side," recalls west side resident Ruth Reese. Various factors helped bring on this migration, which cracked residential patterns that had existed in the city since Reconstruction. Depressed cotton prices precipitated a local housing crisis between 1915 and 1920, as new housing starts came to a near halt. Housing was particularly tight on the east side after the Great Fire of 1917.[7]

Several interrelated developments attracted black Atlantans to the area west of Ashby Street, previously off limits to blacks. After World War I, a number of Auburn Avenue businesses started branch offices on Hunter Street (now Martin Luther King Jr. Drive). The formation of the Atlanta University Center in 1929–30 consolidated all of the city's black colleges on the west side. Most importantly, between 1919 and 1922, black entrepreneur Heman Perry, founder of the Service Realty Company, bought 300 acres west of Ashby for

Curry and Hill haberdashery shop on Auburn Avenue. (Atlanta University Collection, Woodruff Library, Atlanta University Center)

residential use. Perry's Service Engineering and Construction Company began to build bungalow-style houses similar to those opening up to whites in other parts of town, while his Standard Life Insurance Company underwrote the home mortgages.[8]

"They'd go out and buy a piece of land, develop it and build homes and sell it to our people," remembers plumber C. C. Hart. "I had a lot of that work, putting plumbing into new homes that they built. And our people started expanding, getting into these new homes."

In the early twenties, Perry also had a hand in the location of the new Booker T. Washington High School, the city's first black public high school, and Washington Park, Atlanta's first public park for black citizens, in the section west of Ashby Street. As in other burgeoning suburbs on the fringes of town, such amenities attracted prospective residents, like Estelle Clemmons and her family: "Everybody from across town and everywhere else came over to Washington Park. It was a place of recreation and the only park for blacks at the time, you see.

"We used to do things as a family. After dinner on this particular Sunday, we walked over here to Washington Park. And we thought we were something when we could come to Washington Park, because there was the swimming pool there, and there was a pavilion where people used to dance during the week. We had walked by the pavilion, and my mother just turned and looked up this way, and the base of this house was just being constructed. She said to my father—she called him Clemmons—she said, 'Clemmons, I'd like to live up there on that hill.' And he went the next morning to see about it. And he came back and discussed the layout of the house with us, and we liked it. He made arrangements to buy it, and as soon as it was completed we moved in.

"The yards were somewhat larger and the houses were somewhat better. We only had three rooms on Davis Street, and here we had five rooms. And we felt we were going somewhere, you see, having five rooms, with a bathroom on the inside and hot and cold running water. We could bathe in a bathtub whereas previously you heated water on the stove in the kitchen and bathed in the tin tub. But here, to be able to get into a bathtub meant so much. And it was considered a pretty good neighborhood, very much so."

The passage of black Atlantans to the west side did not proceed altogether smoothly, however—not by a long shot. While some whites were accommodating, others strongly resented the movement of blacks to the area, and to other sections where only whites had lived. Throughout the twenties, the Ku Klux Klan and other white supremacists resorted to rallies, cross burning and

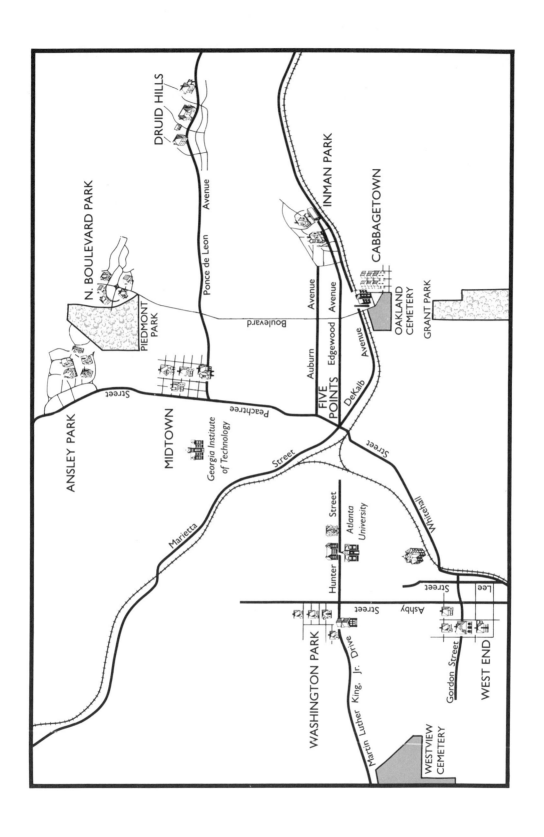

violence to intimidate black families moving into previously white residential areas. "Now, on my street one night," relates Kathleen Adams, who moved to the west side in 1923, "up in the middle of the block above me, a postal worker put up a two-story duplex, and one night they found a small cross burning out on their lawn."

"The Klan would burn a cross," recalls Arthur Raper, who monitored Klan-related activities for the Commission on Interracial Cooperation, "and they would . . . in one place a Baptist preacher who was also a real estate man saw that he could make a pot of money by selling these houses here that had been lived in by whites to blacks who were trying their best and had a little money to get out of the inner city. He was a Klansman himself, but he just liked money better than he liked the philosophy, and so he took the money. And the Klan moved in on that, and they forced this Baptist preacher [to stop]. There was things like that going on."

"On Newport Street," remembers Ruby Baker, "the upper end of Newport and the upper end of Simpson, there were policemen and firemen living. And when the blacks started moving up into the next block, that's when the bombing started. They just started blowing up, throwing bombs on people's front porches and through the front windows, in their yards. I was a girl then, pretty young, and I remember just how it affected me. And it happened in other parts of town, too. The same thing happened on the upper end of Linden Street and on Jackson Street and Boulevard, when they first started moving in up there. They were bombing houses.

"We had a neighbor who was a good friend of my daddy's. And they'd sit up all night with shotguns on the front porch. They'd cut out if anybody just slowed up in a car. They were going to get 'em." "People used to sit up in the window with their guns all night," recalls west side resident Pauline Minnie-field. "The white people bombed a house right there at 333 Ashby Street one night. Colored people were living in it. Just a few of them sneaked back another time to bomb that house, and those colored people were waiting with guns and pistols, and they just went to shooting.

"I'll never forget, one night during the Christmas holidays my brother came home from a dance, and he came in and said, 'Ashby Street School is burn-ing down.'[9] I said, 'Go on, you're always putting on some devilment.' And he said, 'Look out the window.' And I looked out. All I could see was the red sky. And the white people set—or somebody, I'm sure, set Ashby Street School on fire."

As Arthur Raper relates, some of the more liberal white Atlantans took a different approach toward stemming the tide of black migration westward, an approach that did not sit well with Morehouse College president John Hope. "I remember when those bombings happened over there," Raper says, "the Atlanta Christian Council had a committee working on [the problem]. 'Now, we will agree on where the line is where the Negroes will stop. They will move up to this line and they won't cross it, and the whites will stay on this line.' Now, you're going to have whites and Negroes right across the street from each other, or else you'll have them backed up right against each other with their backyards, and everybody knew it wouldn't work. But they were trying to work it out. And John Hope wouldn't cooperate at all. He said, 'I have a right to live anywhere, and I'm not going to sign anything that limits my basic human rights. I'm just not going to do it.' Then the whites would take the position, 'You can't satisfy John Hope. As soon as you do one thing for him, he wants something else.' Well, of course, he did."

Despite violence, intimidation and other efforts to control where they lived, thousands of black Atlantans moved westward and broke the residential color line after 1920. By 1940, fully 40 percent of the city's black population was on the west side. Yet both *de jure* and *de facto* housing segregation persisted for decades. The dual street names of such thoroughfares as Monroe/Boulevard and Juniper/Courtland reflect segregated housing patterns. Realtor associations and the city tried to set formal boundaries for black expansion into the 1960s. Despite the emergence of a large black middle class, black residents continued to reside in comparatively poor housing, and to be discriminated against by lending institutions. And black and white Atlantans today tend to live farther apart from each other than they ever did.[10]

The move to the west side did not break down patterns of residential segregation in Atlanta. It was, however, part and parcel of an overall upgrading of the city's housing conditions during the period. New Deal programs such as those initiated by the Works Progress Administration also helped improve the situation, through the extension of sewer lines and other municipal services, and the installation of screens, cement privies (replacing wooden outhouses), and the like.

The New Deal also provided the means for the first public housing projects in the country, Techwood Homes, then for whites only, and University Homes, for black residents. "It was a totally different concept," remarks Edith Henderson, landscape architect for Techwood Homes. "It was a different concept of the way people could live. It was clearly an introduction of all that was to come. It was really a very exciting thing for the city to have the first and to watch it grow."

Public housing in America had its origins in 1933 when Atlanta real estate developer Charles F. Palmer realized the potential for slum clearance and low-cost housing funds under a section of the recently passed National Industrial Recovery Act.[11] Palmer selected an area just south of Georgia Tech, inhabited by both whites and blacks, for his initial slum clearance effort. "All of the build-ings [there] were just really shacks," recalls architect Preston Stevens, Sr., whose firm, Burge and Stevens, designed Techwood Homes. "They leaked. The floors were rotten. They had no plumbing fixtures in the houses. They had hydrants outside, and they had outhouses in the back for toilets. It was very unsightly and in very poor condition. Chuck Palmer felt that the people living in the substandard houses were living in houses that were as bad as someone eating bad meat, I think is the way he expressed it. And he just had a feeling for those type people, I believe.

"To have people of lower economic income get a decent place to live, that was mainly the reason [for building the Techwood project]. Of course, it did help the city in taxes, tearing down the old shacks that were there." In addition to the promise of better, more sightly homes and increased downtown property values, the public housing venture also provided construction job opportunities during the Depression, and a source of income for Palmer.

After targeting an area to build in, Palmer drew up plans and budgets, and made initial contacts with Washington. He also hooked up with John Hope, president of Atlanta University since 1930 and already interested in developing housing for black Atlantans near the colleges, as Atlanta University historian Clarence Bacote notes: "Dr. Hope had been interested in improving this whole area around the university. He could see how this would be an asset to the university. First of all, you had a housing project that would serve as a labora-tory for, say, sociology and the School of Social Work. It would provide jobs for blacks at the time. And it would eliminate that terrible residential area which was known as Beaver Slide. It consisted of run-down homes. Down in the bottoms it was awful."

"It was a kind of rough neighborhood," recalls Clara Render, an early resi-dent of University Homes. "It was rough. People doing anything they wanted to. I'd visit over here occasionally, but we was always careful to go home before night."

As with Cabbagetown and other colorfully named Atlanta neighborhoods, there existed several stories about how Beaver Slide, located just east of the Atlanta University Center along Fair Street, got its name. "They tells a tale," recounts Render, "I don't know if it's true or not. You know, the police chief was Chief [James L.] Beaver[s], and they rode horses at that time—wasn't no such thing as police riding around in cars. And once they said that it come a big snowstorm and everything froze, and Beaver was coming down that hill and somehow the horse slipped and he fell off and started sliding, and he didn't stop till it got to the bottom, and they called it Beaver Slide. Now, I don't whether that's true or not, but that's what they tell."

A controversy quickly arose when black property holders were paid less by the government for their slum property than their white counterparts. "That land was not as valuable as the land that was purchased for the white project," explains banker L. D. Milton, a University Homes Board of Trustees member. "The white project was built in what was substantially a white area, and University Homes was built in an area which was considered to be mainly Negro. And white land cost more than Negro land."

There were other problems in getting the projects going, too. Local real estate owners and brokers, many connected with slum properties themselves, charged there was already too much housing in Atlanta. Washington dragged its feet on both approval and funding of the effort.[12] The novelty of public housing —a brand-new concept in this country—bred suspicion in Atlanta and elsewhere, as Preston Stevens relates: "Everyone in the country was against slum clearance. It was a different idea completely, and people don't take readily to that. They thought it was communistic.

"After we had been awarded the Techwood Homes project, we went down to the City Hall. There were a great many people there. People were crowded in the back of the room and even sitting in the windows and out in the hall. It was a right hectic time. My partner Flippen Burge and Mr. Palmer made a presentation. And one man got up protesting, saying that it was not only communistic, but that the people wouldn't appreciate it. They would put coal in the bathtubs and put their feet in the refrigerator to keep cool, and that they just would not appreciate it."

"The average citizen just couldn't imagine that many people living that close together," adds landscape architect Edith Henderson. "They couldn't believe that it would work. A lot of people thought those projects were going to crop up every six inches all over the city."

"But," states Preston Stevens, "the Council approved it. Then there was nothing to it, the people had to sell the property. That was the law. So the property was bought and the buildings were wrecked. Now, when Mr. Harold Ickes, the Secretary of the Interior, came down, he dedicated University Homes first. Chuck Palmer said that when Mr. Ickes pushed the plunger to detonate the dynamite under one of the buildings at University Homes, the planks flew high.

But at Techwood, he pushed the plunger under an old shack, and a very slight sound was made. Mr. Ickes turned and said, 'Must be getting a little weak.'

"At any rate, we went on with Techwood, and Techwood was designed as one of the best that now exist. The government sent some people with a slum clearance organization from Washington down, and they advised us about how they wanted it built so as to stand up over the years. It was built of reinforced concrete, brick on the exterior and limestone trim, the interior corridors of glazed tile. It was all built so as to stand up very well. I think the government required [the city] to build them both [Techwood and University Homes] of the same type construction.

"After we made our sketches, the government came down and they decided on our space requirements for each apartment. They wanted something that the people would be comfortable in, which they had not had before. So they had heat, which they had not had before. They had plumbing, which they had not had before. They had electricity.

"We had several schemes for it. One of them was like houses. And some of them were high-rise buildings—I say 'high-rise,' about six or seven stories. But we finally came down to buildings two and three stories high so they would be walk-up, which made more sense. And we separated the buildings so that there would be playgrounds in between. We always thought that the place would be full of children. We put trees back of the sidewalks instead of having trees on the curb, so that children playing wouldn't run out and get run over by automobiles. At this time, these trees are beautiful trees, probably eighteen inches in diameter, oak trees. The planting that we did at that time looks beautiful right now."

"We set it up," adds Edith Henderson, "so that the entire design plan would be an evergreen one, that in various times of the year there would always be something in leaf color or in flower. The housing, the entire housing concept, [was to] be absorbed inside the city as if it were a park—that it would not be shut off or shunted over into a corner, that it would be a part of the regular life of the entire city, that the setting would be so carefully done that it would be pleasing to everyone and would fit in well—never be a sore thumb or stuck in a back alley or some leftover land—and that it could be done so well that the people in it could be proud of it."

Due in part to the fact that Techwood and University Homes were models for the entire country, early tenants were selected with the same care that went into the building design. "At that time," remembers University Homes resident Lula Daugherty, "when you put in your application, they screened you.

Slum housing with Spelman College and University Homes in background. (Library of Congress)

I mean, you know, they found out your reputation, how you paid your rent, and what kind of neighbor you had been, and all such as that. And then they sent somebody out to interview you and see what kind of housekeeper you are— what they don't do now. Even you had to tell them what church you belonged to. And when they done that, then if you had a good reference, you moved in."

"Oooh, they didn't just have any- and everybody in here," says Clara Gibson of University Homes. "They didn't want nobody to come in raising sand and tearing it up. They wanted, well I'll say some of the nicest people they could find to put in here."

"The housing project was, in those early years, not housing the poverty stricken," relates Atlanta University librarian Hallie Brooks. "There were many middle-class blacks who had apartments in University Homes. They were people working in insurance, they were the social workers, the teachers. That is not to say that it was not filling a need, because these middle-class people did not have any money either."

"The people that moved in there at that time were mostly young couples like myself," echoes Waldo Roescher, an early tenant of Techwood Homes. "They were mostly middle-income, from middle-income families, all suffering from the effects of the Depression, having a hard time finding a decent job or getting decent pay. There weren't any illiterates in there, people that had never even graduated from grammar school, for instance. Everybody that I knew that I ever met while I was living there had at least a high school education and maybe some college. There were quite a few postal employees living out there, sales people, a variety of jobs, just whatever they could get to get a paycheck.

"There was no stigma attached to it at all. I mean, everyone realized that the people who were living there were living there because of the Depression. We all were happy to be in there."

News of the new projects spread through the papers and by word of mouth. "A friend of ours told us about it," remembers Clara Render, "and so we came over and put in an application. And, as soon as they opened, people started to talking about how they had to live here. They told more different tales about it —that you had to go to bed by nine o'clock and you couldn't have no visitors, and I don't know what all they said. So the first time they sent us a notice to come and select a house, we didn't come. And so a friend of ours moved in that apartment right joining this one, and we came down here to visit them, and we found out, you know, it was all just something they were saying. Then I went back and put in again. I put in in September, and we moved in on the eleventh of November in '37."

The new tenants overwhelmingly found the projects to be a great improvement over their previous housing. "I moved in here in November when it began to be cold, and I didn't have to get up and make a fire," recollects Clara Render. "When I got up, the house was *warm*. I didn't have to get up and make a fire. And when I got ready to take a bath, I didn't have to heat no water. So, you know, when you're not used to things like that, you really appreciate it." "It was nice," exclaims Lula Daugherty. "Now, I was in heaven and still living, because I hadn't lived in a house like that before in my life."

As one early tenant recalls, some University Homes residents were so pleased with their apartments they figured they must have been intended for the white inhabitants of Techwood: "These was supposed to have been Techwood and the ones at Techwood was supposed to have been over here. They was working on both of them at the same time, and they said they got the plans mixed up. So, they put the nicer ones over here by mistake."

For many tenants, the projects provided their first indoor plumbing, steam heat and electricity, their first refrigerator and cabinets. Both University and Techwood Homes soon developed a backlog of applicants. Some people, like Waldo Roescher, used personal connections to get in: "You had to have a regular job so you could pay the rent they charged you according to your salary. I couldn't have qualified financially at the time we got in because I didn't have a regular job then. But my father-in-law was a friend of somebody out there in the housing administration, and he guaranteed our rent. That's the only reason we got in."

The same scrutiny taken in screening applicants continued after the early tenants moved in. "To see that you kept up their house," remembers Lula Daugherty, "when you moved in, you had a certain hour. If you were going to move in at nine o'clock, you were there at nine o'clock. And when you got there, there was somebody from the office to go over your belongings and spray them, before you put them in there. They was just seeing that you didn't carry any bugs, or any bedbugs, or no kind of bugs in. I appreciated it.

"Our manager was Mr. Maron, and our superintendent was Mr. Alexander. They lived in here. But, you see, now they don't live in here and they don't care what happens. And people had to keep their children out of the street. They had a certain time for those children to go in. If they caught them on the street, they would carry them home." "It wasn't no strict rules," adds Clara Render. "You just wasn't supposed to be too noisy at night, you know, disturb your neighbor."

If anything, the restrictions were tighter at Techwood Homes. "They had

Swimming pool at Techwood Homes. (Special Collections, Emory University)

rules and regulations like lights-out by midnight every night, a curfew more or less," recalls Waldo Roescher. "No cutting up out in the yards or anything like that. Of course, you weren't supposed to have any loud parties or things like that, which we did.

"They had a man named Driggers who was in charge of the maintenance facilities there, and he was more or less kind of a guard, you might say. He went around to make sure that everybody had their lights out and their radios off by eleven or twelve, whatever the hour was that we were supposed to be in bed. He'd walk around the whole complex and sometimes come up in the hallways, looking and listening. And on weekends we'd get together and pool our resources, whatever we had, go up to Southern Liquor Store and get a little refreshment,[13] and then we'd go to one house and have a little party. Everybody would keep a watch out, and all of a sudden you'd hear somebody say, 'Jiggers, here comes Driggers. Turn out the lights!'

"Oh, it was a big joke. If you disobeyed the rules, you'd have to go see [manager] Peter Lynch and he would 'counsel' you—I mean, he'd say if this kept up, he was going to throw you out. In my particular case, I was in boarding school all my life and I was used to rules and regulations, so it didn't bother me a bit. Some of the others kind of complained sometimes about the regulations, but they knew they had to comply with them if they wanted to stay there. And they sure wanted to stay there, because it was a nice place to live."

Both Techwood and University Homes residents quickly organized tenants associations, and sponsored regular block dances, carnivals and other social activities. Despite the advantages of the projects, however, many residents moved out when they were able to buy their own home. "And, you know, that was one thing Mr. Maron used to encourage them to do," remembers Clara Render, "was to get out and buy them a home."

"See, all these teachers moved out," recalls Clara Gibson, "when they started making a better income, because in the housing projects you can only make so much. If you make enough so you can move out and buy, well, anybody that could would want to do that, because you can live here as long as I have and still not own anything."

A housing shortage right after World War II kept many residents in the projects even though their incomes had risen over the allowable level. Waldo Roescher was one: "A lot of us living there were over the income limits. We were living there only because they allowed us because they knew we couldn't find any housing outside of the apartments. See, that was in 1945, and we got thrown out in 1949. They just told a lot of us that we were way over the income limits, and that we'd have to find another place to live."

The scope and character of public housing has changed drastically since the nation's first projects were inaugurated in Atlanta. Other changes have been equally sweeping. As late as 1940, the median value of an owner-occupied, single-family house in Atlanta was $3,320, a far cry from today's prices. Outdoor toilets and plumbing are for the most part a thing of the past. The Plan of Improvement, instituted in 1952, more than tripled Atlanta's boundaries, bringing such communities as Buckhead and Cascade Heights into the city. The development of the interstate highways and MARTA, changing employment patterns, and sprawling suburbanization have all significantly altered the city's residential landscape. "Oh, it was very much different," states Clara Gibson. Adds Pauline Minniefield, "You would be amazed."

Kathleen Adams

Kathleen Adams was born on Auburn Avenue in 1890. While many of her memories take place before the period described in the rest of this book, they provide a fascinating portrait of Auburn at the turn of the century.

Many businesses had been established along the street, beginning up at Peachtree, about three doors from the intersection. There were tailor shops run by young Negroes. Coming further down the street we had a jeweler. Also in that block near Ivy Street [now Peachtree Center Avenue] there was a dry cleaning and dying works.

Coming further down the street was the John Smith Carriage and Buggy Shop. There we had his best workman by the name of Morgan, who was an upholsterer and carriage trimmer, a very interesting and outstanding job for the minority group. Going further down the street, this Charles Morgan put up the first brick building on Auburn Avenue built and engineered by Negroes. In that building he ran a feed and grain store.

Then we came to the old Wheat Street Church, down on the corner of Fort and Auburn. It was one of the finest churches that our group had, the first edifice that had gas lights, a large chandelier. It had a brass rail along the choir loft, red velvet curtains, and beautiful frescoes on the side walls.

The first two physicians—Negro physicians—coming to work in Atlanta lived along the strip between Hilliard and Yonge Street. Atlanta's prestigious dentist, J. R. Porter, also lived in that particular block. Strange to say, on the other side of the street there were cottages that were mostly rented. There had been a glue factory in the settlement, and these little houses had been built for the workers in that factory. But as the German-Americans moved out— German-Americans had lived on Auburn Avenue in the beginning—these cottages were rented out more or less to what we now call the underprivileged. They were neat little places and the occupants kept them beautifully clean.

Beginning at Jackson Street and going up to Boulevard, you had what was called "Negro Peachtree." It came by that name because the houses in that strip were small replicas of a row of houses along Peachtree Street where Davison's department store [Macy's] now is. That is the block where Martin Luther King is now buried. My father had the opportunity of breaking that block in 18-and-84 and taking our group out that far on Auburn Avenue.

When I was a child, across the street there was what we called the clubhouse. The house was a replica of the house that's on the corner of Piedmont and Ponce de Leon [the present Mansion restaurant] now. The Negroes took that property and tried to match it up with the Piedmont Driving Club. So when I was a small child it was nothing to see the rigs and buggies come riding up with a gentleman and his lady, to lift her out, and they would walk up the few steps of the terrace into the *Negro* Driving Club. It was really a sight.

The first people who went in there on Auburn were those little boys that had been, let's say, eight to ten years old when they came out of slavery, and naturally they had dreams and they wanted everything to be just like they had seen other people have. They were well trained by the American missionaries. They had all the accouterments of any other race. Even to their dress, they were formal. Whatever they did was on the formal side. Their stores were kept meticulously. Their businesses were monitored and run according to sound business principles. They had a certain pride and dignity as they stood in their store doors or they walked the streets.

Now, you should have seen Auburn Avenue on Sunday morning when the people were dressed to go to church. The women wore their taffetas. The grandmothers, of course, wore their alpacas and even their brocades on the place Sunday. The women's skirts at that time were what you would call the bellback, which gave you that flow, and as they walked down the street those skirts had a certain bounce to them. And beside them were their spouses, and if they were in their thirties or even into their forties the men had on their striped britches, two-button cutaway coats. My father had a law education and he deemed that he needed the type of coat that the lawyers in the other race wore. So, he had this Prince Albert, and he walked down Auburn Avenue in his striped britches, his Prince Albert, his Stetson hat and his walking cane and, in winter, his tan gloves. Everything formal. And all of his associates in like garb.

A lot of projects went on that you would call on the social side. Bethel was building its present church, and there was a member who gave concerts and little Tom Thumb weddings and things of that sort that interested small children. It wasn't anything for us to be learning a new drill, the hoop drill or whatever, for one of these concerts, to go where they brought us as small children together socially.

By the time you were fifteen you had learned how to play cards and you would have little card parties maybe once a month. I remember when I was in the eighth grade our class formed a little club and we called it the Friday Afternoon Social. We would meet on Friday afternoons and have a little card party.

Then you got to sixteen years old. That was the time your parents let you begin to have a young man come in and take you to a party. So the boys formed clubs and we had two or three nice clubs of boys. One was called the Acadians, and that was supposed to be the most exclusive club that we had around and about. Then the group right under us formed and had a club called the Emission Club, and later on there was a club called the Joymen in Atlanta. These boys of course were high school boys then, and into college. They would get work at the Capital City Club and Piedmont Driving Club as workers in the wine room or checking hats and coats.

These clubs would give seasonal dances, and this Acadian Club in 1913 asked the Emission Club to join in with them and they rented the hall at the City Auditorium and gave a citywide ball, debut party for the girls. They called it the Debut Ball. See, the parents of the other young ladies would give them their debuts, but our parents of course were not able and had nowhere to give a big ball. So these boys got together and gave this big affair for the young ladies. And it's something that we never forgot. I still have the lace off of my gown that night.

Everything in that period seemed to have been . . . the best that I can do, the best that I can give to my race was the ideal.

Chapter Three

Transportation

"Atlanta was noted for its railroading," exclaims redcap porter and train attendant Matthew Housch. "In fact, when I was in elementary school, it stated in our geography that Atlanta was the railroading center of the South. Back during the late twenties and early thirties we've had 224 trains daily coming in and out of Atlanta, just as I believe the statistics say it's forty planes per hour leaving Atlanta today. You could get a train in Atlanta anywhere you wanted to go in the United States, right here in Atlanta, just like you can get a plane out of here now."

The railroads made Atlanta. Founded as the community of Terminus in 1837, the young city quickly became a leading Southern rail center, a fact not lost on General Sherman and his men in 1864. After the Civil War, the railroads played an even more prominent role as Atlanta became the hub of the regional economy. In the 1920s, they spent a hundred million dollars a year in Atlanta and were the city's foremost employer. The railroads left their mark everywhere—from the sprawling Inman Yards just northwest of town to the shops near Pittsburgh and Mechanicsville to the eight trunk lines coming under the viaducts to the Union and Terminal Stations.

"Back in them days," declares textile worker Alec Dennis, "if you worked on the railroad, man, you were somebody." During the twenties some 20,000 people worked at a wide range of jobs in Atlanta's railroad shops, yards and stations, as well as on tracks and trains. "Those who were working on the road," states Matthew Housch, "if they weren't on the train working they would be at the Pullman shops or the railroad shops or on the tracks working."

For those who actually worked on the trains—the porters, engineers, firemen, conductors and others—uncertainty was a way of life. "You didn't know when you was going out," explains engineer and fireman H. Waldo Hitt. "The call boys would call you. They'd call you over the telephone. The call boy would tell you when he called you, said you got so long to catch the streetcar leaving

Decatur at two o'clock, say, or three o'clock or four o'clock. Then you'd have to do a little running to get up there to catch that car. You'd have to get up and catch the streetcar or else drive your old car to Inman, all hours of the day and night, and take a train out."

"My brother-in-law was a hostler's helper," recalls Housch. "When the engine was ready to go out these fellows would go in and get these engines and bring them to the station, where you could connect the train. They would bring the engine in from the roundhouse, and the roundhouse was where you cleaned the engines, turned them around and so forth." "The engines would be serviced," adds fireman and engineer J. R. Spratlin, "and we'd carry them back to Terminal Station to go out again."

Erected in 1905 on Spring Street, at the present site of the Richard Russell Federal Building, the Terminal Station was a bustling hub of activity in Atlanta for decades. "You'd go in there," relates Waldo Hitt, "there'd be a crowd sitting on the seats there and the bags all around them and the kids all a-crying and a-hollering and running up and down. That station had great high seats in it, and the seats was back to back, had little grills all along where the steam heat come up. No carpet on the floor, just an old tile floor. They kept it clean—not just pretty clean—they kept it clean for that day and time. You'd go into the waiting room and there was the tickets, the ticket agent standing there to sell you your ticket. And then the man would come out and call the trains and let you know when they was going so-and-so. He'd commence to naming the stations all up the road.

"We'd get the Airline Belle out of Toccoa, which was a little local train, had about three coaches, little steam engine. We'd come to Atlanta and then walk down Mitchell Street and turn there to go to Rich's, or right down there to Bass's, and there was a Kress ten-cent store. And Mama would get all of our overalls and shoes and underwear, long underwear, for the year after the men who worked on her farm had sold the cottonseed and paid the taxes. That's as far as we ever got, all day long, right in them places.

"And then when that man would say that Airline Belle, we'd grab our sacks of goods we'd bought and take off, go get us a good seat. And then you'd go down to gate so-and-so, and there'd be a man there to look at your ticket. There was one of the best fruit stands I've ever seen in my life, had the prettiest bananas and apples and pears and grapes. It was run by the Union News Company. It was a Greek run it, and he kept all those apples shined. We'd beg Mama to go buy us one of them apples or a banana or a box of Fig Newtons.

Terminal Station. (Atlanta University Collection, Woodruff Library, Atlanta University Center)

I thought if I ever got twenty cents in my life I'd get me a whole box of Fig Newtons.

"Then they had a lot of colored men. There was one big colored man I know that would slice cake and put it on little paper plates, and you'd pay a nickel or a dime and buy you a whole piece of cake from him. He would have the best chocolate cakes or anything I had ever seen in my life. And they had the red-caps, which was the porters. You'd give him a dime or a nickel or something—I never did have one to do it—and he'd carry your baggage down to the train."

The all-black redcaps "didn't have a salary then," recalls Matthew Housch. "We was only working for tips. During the time of 1937, I believe, the red-cap porters went to Mr. Randolph, and they formed a union.[1] And after they became organized, the first salary was given to the redcaps here.

"We were assigned to various trains as redcap porters, and as the trains come in, we would serve. Some weeks we would serve the coach part of the train and some weeks we would serve the Pullman part. Winter and summer we had to stand and wait on the passengers to come out, in order to bring their bags up in the station.

"We had a lot of hustling and bustling at the station there. With Christmas or holiday season, trains were crowded out. And people had to wait sometimes a good while before we could get their bags to the front of the station. During the Christmastime it has been at least twenty to thirty minutes before a passenger could get their baggage. They would become dissatisfied and make complaints [about] why we were so long with their bags, or it seemed as if the porters had run away with their bags. So you had to be on your p's and q's all the time.

"You had a sign up in the waiting rooms: 'Colored Waiting Room' or 'White Waiting Room.' In our waiting rooms here in Atlanta, if a black passenger—which I have seen—made a mistake and went through the white waiting room, why they were harshly spoken to: 'Go where you belong. You don't belong here. You belong over there.'

"I saw one situation, I believe it was in the thirties. There was an Indian woman, a foreigner, very dark, went into the white waiting room and sat there, and they wanted to move her and she refused. And they sent for the super-intendent, I believe, and there was a lot of controversy come up about it. I will say this, most of the time you could be as dark as dark could get and if you spoke any other language you could get by. But, as long as you were an American Negro, if you spoke well or didn't speak well, you was very, very segregated."

Segregation also prevailed on the trains, in the dining cars and the club cars,

Segregated Terminal Station waiting room, 1940s. (Atlanta University Collection, Woodruff Library, Atlanta University Center)

on Pullman cars and in coach. "They would take the passengers and separate them," relates train attendant Henry James. "All the blacks would be in the front and the whites on the back. The first car on the train, we'd call that the colored car, all the colored people would be in that car."

It was up to the white train conductor whether black passengers would stand or move back into the rest of the train if the first car got too crowded. Train porter James Colvard recalls: "If they didn't stand up, they would back them back and then tie a curtain, hang a curtain across the coach. Called it the dividing line." "If they didn't have a sheet or something," adds Matthew Housch, "they would have to put up newspapers to divide the whites and blacks. And in the dining car, service would be the same way, because they had curtains in there. The whites would eat first, and then at the decline of business of the whites, the blacks would come in and they would pull that curtain. And they would ask most times about how many black passengers wanted to go to the diner to eat, and we would tell the conductor.

"And most of our conductors—I don't say all of them—were very nice about it, and then some were a little off about it. Some really have stated, 'Well, we stop at such and such a place and you can get some lunch there.' It seemed as if conductors—just a few of them—didn't care for the blacks to go through the white cars to the dining car. But a lot of conductors, they would be very nice and tell the blacks, 'Well, you can eat at such and such a time,' and then the curtain would be drawn."

Most black passengers did not ride in Pullman throughout the period. When they did, they were sectioned off in what was called the "Lower 13." "During that time we had very few blacks riding in the Pullman cars," remembers Housch. "A lot of times blacks have gone to the Pullman ticket office and they would say, 'Well, we don't have anything open.' And I've known several berths to be open. People would be in coach and say, 'I applied for a reservation but they told me nothing was open.'"

The Pullman cars occasionally carried celebrities, fondly recalled by both black and white trainmen, like conductor C. R. Adamson: "I carried Jack Dempsey. I've had him on my trip and he had me to come in his room and talk with him. I've hauled President [Franklin] Roosevelt. He asked me to come in the drawing room and have a talk with him. He wanted to find out how I liked my job and what my work was and everything. The Seaboard Air Line railroad organized a trip a year for the presidents of colleges and banks to go on a tour as their guests. The first trip that they had I caught as the conductor. And then for the next five years they requested me as the conductor for their trips. I felt more like I was a rich man on those trips than I ever was."

The appeal of railroad work extended well beyond hobnobbing with famous passengers. "I liked the pay and I liked to be the boss of the train," recalls conductor J. H. Bond. For many, like brakeman and conductor Fred Ferguson, working on the trains was the realization of a lifelong dream: "I was born in sight of a railroad and I've loved trains all my life. I was about three years old and I could get up on the hill above Grandmother's house and see the trains go by. In high school at Rockmart the teachers gave me one seat along the wall because they knew I was going to get up when the whistle blew and see what engine it was."

Waldo Hitt was another whose boyhood dreams came true: "I had my mind set on being an engineer. It was no question about it then. You couldn't have got a better job in the world, as far as I was concerned. There wasn't nothing I didn't like about it, nothing.

"Especially with steam engines, you'd be riding along and you waved at everybody and everybody waved at you. And you'd have places up and down the road that at night they'd turn their lights on or wave their lights, their lanterns, at you, open the front door where you could see the fire in the fireplace as the train would go by. You didn't know who they were, but they were people who'd lived there all their lives with trains going by. You'd go in, you'd take you a bath and go to bed, you felt like you'd done something. I just liked it all."

Like policemen, streetcar men and other workers of the time, many railroad men started out on what was called the "extra board," working only when called, and subject to the seniority system, technological changes, and the ebb and flow of the Southern economy. "You had on the railroad then," recalls Hitt, "what they called a peach season, and they'd run a lot of peach trains. And getting to fire a peach train, which was a through-train and going all the time, you didn't have to stop and do any switching. A little after peach season you had a watermelon season. They'd run some solid carloads, fifty-car trains of watermelons. And then in the early spring you'd have a fertilizer season, you'd haul a lot of fertilizer. And that's what you'd look for, those seasons that helped the extra man and let you make some extra money."

"They'd call the roll," remembers porter Dexter Gray. "They let you know how you stood on the roll, on the roster, when you went up for sign-out. If he didn't need you today he'd tell you when to come. I've been up there and the fellow who would sign out would say, 'Gray, today's Monday. Call me Thursday. Nothing doing till around Thursday.' You'd call Thursday, or you'd go up Thursday. He'd say, 'Check with me in the morning.' Then you know you're getting close. Then next you'd go up there. He'd tell you that day, 'Better call me at two o'clock.' Call him at two o'clock, he'd say, 'Well, no, you're first out tomorrow. You call me and check with me tomorrow.' Then you get an assignment the next day. When I got a regular job, I knew when I'd be going out and when I'm coming in."

"Man, it took us a lifetime to stand for a regular job in those days," relates brakeman and conductor Fred Ferguson, "where we'd have enough seniority to build a job up. You hire like I hired—on December 21, 1924—work the extra board and stay there until enough men go off from the top to give the younger men a job. When a job comes open, they put it on the bulletin board that a vacancy exists. If nobody older than you bids on that job, puts in a claim on it, you'll get it. And it took a long time to do it."

For some, the wait was forever. A black hostler's helper always remained a helper, black porters or brakemen could not make it to conductor—"the boss of the train"—and black firemen were barred from being engineers by Southern custom, craft restrictions and railroad regulations. "At that time they couldn't promote a colored man out there," recalls Waldo Hitt, "and he stayed what they hired him. If they hired him a laborer, he was a laborer. And you didn't question that then."

In 1924, there were over 10,000 black railroad workers in Georgia, more than in any other state. At the outbreak of World War I, black firemen comprised 80 percent of the firing force on the Southern Railroad, 90 percent on the Atlantic Coast Line and the Seaboard Air Line.[2] "Actually, there were more black firemen at one time than there were whites," states Matthew Housch. "They were mostly blacks who did do that."

One of the main reasons that black firemen predominated in the early twentieth century was that until the advent of mechanical firing engines or stokers in the 1920s, a fireman's job was hot, hard and dirty. White fireman J. R. Spratlin describes the early days: "It's a real job firing an engine, it's a darn hard job. I was using a scoop and there wasn't no eight-hour haul then, there was twelve hours, sometimes sixteen. And I've burned between here and Chattanooga many a time anywhere between fifteen and twenty tons of coal, and then get back in the yard sometimes [after] sixteen hours.

"You'd put the coal in, then you'd clean up the deck. There was always some falling on the deck. When I first started, they used to have them old chain doors, you opened and closed them doors by hand. You just reached to pull it, throw it open, throw in the fire and then close it just a second or two, and then throw another. You didn't have time to sit down good. You'd kind of lean over the seat box a little bit and watch for a little bit. When the black smoke quit boiling, you had to get down and fire some more. On them hills, up a long grade, you had to be firing nearly all the time.

"And we had to shake and clean out fires, shake the ashes. We had fire cleaning places where we stopped that you always cleaned the fire—Dallas, Rockmart, Rome, Sugar Valley. Them old ash bins, you'd have to get out and rake it out of the pans, you know, it wouldn't fall out. Pull the rake out of the fire, it'd be red hot. It wasn't no fun.

"I've wondered a lot of times how my lungs were maybe affected from that dust that I inhaled from those engines. See, that coal, we kind of tried to keep it sprinkled down with a hose, but you're so doggone tired of firing when you got through throwing in the fire, you'd want to rest a lick in place of sprinkling coal. When you'd come in, you were so dirty they couldn't tell whether you was a black man or a white man sometimes, down in front of that fire door and dust from the coal flying up in your face."

Of course, one could tell the difference. The Brotherhood of Locomotive Engineers and other railroad brotherhoods had constitutional clauses barring black workers. In the early twentieth century white railroad workers and their unions moved beyond excluding black workers from certain occupations to actively seeking to eliminate blacks from positions they already held on the railroads. In Georgia, this new stance culminated in a violent strike on the Georgia Railroad in 1909, when white firemen and their supporters up and down the line tried to remove black firemen from the Atlanta to Augusta route.

White railroad men often sought the dismissal of their black counterparts. The railroad companies in contrast generally tried to maintain their low-paid black labor, weakening unionism in the process. A series of compromises such as the Atlanta Agreement of 1921 reduced wage differentials between blacks and whites, and established different quotas for black and white firemen and other workers on the various lines.[3] "Ever since I can remember," says Waldo Hitt, "they had it fixed that colored men would have a percentage of the passenger trains. It was so many trains they'd run, so many of them had to be colored jobs firing. And they kept them jobs, they stayed on them years and years."

Yet white pressure and improved employment opportunities elsewhere contributed to a great decline in the number of black firemen and other railroad workers over the years. Because black workers were barred from certain occupations, whites would fill job vacancies. Train attendant Henry James explains:

"There wasn't any black engineers. Since a black fireman couldn't be an engineer, he wasn't a 'promotable' man, he couldn't get no higher than fireman. Say you had seniority but since you wasn't a promotable man, a white fireman could take your place, see, because they had to have more engineers. You had to be a fireman before you could be an engineer." Between 1928 and 1949 *no* blacks were hired on a Class 1 railroad anywhere in the country as a fireman, brakeman, trainman or yardman.[4]

Black railroad workers had different reactions to their circumscribed position. Some, like James Colvard, accepted it as part of the larger segregated society: "Well, I didn't think anything about it, I didn't think anything about it. When I got off a job I'd hunt another one, do a little work elsewhere. I just had to work. You would go and plow if you wanted to, pick cotton, chop cotton, anything, but you would come back when they called you back to the board. Of course, the white firemen done the same thing, you know."

Others, like Henry James, felt more bitter: "I didn't feel good over it, I didn't feel good over it. I would say to myself, 'It's a darn shame, it's a darn shame. I'm doing the conductor's work and getting $2.37 an hour.' And then I'd hear them talking about checks probably for $300, $400, on paydays, you know. And mine would be a hundred and something, and I'm doing the same work that he's doing. No, I couldn't feel good over that. But what could you do? Couldn't do nothing about it."

"Really, we have struggled," states Matthew Housch. "But during our struggle it's brightened up some because now it seems that any position you want, you can get it with the railroad. Fellows I know [who] went with the railroad since I came off in 1950 started as porters and they're engineers now. I had a family and they didn't have families, and I couldn't work one or two days a month and take care of the family when they began to cut off help and cut off help. But they stuck with it, and now they have become firemen and engineers and brakemen and so forth."

"See, these niggers have taken over since I retired," states a former white trainman. "Well, I don't feel too good about it. You can't get along with them, never have been able to get along with them. Back when I was there, we'd tell them no, and that was it. Later on, they'd tell you what to do. They didn't do that back in my days."

Changes in racial employment policies and practices are among the many sweeping transformations on the railroads since the 1920s. One of the biggest changes was the shift from steam-powered engines to diesel, beginning in the twenties and accelerating in the World War II era. "The economy of the diesel wasn't in their attractive power particularly, but the service that they can perform," recalls Samuel Young, former chief executive officer and general manager of the Georgia Railroad. "Steam engines spent a great deal of time in the shops under inspection, being overhauled and worked on, very little of which was necessary for a diesel. So a diesel unit would work many more days in a year than any steam engine would. And another element, especially favorable to the Georgia Railroad, was the price of coal. We had to buy coal and have it shipped in over a foreign line. We paid the Louisville and Nashville more money freight on our coal than we paid the mines for the coal. And of course the diesels ran more economically in their operations as well as in their maintenance than the steam engines had.

"And so I was glad to get rid of the steam engines, because I knew we could make more money with diesel power. If I remember correctly, we bought fifty-two diesels to replace 105 steam engines. We sold thirty good steam locomotives to a scrap firm located on our tracks at Oakland City for less money than enough to buy two diesels. Many of the steam engines that we scrapped were very fine engines, but there was no market for them because other railroads were buying diesels at the same time. Course, I was disappointed that we could sell them for so little money, but it was an economical thing to do."

Yet many former railroad men, like Waldo Hitt, lament the passing of the steam era: "Diesel was good, there's no doubt about it. It handled more stuff, handled it better. And they can be a whole lot faster. But I come up on steam and I liked steam. I thought the steam engine was the best piece of machinery to be built in the world.

"It was a different thing running a diesel and a steam. Running a steam engine, you felt like you was master of something. But a diesel, you just got up there and run it, just drove from one end of the road to the other." Echoes J. R. Spratlin, "Them diesels you just set up, ain't no science much to them. There's a science in running a steam engine. You take a good steam engine and the valves are good and square, and you get on a hill and hear them cracking. I love it."

"On a steam locomotive," reminisces Hitt, "the engineer waved at everybody, and if they didn't wave at him out in the field or sitting on the porch, you thought there was something the matter with them. But now, this day and time, on the diesel you don't pay no attention to nobody, like riding up and down the road in your automobile. You don't wave to nobody much."

Compared to the boom days of the twenties, when well over 10,000 railroad passengers a *day* came through Atlanta, nobody much rides the trains anymore, either. Federal subsidies of alternate forms of transportation, the rise in inter-city bus traffic, technological changes in transportation facilities, and out-dated work rules all contributed to the decline of passenger train service. "The time came," recalls Samuel Young, "when it was very unprofitable to handle passengers. By 1930 we were losing substantially. So we got rid of the passenger service as quick as we could. And we were more successful in Georgia than some other railroads were in other states in eliminating passenger business.

"People were not traveling on trains, they were beginning to fly and drive their own automobile. The last train that we got rid of on the West Point route was a train that operated between West Point and Atlanta, arriving in Atlanta about 8:15 or 8:30 in the morning. We applied to the Public Service Commission to get rid of that train, and at the public hearing before the Public Service Commission there were forty-two living in Palmetto and Fairburn that came in to object to our taking off the train. And they all came to Atlanta that morning in their own automobiles to attend the meeting."

In 1927 there were 326 passenger trains passing through Atlanta daily, at mid-century 110, by the 1970s but a handful, although freight has maintained a significant presence in the city. In early 1972 Terminal Station was razed, a few months after Atlanta's Union Station suffered a similar fate. "I hated to see the passenger trains going," says C. R. Adamson, reflecting the view of many retired railroad men. "And when they tore down that Terminal Station, it just made me feel so sad to see it go. They could have made it a central place for everybody to come to Atlanta to see that station, they could have beautified that place to no end. And it just makes you feel bad to see it torn down."

Matthew Housch

Matthew Housch worked as a redcap porter at the Terminal Station until 1939, when he started as a train attendant. He was on the initial run of the Southern Crescent from Atlanta to New Orleans.

As a boy, I long wanted to become a part of it, and not having any dreams that I would. But my dreams did come true. It did come true in my middle years of life. My affiliation begun in the early thirties at the station, which was

[as] a redcap porter. I was in my late thirties when I begun working with them. And I really enjoyed the work, worked on up till '39. I made my first run on the road, which was from Atlanta to Jacksonville, Florida, after which I was one of the first ones to become initiated with the first streamlined [trains] the Southern put on. And I made its initial trip from Atlanta to New Orleans. I came off in around 1950, I believe, off the road.

During the time of the redcap I met my wife. She was an Alabama girl and was going to teach school in Savannah. In the afternoon I met one of our trains coming from Birmingham and brought this young lady off the train, and, to my surprise, she had to wait over until eleven o'clock that night to catch a train to Savannah. So we begun talking, and after talking we—at my break, we had dinner. And after having dinner she asked me to call some friends of hers, which were some young men in Atlanta she knew, and I called about five or six times and never could get in touch. So we continued to talk at my convenience hour, and she decided—I asked her, rather, to write me when she was situated.

So when she got to her station she wrote me and I wrote her back. Actually, I liked to not given her my address, because I didn't think about it until the train was getting ready to pull off. Then I grabbed a little cup, little water cup, and scribbled my address on it, and she kept it and wrote me. She came to Atlanta from September to December three times, and on the fourth time she came into Atlanta we got married.

Our duties were to meet the trains and wait until the people come out of the cars to bring their bags up. And you had to clean the station area, the front part of the station, the steps or in the waiting rooms, to some extent, you had to clean that, and out in the hallways which you would travel going from the waiting room down to get on the train. Carry the bags, clean the station. And, by the way, you had to be responsible persons there. All of us had to be responsible persons because of the fact that there had been fellows who weren't responsible, had gone in people's bags and got off their jewelry and other materials which they had, and then a suit was filed against whatever terminal company it had occurred. I don't remember any of that applying to us in Atlanta.

I enjoyed the work there, waiting on people and meeting different people. During that time we met people who were up in society very much. And we were very glad to serve them and to bring their bags up. I think I have met some of the top people of the country, such as the late Mr. Bing Crosby and the late Mrs. [Mary McLeod] Bethune. I did have their autograph. And I've met several other movie stars and also Mr. Gene Tunney. I became closely associated with two of our former governors, which were Governor [E. D.] Rivers and Governor Eugene Talmadge. We became very much associated with each other. I enjoyed talking with them and enjoyed waiting on them and carrying their bags up.

At one time, when you become a train porter, if the conductor wanted a certain man to go with him, they would let him do so. And they didn't altogether respect the seniority rights of the train porters, because this conductor says, "I want 'X' to go with me on my run. All the time he is my porter." And then that was just it. But when we become unionized they had to honor the seniority rights. Regardless of whether the conductor wanted that man or not, he had to accept him as a porter.

This change came during the time that I entered the railroad, running on the railroad, which was around '39. The union then negotiated with the railroad and said, "Now, this man should get so much pay for 240 hours per month or so many miles per month, whichever was the greatest. That's one good phrase which the union did bring out: "whichever was the greatest," which gave you a pretty decent salary at the particular time.

It seemed as though the better coaches went to the white passengers. A lot of times windows were possibly cracked, seats weren't cleaned so very well. Actually, I've seen people put paper down to sit on those seats. They should have been clean, but when they got in a rush they would just go and grab up a car whether that car had been cleaned or not, because to get a real clean car sometimes it would entertain the train's lateness a lot. Sometimes they would just see if any paper towels or tissue was in the rest rooms, and then let it go.

And then a lot of times the whites would have air-conditioned cars and the blacks would have the non-air-conditioned cars. At that time, they would have to place ice under the cars to make them cool, it was a cooling system which worked by ice. A lot of times they didn't have enough ice under those cars to make them work.

Some of the white employees was good and some weren't so good. For instance, on several occasions the conductor would send you up in the station after some report or something from the ticket window, and you were very harshly spoken to, I well recall, by the ticket agent or some other white employee when you went into the white waiting room to pick up these things, especially if you didn't work at that terminal. They would ask you, 'Boy, what do you want?' or 'Uncle, what do you want?' See, you were always 'boy' or 'uncle' to them.

If you resented them calling you 'boy' or 'uncle,' well you would be a slob-sob the rest of the time with that employee. He'd say, 'That so-and-so, he's hateful,' or 'He's trying to be smart. Well, I'll get rid of him.' And actually they did get rid of you. I've seen a lot of fellows beg back for their jobs, and eventually they did get their jobs back. Sometimes they would go higher than the regular officials of the Terminal Company and they would state their case to them. And I have known fellows who have gone to the president of the Southern Railroad and state their case. Right here in Atlanta I've seen it happen. Later on, when we did form the union [the Brotherhood of Sleeping Car Porters], you just couldn't get rid of that particular man. The union would bail you out in such hard situations as that.

That was mostly back in the thirties when that happened. And, all of the white employees were not selfish. Some, I should say, were liberal, and some were not. As this hatred-ism seemed to get a little quieter, the people seemed to get along much better and understand each other, which was very good, I think.

I wish that the time would come that really the trains would come back. Though the railroads say they are losing on mail and passengers, that is a matter of opinion. I can't see it, but maybe they are. I really believe that if the trains were running as they were, or even if half of the trains were running, we would have less unemployment, period.

"That old Terminal Station was nice," recalls Waldo Hitt. "In its day, it was a crackerjack. They had just a little parking area out there in the front. Everybody rode the streetcar up there. And the streetcar was the way you got around in Atlanta.

"A lot of railroad men lived out around Little Five Points, because of the streetcar service. You could catch a car there most any time. You could just walk up there on DeKalb Avenue and catch the Decatur car. The Inman Yard car, it run all night long and it made connections with these Decatur cars and all at Five Points. There was very few railroad men that owned automobiles, very few poor folks that owned automobiles, and especially you didn't have two. And if you had an automobile, you didn't want to take it out there to Inman and let it sit all day and night if you were going on a freight train, and get cinders and dust and old smoke all over it, see. You'd ride the streetcar."

"Back there in 1913, '14, '15, along up in there, all the city of Atlanta rode the street railway," states streetcar conductor I. H. Mehaffey. "The mayor of

Atlanta rode, and the police chief, he rode, Sheriff Lowery rode—he was a grand old man—most everybody rode the street railway."

In 1913, Atlanta's extensive streetcar system, owned by the Georgia Railway and Power Company—later Georgia Power—carried over 57 million passengers.[5] The streetcars passed through working-class neighborhoods to get to the Inman Yards and other work sites, helped develop Inman Park and other residential communities, ran out to recreational areas like Grant Park and Ponce de Leon Park[6] and furnished access to downtown Atlanta.

In the teens Georgia Railway and Power only hired white men raised in the country as motormen and conductors, in part to get employees with no union background. The company held huge hiring days, vividly remembered down to the date by former streetcar men like A. J. Shupe: "I grew up in Putnam County, Eatonton, Georgia. We farmed, gristmilled, sawmilled, and dairied. I had a good friend here, G. C. Patrick, and he got after me to come up here and go to work for the power company. So I left home the fourth Sunday in July, 1919, came up here.

"They were hiring down there then on the second and sixteenth of each month. I missed the sixteenth and I had to wait till the second day of August to get hired. And Mr. Patrick give me a note to Mr. G. C. Cobb, who was hiring. He told me just to push—I'd never seen such a bunch of men down there. And every time they'd open the door, they'd let one in and then they'd interview him and he'd come back out. So I worked my way and got right up to the door, and he opened the door and said, 'Well, that's all, men.' So, I handed him my little note and he closed the door. And directly he come back there, and he says, 'Come in here, boy.' And he says, 'Do you want to work?' I said, 'That's what I come here for.' And so they hired me. There were thirty-five of us hired that day. That was on a Friday, and he told me to come back down there Saturday morning and get my badge and all."

In the days before the union became well established, hours were long and working conditions hard for the city's streetcar men. "A beginner had to take what he could," recalls I. H. Mehaffey. "Where there was someone off sick, you was selected off a list of extra men. And each morning, if you had early report, why you'd get there at 3:30 and stay on till they called you or at least they didn't need you. Then you went on back to your boarding place and would come back at 11:00 and report again. Then 3:30 in the afternoon for the evening work, you had to report. Three times a day that you would report, but didn't get any time for reporting.

"If you did work, it would be around eleven or twelve hours a day. What we

Streetcar riders. (Courtesy Atlanta Historical Society)

called a day run was a two-time run. You'd go to work at 4:30 in the morning, get off at about 11:00, and go back at 12:00 and off at about 7:00 that night. That was a day run.

"Then we had a tripper run that would go to work about 5:00 or 5:30 in the morning, get off about 7:30 or 8:00, come back at about 10:30 and work until about 1:30, and be off until about 5:00 that afternoon, and come out and work till about 7:00 or 7:30 that night, a three-time run. An evening run was one that you would go to work about 1:00 and work till 5:00 and be off an hour, and come back at 6:00 and work till 12:00 or 1:00 that night. It was all just straight pay, for the actual hours that you put in, no overtime. Being a divided run, why, it would use up a lot of your time. You didn't have time to go home, maybe, and you had to get a sandwich or something and be back in position to relieve your relief man at the proper time."

"They were telling tales that children asked, 'Mama, who was that man in here last night?'" laughs motorman Lloyd Adair. "You couldn't hardly spend no time with your family hardly at all. And you'd get awfully tired—I'll tell you that now—standing up all day. At a nickel apiece, you were taking and hauling a lot of people back then. If you got fifty dollars of a night at a nickel apiece, you was a-working."

"They had the old hand-brake cars," remembers conductor T. Ross Couch. "The motorman had a lever just like a grinding stone up there for hand brakes. If you were running fifteen or twenty miles an hour, it'd take you fifty feet or something to stop one of them things. You couldn't stop one of them just sudden." "You just couldn't stop a streetcar," says Mehaffey. "Sometimes I've seen them be going forward on a hill and come to a dead stop and just slide all the way back down the hill. I did that with me, I'm talking about myself. And I've heard others say the same thing, that they wished they could just see Stone Mountain out in front of them instead of what was out there to stop the old streetcar from sliding."

"I was going to Buckhead one morning," remembers motorman A. L. Nelson, "and the car in front of me had froze up. And I throwed on the brakes and I didn't have no brakes, and I went right on into that other car. Another time, I was pulling on this East Point, Hapeville and College Park line and the superintendent, Mr. Grubbs, come out and said, 'Nelson, we haven't had an accident on the whole system today, let's make it a day without an accident.' I said, 'Okay.' I went on and went under the underpass on a private right-of-way to Hapeville, and there was a high bank up on my right. I looked at my board to see what kind of time I was on, and just as I hung my board up and looked in front of me there was an old cow come down that bank. I hit her, knocked her over on the other track. They had to go out there and kill her. I had to tell Grubbs I had an accident."

"When I first come here," relates motorman M. Y. Rutherford, who later joined the Atlanta police force, "the old streetcars wasn't enclosed. The inside, the passengers was, but the front and back was all open. The platform just had a vestibule around it, and take a cold, windy day and you'd freeze to death out there. I'm telling you, it was chilly."

According to motorman H. E. James, "In the early days they had some of the superintendents that made statements that men was cheaper than glass. We had some pretty rough foremen around, and supervisors. We had a lot of them that would climb up in the trees and hide around the posts to pimp on, to spy on the men, to see whether they was running ahead or smoking in the cars, and all such things as that."

Lloyd Adair had one such encounter with a supervisor one morning on the Emory route: "It wasn't daylight. I was going up the street and I saw something move up there. I don't know how I come to see it, but anyhow it was behind that hedge on the side of the road there. I couldn't imagine what would be a-jumping and hid behind it, fallen down behind it. I stopped and went over there and peeped over it, and it was a supervisor.

"I said, 'Bill, you just as well go on back to town. You ain't going to catch nobody today. I'm telling every man I meet where you're at. You ain't going to get nowhere today. Go on back.' He said, 'No, don't do that. Don't do that.' But I did."

These types of conditions helped prompt Atlanta motormen and conductors to go on strike in 1916 and again in 1918, eventually gaining union recognition. Heightened competition with the automobile, as well as with privately owned jitneys, also contributed to company officials seeking a more amicable labor relationship with the streetcar men. Between 1916 and 1925, the number of motor vehicles registered in Fulton County swelled from 6,301 to 47,433.[7]

Increased automobile traffic, especially along the crowded streets of downtown Atlanta, helped bring on a number of accidents involving streetcars, such as one which befell M. Y. Rutherford on the Peachtree and Whitehall line in 1928: "I came up Whitehall Street one afternoon in the rush hour. Just before I got to McDaniel an automobile passed me on the right. Well, I didn't see him till he got tangled up in the corner of that trolley, and when we stopped he was headed back to town on the other track. There was no way for me to stay away from that automobile. So I decided, 'Well, I'll quit this job. I'll go down and see if I can get on the police force.'"

Passengers could also present problems for the streetcar men. "They'd slip

Mechanics at Beaudry Ford, 1916. (Courtesy Atlanta Historical Society)

by you," says T. Ross Couch. "You'd sometimes get a big crowd standing and all, you know, it was hard to keep up with them." "Occasionally someone tried to tell you that they had already paid," adds I. H. Mehaffey. "And especially if a drunk would get on, why he would feel like he had already paid. Then sometimes you'd have a drunk that would get on and go to sleep. It was quite embarrassing to try to wake him up. Of course, we all learned the tactic of waking up a drunk man—not to be in front of him, always get behind him and just put one finger on his forehead and press his head backward. It wasn't long to where he couldn't stand the pressure and it would wake him up."

Motorman Sanders Ivey, who later joined the police force, recalls one way to deal with unruly passengers: "The streetcar man's best weapon was what he called a switch stick. It was a rod about two and a half feet long. On the old tracks, you'd take and open up a switch and you could turn [it] to the right, you know. And you could pull out that switch stick and you could knock somebody cold with it. Some people did that."

The streetcars were where black and white Atlantans most frequently rubbed elbows. They thus provided a daily reminder of the inequities and tensions of a segregated society. In 1891 the Georgia legislature passed a street railway segregation law. In 1906 the city added its own local Jim Crow ordinance, creating an informal dividing line between black and white passengers. "The sign was in the front of the trolley," recalls one resident, "'Colored seat from rear toward front. Whites seat from front toward rear.'"

"There was no [racial] trouble at all in those days," declares motorman M. Y. Rutherford. "If they would sit too far up in the car the conductor would ask them to move back. Well, they'd get up and move back without any arguments. No trouble at all." A prominent white professional man adds, "They had the Jim Crow law and blacks sat in the back. And they didn't resent it, seemingly."

Yet, in fact, the segregated seating system bred constant friction. "The whole, total way of life was there in this accordion movement continuously to obey the law," observes sociologist Arthur Raper, who monitored the streetcars for the Commission on Interracial Cooperation in the 1920s. "There were all sorts of needing to move back and move up and keep that line, that imaginary line. And there would be all kinds of things happening, some of which had the elements of direct physical brutality."

"I ran on the river line about fifteen years," relates Lloyd Adair, "and I worked seven or eight of that at night. And every Saturday night come, we had a few fellows from around Center Hill and Riverside, boys that would get drunk and think they'd have to whip a nigger, you know. And they'd get back

Interior of bus, 1941. (Special Collections, Georgia State University)

in the black section—they had to sit from the rear, you know, toward the front —and get it started. Then you'd have to get in there and get them out and take care of them. That was about the worst thing.

"I've done a little meanness with those fellows, I'd get so aggravated. One of them had give me so much trouble I couldn't stand it. Just as he got on the bottom step I give him a little shove with my foot. 'Go ahead.' That was pretty mean, I guess, but at the same time you'd done been in it. We had a bunch that would try that every Saturday night over on the river."

"That river car was the worst so far as racial conflict was concerned," echoes nurse Ruby Baker, "because it was going from town to a poor section of whites out there at the river. When we lived on Newport Street we rode the river car. And I remember the night we graduated, coming from the Auditorium. My mother stepped up on the step on that river car and a white guy come up and shoved Mama back like that, got in front of her. And it was a boy in my class, Marion Allen, he grabbed him in the back of the collar and the guy come out of his coat. The motorman was trying to hold my brother and Marion Allen and a lot of those boys—all of us getting on the car—back. And he opened the other door and let that fellow out, and he took off. See, you weren't supposed to get on the trolley in front of a white person. He wasn't even there when we started boarding, you know.

"They was really poor white trash out there. And they would take one to a seat, and there was always conflict, there were fights always erupting. Of course, they would end with putting the black person in jail, it was always his fault, you know."

"I put a colored woman and her son off one night," remembers conductor Adair. "A white fellow had asked her to get back and she'd cursed him. Him and her got into a fight. Then the whole carload was about to get into it and I decided I couldn't whip all of them to make them leave her alone. I'll just put her off to get rid of her."

Racial tensions on the streetcars, and later the trackless trolleys and busses, extended well beyond the river line to every route in the city. "If there was one white person sitting back there in the back where the colored ought to be," remembers blues musician Roy Dunn, "the Negro couldn't sit down till that white person got up and went to the front. He'd better not ask him to go up there, he'd get beat to death. You just stand up and hold to the rod until that white man get off and then you can get over there and sit down. Even if there's no space for you to stand back yonder, you'd better go back there and stand— don't stand up over that white man. I'm telling you what I know."

"It was miserable," seconds schoolteacher Pauline Minniefield. "Everybody was packed back there, and all those empty seats in front. But, you see, you couldn't sit in front of some old white woman or man that'd get on and sit for the heck of it right middle-way of the doggone streetcar, and you'd have to stand up. And sometimes, people would say, 'I've been standing on my feet all day. Dogged if I'm going to stand up here all night.' And they'd sit down."

Such occurrences happened well before the famous Montgomery bus boy-cott of 1955–56. "Sometimes we'd have arguments, little specks on the bus or the streetcar," recalls domestic worker Alice Adams. "Some peoples would just get determined: 'I'm not going to work all day and stand!' Well, sometimes we had flare-ups, but not too much because we knew what we was supposed to do and we did it."

"Now some white people," states Roy Dunn, "was decent enough to when he come on the streetcar and seen it was full up, he wouldn't come on back there and make the nigger get up. He'd just stand up and hold to the rod up there in the front, till somebody got off there and then he'd sit down." "I used to go towards the rear," remembers white schoolteacher Evelyn Witherspoon, "so that I could up and move forward when some black people started getting on. I could do that and let two black people sit down. I knew that it just wasn't right or reasonable to force them to stand in the aisle."

Some streetcar men, like Ross Couch, also tried to be civil to both black and white passengers: "Maybe the back would be filled up with colored, maybe old colored widow women standing up in back, and there would be vacant seats up towards the front. If it got that way, I'd just stop the car and ask them if they would mind moving up, or vice versa, whichever one happened. Even back then I knew it was wrong, people doing that, sitting back there like that."

But for many black Atlantans, the motormen and conductors were a major part of the problem. "The Negroes knew that the white conductor had ready access to the police," states Arthur Raper. "All the conductor needed to do was blow his whistle. The policeman was just simply there to carry out the conductor's instructions. There were no Negro conductors, all white men con-ductors, and most of the conductors were people who had come in from the farms and from the hills and whatnot. They were sort of the same people as most of the police were, although maybe not as 'city-ized' as the police were."

"I recall going to one of our NAACP meetings many, many years ago," re-calls chauffeur L. D. Keith. "I shall never forget it. Something happened on the car between a Negro girl and the conductor, maybe over the fare. But

Filling station, 1939. (Photograph by Marion Post Wolcott. Courtesy Library of Congress)

whatever happened, he came back to slap this girl. And my uncle, he jumped between them and caught the motorman's hand. So he called a policeman, and the policeman made a case against the Negro girl and did not make a case against the motorman. And when we attended court, during the next week I believe it was, the judge settled the case by dismissing it. But he so stated that had not the colored girl given this white motorman a deal of trouble, he would have never hit her." Such incidents prompted black community leaders to regularly call for black streetcar men and later bus drivers, especially on the lines that serviced largely black neighborhoods. Yet the work force remained all-white until the mid-1960s.

Black Atlantans developed a range of personal responses to the system. "Every time I saw a streetcar coming and people standing up on there," recalls Roy Dunn, "I didn't get on. And I'd tell the people that I worked for, 'Now, if the bus is crowded, the streetcar is crowded, I'll be late because I'm going to walk. You just have to come pick me up.' But, when I saw some empty seats back there when it pulled up to a stop, I got on. Do you see what I mean? That's the way I did it."

"I boycotted the streetcar as much as I could," states Benjamin Mays. "But when I got on the streetcar and I had to sit in the back, my body was there but not my mind." "There were some Negroes, like Martin Luther King, Sr.," adds Atlanta University history professor Clarence Bacote, "who would *never* ride the streetcar, would not suffer those injustices."

"We tried to have peace," says Alice Adams, "and then sometimes you couldn't have it. But anyway, we hung in there—I did. And eventually it changed where you can sit anywhere you want. We didn't have as much trouble about desegregating the busses as they did in other places. But it wasn't so easy."

After an organized desegregation effort led by local black ministers, and a federal court order, Atlanta's transit system was integrated in the late 1950s. The first black bus drivers came on board in 1965. There were other major changes, too. The late 1940s marked the demise of the inter-urban routes and of the streetcars themselves. The interstate highways further cut into public transit. Following a 1947 Securities Exchange Commission order requiring the company to drop its transportation holdings, and a series of strikes—the first since the teens—Georgia Power sold the system to the Atlanta Transit Company in 1950. "My gosh, it's just different," states ex-streetcar man Couch. "Way it is now and how it was then. It was a different proposition."

H. Waldo Hitt

The son of a railroad man, Waldo Hitt worked over fifty years on the railroads himself, retiring in 1972.

I started about 1918, '19, as a water boy, with my father. My father was a B-and-B foreman, and I was working with him, which I maybe was making fifty, seventy-five cents a day, just carrying water and staying out there especially all summer. That was railroad work, building trestles and water tanks and depots and repairing depots and platforms and all such as that.

And I'd carry water then for all of them. They were always a-hollering at the water boy, and they'd holler, "Water! Water! Water boy, where are you? Turn your cap around so I'll think you're coming instead of going," and all such as that, you know.

He had colored men working for him that used to just . . . man, I could stand and listen to them all day long call timber or laying rail or loading stuff, heavy stuff. And he had one Negro—I never will forget his name, John Barnett. He was a timber caller, and he could sing better than anybody I ever heard in my life, I thought. Whenever they was handling heavy timber or rail, he'd sing something and they'd follow it, and in the time of it they'd pull. Then they'd just be a-working, digging in a ditch, a drain ditch or something, and they'd just get to singing. It was hard for them to get a drink of water sometimes, getting me to leave. I'd hold still and listen to them sing.

Papa had a colored man, Will Howard, that was a good worker and Papa thought a lot of him, he could depend on him. He didn't have to stand over him. He wanted to give Will a little better job and let him make a little more money. He couldn't do it. He just changed his name, called him J. W. Cornelius, and hired a J. W. Cornelius. His check come 'J. W. Cornelius.' And it was the same one, just changed the colored man's name.

I went to firing when I was sixteen years old, but I was supposed to be twenty-one. And about all the questions they asked the firemen then was, "How old are you?" You would say, "Well, twenty-one." Then they would ask you, "Do you have a strong back?" You'd say, "Yes." "Do you have a weak mind?" You'd say, "Yes." "You've got a job." But that's about all they asked them then. They knew everybody they was hiring before—the trainmasters.

I was sixteen years old in February and I went to firing in May. That was 19-and-23. I fired some with a scoop. I fired local freights with a scoop and switches with a scoop and some through-freights and some passenger trains. Before 19-and-26 and along in there, I'll say 1924 and '25, them boys were firing with a scoop. They didn't have a mechanical firing engine or a stoker, we called them.

They had more to do than a man could do in this day and time. They don't make men like that today, because they did a lot of shoveling of coal, and they'd just fire it with a number two scoop—long-handled number two scoops. And they fired that engine. They put that coal in that firebox.

And there was better firemans and sorry firemans. I got the chance to ride the road and do my learning with the better men, and I had a better chance. I had a better chance than a lot of men had out here on the railroad, because my daddy was ahead of me and he knew them all. They all knew him.

My first passenger train that I ever fired on—I'll tell you why I remember it so well. I didn't have a regular job. I was just working extra. And the trestle across Tallulah River burned off, and my daddy, of course, had to put the timber back on it. It didn't burn the steel. And that was August the seventh, 19-and-24. And the shop foreman got me to fire the little passenger engine that ran from Toccoa to Elberton and back. A fellow, Sisk, Jesse Sisk, was the engineer—a mighty good man. They took some cars and they brought passengers across the little covered bridge from the South Carolina side to the Georgia side late that afternoon, and I fired with about two cars, two coaches and a boxcar or two, all the way to Atlanta.

Well, I thought that was the greatest thing in the world. I wouldn't have swapped jobs with President Roosevelt—whoever was the president then. He didn't have a job. *I* had the job. I wouldn't have swapped with him for nothing. That's what I wanted to do all my life. I loved it.

Then, when I was promoted, I just got a message. That was in 1936. It was put on the bulletin board that I was promoted—yard engineer at Toccoa. They didn't need road engineers, they needed the yard men. And then I transferred to the mainline.

My first mainline trip was on a freight train from Atlanta to Greenville. I remember it mighty well. The boy's still living that was firing for me—a white boy. His daddy was an engineer and he'd just been hired out maybe a year as a fireman. I was not only nervous, I was scared. I'd think about certain places. I thought about that mountain the minute I left Inman out there and got out of the yard, and I thought about that mountain, was I going to be able to do it. I didn't say nothing to nobody. I didn't say nothing to the fireman. But I worried about it.

I made it down the mountain a lot of times after that, too. Then the war come along, the Second World War come along, and I was put on the engineer's board and worked regular then. I was never cut off no more. I was an engineer from then on.

I know when I was put on the engineer's board, I caught several of the through-freights and they'd have them colored firemen. They knew more about running that train than I thought I'd ever learn. They knew about handling it, what they could do. I'd just tell them, "Listen here, now. You want to go to Greenville just like I do. You'd better get in here with me." And they would tell me just what to do, tell me, "Now, you can't go yonder without delaying that passenger train. You'd better head in over here." And they saved me. We had a good bunch of colored men.

When I was a boy, my daddy didn't know anything about steam engines, but he could just about tell you what engineer was blowing that whistle. It was just about that way with all of them. You had your own style. I just blowed it and tried to be different from anybody else, put a little toot on the end of it.

I was firing the Crescent Limited with engineer Lawrence Couch, he lived about twelve miles this side of Greenville, South Carolina, had a farm. His first wife had died and he had married a right smart younger woman than he was. And he stayed in Atlanta every two or three trips and then he'd go home. But whenever he left Greenville on Number 35, which left over there about two every other morning, he'd be coming around that hill there and he'd go to blowing a certain little blow. And his young wife would be standing in the window, a-waving at him.

So the first trip I made [as an engineer], we left Greenville just ahead of him. We come around there and *I* woke up his wife and she waved at *me*. Then he come along and she didn't get up and wave at him. She thought she'd already waved at her husband. I'd heard him blow it so many times, I fixed it where she couldn't tell the difference. But we laughed about it.

[One time] I was living in Toccoa, and I was firing out of Atlanta, working out of Atlanta, and I was deadheading back and forth, and had a room out at Inman. And I got Number 29 out of Toccoa one afternoon about one o'clock coming down, to come out on my job that night. I was sitting up there about half asleep and here come the flagman. And he talked real low and down in his throat, and he leaned over to me and says, "Do you want to see Mae West?" I said, "Yeah, I want to see Mae West." I didn't know what he was talking about.

He says, "Just get up and follow me." He says, "Now, don't make no scene." Well, I got up and followed him. And as we went back in the Pullmans, he says, "Now, she's sitting on about the fourth seat back yonder." Well, there sat Mae West.

I walked by, looked out of the corner of my eyes at her. And then in a few minutes I come back through there and kind of cut my eye around at her. And that really was Mae West. That was a great thing. She didn't look no better than the rest of the good-looking women, but that was Mae West. She looked better because she was Mae West. And that was—to brag about it when I got to Inman and tell the engineer and tell the crew and let them try to prove me out I was a liar and all such as that.

The better people rode them. I can remember when Number 30 used to leave Atlanta at 6:30, and you'd come out there to Peachtree Station and there would be a new married couple with all the wedding party with them down there on the landing, throwing rice on them and everything, get on the train and go to wherever you're going, on their honeymoon. Everybody'd be dressed up, hollering and a-whooping. But that was the way to go then.

You get an old railroad man started, he can talk railroading all day long. It gets in your blood, and that's it. As my daddy used to say, once a railroad man, never worth a cuss at nothing else. That's the way it is, I think.

Chapter Four

Commerce

Since the days of Henry Grady, Atlanta has been a city of boosters. "Atlanta was a small town with big ideas," states architect Preston Stevens. "A rival Chamber of Commerce said that if Atlanta could suck as hard as they could blow, it would soon be a city on the Atlantic." In the late twenties the Chamber of Commerce launched the first "Forward Atlanta" campaign, advertising the city in national publications and bringing hundreds of companies to town. There were other local business success stories, too, from Coca-Cola and other corporate giants to the black-owned firms on Auburn Avenue. Yet beneath the surface of municipal self-promotion and commercial prosperity lay a more complicated situation.

Atlanta boomed during the twenties. The city's population swelled from 200,000 to 270,000. The Biltmore Hotel, the Fox Theatre, City Hall and the Sears Building all went up during the decade, as did downtown office buildings and department stores. Robert Woodruff assumed the helm of the Coca-Cola Company. The construction of the Spring Street, Pryor Street and Central Avenue viaducts and the development of plazas and commuter suburbs all signalled the emergence of "Automobile Age Atlanta" and a growing middle class.[1]

The symbols of prosperity existed alongside more troubling economic signs, however. As the hub of the regional economy, the city had experienced boom-and-bust cycles throughout the twentieth century. After World War I, washed-out land, plummeting cotton prices and the boll weevil combined to create a major agricultural depression in the Black Belt South, with ripple effects in Atlanta.

"The plantation was already crumbling," explains rural sociologist Arthur Raper, research director for the Atlanta-based Commission on Interracial Cooperation, "and then came the boll weevil and that just knocked it down. It just simply went broke. People just simply had no jobs, and they just left there as virtual refugees. And that was well before the thirties.

"Cotton in Atlanta had been a tremendous factor, and there just wasn't as

Salesmen at Rhodes-Haverty furniture store. (Courtesy Atlanta Historical Society)

much cotton coming in. These people who had been pushed off the land and refugeed got into Atlanta. They were hungry, and they were not educated. They'd never voted, they'd never paid taxes. Here they were in the middle of Atlanta. It was a drag on the welfare facilities and all the rest, on the health of the community, on the spirit of the community. It was a very demoralizing period for Atlanta to go through the boll weevil period."

Another unfavorable development was the much ballyhooed Florida land boom of the twenties, which attracted many young ambitious Atlantans with capital. "It was really the craziest thing you ever heard about," exclaims businessman Duncan Peek. "People down there, on paper, were making fortunes overnight. But actually they wasn't making fortunes. It was mostly on paper. But it created a tremendous impact on the city of Atlanta, and millions—not millions, of course, but many of them went to Florida."

"A lot of Atlanta people went down there hoping to make a lot of money," recalls banker Baxter Maddox. "But they didn't have too much success. I remember a friend and I went down to see about making some money. We heard about how rich they were getting. But then we saw them coming home and they didn't have that kind of money. Those deals didn't go through. They didn't make the commissions they thought they were going to. So most all that I know came home."

Both the decline of cotton and the Florida land boom influenced the decision to start up the Forward Atlanta campaign. Duncan Peek, then with the Jaycees, relates: "The people going to Florida and the somewhat slowing of business, and then along about that time we had, I believe, eleven-cent cotton, and there were just facts like that that convinced these real leaders of Atlanta that something should be done."

The "real leaders of Atlanta" were a select circle of prominent white businessmen who wielded tremendous influence over municipal affairs. "A very small group of very close-knit, civic-minded men really started the Atlanta spirit and Atlanta growth," states Peek. "And politics and the Chamber of Commerce and these commercial leaders and financial leaders, all were more or less a caucus in those days because they did work so closely. Whenever they sponsored something, as a general rule the city was right there with them." "They were the leaders of the city," adds Baxter Maddox, "and they might meet at the various clubs, or maybe at somebody's house. I know they used to meet a lot—I've been present at the Capital City Club, Driving Club. They used to have meetings at those places."

In August 1925, the Chamber of Commerce approved a promotion plan outlined by its president, publisher W. R. C. Smith. "I believe it was Mr. W. R. C. Smith," recalls Peek, "that said that it was a foolish thing to sit idly by, that we ought to go out and let the people know what we have here and publicize Atlanta, advertise the qualities and advantages of Atlanta. And then a group of these people in the Chamber of Commerce got together and decided on the Forward Atlanta campaign."

The Chamber of Commerce approved the slogan "Put Atlanta on your payroll for a year," and began a subscription drive to raise $250,000 for the campaign. On October 6, 1925, some seven hundred volunteers kicked things off with a torchlight parade down Peachtree Street. Duncan Peek took part in the drive: "My organization, the Junior Chamber of Commerce, which of course was composed of a group of young men, were asked to furnish people to go out and solicit. And they went out and asked the businesses of Atlanta to contribute to the Forward Atlanta advertising campaign. And they came through beautifully. There's no question about that."

Subscribers pledged $85,000 to the campaign the first day, $668,000 by October 10. "Once they raised the money," relates Peek, "a very blue-ribbon group of men sat down and directed the whole campaign. And the campaign was directed at the people that they felt if they could impress those would do the most good. It just brought out Atlanta's advantages as a distribution point, emphasizing the fact that we had a great climate, a great labor force, and just bringing forth the real outstanding points of the city. And it was in the leading trade papers and *Forbes* and *Fortune* and magazines where the right kind of people would see these things."

On February 20, 1926, the first ad for Atlanta appeared in the *Saturday Evening Post*. Many others soon followed, as Duncan Peek recalls: "The ads were phenomenal. I've never seen anything to this day that compares with the interest-catching depicted on these ads, the things that they said and the pictures that they presented on them. I remember one of them, it was a great outflowing of all the logos of the various concerns, just hundreds and hundreds of these things, flowing across this page, coming South.

"I recall one on transportation where they had a picture of a truck, and in the back end of that truck was a pair of lady's slippers on a pillow. Now what they were trying to depict I don't know, but it was an attention-getter. There's no question about it. And all of the ads were that kind of thing, all of them were just marvelous."

The ad campaign was one of the first of its kind in the country. The Chamber also developed additional promotional materials and sponsored recruiting visits

EXTREMES

Shoe and Leather

The shoe business has swung from one extreme to the other. From twice-a-year selling it has gone to twice-a-week selling. From staples to high novelties. From few salesmen to many.

But one extreme may be as bad as the other. There is an ideal mean.

Present-day marketing calls for decentralized production. The goods should no more be made at one central point than they should be distributed from one central point.

In the South, Atlanta is the ideal point for your factory branch and your branch factory. Here you find economies in labor, power, taxes and many other basic items. And from here your men and your shipments may be most efficiently routed over the rich Southern territory.

′ ′ ′ ′ ′

The Atlanta Industrial Bureau is ready to give you the facts and figures without charge or obligation, and in the strictest confidence. Write

INDUSTRIAL BUREAU, CHAMBER OF COMMERCE
9188 Chamber of Commerce Building

Send for this Booklet!

It contains the fundamental facts about Atlanta as a location for your Southern branch

ATLANTA
Industrial Headquarters of the South

Forward Atlanta ad. (Courtesy Atlanta Historical Society)

to other cities. In 1926 alone, Atlanta added 169 new firms with nearly 5,000 jobs, prompting the Chamber to extend the campaign for an extra three years. By the campaign's end, 762 firms totalling 20,000 jobs had come to town, although it is unclear how many actually came as a direct result of Forward Atlanta.

"There was lots of big national firms that moved here," recounts Peek. "This is one of the stories that was told, that Chevrolet in 1926 said that they had no interest in locating anywhere at any time in the future. And then in 1927 they received a communication from Chevrolet saying that they would like to pursue further the idea of Atlanta for a plant. And then in 1928, Chevrolet moved to Atlanta. Nabisco is one of the ones that moved here. They built this tremendous plant out here on the railroad on the south side. I remember the Southern Railway sent some of their people down here from their headquarters in Washington. And now they have two tremendous buildings that they built along about this time, over where the old Terminal Station was. And that's the kind of thing it was."

"They opened many, many branch offices in Atlanta," echoes Baxter Maddox. "Many, many men were moved to Atlanta, sent here, and then when their companies wanted them to move to another city, they didn't want to leave Atlanta, and they'd look for another job in Atlanta rather than move away. We used to call it a branch manager's graveyard, because once they got here, they didn't want to leave."

Atlanta-based firms also grew during the Forward Atlanta years. "I think it was just a normal thing that the local concerns would expand," states Duncan Peek. "Of course, that's what the city fathers thought, the Chamber of Commerce people thought—if they could get people to come in like that, it would help the whole economy. And some of our young concerns there have gone on to be great outstanding national concerns.

"I remember Herman Lay very well when he came to Atlanta from Nashville. And it was along about this time, right in this time. But Herman came here individually selling peanut butter sandwiches. And then the first thing you know, he had built a plant out on Boulevard and H. W. Lay Company, a large plant, going out there. And then they merged with Frito in Dallas, which is Frito-Lay Company."

Forward Atlanta stressed the city's position as a distribution center with extensive rail and trucking facilities. It also coincided with the arrival of a new form of transportation that would be linked with Atlanta for years to come— aviation. Some of the same Junior Chamber of Commerce members active in the Forward Atlanta campaign also helped pioneer aviation in the city, along with future mayor William B. Hartsfield, then head of City Council's newly established Aviation Committee.

"I think Mayor Hartsfield did more for aviation than any one individual," states John Ottley, then an Atlanta *Journal* reporter and a member of the Junior Chamber Aviation Committee. "When he was in City Council, he recognized what it would mean to have Atlanta an air center as it was a rail center. And he worked so hard for it that he lost a race in City Council even, at least one time. Because in those days the things that people wanted in City Council were sidewalks, streetlights, things of that kind, and to spend money on Candler Field or aviation was something way out there.

"It was Candler Field in those days. Candler Field was in the center of the racetrack. Nobody was flying then. It was just some stunt pilots and daredevils and that sort of thing."

In the late twenties Hartsfield led the effort to get the new Southern airmail route through Atlanta. John Ottley relates: "Secretary of Commerce McCracken came South to look into the terminus of a New York–Southeast line. Birmingham was all set up for it. And he just agreed to come through Atlanta and sort of say hello and look things over, but it was really all set for Birmingham. So Mayor Hartsfield was responsible for getting Mr. McCracken and various prominent people in Atlanta together, and got them together enough and sold enough on Atlanta to where Atlanta became the Southern terminus and the air center that it is now rather than Birmingham, Alabama.

"Pittcairn Aviation opened the airmail route May 1, 1928, from New York to Atlanta. There were several competitors and they dropped out. But that was the original one. It later spread around the country and became Eastern Air Transport, then Eastern Air Lines."

In addition to shoring up Atlanta's economic base, these promotional efforts had other effects as well. As attorney Harold Sheats remarks, "Atlanta, the whole South, even in the twenties and thirties was sort of suffering from an inferiority complex. And the Forward Atlanta campaign pretty much broke the ice." Duncan Peek is even more effusive about the campaign: "It simply really picked the city right up at that time. That was the beginning, in my estimation, of Atlanta becoming a great city." The campaign also established a reference point for later municipal promotions.

Yet there was plenty that Forward Atlanta did *not* do. Local trade unionists resented the fact that the campaign ads mentioned pliable labor and comparatively low wages as reasons to consider Atlanta. Despite the assertion by one

Candler Field, 1920s. (Courtesy Atlanta Historical Society)

Forward Atlanta participant that the black community was "more or less en-
thused over the idea that jobs would come to Atlanta," campaign coordinators
did not include any black citizens in the effort, did not solicit a single black
company, and made no effort to gain jobs for black residents.

Not that there weren't any black-owned businesses in town. On the contrary, Atlanta had long been a mecca for black commerce. At the turn of the
century black businesses clustered near the downtown business district. Many
of these concerns served both whites and blacks. After the introduction of Jim
Crow laws and the Atlanta Race Riot of 1906, however, most black enterprises
were edged out of downtown and began catering to an all-black clientele.

The hub of black business became Auburn Avenue. "Every type of business
that an individual Negro had sense enough to run," exclaims banker L. D.
Milton, "he first headed for Auburn Avenue because that was the hotbed of
Negro activity. It was the hotbed." Adds Atlanta *Daily World* publisher C. A.
Scott, "That was the leading business street in this country for our people."

By 1920, there were 72 black-owned businesses and 20 professionals located
on Auburn; by 1930, 121 businesses and 39 professionals.[2] "You could get anything you wanted on Auburn Avenue," states plumber C. C. Hart. "You could
get it on Auburn Avenue among your people. Barbershops, restaurants, drugstores, eating joints of all kinds. That's why it was so sweet. I think we had
one haberdasher over there at that time. A filling station. A jewelry store and
banks. Beauty shop. Had a tailor shop, pressing clothes, dry cleaning plant.
Jackson Appliance. The James Hotel. Anything you needed for your livelihood,
it was found on Auburn Avenue.

"And another thing, we owned Auburn Avenue. Most all the businesses
down there were owned by the people who occupied them. We owned our
businesses, we owned the land. We wasn't tenants."

In many ways Auburn Avenue "was the pride and joy of black people," in the
words of nurse Ruby Baker. The avenue's businesses provided jobs for black
residents that otherwise were scarce or nonexistent. For outside of menial or
domestic labor, employment opportunities for black Atlantans were extremely
limited throughout the period between the world wars. There were no black fire
fighters or police officers, and hardly any sales personnel or clerical workers.
"This sounds silly but we had a hard time getting them to hire Negro drivers on
garbage trucks," relates Atlanta University professor Clarence Bacote. "Whenever you saw a job for the state or the city, it would be a white man supervising,
the Negroes doing the hard work." Trade after trade, shop after shop, blacks

Barbershop, 1936. (Photograph by Walker Evans. Courtesy Library of Congress)

were excluded from all but the lowest paying, hardest, dirtiest jobs—"nigger work"—by a combination of custom, craft restrictions, and law.

Even when blacks performed the same work as whites, they generally received only a fraction of what a white worker would get. Throughout the period black teachers, construction workers and others made less than two-thirds of what whites in the same field got paid. "When white folk were getting a dollar and a quarter an hour," recalls musician Roy Dunn of his days as a truck driver in the 1940s, "I wasn't getting but seventy-five cents. I'm driving a bigger truck than he got, I got more work to do, I'm hauling heavy stuff. I have to help load and unload his truck. The white man backed it in there and the niggers unloaded it. He didn't put his hand on nothing but the steering wheel.

"And when you get ready to eat lunch, all the white folks sit off right up here under the shed. The niggers had to get back there in the corner out there in the sun, or go out on the street somewhere. And payday, on Friday you had to line up. The man called your name to go up to the office and get your money. All the white folks in line ahead of the Negro. Didn't nary a black man go up there in that line to get his check. Everything come in that place, the white man get it first. A colored person just had it bad on the job, anywhere."

It was only in the 1940s that very small numbers of black residents began to move into sales counter and other previously off-limits jobs in white-owned establishments. Clark College dean of women Phoebe Hart recalls how a white shoe merchant on Auburn Avenue changed his hiring policies: "Talk about boycotts now, we used boycotts back then at Ebenezer Baptist Church in the early forties. I can remember a business on Auburn Avenue. Pastor King [Martin Luther King, Sr.] went into the organization and looked things over. He saw these white girls in there. He said, 'I have a number of girls in my church. Would you give one of them a job?' He said he wasn't hiring Negroes. He said, 'But you can hire them, you can.' The man just shrugged his shoulders. He said, 'Oh yeah, oh yeah, you can hire them.'

"He went back to church the next Sunday, he said, 'Let me tell you one thing. That man is employing these white girls here and your sons and your daughters could be working in there, and we could be giving *them* help.' And there was a boycott. We looked up and the store was closed.

"King was riding out here on Martin Luther King Drive, which was then Hunter, and he saw this store just across Ashby. And he told his wife, 'You know, I believe that's that same guy come out here.' He got out, he went in, and this young lady, colored, said, 'May I help you? What would you like to have?' He said, 'You clerk here?' She said, 'Yes.' He said, 'Where's your boss?'

So he came out, he looked at him and he knew King knew he knew him. He said, 'Oh, yes.' [King] said, 'I want to congratulate you, I want to shake your hand.' And he shook hands. He said, 'Now you're all right and you're going to get some business.'

"We went to church the next Sunday. I never shall forget, he told us, 'If you don't buy, why but a pair of—now, you men, got to have some shoestrings. You get over there and buy some shoelaces, shoe polish. Don't come into this church not looking right. Go over there and everything you buy will help create two or three more jobs for black boys and black girls." He said, "Now, the man's been fair. Let's be fair with him.'"

Black shoppers also faced discrimination. "Although you were spending your money at Rich's," recalls social worker Nell Blackshear, "you drank out of a fountain marked *white* and *black*—in Rich's, and Davison's, and Keeley's, and High's." "Oh, it was just terrible," recounts Ruby Baker. "I can still remember how you would go into a dime store to be waited on, and some cracker would come up and you'd just have to wait. You know Christmas rush, you were buying these little presents for family and friends, and you could not get waited on, because they waited on the whites first."

"My wife went into stores," says Butler Street YMCA director Warren Cochrane, "and she'd have to wait until all the whites were served. You couldn't try on things in stores. If you tried them on you had to buy them." "If you wanted a hat," adds teacher Bazoline Usher, "you bought it by looking at it, or a dress. You'd have to give your size. And there were those who did not go downtown to try on any of the clothes in the stores. They'd have them sent out, and then they'd try them on and send back the ones they didn't want."

According to Phoebe Hart, one downtown department store eventually did adopt a different policy, allowing black shoppers to at least try on clothes, although still within a segregated framework: "Rich's has always been very, very broad, much more so than some of the other stores. Back even in the forties, '41–'42, I'd be fitting in one area and the whites would be fitting in another."

Personnel in the downtown stores also followed the common practice of not using polite titles with black customers. "One of my favorite stories," relates Julia Fountain Coles of Morris Brown College, "is the time my mother took her three daughters down to buy some shoes at one of the shoe stores downtown, and they gave us the best possible service and waited on us. And as we were going out the door he said, 'Auntie, I sure enjoyed waiting on you, and I hope you come back.' And she threw her arms around his neck and said to him, 'I *wondered* where my sister's child was.' So, we fought it in our own subtle ways."

Atlanta University professor E. A. Jones also challenged the manner in which he was addressed by a white-owned establishment: "Back in the early thirties it happened, when I was buying some furniture. They sent me a bill, addressed me as, 'Dear Edward.' I wrote them back and said my name was Jones, that if he couldn't address me as he did all of his other customers—that is, the white customers—then we couldn't do business. And so, when I gave my last payment I wrote, 'Now, you can expect not one penny out of me, and I'll see to it that my colleagues are also alerted to the fact that you treat your black customers differently from your white ones.' He never answered that letter, but the next time he sent out a sales announcement, it was addressed to 'Mr. Edward A. Jones.'"

Again, the Auburn Avenue businesses provided an alternative. "There are plenty of people," relates Phoebe Hart, "who have never been to pay a light bill or a water bill anywhere other than Yates and Milton drugstore. The bills were paid there. The post office and your Christmas shopping and all—you see, they brought as much business down there that kept you out of having to take the slurs and all of downtown."

Compared to their white counterparts, most black businesses were quite small establishments serving the daily needs of the community. "Small businesses, mostly that's the type of business most black people are in," states barber Dan Stephens. "It wasn't as difficult then as it is now. You get your place, your location, and you apply for your license. And whatever business you decide to be in, you get whatever it took to operate your business, and that was just about it."

"I started out in 1925," relates plumber C. C. Hart. "Back in those days, I didn't need no whole lot of money to start a business. I didn't start no big business, I just started from a shoestring. My first business I had on Auburn Avenue was just a little place, little hole in the wall. That's where I started from. Then I spreaded out, got in a bigger business. Most all of them started that way, on shoestrings. A man started on a small basis and grew, took what they made and put it back into the business, and went forth from that."

A few women also owned Auburn Avenue businesses. "I can recall when Mrs. [Geneva] Haugabrooks went into [the undertaking] business in 1929 or thirty-something," remembers barber Dan Stephens, "and she was very progressive in her business." "There was a need for seamstresses," adds Ella Martin, who ran the Poro Beauty College on Auburn. "There were quite a number of restaurants owned by Negro women, black women. And I remember Ma Sutton had one of the outstanding restaurants at that time. She was nationally and internationally known for her little cafe on Auburn Avenue.

"The Poro system of beauty culture was founded by Annie M. Malone. It is the oldest system of beauty culture for our race, the black women. I worked with them in St. Louis, in the mail-order department. I used to open up all that mail and see all that money coming out and all those big orders coming from Atlanta. And of course Auburn Avenue was *the* leading business section for Atlantans, and on Auburn Avenue in October 1930 we had the opening of the Poro branch of Atlanta, Georgia."

Many of the country's leading black-owned financial establishments also had branches on Auburn Avenue. Along with Atlanta's own black lending institutions, they combined to make Auburn a national center of black commerce. "You found colored finance there that you didn't find anywhere else in the country," states C. C. Hart. "People could go into our banks and into our insurance offices, and borrow money to build their homes that you couldn't borrow anywhere else in the country among colored people." "Auburn has really been the street," adds Dr. Homer Nash, who opened his practice there in 1910. "You had Standard Life down there in the Odd Fellows Building, and the Pilgrim Health Insurance Company, and Chatham Mutual Insurance Company, North Carolina Mutual Insurance Company. Atlanta Life has always been here on this street."

The Atlanta Life Insurance Company was the city's oldest major black-owned financial institution, founded in 1905 by ex-slave Alonzo Herndon, Atlanta's first black millionaire. "Old man Herndon came here and got into the barbershop business," relates banker L. D. Milton. "He bought him a place on Peachtree Street. Built him an outstanding shop, for a Negro, on Peachtree Street. And the white people started flocking in there. So he grew to be the outstanding barbershop for white folks in this town. Well, Herndon made so much damn money in that barbershop till he started in the insurance business. And he found a little colored company in town that he bought into, hired him some good Negroes who had been in insurance to run it, and he built it and then added other little companies to it until he made it an outstanding company."

Herndon helped set a standard for local black entrepreneurship. Atlanta's second black insurance company, Standard Life, was formed in 1911 by another enterprising man, Heman Perry. "He was a powerful man," remembers L. D. Milton. "He had come here from Texas and started Standard Life Insurance Company and took that company to be a strong company. And as he built up that insurance company, he got ambitious and wanted to do other things."

Interior of Herndon barbershop, 66 Peachtree Street, ca. 1915. (Courtesy Herndon Foundation)

Overleaf: Atlanta Life Insurance managers, 1921. (Courtesy Herndon Foundation)

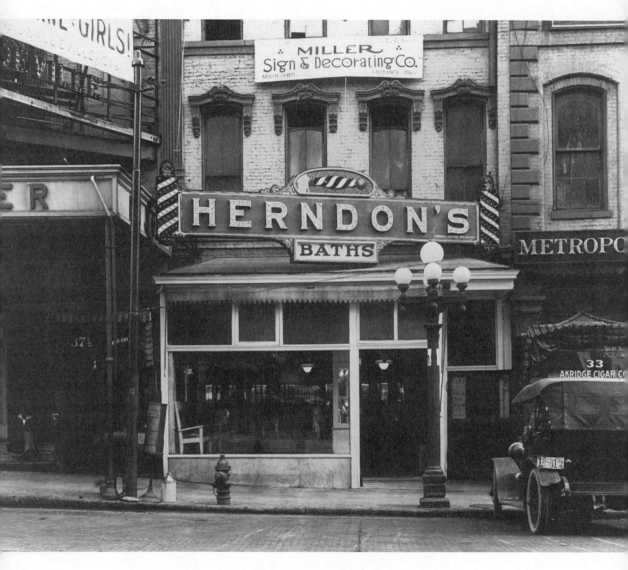

Marietta Street barbershop owned by Alonzo Herndon, 1916. (Courtesy Herndon Foundation)

Perry set up an umbrella organization, the Service Company, getting involved in real estate, construction, engineering, fuel, printing and the laundry business. He also acquired the Gate City Drugstore and started the Citizens Trust Bank, which opened its doors in 1921.

Yet, in the words of L. D. Milton, "Heman Perry tried to expand himself too much." "All of those enterprises failed because he had too many things at one time," adds longtime Auburn Avenue resident Kathleen Adams. "Before they could get one thing started, why, they started something else. And all of those things just broke them. These organizations died out by, oh, '26 or '27."

While his operations eventually went under, Perry's influence lingered on. Through his realty and construction companies, Perry helped develop the west side of town for black residents, who secured home mortgages from Standard Life.[3] "When people wanted new homes, they'd come west," relates C. C. Hart. "They were expanding, they were getting into something new. I mean, it was a step up."

Citizens Trust Bank also supplied home financing and provided capital for black businesses, both difficult to obtain at white-controlled banks. "It didn't matter what the law said," states Atlanta University professor Samuel Nabritt. "You couldn't get it because nobody would give you the loan. They could restrict you living by simply economic control of money, where you borrowed."

In addition, Citizens Trust attracted ambitious young men, many connected with Atlanta's black colleges. One of these was L. D. Milton, who came to teach at Morehouse in 1920 after graduating from Brown University: "The bank was opening, Citizens Trust, and I had acquired three shares of that stock, and I went down to talk with the officers of the bank about getting me a job. At first they said, 'No, you don't have anything about banking.' I said, 'Well, you don't know anything about me.' They evidently got in touch with Brown University and then got in touch with me and told me to come down, they wanted to give me a job.

"Dr. John Hope [then president of Morehouse College] begged me to change my mind and come back to Morehouse. I subsequently did, [and I] accepted the job in the bank. They set the time of my classes at 7:30 in the morning. But I did that, [then] went to work in the bank in the accounting department. And I learned how to run the accounting department.

"I was at Morehouse and I was at Citizens Trust Company, and I was head over heels in both places. There were no [black] majors in economics except for majors that we began to turn out at Morehouse College after my third year on the faculty. They kept me on that faculty eighteen or twenty years."

In 1923, Milton left the bank and entered the drugstore business with associate Clayton R. Yates. "Yates and I bought an interest in Gate City Drugstore, which had become Service Pharmacy, and which was then owned by the same people that owned Standard Life and owned control in the bank. And Yates and I finally agreed to get together and buy the drugstore from them, with the assistance of the wholesale druggists to whom the drugstore owed money.

"We had to go through the wholesale druggists who had loans on that property, and make arrangements with them to take charge of those loans. And they gave us a tight package, requiring us [to] pay them everything we owed them in about a year and three months. But instead of that, I paid them out in nine months. Now, when a white man finds out a Negro jumps up and pays him a debt far in advance of that debt, they say, 'Umm-hmmm. I've got myself a good nigger here.' And they went on then to even loan us money to pay out other creditors that we had.

"And we developed crowds of people coming to that drugstore. On Sunday, my Lord, you couldn't get in the drugstore for the people piled in there. After one year, we were opening our second drugstore, on the west side. In subsequent years we opened three more stores until we had five drugstores in the city of Atlanta. No white chain in this town had as many drugstores as we had."

In 1927, Heman Perry's enterprises went into receivership, and L. D. Milton returned to the bank, becoming president shortly afterwards. Vice-president was J. B. Blayton, the former auditor of Standard Life and the first black CPA in Georgia, while Clayton R. Yates served as chairman of the board. Citizens Trust joined the Federal Reserve in 1936, the first black bank in the country to do so, and became a major force in the black community.

According to Reverend William Holmes Borders, pastor of the Wheat Street Baptist Church, black ministers helped the bank grow: "The preachers made Citizens Trust Bank. They put in deposit that Monday morning. Around 11:00 o'clock the lobby would be full of nothing but preachers. And the people, seeing their preacher deposit God's money from the churches in Citizens Trust, put their money into it and helped to put it over, in a great way."

Quickly Citizens Trust became one of the leading black banks in the country. "The bank was a powerful negotiator for Negro businesses in the city of Atlanta," states L. D. Milton, "and helped these businesses to grow and to get started and expand. Oh, there were gracious plenty of businesses started."

One of the most prominent of those businesses was the Atlanta *Daily World*. Founded in 1928 by W. A. Scott, the *World* became the nation's first daily black-owned newspaper in 1932. "I started that paper," recalls Milton. "W.A. went to

Morehouse College while I was teaching at Morehouse, and that's how he got to know me. I had a printing company, which I took from Perry and his crowd when they failed in running the printing company successfully. And when Scott knew that I owned that printing shop, that is, my bank owned that printing shop, then he came to me to let him use it. And so I let him use the damn equipment. I didn't charge him a damn thing for it."

"I quite often say of W.A., he could sell an Eskimo some ice," relates Scott's wife, Lucile. "And he went in and negotiated with Milton at the bank, and he got it for almost an unbelievable rental."

In 1934 W. A. Scott was murdered. His brother C.A., who took over the *World,* describes some of the reasons for starting a black newspaper: "The Atlanta *Constitution,* in 1928 their policy was to put all the black funerals and deaths at the bottom of the back page and the whites on the top half of that back page, and a big black line separating them. Well, that was discrimination in a way and we didn't like that too much. And at that time they spelled 'Negro' with a little 'n.' Well, I knew 'Negro' was a capital noun and it ought to be spelled with a big 'N.' So that had something to do with starting the paper. And we wanted to inform and inspire and create jobs.

"We never tried to cover the general public, but [only] news that would have been primarily important to black people. In other words, our policy geared the news to the black community. Just all news, their crime and their business meetings, Chamber of Commerce, things like that. The church news, social news, just all the news we can get."

Originally a weekly, the *World* quickly expanded its production and spawned a chain of newspapers across the South. C. A. Scott explains the reason for expansion: "We realized we had to create more business, and we had to keep people employed for a week, couldn't do it. And at that time businesses didn't believe in giving a black paper any advertising. A few Negro businesses did, but you couldn't hardly get any from the general businesses here." In contrast, according to L. D. Milton, "Right now, there's not a white bank in this town that doesn't advertise in the Atlanta *Daily World,* not one."

There have been other changes in black commerce as well. The civil rights movement of the 1960s brought some new employment opportunities and enabled blacks to shop where they wanted to, without discrimination. At the same time, black commercial strength has been diluted. "You see," explains Dan Stephens, "we've kind of spread things out. We're going to the white business where we used to carry to the black. You can go certain places and we go there and spend our money, whereas previously we couldn't go there. So, this

has hurt in a way. This has helped some and it has hurt some. I think sometimes that black business was more successful when we were segregated."
Adds Ella Martin, "The people, black people, own jobs, but a lot of them don't
own businesses like we did at that time. So, in those days it was really 'Sweet
Auburn.'"

Ella Martin

*In 1930, Ella Martin opened a beauty shop on Auburn Avenue, applying
the techniques of the Poro system of beauty culture developed by Annie M.
Malone. She also started the Poro Beauty College and organized the Georgia Beauty Culturists League.*

I've been fortunate, and that's why I want to be helpful in the community
in which I live, in any way possible.

I was born in Tuckerman, Arkansas, just at the turn of the century. I went
to St. Louis, Missouri, and stayed there quite a while. I had a lot of experience
in different fields before coming to Atlanta. I met Mrs. Annie M. Malone of
Poro College in my early years and worked with her in St. Louis, in the clerical
division. She was very successful. In fact, she was the only [black] millionaire
woman at one time, from these products and the training of beauty culture for
our group of women. And it was through her that we learned to be thrifty and
to be helpful and useful in our community in all areas.

And from there, I went to Chicago, Illinois, working for a furrier, in the
office there. I took care of his books, I did all the payroll. When they needed a
loan from the bank, believe it or not, "Let's send Ella. Ella can get it for us."
Now these were the other race, you know, whites, and a big place at that. And
I stayed with them about five years, until I married. I married an Atlantian, a
Georgian. From there we went to California to live, from California to Atlanta.

I needed some work to do when I came to Atlanta. Having known Mrs.
Malone for years and knowing just what Poro meant in Atlanta, from the use of
her cosmetics, when I was coming back from California I stopped in St. Louis
to see Mrs. Malone. And I was telling her that I was coming to Atlanta and
I would need some work to do. Because at that time, you know, 1930, it was
during the Depression when it was its highest.

She considered it and she told me that she was due to come to Atlanta with her moving picture show—she went through the country with a moving picture show showing the workings of the college there in St. Louis in all its details— and that she would be stopping over on Boulevard with a family, Dr. and Mrs. Birney. I said, "Well, that's just around the corner from where I live." So, she did come. I persuaded Mrs. Malone to open a branch of the Poro system.

I was fortunate to get in the Odd Fellows Building on the corner of Bell Street and Auburn Avenue. At one time a bank was located in that particular spot. And a man by the name of Mr. Price had a coal yard out on Simpson, but he would bring his little different nuggets of coal on display. And the place was just filled with little—with Mr. Price's coal to show what he had to sell. And it had to be cleaned up. We did rent the place but, boy, we had a time getting it cleaned out and then—well, it had been used for a bank and it had teller's booths still in there. So we had to spend, Mrs. Malone had to spend, quite a bit of money to get the place renovated. But that's where we started. October the thirtieth is when we started business on Auburn Avenue. And I've been on Auburn ever since.

At one time there were no laws governing beauticians doing work in their homes. And I knew quite a number of these women were here. So I first went to the cosmetology—the board there in the Capitol and talked with—they had a barber board, but no cosmetology board, and I asked them what the requirements were. So he says, "Well, you tell those people who know the work . . . now, if they will come and pay seven dollars and get their license, then you can go ahead and operate with them." And that's what we did.

Now, he gave us a certain time—after a certain month, then those that wanted to go into the business and didn't have their license would have to take a state board examination. So that meant that they would have to go to school somewhere to get prepared. Because they knew—not the science of it. They knew how to shampoo and press, they did beautiful work like that, but manicuring, facial massaging, and hair and scalp treatments and the science of it they did not know.

We had to get these people prepared and ready to take care of the customers when I opened up. They had to know all this. So, believe it or not, my first class was given on Howell Street, in Mrs. A. D. Hamilton's boy's poolroom. They had a beautiful big poolroom, and I had my first class in that poolroom in their house. We started with dummies. These dummies had little heads of hair weaved on. And they practiced their curling and their pressing, the heat, and then they came to use chemicals, you know.

I was very fortunate. When I came to Atlanta, I was married in a family that was well-known people, highly respected, and that helped me quite a bit. I was thrown with the right people, and with my training I didn't have too much difficulty. I had so much experience in office work that I had no problems with the government, because I knew how to keep strict records and how to file on time. And seeing how money was handled and was gotten, I think that helped me. I wasn't frightened.

When I first started out, Mrs. Malone backed everything, she financed everything. I was paid by her, and she allowed me monies to have a janitor. And I had a little fellow, we called him Keystone, ran the building. And Keystone, oh, he played the numbers but he couldn't write his name. So I said, "I will never give you a check until you learn to write your name, sign your name. If you can learn everything else, you can learn to sign your name." I started teaching him how to sort of read and write, and to write his name so he could sign it to get his check.

You know, when I came here, we were trying to get everybody organized, in any profession. And there was so much work to be done for the community from organization that I organized. The Atlanta Beauty Culturists League was my first chapter to organize. And we wanted to go through the state and organize all the beauticians. To be recognized by the national as a state organization, I had to have seven chapters at least. So we just continued to grow and grow and grow from city to city here in Georgia. And, when we got the required number for a state organization, I was elected their president and served for twenty-two years.

We would encourage the people. Some beauty shops we would use for the people to register to vote, to get them interested in voting and to get them registered, and after getting them registered, to try our best to get them to go the polls, educate them to go to the polls to vote. So that was one of the things.

Another thing is, we gave a lot of free service at times for children. The Grady Girl's Club, we used to do all of the girls' hair, free of charge, and when they would put on their little shows they had to have models, and we would do their hair, free of charge. And then the old folks' home, we'd go out there and make those ladies feel good. Now, if you want to make a woman feel good, just improve her appearance. Just giving them a good shampoo was healthful for them, made their little blood circulate. And then, when you put a little powder and paint, little color on them, the women just felt good. We've done quite a bit of that work, in that capacity.

Now at one time I had a little boy on Auburn Avenue. He would come and look at me through the glass window. He was a pretty little boy, but he was so dirty, looked like that little thing hadn't had a bath in I don't know when. And I used to tell the girls, that was way back there when I first started the shop, "I bet he's a cute little fellow, if I could just get him in here." I said, "I'm going to buy me a big tub. My mother used to bathe me in a tub back there in Arkansas." So I got me a big tin tub and put it in the back of my shop, and I said, "Now, he's going to make friends with me one day, and I'm going to get him in here." I called him "Sonny." Every time I got up from my desk to speak to Sonny—he was about four years old—oh, he'd run off just like a jackrabbit in a briar patch.

So one day, it just looked like he said, "Well, I'll just go on in here and speak to this lady." And he did. I told him how cute he was, and I said, "I bet you're a pretty boy if I can just get some of this dirt off you." The place was filled with customers but I had a little vacant spot back there. I got this tub and filled it full of warm water, and put some marbles in there for him to play with, and plenty of soap. I got him undressed and got him to get in this tub of water. And if you want to know how a good warm bath feels, penetrating through all of that must and dirt and oil on the little fellow, he started whistling all in the tub. Oh, he just started whistling. Oh, he whistled and he whistled. And everybody in the beauty shop was really interested. Well, we became very good friends. From that day, we were very good friends.

I've had a lot of experiences like that on Auburn Avenue.

Of course, few black women got to run their own business like Ella Martin. In 1930, over 21,000 black women, or 90 percent of all black women employed in Atlanta, worked as domestic workers of some kind. Fifty-seven percent of all black women in Atlanta worked, compared to 20 percent of white women, meaning that *every other black woman in the city labored as a domestic worker*.[4]

"Black peoples didn't have any other field to go into," explains Dorothy Bolden, who in 1968 organized the National Domestic Workers Union. "You didn't have no other avenue to go down. I became involved when I was a young girl in Atlanta, nine years old, back in the early twenties. My father was a chauffeur and my mother was a cook. And when she wasn't in her cooking job she did laundry at home. That was a tradition of black women to pick up laundry during the week and do it at home and deliver it back to the employer. You'd iron and get a bundle for a dollar seventy-five or two dollars, and you did

Domestic workers, 1939. (Photograph by Marion Post Wolcott. Courtesy Library of Congress)

everything such as linen, napkins, tablecloths, shirts, sheets—a whole family washing of a white person's family. And back in those days we didn't have a washing machine. We only had the tubs and the rub boards and the big black pot to boil them in."

"I would go in," recalls Alice Adams, who began domestic work at the age of fourteen and stayed with the same family for some forty years, "fix breakfast, fix the midday dinner for the children, cook, at six o'clock serve dinner, wash the dishes. Every day I would have to go in and do the light cleaning, like dust and make the beds, change the beds, and keep the closets straight. Next morning, back in the same routine. I would leave home early in the morning, [be] on the job at seven, leave this job at seven, then get home around eight. You'd leave home in the dark, get back at dark. You never knew what home looked like. The family was very nice, but I'll tell you what it was—long hours and little pay."

The low wages domestic workers received meant that even white families of moderate means could afford a maid, and many families had more than one servant. "I came from a rather modest background," relates Georgia Tech professor Glenn Rainey. "My father left home early and lived pretty much the hard way. We had five children, but we always had a servant, as far as I remember. It would be some black woman who'd come in and work for a dollar and a half a week, fifty cents a day, maybe, at the most."

Lula Daugherty, a resident of the University Homes housing project, actually worked for a white family who lived in the Techwood Homes project across town: "They were running a florist shop over on Ponce de Leon. I washed and ironed and cleaned up. And when I got through, that woman handed me fifty cents and car fare. Now, you can believe that if you want to, but that's true."

In addition to wages, many employers supplied food, clothes and other items to their servants, and frequently spoke of their domestics as "part of the family. You looked after them like you did any other member of your family." "The people I worked for," states Willie Mae Jackson, "have been very gentle. And the things that they've done for me were sometimes more than my salary. At that time, the children didn't go to school in the summertime unless you paid extra for that, and she said, 'Well, Willie Mae, you want to send your children to summer school?' I said, 'I got to, otherwise I'm going to have to go home and stay with them, because we're both working.' So she'd always just write a check for to take it to the school. And of course it wouldn't be paid back, that'd just be a gift she'd give me and the children."

Some employers helped their maids put their kids through college, acquire

Domestic workers boarding a streetcar, 1939. (Photograph by Marion Post Wolcott. Courtesy Library of Congress)

a house, or even, as in the case of attorney Louis Geffen's family, move on to a new career: "We had a young black woman who came to work for my mother. And my mother trained her to do the kosher cooking. And she became so proficient at it that she eventually became *the* Jewish cateress of Atlanta. She was the main cateress that supervised the cooking and the preparation of the kosher food that was used at the Ahavath Achim synagogue for many years."

Yet, despite the very real personal ties that often existed between employer and servant, there were distinct limits to such paternalism, as Dorothy Bolden notes: "You're part of the family till somebody gets there. And that part that you was would vanish when somebody else came around. Her attitude would change and her conversation was 'niggers.' And then, the excuse she would make was, 'Oh, I didn't feel good today, the company got on my nerves. I just wasn't too myself.' And you had to listen to those lies.

"You had to walk a chalk line. And if you talked back in those days, you was an uppity nigger, you was sassy, and you was fired and put out. And where would you go, you didn't have nobody you could call back to get any reference. They could lie on you quicker than anybody could lie on you. 'You stole something.' You never touched anything in that house."

"One of my neighbors in Summerhill," choruses Willie Mae Jackson, "she was working for this family and the lady lost her wedding ring and she fired this girl, thought she had it. But she was a real nice person, she found the wedding ring on the ground outside the bathroom window and then she remembered putting the ring on the window and the girl was rehired. So this girl was fired for that. They used to would just fire you in a minute for just different little things."

"And you never talked back to your employer," states Dorothy Bolden, "regardless of how angry you got, because you needed the money to survive. They had the advantage over you, you was locked into a system that we didn't create, but they created. And nobody knows how ugly that system was. It was always attempts made on black women from white men, always. Sometimes he had a knack for patting you on the back, not on your back but on your behind, and telling you that you was a nice-looking black gal and this type of thing. And I resented that."

The long hours away from home often meant that a maid devoted considerable time to the children of the white family, at the expense of her own. "I had an old grandmother come into my office not many years ago," remarks pediatrician Leila Denmark, one of the city's first women doctors. "She said, 'You know, Dr. Denmark, I've lived through two generations rearing white children but I never had time to rear my own. I never had time for my own child.'"

"You gave as much love to their children," adds Dorothy Bolden, "that you would give to yours, almost. You respected the child and you protected the child in that home while you was working. That child was top priority in that home and you had to give that child comfort, cause their mama and daddy was gone all the time. If they stubbed their toe, you had to kiss it and comfort that child, pet him, and let him know somebody cared.

"You stayed up until about one o'clock at night cleaning up your house and got up the next morning at five getting things prepared for those children to get up and send themselves to school, by themselves. If one [of your children] got sick, you had to keep the oldest child home. You couldn't afford to stay home, so they stayed home and kept the children. So how much education did some of those children get? None."

Alice Adams

After coming to Atlanta during the Depression, Alice Adams spent her entire working life as a maid for a single family in Druid Hills.

I came from Jasper County, Monticello, Georgia. I came to Atlanta when I was fourteen years old, just a kid, and I got a job working with some peoples, fourteen years old. And I worked for forty years. The same family.

I wanted to come to Atlanta and work, so that I could help my parents. My father's health had began to fail. He couldn't do anything on the farm. My aunt asked him to let me come to Atlanta and work. And at first he didn't want me to do it. But eventually he decided that he would. So, I came up here and got a job.

My aunt sent me to these people. He was an official of the telephone company and she didn't work. She'd go out and she'd go to town and visit. She'd go to meetings. And they wanted a cook. And my aunt sent me up there. It was on a Thanksgiving day. She wanted me to cook a turkey for Thanksgiving.

*Domestic worker and child, 1939. (Photograph by Marion Post Wolcott.
Courtesy Library of Congress)*

I had said that I wasn't going to start cooking, but when she asked me could I cook a turkey, I told her, "Yes, my parents raised turkeys." And so I fixed their turkey and she enjoyed the meal, the Thanksgiving dinner, that day. And from then on I was in the kitchen until the end.

I had to feed the children, give them their meals, see that they had their bath and rest, and then at night serve their six o'clock meal. I would get out the laundry—set it out. For a while we had a wash lady and she would come in and pick up the laundry. And when their laundry came in, I'd have to check the laundry. Keep the children's clothes checked, keep her clothes checked and his shirts checked, and see that there wasn't any lost. And if so, I had to report it.

I didn't have laundry to do, but I had to cook. Now, I enjoyed the cooking because I loved to cook, and I still like to cook. I would serve the parties. Sometimes on Friday I would have to serve a party—make sandwiches and serve about twenty-five or thirty peoples a luncheon, and from that fix dinner. That I enjoyed because I loved entertaining. But you didn't get any extra pay for serving parties. That was in your work. You just had to serve extra peoples.

I didn't just cook, I kept house and kept everything in place and raised them two boys. The relationship between me and the boys and the boss man and the boss lady was fine. Those boys obeyed me almost more than their mother. They obeyed me.

Lots of them when they get in their teens and start going to these different proms and dances and things in high school, they wanted you to say "Mr." and "Mrs." But my peoples never did. It was "Charles" and "James" until James died. I never said Mister nobody. Now, when they began to go to fraternity, once or twice some of his friends would call and they'd say, "Is Mr. Charles or Mr. James there?" Because they knew that I was the housekeeper and I took care of them as children. And I'd say, "Oh, you want to speak to Charles or James." I never said "Mr." They called me Alice, and was I going to say Mister?

They was lovely people to work around. They treated you as peoples. I had vacations with pay and sick leaves with pay. She was one of the loveliest people you could be around. She'd help me if I needed money for house rent or if I needed money for clothing. The onliest objection was long hours and little pay. She was willing to do anything to help me—but the money. Four dollars a week. Just no money. And everybody was doing the same. They all was that way.

I tell you when I started getting disgusted, during World War II. That's when

President Roosevelt, he give orders for all domestic workers to be paid a minimum salary. One morning I got the paper, and I showed it to them. She said, "Yes I know it. We're going up on your salary, we're going to raise your salary." And so, they did.

But still, I wasn't happy at the long hours. I worked from seven to seven. It didn't seem so hard, but the hours was long—just long hours. Now, we was off for half a day on Sunday, the same thing on Thursday. Now, do you know what half a day was? You'd get off at one o'clock, get home around three. Well, I did that for about twenty some-odd years. I couldn't go to church because I had to work. I wanted to go to church and I wanted to visit friends and take care of my house. And you didn't have time, you just had to work.

What you did, you had to do at night. You know, every church used to have a service at night, and that was the only time you could go. And then sometimes you'd get to church and the church was so crowded you couldn't get a seat. And I was determined to have Sunday off to go to church at day and not at night. I had prayed and asked God to provide a way for me to go to church on Sunday. Because I was reared up in Sunday school going to church, and I was just tired of it. I wanted time off.

One Sunday there was a program at the Wheat Street [Baptist] Church and I wanted to go to that program, and I was too late getting home. Well, that didn't make me so happy. So that Monday morning, I don't know how it happened but I was late getting up. I didn't wake up until six o'clock and I was supposed to be on the job at seven, because I was supposed to have his breakfast ready so he could be at his office at 7:30. There was no way. So, I said, "God has a way of answering."

I didn't get there until 7:30. He had left. So I thought, "Well, this is it." When I walked in, she said, "You're late this morning." I said, "Yes. I wanted to go to a program yesterday and I couldn't and I just got so upset!" She said, "Well, why didn't you tell me?" I said, "Well, I'm telling you now. I'm not going to work anymore on Sunday, not anymore on Thursday. I want every Sunday off and every Thursday off." She said, "No, I can't do it because I never had to cook, I've never had to wash dishes, and I'm not going to do it. Now, if you want to be off every Sunday and Thursday you get somebody to work in your place." I sat down. I said, "Now, listen. That is your job. You get them." I was determined right then to get some of my wants, or quit the job.

She said, "Well, you tell my husband." I said, "I didn't hire to him, I hired to you." So, she looked like she studied it over. Eventually she said, "Well, Alice, we have decided to give you every other Sunday off and every other Thursday off." I said, "Well, I wants every Sunday and every Thursday. And it's that or I'll have to quit because I want to go to church." She said, "Well, if you want to be off, I'll let you off." From then on I stopped working on Sunday and I stopped working on Thursday. If you ask for it and act right and intelligent, you'll get it. But you have to ask for it.

Like many domestic workers, Alice Adams took the streetcar to work.

You had to go in the front and out the back. And if there was a seat vacant and the other side didn't want to move, you had to stand. After standing, working all day, there you were. You couldn't sit with this white person. If they didn't feel like moving, plainly speaking if they were just too mean to move, you had to stand there, unless you wanted a fuss.

And I never understood. Look, you're going in their house, cooking for them, cleaning their beds, cleaning their house, doing everything, and then you couldn't sit by them. This is what I never could understand.

Sometimes some people, black, would get on the bus. They knew the law that the black people was under and still they would ask that white person to move up. And they'd say, "Well, if you don't move I'm going to sit here." And then they'd use some kind of profane language and get up. But I never was afraid to ask somebody to move. If they didn't move, I wouldn't say another word. I'd just let him sit.

In 1969, when she was close to retirement, Alice Adams joined the recently formed National Domestic Workers Union.

Eventually, I had a friend that had joined this domestic union. She said, "A lady by the name of Dorothy Bolden have started it." So I said, "Well, good, where do they meet?" She said, "Wheat Street Education Building." I said, "I'll go."

I knew it wouldn't be very much longer that it would help me, but I could join and help somebody else. And so that's just what I did. I joined. I met Mrs. Bolden and I seed that she meant the same thing that I wanted—stop long hours, and more pay.

And so, after I retired, I continued to work for Mrs. Bolden in the National Domestic Workers Union. And it's a wonderful thing. But I tell you, doing do-

Domestic workers waiting for streetcar downtown, 1939. (Photograph by Marion Post Wolcott. Courtesy Library of Congress)

mestic work you've got to hang in there. I hung in there. I don't know how I did it, but I did.

The labor of domestic workers helped free up many white women to pursue club work, careers or other activities. "My office was in my house," relates Leila Denmark. "I had a maid that was there and had breakfast on the table in the morning and had things put away at night. But that was a different era."

In the teens and twenties growing numbers of white women entered the work force, primarily in office jobs. By 1930, there were over 9,000 white Atlanta women in clerical positions, compared to only 180 black women.[5] Yet for many, clerical jobs were as far as they got. Unlike black women, most white women in the labor force quit work after marriage. Those who continued working often were relegated to certain positions, denied access to others, and routinely received less pay than men doing comparable work. "We had four of us working in the office," recalls Southern Bell systems analyst Marie Townsend. "Two men and two women. The men got about a hundred or more dollars a month back then, and that's when money was worth something. We were all four on good terms with each other, it's just that when time for promotion or anything else came you knew that you weren't going to get it. You liked the man, it was the system you didn't like. I think all of us protested it privately, and we didn't do it openly because there were too many other women that were ready to take our places. Those were hard days for women in business in big companies."

Mamie Kimball had a similar experience at Sears, where she began work as a claims adjuster in 1933: "If men went to work in the same job as women, they got the same pay at Sears. They got the same pay, but naturally they got promoted up. I noticed men had more opportunities but I didn't let it get me confused and unhappy, because it seemed to be the custom of the land. And I just figured a woman had to prepare herself to do a job maybe better than a man."

"Of course," says Marie Townsend, "if you want to go into the marriage situation and community property and stuff like that, there were a great many inequalities in the law. There was no way in the South for a long period of time for any married woman to work up a credit rating. It didn't make any difference whether she was working or not. Some cases that I knew at the telephone company where it was bad was when women had good jobs but they'd been married. They might have even left their husbands, but because they were married to him and maybe did not have a divorce, they still could not get any credit, although they might be supporting the children."

"As a working female, single," adds bookkeeper Marian Doom, "I couldn't get hospital insurance until Blue Cross/Blue Shield came in. No insurance company would give a single woman insurance at all. Only through your husband could you get it. Mother sold life insurance, first for the Fidelity Mutual Insurance and then for Prudential. Men would rarely listen to her because she was a woman, and women didn't have the money. So she had a pretty tough time trying to sell it."

Very few women entered the professions or owned their own business. "It was most unusual," states attorney Mildred Kingloff. "There were very few women in the law school. I don't suppose there were more than two or three women in the class. I just really don't know but I would say the number of women lawyers [in the late 1920s] would certainly be in the neighborhood of less than ten. Like Ivory soap, 99.9 percent men and the other one-tenth of 1 percent women."

When they did enter the professions, women frequently worked in what were thought of as "women's fields." Women attorneys often practiced family law, women physicians were far more likely to be pediatricians or gynecologists than surgeons, and women reporters, like Yolande Gwin of the *Constitution*, regularly covered the "woman's angle" of current events: "I would approach [a story] as to what I would like to know about the subject, and what I think any woman would like to know about the subject. I remember Mrs. [Eleanor] Roosevelt came to town one time and [Ralph McGill] was on the story, too. I was on it, to do the woman's angle of what she was doing, and then he was doing the main story. The main story was about her comments on the [public] housing situation and how it had grown and the future of housing. I had something else, you know. I remember one part of my story. I mentioned her hands. She had the most beautiful hands I think I've ever seen in my life, and she gestured with her hands so much, you know. And I played that up because that was really interesting, I thought."

In business, too, women often catered to a female clientele. "Beauty salons and dressmaking places, we had those at the time," recalls corset shop employee Cassie Dollar. "There were several places in Atlanta that did a lot of dressmaking for people. Of course, women were head of those. There were a lot of people who were in the millinery business and made hats at that time. That was a big business in Atlanta in the twenties and thirties, well up into the forties. Everybody wore a hat to match their costume.

"There were several tearooms. We said tearooms years ago because it was only open at lunchtime and was kind of light lunch, and ladies shopping downtown would go in there to eat."

Cassie Dollar went to work for the corset concern of Eager and Simpson in 1927: "Miss Eager and Miss Simpson decided to go in business for themselves, and they did that in 1919. It was a small business, but they had very good trade, what I would call the carriage trade, because they had the best families in and around Atlanta that would come to them. And Miss Eager made corsets for a lot of people around town. She cut her own patterns and fixed those.

"People always called up and wanted to see 'Mr. Manager.' They never wanted 'Mrs.' or 'Miss.' They always thought the head of the firm should be a man. Well, we'd just tell them that it was a lady. Well, yes, they'd speak to her, but they always seemed a little bit surprised."

When women did enter untraditional fields, they sometimes faced resistance from their male counterparts. In 1942, Louise Chandler opened up the city's first woman-owned dry cleaner: "When I went into business, the men completely ignored me. I was a widow woman and they knew I'd soon fail. I'm just supposing they thought that, but nobody came to see me.

"I wanted to promote my business. So, I met this man at the telephone company, he was a customer. He said, 'Why don't you advertise in the Yellow Page?' So, I took his advice and started advertising. Well, immediately, I had a visit from the good cleaners in the city of Atlanta, who told me that that wasn't ethical to advertise. They had an agreement among them to *not* advertise. And I said, 'Well, I don't have an agreement. Where were you when I needed you?' So, I continued to advertise. And it immediately started making money."

Despite such occasional success stories, the woman in business and the professions remained restricted by custom and law throughout the period between the world wars, and beyond. "All of the laws tended to protect her," states Mildred Kingloff. "She was really not permitted to come out into the real world of business, as a protective feature, I guess. She was not permitted to be on a jury. Why? She was busy looking after her husband's needs and bearing children, looking after the home."

The situation changed somewhat during the World War II years. The war itself expanded opportunities for some women in both the public and private sectors. "And, of course," recalls Mamie Kimball, "business and professional

Dry cleaning establishment, 1944. (Special Collections, Georgia State University)

women were working hard for some changes in legislation. I know that they changed that rule they had when I first went to Sears, that if they had to lay off, they could not lay off a woman just because she was married and her husband was working. And many things improved slowly over the years."

Louise Chandler

Born in 1904, Louise Chandler opened the city's first woman-owned dry cleaning establishment in 1942, after the loss of her first husband. She later became involved in real estate, Baptist Business Women, and the Business and Professional Women's Club.

I never followed the crowd. I always wanted to do what *I* wanted to do. I grew up in Douglas County, a suburb of Atlanta now. I did not have too much formal education because in my day people went to school and they came home and they married. I finished high school and was going to be trained to be a teacher and then I decided I wanted to be a lawyer. But then along came this handsome, well-to-do young man and I was told to either drop the man or drop the school, so I dropped the school. I decided to marry because if I hadn't married this man, I think I'd have just died.

At that time, back in the late twenties, there was no opportunity for a woman other than teaching. No nice lady went into business. And I would not have been allowed to, because my father was one of those men that did not believe in women working. I have two sisters and they've never worked a day in their life. And my mother never worked a day, because she thought money fell off trees.

The reason why I went into business was that I found myself in 1942 with two choices. I was left alone with a child who was in high school, and I either had to go back home and listen to my father tell me what to do, or I had to go to work. And of course there weren't many opportunities then because I was thirty-eight years old, and nobody but nobody would hire an old lady of thirty-eight with no business experience. I had no business experience whatsoever.

I had just a little money. And I had seen this ad: "A dry cleaning place for sale. Will train." I thought, Well, I can learn anything. So I went home and asked my father to let me borrow some money. He said, "No daughter of mine will ever go out in this world." Then I had a brother who was an engineer in the Highway Department. I thought he had a good bit of money and I asked him. He said, "You go home where all women are supposed to be." And I didn't do it.

You want to know how I got the money? Well, I came out and looked at this place of business. It was very small but it had a good reputation. It happened it had the same name as my mother's maiden name. So I went down to the bank and I had . . . I had never had a charge account. I didn't know anything what to do. I just told them I wanted to borrow the money. He said, "What collateral have you got?" I hardly knew what collateral was. I said, "Well, if I fail, you've got a dry cleaning place." He said, "Well, I think I'll take a chance on you." And I'll ever be grateful to this man for having trust in me. Of course, my family kind of ignored me and my lady friends and personal friends ignored me because I was an oddity at that time.

I immediately started taking all the national magazines and I immediately joined the National Cleaners and Dyers. Not only was I going to the cleaners [conventions], but I was also studying at Mercer extension at that time to work on religious work, because I thought if I failed I could always go do religious work.

Now, the salesmen were nice to me because they knew I liked to have new ideas, you see, and would buy things that the men would not buy. I would venture out. You might be interested to know I was the first one that ever started the one-hour cleaning. A man could come in my business. I'd give him a *Constitution* and sit behind the curtain, and we would half-sole his shoes, wash his shirt, take off his clothes, wash everything he had on, block his hat, and he would be gone in an hour. And you'd be surprised how many did that, because you couldn't buy clothes in those days, you know.

My [second] husband went to Maryland and studied at NID, that's National Institute of Dry Cleaning. He went to the leather and suede shops and learned those things, and came back and taught the help. They had to come to me then to do their suede and their leather and their draperies and their pillows and all the services I was offering. Basically all the average dry cleaner was doing in that day was pants, shirts, overcoats, and coats.

We even benefitted from the pawnshops. Everybody would . . . all the men would leave and they'd pawn everything they had. Well, the pawnshops —there's a law that it has to be clean, you can't sell anything that hasn't been cleaned. We even cleaned [for] all the pawnshops, you see.

I did not try to take advantage of anybody but I just happened to be at a point and a place and a time that I could benefit by it. I was not in business when the things were frozen [during the war]. For instance, the man that owned the cleaners, they gave him an order. Okay, he had to fill it out and he could not go up any [on his price]. I came in with all these other services. I had to go down to OPA [Office of Price Administration], said I'm starting and showed them all the new services I was starting. And they said, "What do you think you should charge for them?" And I put my own price. See, I was not restricted, because this man had not been doing any of those at this place.

We had met this nice black man who brought us cleaning, who was a church leader, and he asked us to come out and do some work at his church, and we did. He was a tailor and he became my husband's tailor. And we started renting tuxedos. Then we let him do the repair work on the tuxedos, and we would dry-clean them, and he would deliver them, see.

I think I was the first one to ever promote the individual as to dignity. In other words, everyone was a manager of something. I had a bonus system. I never lost any help, no one ever laid out. The men thought I was the silliest thing in the world. They couldn't hire my people.

Even the union. They tried to unionize. He would meet them on the corner. I happened to know the head of the union at that time. I went down there one day and I said, "Well, I hear you're trying to unionize my shop. Why do you stand down here on the corner like a criminal? Come on up there and tell them what you've got to offer, and if they want to join, let them join." He came up, and they wouldn't even listen. See, the dignity of the individual is what helped —you can't step on somebody else and get anywhere. You've got to carry them with you.

I was the first to give the black an opportunity to wait on the counter in a dry cleaning [place], the first one to mark the cleaning and mark the clothes. It was a matter of I couldn't get anybody else. How's that—just couldn't get anybody else. During the war, the white girls were going off to war, and they got first chance. We had a lot of smart black girls. I tested them out and they wrote a pretty hand and I trained them.

Some of the ignorant people quit trading with me. They wouldn't come back to the building. We had a cash-and-carry price which was cheaper than the pickup and delivery, and they wouldn't come, they missed the advantage of the cash-and-carry. And lived in this neighborhood but they would not come back because they resented that, don't you see. But it didn't bother me. I just didn't worry about it. It was their problem, not mine.

I had belonged, before I went into business, to the Woman's Club, the Garden Club, the bridge club, all the clubs, and they didn't do anything but just talk. And then I was the head of the Baptist Business Women, there were three thousand of us, and I needed a good secretary. And I asked this girl would she be my secretary. She said, "Yes, if you'll join Capital City Business and Professional Women's Club and help me. I'm going to be an officer next year." And I got in there and I found what a wonderful organization and what a program they had. This was in the fifties.

So, I do say this as advice: If any woman wants to go into business and make a success, she has to go into something different and be willing to take the slights and slurs, because after all, just admit, this is a man's world. But just smile at them and pay no attention to them and go on and make a fortune. And then they'll love you.

Chapter Five

Education

Several different issues influenced the development of Atlanta's public schools during the period between the world wars. As enrollment dramatically increased, persistent financial problems plagued the system, especially during the Depression years. Budget constraints often came into conflict with teacher demands, increased services, and curriculum innovations introduced in the 1920s under the administration of Willis A. Sutton. Despite the opening of Booker T. Washington High School, Atlanta's first public high school for black students, glaring racial inequities in facilities, supplies and salaries persisted throughout the period.

"Things were at a low ebb during World War I, things were very low here," states Bazoline Usher, who taught at the Houston Street School and later became assistant principal of Washington High and principal of David T. Howard Junior-Senior High. Only about half of Atlanta's student age population of around 40,000 attended school in 1910.[1] The need to contribute to the family income, accompanied by loosely monitored and inadequate child-labor laws and the lack of a compulsory attendance law, kept many poor children away from school, as did an out-of-date curriculum and the absence of free textbooks until the 1920s. Evelyn Witherspoon, who began teaching at the white working-class English Avenue School in 1918, recalls another burden for the poor: "During those years and longer it was necessary for the parents to buy supplies for the children. The first-grade supplies cost a little over a dollar, about a dollar and a quarter. It was a package of drawing paper, a ruler, little scissors, tablet and pencil which they brought to school the first of the year. It was a requirement. I don't know how the parents managed, because we have certainly always had very poor parents, but somehow they got those supplies together and furnished books, too."

Black children were far less likely to attend school than white children. While Atlanta's black colleges sponsored private high schools, there existed no public high school for black students in the city until Washington High opened in 1924. In fact, in 1913 the Board of Education tried unsuccessfully to abolish the seventh and eighth grades in the city's black schools, on the grounds that those grades were unnecessary for future manual laborers. Walter Bell, visual education director for the system, later to become schools historian, recalls: "Back in that day and time, a good-sized group of blacks may have started in the first grade but by the time they had gotten to the seventh grade, the vast majority of them had dropped out. It was necessary in order to live for both the black girls and boys to go to work. The boys went to work as delivery boys, the girls as domestics, and so they dropped out, one by one."

When children did go to school, it often was in overcrowded, dilapidated, even unsanitary buildings, with no cafeterias and very meager facilities. "The buildings for blacks around 1918, 1920," says Bell, "they were really deplorable. And a lot of white schools were in pretty bad shape, too, but not nearly so bad as the black schools." "Those schools at that time," recalls Bazoline Usher, "they were just like boxes, nothing but just plain boxes, four rooms downstairs and four rooms upstairs. All the children in the neighborhood had to go to that school."

Because of overcrowding, many children of both races had to attend schools with double sessions, each lasting only a part of the day. Responding to pressure from middle-class white parents, in 1914 the Board of Education eliminated double sessions and restricted class size to forty-five students—in the white schools only. Even so, according to Evelyn Witherspoon, "Forty-five looks like all the children in America the first time you face them. And they can really be a big handful because if you have two or three problem children, they can pretty well disrupt the class. With that many children in the room, it was more time devoted to discipline than to teaching, really.

"In my earliest days corporal punishment was permitted, and there were just a few times, I guess not more than five or six, that I ever asked to have a boy switched. I let the principal do it. Nearly all principals were stern disciplinarians. They didn't joke with you at all. If the child was tardy he might be sent to the office because that was a hanging crime, especially with Miss [Lula] Kingsbery, [principal of the English Avenue School]. She would say to the child, 'You're giving this school a black eye,' and that child might sit in her office for two or three hours to pay for it.

"I sometimes think Miss Kingsbery was raised up on an Army post because she conducted everything in such a military sort of fashion. She had very strict rules. And Miss Mamie Pitts at J. Allen Couch School was very severe. Even

Miss Wentworth at Fair Street School wanted it done just right. She was a little more lenient, but I never talked with a principal that was easy, never did."

Strict discipline extended to the flagship schools of the system, Boys' High School and Girls' High,[2] the training grounds for many of the city's white community leaders. Harvard graduate H. O. Smith headed Boys' High for over a quarter century. "I remember H. O. Smith as being what I conceived of the typical old-fashioned schoolmaster, who insisted on very high standards and got very excited at his students when he found them falling short or involved in activity which he didn't approve of," states sociologist John Griffin. "For example, smoking was against the rules, and if a young man was caught smoking in the toilet area or in some other part of school ground he was subject to being sent to Mr. Smith's office. Then Mr. Smith would explode and that student would be very, very sorry that he'd had to go there. I can see his red face screaming at students right now."

"One time I asked to be excused from Christmas exercises," recalls businessman and reporter John Ottley. "A friend and I wanted to open a fireworks stand at Five Points, and I asked him if I could skip the Christmas exercises, and he said no, I couldn't. So I sneaked off anyway. And he came by during Christmas and asked me if I did leave early. So I said, 'Yes, sir, I did.' And when I got back to school after Christmas he suspended me for the week. But my mother called him and said, 'Mr. Smith, John should be punished, but you're punishing me instead of him, because he's staying at home, bothering me. Can't you think of some other way?' So he agreed to keep me in every afternoon and give me some extra work to do. That's the type of man that he was."

Jessie Muse, Girls' High principal from 1912 to 1938, was a similar figure. "She was a very dignified person and had [such] an air of authority about her that you knew she was top-notch just by meeting her," recalls systems analyst Marie Townsend. "She was a very strict disciplinarian, but a very fair person, a very good person to be principal of the school.

"Seniors always had a luncheon and a program about the class that was going to graduate. We had it at the Ansley Hotel. During our senior luncheon those of us on the program that were sitting up where Miss Muse sat were told to eat our chicken the way that Miss Muse ate her chicken. So we used a knife and fork. Well, all down the floor were all our classmates and even the faculty, and they were all using their hands.

"Academically, it was a top-notch school, and anybody will tell you that. A good many of them went into business, mostly as secretaries and clerks and

Varsity Team. Basket Ball 1921

Girls' High School varsity basketball players. (Courtesy Atlanta Historical Society)

things like that, some of them into selling jobs, right out of high school. But many of the girls went to college. Even at the time they were taking Girls' High graduates at any college in the United States. I don't know of anyone who is not proud to have graduated from Girls' High, because it meant something in the business world, it meant something all over at that time."

"The schools prided themselves on discipline and classical studies and that sort of thing," relates Georgia Tech professor Glenn Rainey, a Boys' High graduate. And, while both schools offered general as well as college prep courses, the curriculum emphasized classics, mathematics and languages, especially at Boys' High.[3] "Boys' High School had Greek from the beginning," states H. Reid Hunter, assistant superintendent of the Atlanta Public Schools from 1921 to 1944, "and you could not graduate from Boys' High School unless you had Greek. And one of the big fights that occurred in the Board of Education one time was that, in the late twenties, a Boys' High student, a very brilliant student, had finished all the work, except he didn't take Greek and the faculty notified him that he would not graduate because he hadn't had Greek. Well, that caused quite a protest from the boy's parents and they appealed to the Board of Education and they had a public hearing. So, the Board of Education passed a rule that they would no longer require Greek for graduation from Boys' High School, but they could substitute Latin in the place of Greek."

Such traditions fostered a high degree of school spirit among Boys' and Girls' High students and graduates. "Oh, it was fierce," recalls Glenn Rainey. "We loved Boys' High. There was this great loyalty, ready to die for the school and so on. After the game against Tech High, you would go down the streets with your fists clenched and ready to fight and die."

School spirit often shaded into snobbery toward students at Tech High School and Commercial High, established in 1915 as the city's only coeducational high school.[4] "Boys' High students and faculty had the tendency to look down on Tech High," states H. Reid Hunter, "because they said that Tech High was kind of a vocational school and they called them smithies, blacksmiths. And Boys' High would sometimes rub it in that Tech High people didn't rank with the Boys' High people in scholarship and so forth, but the program of studies at Tech High was such that they prepared students for college just like the Boys' High did, and that was one of the fine things about the old Tech High, it did give training in technical subjects and at the same time prepared students to enter any college."

Ironically, after fire destroyed the Boys' High building in early 1924, Boys' High and Tech High were combined on one campus, at what is now Henry

Basketball game between Tech High and Boys' High, 1919. (Courtesy Atlanta Historical Society)

Grady High School, across from Piedmont Park. The move, which also reflected the migration of middle-class whites to the north side of town, aroused strong emotions from loyalists to both schools. "One of the great fusses in Atlanta for a long time," remembers Hunter, "was the merging of the two schools. The Boys' High alumni didn't want it and Tech High alumni didn't want it and the faculty didn't want it. So they kind of compromised by putting them both in the new building, but letting each one keep its own identity."

Social snobbery also existed within Boys' High School, as John Griffin notes: "There was kind of an elite group of students who tended to come from the more upper-middle-class homes in the city, but not exclusively, who were members of high school fraternities. And these groups would have regular meetings and a great deal of social activity. This would include their annual dance, which would be put on at some place like the Druid Hills Golf Club or the ballroom of the Georgian Terrace Hotel or some other place. And we all wore tuxedos. This was a great event, this spring dance of the fraternity, and we made much of these events."

"I was not in a high school fraternity," declares attorney and school board member Devereaux McClatchey, a graduate of Boys' High. "They tried to be like the college fraternities. They were very snooty and got off to themselves and the rest of us just felt out of it. You could have guessed who would be the boys in the fraternities, the boys who were able to shine at dances and dress right and who had big cars, who belonged to prominent families. They lived out Peachtree and out that way. Well, that's the type of boy that you would see. And later, when I was on the board, I was personally responsible for doing away with high school fraternities."

In 1934, the Board of Education outlawed fraternity and sorority meetings, insignia, and solicitation for membership on school premises, and prohibited mention of such organizations in annuals or other school publications.[5] Still, while their influence certainly waned, high school sororities and fraternities continued to exist in some form throughout the period.

Several important changes took place in the system around 1920. After the charter amendment of 1918, school board members were elected on a ward basis rather than appointed as previously, thus becoming somewhat more subject to local political pressures. A compulsory attendance law went into effect on January 1, 1920. Free textbooks and strengthened child-labor laws followed later in the decade. Also, in July 1921, Dr. Willis A. Sutton, principal at Tech High, became school superintendent, serving in that position until 1943. "When Dr. Sutton became superintendent," states H. Reid Hunter, "corporal punishment was used a great deal in the schools. He didn't say you shall not have corporal punishment, but he said any case which involves corporal punishment, the facts of the case should be put in writing and sent to him for his review. That policy put the brakes on too much corporal punishment, and soon after the board passed a rule not permitting corporal punishment at all.

"When I became a member of the superintendent's staff, there were not many health services operative in the school, but as time went on there were. The City Health Department provided physicians and public health nurses for an annual medical examination of school children and then the follow-up work was done by the public health nurses. Mr. Cater Woolfolk, the founder of the Retail Credit Company, subsidized an experimental program for dental services, dental inspection and follow-up care of the teeth. And the Board of Education took it over, and they established the dental clinic at the office of the board."

A strong adherent of modern progressive ideas in education, Sutton became president of the National Education Association in 1930 and brought a number of curriculum changes to the Atlanta system. "The Atlanta schools were just frankly a little out-of-date," asserts H. Reid Hunter. "The program of studies was rather restricted. When Dr. Sutton became superintendent the program was greatly enriched. New subjects were introduced. For instance, music—instrumental music, bands and orchestras and glee clubs were introduced. Also the introduction of courses in arts, ceramics and such was made part of the curriculum."

Such innovations did not go unchallenged by some school board members. "They had a very narrow viewpoint," states attorney Louis Geffen, himself a school board member in the thirties. "They felt that he was adopting ideas from the North and that he was abandoning some of the conservative principles that we had here in the South, and that he was making education too expensive and that the city could not afford it."

There were other battles over curriculum, too. While apparently the teaching of evolution never was a problem in the Atlanta schools, religion-related issues did arise periodically. In the teens various groups attempted to increase Bible readings and other religious activities in the classroom. The rebirth of the Ku Klux Klan in 1915 contributed to an increase in anti-Catholic assaults on the schools. Between 1922 and 1924 Klan leaning school board members Carl Hutcheson and Julia O'Keefe Nelson attempted—generally unsuccessfully—to ban books which mentioned the contributions of the Roman Catholic church in the history of Western civilization. In addition, former school board member Walter Sims charged during the 1922 mayoral campaign that the Roman Catholic church sought the destruction of the public schools, and Catholic Julia Riordan, principal of the Davis Street School, lost her job the same year in part because of her religious affiliation.[6] "Now two teachers were fired," states Evelyn Witherspoon, recalling yet another incident, "and I think they were veteran teachers. I think they had both been teaching more than twenty years, and the Board of Education would not say why. But the rumor had it that they were Catholic and had been teaching their religion in the schools."

In 1921, the black community provided critical support for a four million dollar bond referendum, with the insistence that the city build its first black public high school. "There was considerable demand on the part of the colored leadership to be assured that if they voted for the bond issue, they would be given a high school, a good high school," recalls H. Reid Hunter.

Black Atlantans had long struggled for better public education. In 1902 and 1909 the black community had supported bond issues in hopes of gaining school improvements, only to be rebuffed when the final allocations came. In 1910, Atlanta blacks had petitioned the school board for higher black teacher salaries and better accommodations. In 1917, local NAACP leaders came before the Board of Education to plead their case for improved facilities, again without success. At that meeting, however, school board member and future mayor James L. Key pleaded "guilty to every word these men have spoken. I shall fight for the rights of these men." Still, as late as 1923 there were 11,469 black children enrolled in the system—with only 4,877 seats assigned to them.[7]

While black Atlantans had been effectively eliminated from voting in the Democratic primary where it really counted, they could take part in special elections, such as school bond issues. Mindful of earlier snubs and suspicious of white promises, black Atlantans twice helped defeat school bond measures in the spring of 1919. Two years later, another school bond referendum came before the public, and once more the black community was approached for its backing. "Mayor Key went to the blacks in 1921," notes Walter Bell, "and told them that he realized that they had not been treated fairly and that if they supported the new bond issue he would guarantee—he would personally guarantee—that they got their fair share of the bond money."

After passage of the bond referendum, Sutton brought in two experts from Columbia University's Teachers College, George D. Strayer and N. L. Engelhardt, to make a comprehensive survey of the city's schools and to recommend a building program. The Strayer-Engelhardt report stated that existing schools were overcrowded, dilapidated and suffering from inadequate sanitation facilities, poor lighting, and insufficient recreation areas and equipment. The study also criticized the school board for not supplying free textbooks and for leaving the burden for providing school lunches to the local PTAs. Among other things, Strayer and Engelhardt recommended that the schools adopt junior high schools and introduce kindergartens throughout the system, and that various schools be repaired, demolished or constructed.

They also proposed building the city's first high school for black students, in an area newly zoned and targeted for an expanding black population, just south of Hunter Street, now Martin Luther King Jr. Drive, near Atlanta University. In the fall of 1924, the doors opened to Booker T. Washington High School (which originally also contained seventh and eighth grades), at the time one of the finest buildings in the system. "We had a good physical plant," recalls E. T. Lewis, who began teaching math at Washington High in 1929. "It was better than some of the white schools physically. We got, well, practically everything that we wanted in that one school. I guess it was about twenty years later before we got the gym that was supposed to have been built with the school itself. And the study hall, we never did get that. And the library that was in the plans was never built. They partitioned a couple of rooms and made the library out of those rooms. But the plant was well built and well heated and we had everything new. It was nice."

Washington High incorporated features of all the four white high schools, providing both academic and vocational training, on a coeducational basis. Associate school superintendent J. Y. Moreland, who graduated from Washington High, recalls: "We took foreign languages, a couple of years of biology, a year of chemistry, physics, algebra, trigonometry. And for those of us who wanted to, we went a little beyond that and took a little calculus. And of course English composition, history, economics."

"They made a survey to see what employment opportunities were open to blacks," states Walter Bell, "and the vocational courses at the Booker T. Washington School were given to meet those particular needs." "Then, as now," adds Dr. Hunter, "a great majority of the brickmasons in Atlanta were Negroes, so we had a class in brick masonry. They also had a class in tailoring. One time a lot of the tailors in the Atlanta area were Negroes. We had a course in home nursing for girls that was very practical. And we had several courses in cooking, not just nutrition but cooking and cafeteria management."

The only public high school for black students in the metropolitan area, Washington High soon became seriously overcrowded. "The only [negative] thing that I can say," recalls Flossie Jones, one of the school's first teachers, "was that it wasn't big enough for the crowd that came, because everybody who had been denied an opportunity to get a high school education was flocking there. And they came not only from the city of Atlanta but from the surrounding communities—East Point, College Park, Decatur, Marietta. None of those places had high schools for their blacks, so those whose parents were able to get into Atlanta any kind of way they could get them in, they were in Washington High School, too."

"You had a large reservoir of black children who were eligible for high school because they had finished elementary school, but some of them hadn't been in school in five, six, seven years," recalls E. T. Lewis. "When I started teaching one of my first twelfth-grade classes consisted of several people that I had finished elementary school with myself. We finished elementary school, they couldn't go to high school, they stayed out and did various things the four years that I was in college. Washington High School opened in 1924 and they started in junior high school. So, when I started teaching in 1929, they were in the graduating class of that year. I had some boys in the eighth grade eighteen, nineteen years old.

"It wasn't but a few years later that the school was overrun. I know by 1935 we had almost 6,000 students in a school that was built for 2,000. And we overflowed the main building. We built wooden structures in the back, we called them portables. And we taught over 2,000 people in portables at one time on that campus." "Some of the students came to school on double sessions," states Bazoline Usher. "Some teachers would have the group of students come in the morning; they might have sixty-five in the morning and they might have seventy-two in the afternoon session, coming in at 11:30."

"I taught there for ten years, from '37 to '47," relates Estelle Clemmons, "and I don't think I ever had a class with less than fifty children in it. I had one math class with seventy-five students in it. There was actually no space for me, hardly, inside of the room because students were all doubled up two to a seat. And this was a small room. I remember I actually prayed every day, and I would say, 'Lord, help me to get out of a situation like this,' because I wanted to do my best and I didn't feel that I could do my best by my students in such crowded conditions.

"We didn't have enough books. During those ten years that I taught there I never had enough books to go around in a single class. And the books that we did have were usually old books that had come from other schools, the white schools predominately. I remember one day in March—you know how windy it is in March—a big truck drove up behind the main building piled up with a lot of books. And because of the wind, some of the pages blew out of the books all over the campus. And I said to myself, 'This is what is being sent out here for our students to use.' And it hurt, it really did hurt."

Washington High originally had no auditorium, no athletic field, and limited supplies for sports. "We would go practice basketball in the Sunset," remembers J. Y. Moreland.[8] "You had to walk over there and make the fire in the potbellied stove to get the place warm. We kept on our coats and pants and everything until we ran long enough to get warm. And after we finished practicing basketball, our coach, Coach Baker—God bless him—would give us the nickel or the dime to buy the wienie or to use that nickel to ride back to the Fourth Ward. Many's the night we walked back—no shower, no nothing—just walked on back to the Fourth Ward and got in that tin tub and took your bath. There were no facilities for such at the school."

Black schools lagged considerably behind their white counterparts throughout the period. As late as 1940, the average per pupil cost for white students was $95.20, more than three times the amount expended per black student. In 1942, there were over ten times as many books in the white junior and senior high schools as in the black junior and senior highs. According to an Urban League report issued in December 1944, the great majority of black schools still lacked kindergartens, auditoriums, gymnasiums, and cafeterias.[9]

"Some of the people in the Board of Education back in the twenties," recounts Walter Bell, "stated very clearly that as far as providing facilities and supplies and material in the schools that what they should do is take care of the whites first, and if there was anything left, they'd give it to the blacks. And that's about what happened. In many, many cases, the whites had more supplies, more books, more of everything than the blacks had."

"They made the good showing for themselves, with the meager materials they had to work with," states Bazoline Usher of the city's black teachers. Washington High School certainly attracted a select group of committed teachers. "We had one of the best faculties of any high school in this city, white or black," asserts E. T. Lewis. "They got some teachers from the private high schools [affiliated with Atlanta's black colleges]. Also, we got teachers from the graduating classes of all of the colleges here in the city. And since teaching was one of the best fields open to the Negro at that time, we were able to get top graduates from all of these schools.

"You didn't have the turnover like you did in the white schools. For example, when I was teaching at Washington High, there were at least six people in the math department who had between twenty-five and thirty years' experience.

When it comes to Negroes, we had the tendency to stick to teaching for two reasons: one, we couldn't find anything better, and, two, we loved it."

"The faculty was a very resourceful group of people," remembers J. Y. Moreland. "They would go out and get things that they needed to teach us with. All our teachers worked closely with Morehouse and the other schools in the Atlanta University system and they got things there that they needed."

Pacing the faculty in resourcefulness and dedication was principal Charles L. Harper. Formerly the principal of Morris Brown College's high school and the Yonge Street Elementary School, Harper was active in community affairs and at different times headed the Gate City Teachers Association, the Georgia Teachers and Educational Association, and the Atlanta chapter of the NAACP. "He was recognized as a leader by his faculty just as he was recognized as a leader among the colored citizens of Atlanta," states H. Reid Hunter. "He was a good administrator and he was always a great champion of the things which would improve Washington High School."

"We didn't have an athletic field," recounts J. Y. Moreland, recalling one of Harper's efforts, "and he worked it in such the way that he got the WPA to develop the athletic field. We had no fence around our field, we had no bleachers. And he directed us on the campaign to raise the money to put up the bleachers. On Saturdays we would sell things and we would go downtown and seek contributions at various locations. He told us that we must do for ourselves what others may not do."

In a similar vein, Harper organized black community support to raise funds for a statue of Booker T. Washington, modelled after the famous one at Tuskegee Institute, to go in front of the school. In other ways, too, Harper was an inspiration to a generation of black students. "He was a man, I mean a real man," relates J. Y. Moreland. "He wouldn't back down to anybody because of race, creed, wealth or anything. He was a scholar. And he had a dedication about him, for his race, for his people, a commitment that he had to guide us and push us in certain directions." "He literally preached, 'Educate the black youth,'" adds Flossie Jones. "He preached teaching morning, noon and night. I can see him now, standing up and shaking his head and saying, 'We've got to get the best for these our boys and girls, we've got to give them the best. Teachers, go in your classroom and *teach*!'"

"He was a very influential man in this part of the country," states Walter Bell, "and he is the man, in my opinion, that was largely responsible for making Booker T. Washington into such a famous institution." "The record is out and you can't hide it," boasts teacher Pearlie Dove, "there are students who went to

Washington High School who are in very prestigious places now, and who have done very good work, despite the limitations that we had." And to this day, many of Atlanta's black community leaders are graduates of Washington High.

The development of Washington High School, a more appealing curriculum, the new compulsory attendance law, tighter child labor legislation, and Atlanta's overall population growth led to a boom in school attendance during the 1920s. Throughout the decade enrollment increased by an average of 2,000 students a year.[10] "There was a campaign on for several years to promote good attendance," remembers Dr. Hunter, "and it had good results, both for white and colored students."

By 1940 approximately 65,000 of the 71,000 student-age children in Atlanta were entered in school.[11] The great increase in students put additional strain on an already financially distressed system. Despite city charter amendments of 1918 and 1922 that guaranteed the schools a fixed percentage of municipal revenues, the Board of Education chronically ran out of funds in the fall, and had to apply to City Council for supplemental appropriations to pay teachers' salaries. In 1926, after one such shortfall, a group of local capitalists offered to lend the school system $500,000 with the stipulation that an advisory committee of businessmen work with the Board of Education on the management of finances. The following year the advisory committee called for the elimination of free textbooks, kindergartens, the teacher salary scale, and music, art and guidance programs, as well as the night schools providing services to many illiterate adults within the black community. The school board refused these demands, and in fact continued to introduce such improvements as cafeterias —mainly in the white schools.

The financial situation got even worse as the Depression hit. "There was a shortage of funds to operate the city and a shortage of funds to operate the public schools," recalls Dr. Hunter. "A lot of suggestions were made to curtail the budget and the people who were in support of cutting funds for the schools said, 'What you need to do is do away with all these fads and frills and stick to the fundamentals, the basics.' Well, Dr. Sutton said, 'We've got a good program of studies. We've got a lot of electives in it, we've got the arts and crafts and music and all like that, home economics, bands and orchestras, physical education. We've got a good program, we want to keep it intact.' Well, the outcome of all this discussion was that the teachers stood by the superintendent and the Atlanta [Public School] Teachers Association [APSTA] discussed it in their meetings and said that instead of tearing up the program and wrecking the whole system, give the teachers a reduction in salary."

In February 1932, the APSTA voted to take a major pay cut over and above the wage reduction already in effect for municipal employees, rather than dismantle special programs and departments. "That was when the Teachers Association held a meeting to debate whether they would go on strike," remembers Evelyn Witherspoon. "Well, one teacher after another protested the cut. And Miss Allie Mann, she was in Girls' High School and was president of the Teachers Association, she said, 'They cannot pay our full salaries. The money is not there because taxpayers are having to lose their property, they can't pay their taxes. And we would only hurt the children and we can't do it.' And we had a pretty stormy meeting, it lasted until about 7:00 or 7:30 in the evening, when we finally agreed that we would not hurt the children that way. We would go on teaching.

"So we were paid the reduced amount for some time. It was a steep cut. I know I was cut back from about $164 [a month] to, I think, $124." "I was making, on paper, the hundred dollars," adds E. T. Lewis, "but I was only getting paid seventy-six. Twenty-four dollars was going back to the city. Now, we got little receipts for that. Supposedly, we were to keep those receipts and cash them in with the city later on, but the city never did cash those in, so we lost that."

"We had a stub on the check that said, 'Donation forty dollars a month,'" recalls Evelyn Witherspoon. "The reason for that was that if we took a cut, it would be hard to restore our salary schedule. But if we made that donation for as long as it was necessary we would then immediately step back up. And that worked."

Teachers received additional salary cuts in 1933 and 1934. Then things got even worse. "We reached the point," remembers Witherspoon, "that the schools could not give the teachers *any* kind of a check. We were paid with scrip. Now, scrip is only a promissory note. It says, if we ever get the money, we will pay—*if*. You couldn't take it to the bank and get a penny."

Like other municipal workers, teachers had a hard time getting scrip cashed by local merchants without a markup. "Most of the stores, they wanted a percentage for it, for cashing that scrip," states E. T. Lewis. There was, however, one notable exception, Rich's department store. "Rich's did come through," recalls Louis Geffen. "They agreed to accept the scrip for cash. Had not Rich's come forth and done this, I don't know what would have happened because these people would have been unable to pay their rent. They couldn't buy groceries, they couldn't buy clothing, and just absolutely all the necessities of life would not have been available to them."

"Rich's saved our lives," echoes Evelyn Witherspoon. "It saved the public school system. We said that if our salaries ever were restored, we would buy only from Rich's, if they had what we wanted. We would go there first. It was a terrible time. While we were in the thirties it was just a long tunnel, you couldn't see daylight. It did end about the beginning of World War II and prices began going up and salaries were restored." The 1934 schedule of salary cuts was phased out in early 1937, with scrip redeemed by the city around the same time.[12]

Though they accepted the pay cuts without striking, Atlanta's teachers were far from docile. Organized in 1905, the all-white APSTA gradually strengthened ties with organized labor, and in 1919 affiliated with the American Federation of Teachers (AFT), after a lengthy wage dispute. The Atlanta teacher's union quickly became one of the largest in the country, under the leadership of Mary C. Barker, president of Local No. 89 from 1921 through 1923 and national AFT president from 1925 through 1931. Atlanta teachers gained several raises, and obtained tenure and a pension plan during the 1920s.

They continued to exert political pressure into the thirties, as Dr. Hunter notes: "When people were running for office, to City Council or the Board of Education, the teachers would commit them and say, 'Well, what is going to be your policy with reference to giving us a refund on our salaries, to cut this cut in salaries? What's going to be your policy with reference to civil service or tenure or group insurance or pensions?' They would put them on the spot, and they'd go down to the Labor Temple and say to the Atlanta Federation of Trades, 'Now, we want you to help elect our friends, support them.' And it gave the teachers a kind of political clout which before they did not have." Upset by the salary cuts of the Depression, APSTA members played an active role in the 1932 attempt to recall Mayor James L. Key, and engaged in other campaigns, too.

Sexual and racial differentials characterized the teaching staff throughout most of the period. "Oh, you could not be married and teach," states Evelyn Witherspoon. "You had to be 'Miss' somebody. The reason was you could be having the child and leave teaching, maybe in the middle of the year, and they just weren't going to have that. I remember two instances where a teacher lost her job. One was the year I began teaching and we had graduated together from normal school. She was Miss Blackburn and she married at Christmas and was fired. She couldn't go back the first of January. And the second instance was maybe three years later. The teacher was secretly married and hadn't told the principal or the Board of Education. And somehow people in the neighborhood found it out and she was relieved the next day. I was married in 1923 and about that time married teachers were accepted." Yet black women teachers could not marry for some time afterward.

"Back in the twenties," recalls H. Reid Hunter, "the women teachers in the high schools had lower salaries than did the men. The Board of Education said that to attract men, you'd have to pay men more than you did women. They said that men who were employed were married and had responsibilities and their economic position was different than that of women." The new salary schedule adopted in 1919 actually reduced the sex differential somewhat, but still left women teachers getting between two and four hundred dollars less per year than men. For instance, a second-year male teacher received an annual salary of $1,800, while women of the same rank got $1,524. The differences were most noticeable at coeducational Commercial High School, where the teaching load and training of men and women teachers was equivalent. After women teachers mounted a campaign to equalize salaries, the board eliminated sex-based pay differentials effective January 1, 1921.[13]

It took a lot longer to eliminate the considerable salary differential between white and black teachers. Until well into the twenties, black teachers did not even have a salary scale and, despite the efforts of Mary Barker, were not admitted to the APSTA during the period. In 1926 the board did adopt a salary schedule that included blacks, but the lowest paid white elementary school teacher still made more than the highest paid black elementary school teacher, with similar disparities throughout the system.[14] According to Reverend Martin Luther King, Sr., "A white teacher with an A.B. would be paid more than a black teacher with a Masters above an A.B. It was unequal."

In May of 1941, King helped found the Atlanta Citizens Committee on Equalization of Teachers Salaries, an umbrella organization drawing from several ministers' associations, the NAACP, the Atlanta Civic and Political League and the Negro Chamber of Commerce. Shortly afterward, C. L. Harper, in his capacity as president of the Georgia Teachers and Educational Association, threatened legal action over the issue. In 1943, two black instructors did file a federal suit which continued even though one of them lost his job. In response, and in recognition of emerging black political clout, the board gradually adjusted salaries until they were equal, and in 1951 the case was dismissed with no decision ever being reached. "The teachers today receive their salaries on the basis of their degrees and their certificates," states J. Y. Moreland. "And all of them are treated equally."

The World War II era brought other changes to the system. The elimination of Georgia's white primary in 1946 and a public campaign for educational improvements waged by the Urban League brought black Atlantans 30 percent of the postwar bond allocation. The black community still did not receive a proportional share of yearly expenditures, though, and black schools remained unequal throughout the era of segregation. In 1946, coeducation was introduced in all of the white high schools. The following year saw further curriculum revisions and the separation of the system's finances from city government. "It was a gradual improvement," sums up Bazoline Usher, "but still much to be desired. But it was improving."

Evelyn Witherspoon

Born and raised in downtown Atlanta, Evelyn Witherspoon taught from 1917 to 1947, primarily in white working-class schools.

My parents were born in England and reared in the North. My father grew up in New York State and my mother in Illinois. After my mother's mother died, my grandfather came to Tennessee, where one of his married daughters lived. Then a nephew went to work on the railroad and he worked between Chattanooga and Atlanta. My grandfather and his two youngest daughters came to Atlanta, mainly to provide a home base at this end of the line for this nephew. And I was born in Atlanta in 1896. All the people that lived around me, all the grown people, had seen Sherman's men come through Atlanta, and most of my teachers were eyewitnesses.

I remember in 1906, when I was ten years old, seeing a man lynched in front of our house. The race riot broke out in September and I had turned ten in August. I woke up somewhere around midnight and could feel tension in the room. My mother and her sister were kneeling in front of the window looking out into the street. And I got up and said, "What is it?" They said, "Go back to bed." But I knew something was going on and I came to the window and knelt down between them, and there I saw a man strung up to the light pole. Men and boys on the street below were shooting at him till they riddled his body with bullets. I will never forget it as long as I live. And that was the beginning of the race riot in Atlanta.

About two hours later rain came and sent everybody home, and that was a great blessing. But for a week afterward, colored people were afraid to appear on the street.

We had a Negro cabin in back of our house, the kind they had built in the days of slavery, so the slaves would be close to the houses they were working for, and there was a nice couple there, Ed and Henrietta. They had lived there many years. Henrietta took in washing and Ed went to work somewhere, I don't know where. But when the riot began, they shut their door and their one window and didn't come out. And after a good many days' time, my mother went around to the window and asked Ed if they had plenty of food. And he said, "No, we were about out." My mother said, "You can go to the store, and if anybody bothers you, come to my basement and you'll be safe." So a few minutes later he came up these steep front steps—we had twenty-two front steps. He came flying up, around the house and into the basement. My mother came out and faced three teenagers with guns in their hands. She said, "What do you want?" And they said, "We saw a nigger run around here." She said, "You're on private property. Turn around and go back." And they did. They would have murdered him in cold blood, and he was a good man.

I went to a private school, Miss Hammer's School. She was just a well-educated woman who thought she could conduct a school and she did it very well indeed. And of course it was exclusively girls. There were no coeducational schools in those days. And I was in the old Atlanta Normal School from 1915 to 1917. It was really two years of college concentrating on how to be a teacher. I loved children, I got along well with children. We had one or two friends who were teachers and they encouraged me in that direction. And I thought it was what I wanted to do, and I guess that was it.

I went to Faith School in the East Atlanta area the first year. And Faith was half toward Decatur, and a teacher who lived in Decatur was teaching at English Avenue and asked to be in Decatur. So she was given my place at Faith. It really upset me, but I was sent to English Avenue School, English Avenue at Bankhead. I was there five years. And then my mother was seriously ill and I asked to be placed nearer home. I wanted to go to the old Joel Chandler Harris School, but I was sent to what was called Fair Street School. It's E. F. Cook I think now. And I taught there until my little girl was old enough to go to kindergarten. And again I asked to be transferred. I wanted to go to the Joel Chandler Harris School. We were living in West End at the time. But I was sent to [J. Allen] Couch. And I did that fifteen or sixteen years.

So many of our children came from homes that didn't have a book or a

Second grade classroom, 1942. (Special Collections, Georgia State University)

magazine ever at any time, not even a newspaper. A lot of parents were total illiterates. If we sent a note home they often had to find a neighbor who could read it and write it to send a reply.

We had health problems. The school nurse would come and check those children and very often they had to be sent home to have their hair cleaned. I know I had my life threatened once because I happened to be the one who handed the note to the child. The mother came up looking for "that 'ere first-grade teacher," and the principal argued her out of seeing me, because I wasn't responsible because the school nurse wrote the note. But she was furious because she was told there were lice in her child's hair. And it often was the fact.

And we kept a clothing room for emergencies. Very often we got messages —"If you want my child to come to school, get him some shoes," or "Get him a coat," or whatever. So, we had a clothes closet and I think we had a food pantry, too. They would come in in the morning and say, "I ain't got no lunch money," or "I ain't got no shoes," "I can't go to the dentist, ain't got no money." There never was anything at home, just nothing. Home was a shell of a house, maybe three or four rooms, as bare as you can imagine. People often sat on the beds because there weren't any chairs. Nowadays I think the poorest of the poor have better things.

In those days there was no welfare as is known today. It was left to the Associated Charities, mostly through the churches. We had a family that had lived by charity for a long, long time. I visited that family and at the time the mother was twenty-four and I was twenty-four. I was not yet married and she had eight children. She had married at fourteen to get away from an unkind stepmother.

And those little children were dressed from flour sacks. She made their little clothes out of flour sacks. They were running barefooted in December when there was sleet on the ground. Beautiful little children. I had two of them in my room. Later they moved out to live in a tent pitched in a pasture on Bankhead, just below Ashby Street. That's how rural that area was at that time. Every time it rained they had to go to bed to get out of the rain.

She eventually had twenty children. Twenty children. I wanted to adopt the little five-year-old. She was as pretty as an angel, blue eyes and fair-headed and friendly. The first time she ever saw me, she came and sat in my lap. I took her to town, to Davison's, and got her all new clothes. Took her home and bathed her and dressed her up and kept her one night. And she stayed willingly, a darling little child.

We had a great deal of venereal disease in that community. The first time I ever heard the word "syphilis" was in a PTA meeting, the school nurse spoke to us. And I went home and asked my mother if she knew what that was. And she sort of hung her head down and said, "Yes." It was news to me. I didn't know anything about it. I was in my early twenties. She told us of one of the girls who could not even walk anymore, she was so diseased. She said, "Her body is literally rotting." Can you imagine it? Well, off and on I heard of a great many of the teenage girls that were going into prostitution, and they would sell for a quarter. They would walk up and down Marietta Street.

The first thing you've got to do is get the child's interest. And if you can get the interest of that many children in any one thing, then you can move along. That was the time when projects were favored. The farm project was a favorite with first grades. We tried to set up a sand table. Do you know what that is? It's a table with a sandy top. Every room had a sand table, every room. At least every first grade did. And that was converted into a miniature of a community or a farm scene, and the children would build the little buildings or the little trees. Sometimes we would dye sponges green and make trees of them. It was kind of an impressionist picture of a tree.

I had a good friend who taught at Spring Street School and that was number one at that time in Atlanta. She said, "Those rich people come to see you and watch you teach. They will come to visit in the room for an hour. And if they're not pleased, they go tell the principal, and it's really harder than teaching in the slums." She had tried both.

In a way it was nice to be in a rich community. She said at Christmas they might bring you a present worth twenty-five dollars. And you might be invited to their homes. She said she was invited to a rich home, and they had fried chicken. And the first time she put her knife to it, it shot across the table and onto the floor. She said the mother, the hostess, just rang a bell on the table and a maid came in, took it out, and she was given another piece of chicken.

But it was easier to work in slums, from that point of view, and I didn't ask to be transferred to a rich school. I knew teaching was what I wanted to do and I took my assignment and did the best I could do with it.

While the number of students who attended college during the period was very small compared to the present, Atlanta's colleges and universities played an important role in developing the city's leadership. At both black and white colleges in the area, students frequently had close personal ties with their professors, who introduced them to various currents of secular, modern thought, although in a setting where religion was still often very important. White and black students alike engaged in a wide range of campus activities, but their social life tended to be limited and closely supervised. While parallels existed between black and white college student life, there were important distinctions as well.

It is difficult to underestimate the significance of Atlanta's black colleges: Morris Brown, located at the corner of Boulevard and Houston streets; Clark in South Atlanta; and all-male Morehouse, all-female Spelman, and Atlanta University, on the west side of town. Atlanta was arguably the leading center of black higher education in the country, and the colleges left their mark on countless areas of black community life, in Atlanta and beyond.

"This whole matter of social leadership didn't just start in recent years," exclaims Morehouse alumnus and dean B. R. Brazeal. "The most prominent lawyer here was Colonel A. T. Walden, a graduate of Atlanta University. C. L. Harper, a Morris Brown graduate, was the first principal of Washington High School and later became head of the NAACP here. Miss Ludie Andrews at Spelman had connections with teachers of nursing at Grady Hospital. Professor L. D. Milton was teaching economics at Morehouse College in addition to his work at the Citizens Trust Bank. There were ministers who were connected with Morehouse. Dr. Peter James Bryant, who was the minister of Wheat Street Baptist Church, was a Morehouse graduate. And of course there was [Morehouse graduate] M. L. King, Sr., who was minister of Ebenezer Baptist Church."

"The intellectual, commercial and social life of this community has felt the impact of the combined efforts of these institutions," echoes Atlanta University professor E. A. Jones.

The black colleges continue to be important training grounds for future leaders, although campus life today is a far cry from what it was between the world wars. Up until the twenties, for instance, the black colleges sponsored high schools and elementary schools to compensate for the lack of black educational opportunity under segregation. "All the colleges," relates Atlanta University graduate Pauline Minniefield, "Morehouse, Clark, Spelman, all of them, had bigger high schools than they did colleges. You see, there were no public high schools over the state, and people had to come to Atlanta to go to high school."

"Both high school and college students lived in the dormitories," states Julia Fountain Coles of Morris Brown. "We also had a large number of high school students as well as college students who came from all over the city." With the advent of Washington High School, the colleges phased out their high school programs by the early 1930s.[15]

All of Atlanta's black colleges had nineteenth century church-related roots: Morris Brown established by the black African Methodist Episcopal Church and the other four founded by white Northern missionary societies in the decades after the Civil War. Well into the 1920s, many of the board members, administrators and teachers at the latter four schools were white, as Spelman graduate and professor Millicent Dobbs Jordan relates: "Most of the teachers were New England people, and I can remember the names of some because they were very historic. My art teacher was Miss Rose Standish, a direct descendant of Miles Standish. Two sisters there, the Dickinson sisters, were great-nieces of Emily Dickinson. It gave you quite a sense of history. I felt they were marvelously dedicated women."

"I think you got a great deal of missionary zeal," adds Dr. Samuel Nabritt, who joined the Morehouse faculty in 1925. "You had blacks who somehow got the feel that they had innate worth as the result of these missionaries who had come from the North and who lived with them and ate with them and made them feel that they had great capabilities."

However, beyond the campus white faculty members were often social outcasts, as E. A. Jones remarks: "They were looked down on, they were sort of exiles in the white South. Any whites who came in from the North were considered to be damn Yankees who were meddling in the Southern way of life. Teaching these boys and girls—as was the case in these colleges—that they were equal to whites was something that was contrary to the best interests of the South, so that these white teachers were ostracized. And therefore it was thought best for them to live on the campus."

The 1920s marked an increase in the percentage of black professors, including some of the first blacks with advanced degrees or training. John Hope, president of Morehouse from 1906 until 1929, when he assumed the helm of the newly formed Atlanta University System, played a key role in building up black faculty. "Mr. Hope was a Brown graduate," states Dean Brazeal, "and would check on young Negroes who were in Brown, and he employed a number of those persons. Mr. [L. D.] Milton was among the first. I took 'Introduction to Economics and Money and Banking' under him. And when I got to Columbia I found out that what I had been taught held up well. And I didn't have any unusual difficulties at Columbia working for a masters degree and subsequently a Ph.D."

Still, as Samuel Nabritt, the first Morehouse alumnus on the faculty who eventually received a Ph.D., notes, "The faculty was not highly degreed, primarily people that had bachelor's degrees. Mr. Hope always identified young men who were bright and capable and committed, and although there was a lot of inbreeding, he almost handpicked his faculty that sort of inculcated his ideas.

"I always thought of him as being a teacup diplomat. He called me in one day in my senior year and said to me, 'Nabritt, I think you ought to stay out and teach a year.' I said, 'Why, Mr. Hope?' He said, 'Because your father has eight children and with four of you in college it's really asking a little bit too much for him to send you to medical school as you plan.' He said, 'If you were to teach a year, you'd be sharper in the sciences and you'd have a little money and you would relieve the family burden.' And he said, 'I've got a job down at Straight University in New Orleans in chemistry, and I want to recommend you for it.' I said, 'All right, Mr. Hope, I think what you've said makes sense.' And about five weeks later I hadn't heard anything, so I said, 'Mr. Hope, what happened to that job that you had for me?' He said, 'Oh, nobody told you? The head of the biology department here is going to medical school next year, and they've recommended you to stay and teach biology.' So, he shaped my career in a single conversation."

In recruiting such faculty members, Hope was also expanding the curriculum in new, more liberalized directions, while maintaining training for the traditional black professions of teaching and preaching. "In my time," states Arthur Idlett, "blacks were teachers, preachers or insurance men. Half the student body was going in the ministry when I was in school, going in the ministry or going to teach. All right, Dr. Hope saw what was happening to us. Dr. Hope got a fellow from Colgate to come down and set up the science department, and built that science building. He did that in order to influence young men to go into medicine. As time passed, they put in courses to influence students to go into the legal profession." The Atlanta University School of Social Work, which opened in 1920 with an orientation toward black issues and problems, also reflected this more contemporary outlook.

Despite such development, the schools still suffered from small libraries, insufficient equipment, and ever-present financial problems. "Morris Brown was at that time laughingly called the 'soap wrapper school,'" relates Julia Fountain Coles, "because people used to sell soap and things like that to raise money to keep Morris Brown going. We didn't have any rich foundations, any rich uncles and angels and so forth. We didn't have government help and all that type of thing that we have now."

The Depression made an already acute financial situation even worse, even at the better endowed and connected colleges like Spelman and Morehouse. Samuel Nabritt recalls: "Nineteen twenty-nine just happened to be the period when the Home Mission Society cut off all of their support for the Baptist colleges throughout the South. Morehouse was in such a sad financial plight that the faculty had to take a cut in salary. And at one period, Spelman would have to send over their people to cut the Morehouse grass. Morris Brown was rapidly becoming bankrupt."

The economic crisis prompted greater cooperation among the various black colleges. "All of these institutions were threatened with the lack of finances," recalls James P. Brawley, dean at Clark from 1926 until 1941 when he became the college's president. "They were trying to find some way of bringing these institutions together, eliminating a great deal of competition, and to make a stronger center of education here for the black people. In 1929 they formed what was known then as the Atlanta University System, consisting of only three institutions—Atlanta University, Morehouse and Spelman. Atlanta University was changed from an undergraduate college to the graduate college.

"The General Education Board became very much interested in this development and they gave the money for the Trevor Arnett Library, for *all* of the institutions.[16] We had a power plant out at Clark that was failing—every time we had cold weather we almost had to close the school. The General Education Board said, in response to requests from Spelman for money to build a power plant on Spelman's campus, 'What we'll do is build a central power plant, *if* Clark will agree to move over.' And another factor which is often overlooked, the movement of population was from the east and the south side to the west side. And we had sense enough to know that students were not going to pass the university system over here for long and come clear to South Atlanta to go to Clark College.

"But the biggest thing was the opportunity for these institutions to get together and develop a cooperative program, bringing them together so that they could pool their resources and exchange faculty and students." And by the 1940s all five colleges, joined by Gammon Theological Seminary—now the Interdenominational Theological Center—had become part of the Atlanta University Center, although individual school identities remained often intensely separate. Among other things, the establishment of a cooperative center further reduced direct church influence on the schools.

From John Hope on down, the black colleges had an ambience "just kind of like a family," in the words of Atlanta University graduate Bazoline Usher. "The fact that I was young," states Hallie Brooks, who was recruited by Hope to organize the new library, "and many of us were that Dr. Hope had hired in this first [unified] faculty, meant that they were very maternalistic and paternalistic toward faculty. For example, we went to the president's residence to have our hair cut instead of going to barbershops. He did not want us going into a public barbershop. We played games in the residence and Mrs. Hope was a marvelous woman. She made us feel right at home and she interested us in community affairs."

"We got to know one another very intimately," adds E. A. Jones. "We took our meals in a common dining room, usually where teachers sat at the head of the table, much the same as the father would sit at the head of the table in the home. This made for very wholesome contact between teacher and students. And it also served as a very effective vehicle for the transmittal of culture, table manners and that sort of thing, and the correct dress. Students did not dare come down to breakfast in the morning, say, in their pajamas and robe. They had to be fully dressed. By that I mean they wore socks, a shirt and preferably a tie and coat, so that they could leave the dining hall and go fully dressed to class. The college had better control over the behavior and appearance of students than it has today."

The colleges made it difficult for students, especially women, to even leave the campus, as Atlanta University graduate Louise Mack Strong relates: "They were away from home and they felt they had to be strict in order to keep up with them. We weren't supposed to leave the campus at all without permission, and we could only go at certain times. We were not allowed to go off the campus to shop. If there were those that wanted to go shopping, they had somebody to come out and they chaperoned them to town. Coming to a city like Atlanta, you see, they couldn't let those children run around in Atlanta."

In addition to upholding the moral standards of the day, and grooming students who often came from poor or rural backgrounds with little previous exposure to college life, such paternalism also shielded students from the perils and humiliations of a segregated society. Off campus, students could rarely relax, and on occasion got into even deadly serious situations, such as one which befell a Morehouse student who was working a nearby paper route. "He dared to walk in a cafe on Peters Street," recounts E. A. Jones, "and reminded the man that he had not been paid for several weeks. The man cursed at him and said, 'Get the hell out of here.' As he walked out the door, he shot him in the back."

"When the news got back to campus," relates Arthur Idlett, "the students got together and were going up there to beat up that man. We met a professor,

Atlanta University students, 1942. (Photograph by Arthur Rothstein.
Courtesy Library of Congress)

and he said, 'Young men, don't go up there and get yourself in trouble.' So we stopped." "Now, that case went up before the Grand Jury," recalls Professor Jones, "and the Grand Jury didn't even indict him. The man went scot-free."

In 1930, several white men were convicted of the murder of Morehouse student Dennis Hubert, accused of assaulting a white woman. Afterwards, unknown parties burned the dead youth's home, assaulted his cousin, and threw rocks at the Spelman College chapel, and the Ku Klux Klan marched in protest, just as historian Clarence Bacote arrived to teach at Atlanta University. "My experience coming here was quite eventful that first evening," recalls Dr. Bacote. "The Klan was quite strong, and to demonstrate that they were not going to let Negroes get out of line, they staged a parade on the west side. And it was quite a scene. Unfortunately, I was the only one on that campus over there that night. I said, 'Well, this is my reception as far as the South.'"

Such episodes tended to increase the already insular quality of the black colleges. "Atlanta University was an oasis," states Clarence Bacote. "You could live here, at any of these schools, and not suffer the injustices that the person who had to make his living in the city did. You didn't have to face Jim Crow, you had your own group right out here." And, indeed, all of the many activities at the black colleges were integrated, about the only place in town where that was the case. "We definitely took the position," recalls B. R. Brazeal, "that none of our activities would be opened on a segregated basis. We would give a Shakespearean play nearly every year and it was attended by whites. Our football games were attended by whites in those days. I remember once I was at the gate during a football game and several whites came out and bought tickets and said, 'Where shall we go?' I said, 'Well, go anywhere you wish to, the whole place is open. Just go on in.'

"We had a kind of stubbornness when it came to segregation. We would make talks in chapel and even the students would make talks against going to segregated theaters and segregated anything, you see." "Every year I talked to my students," adds Benjamin Mays, Morehouse president after 1940, "and told them that I did not want them to go up in the 'buzzard's roost' to see anybody's show, to see any theatrical performance. And I made it very strong. I said, 'Even if God Almighty came to preach at a white church I wouldn't go to hear Him.'"

At the same time, the black colleges had to balance their ideals with the necessity of maintaining a low profile. "We just didn't go in for much publicity," remarks Dean Brazeal. "That was really a technique of survival. I mean, the leadership at that time didn't intend to have any confrontations. And so a lot of people just didn't even know that the schools were out here." "No, the whites did not know they existed," adds E. A. Jones. "Sometimes in giving your address where you were opening an account, they'd say, 'Where do you work?' 'Morehouse College.' 'Never heard of it.' It would be difficult to find even the most prejudiced white now who would admit that he doesn't know where these schools are. When you mention Morehouse and Clark and Spelman, Morris Brown, Atlanta University, white people take note now."

Arthur Idlett

A 1928 graduate of Morehouse College, Arthur Idlett joined the Atlanta Black Cracker baseball team while still in college. He later became a school principal and retired from the U.S. Post Office in 1972. Idlett moved to Atlanta at the age of four, residing in "a suburb section called Pittsburgh."

My early years of going to school, we didn't have a public school. It's a church out from Pittsburgh called St. John's AME Church, and that was a private school where all the small kids went. The larger kids went to Clark, Morris Brown, Spelman, and A.U. to elementary school, because the colleges had an elementary school at that particular time. In about 1912, the people of Pittsburgh asked the city of Atlanta for a public school. The city agreed to furnish the teachers, provided the community would furnish the building. So we had a native of Pittsburgh named Mr. Green Williams, who was working for the Southern Railroad. He built a two-story, four-room building, which was the first public school in that area. And I went there beginning in the first grade, finished elementary school there. Went to high school at Morehouse College and college at Morehouse.

My first Shakespearean play was *Macbeth*. I wasn't a student at Morehouse at that time—I was in elementary school at that time—but I went over there to see that play. And got interested in Shakespeare then, when I saw *Macbeth*. See, my daddy could read and write, but I don't guess I . . . I haven't ever heard him say that he went to school over three or four years. But he was interested in his children being exposed to speakers. He's taken us to hear the great speakers, black speakers, that came to Atlanta, all the artists. And today I enjoy it, from having come up as a little boy going to that.

My mother and father insisted that I go to school. Sometimes I told them

I was going to drop out of school, but that was my thinking. They said, "No, you're going to college." So I went to college and I've been happy afterwards. I had a lot of friends who were at Morehouse from my particular area in Atlanta. And the first day you entered Morehouse, you were a Morehouse man. If you just stayed there one day, you were a Morehouse man.

The faculty would oftentimes stay after school on their own time to try to put their program over with the students—because at that time, the average man finishing college would have been around twenty-six or twenty-seven years old. And I had some classmates who were in their forties. They graduated around about forty years old.

When I came to Morehouse, Howard Thurman was a student, but he worked in the office, and he registered me. And Howard Thurman became one of the outstanding preachers in the world, among the outstanding ten. Jim Nabrit was a student at that time. Jim Nabrit left Morehouse, went to Northwestern and got his law degree, and then became president of Howard. I was in some classes with Daddy King. I was ahead of Daddy King, but we were in some classes in church history.

My parents always told me that, "We will pay your schooling and you buy your clothes." So we would go to the golf course, we had several golf courses in Atlanta then. And we had black caddy masters. Those caddy masters were in sympathy with young men that were going to school, and they would give you a job every Saturday and Sunday when you come out there. And you could make fifty cents for nine holes, and a dollar for eighteen holes. But a dollar was about what you usually made on Saturday or Sunday, and you had two dollars. Well, at that time two dollars was pretty good money for a student to spend. We had a Thom McAn in Atlanta, and you could buy a pair of shoes for three dollars. You could buy—the veterans came back from World War I, they had a surplus Army store—you could buy those old Navy pants for a dollar, you could buy khaki pants for a dollar. And those are the trousers that we would buy. We would wear that through the week, and on Sunday we'd put on our better clothes, unless they had some special occasion at the college where we'd have to dress up. But you could use your Navy pants plus a coat and a tie and go to class or to the dining hall, because they required that you look presentable.

In 1922, when I was in the second year of high school, Kennan Thompson, who was a friend of mine—we played in the band together—he encouraged me to go out for the Morehouse College baseball team. And in my first year I made third base on that Morehouse College team. And I began to gain popularity. That's another thing that sold Morehouse to me, when I made that baseball team. I didn't have any idea I was going to make the team. I just enjoyed play-ing baseball. But I made that baseball team and I gained the popularity, and I had the opportunity to travel with the team in some cities that I had never been. And I played every year that I was at Morehouse on the baseball team. Made my letter.

The fraternities would try to get the outstanding men on the campus, get the athletes and students. So they started approaching me about it. I had never heard of a fraternity prior to that. I didn't know what they were all about. They started approaching me about joining this fraternity, joining that fraternity. And then they would have parties around the various homes, and invite me to the parties, and you got a chance to meet young ladies, dance with young ladies. And you felt like you had some prestige, you see.

In 1923, Arthur Idlett started playing for the newly formed Black Crackers, as well as for the Morehouse team.

We'd have the excursion trains—that's reduced fare, a round-trip reduced rate on the train—and they carried a baseball team along with them. Mostly some organizations sponsored the excursion, and we'd play baseball. A lot of your secret orders, your Masons, the Elks, and your Odd Fellows would spon-sor excursions and take the baseball team along with them. Then you're coming back that night because the distance wasn't too far. We'd have an excursion to Augusta, excursion to Albany, excursion to Savannah, excursion to Greenville. And we had excursions going to Birmingham, mostly on Sunday. The team would go up there and play the Birmingham Barons on Sunday.

We played in Lumpkin, we played in Hattiesburg, and we played in Meridian, Mississippi. We played Meridian for a week. They could play Sunday baseball in Mississippi, but they couldn't play Sunday baseball in Georgia. So after that Sunday game when we checked up, we just had enough money to pay the hotel bill. And, man, we were having fun out there outside the hotel that night— "How are we going to get back to Atlanta?" And a fellow from Georgia came up and said, "Boys, if all you all can get in a Hudson Super Six—you see this Hudson Super Six over here—I'll take you on to Montgomery on credit and you send me my money when you get back there." We settled for that, and two fellows decided they'd stay there and play with the Meridian team, so that gave us ten men, plus our baggage, coming from Meridian. And some places they were working on the road and had that old rock that you had to push through, but we got back to Montgomery. Our manager was a big man in the Elks, and he fooled around there in Montgomery and got enough money from the Elks to bring us to Atlanta.

Now, we said we weren't going back anymore, because we got stranded, and I came back and started working with my daddy. And I was on my job, and I saw one of the players. "Man, we're going back to New Orleans." And I went and told my dad, "I'm going back to New Orleans."

Small towns produced some beautiful women. They were in these small towns, and you were a baseball player—man, they were crazy about baseball players. See, the only recreation there you had was baseball and parties and dances. You had either a Masonic Hall, Elks Hall or Pythians Hall, and you were able to have a dance at all those places. And sometimes, musicians would be barnstorming, too, and they would ride along with the baseball team. The bands would operate just like we were operating, on a percentage basis. A lot of times the band would be at the baseball game playing while the game was going on, to drum up crowds for the dance that night and help the baseball team. And the visiting team and the home team would be dancing, see, to get the folks to dance. And you'd meet all them girls around the game. That was fun, man. We had several fellows that married some of those girls. Yeah, living with them now.

My daddy being a carpenter, he would have a job for me every summer. One day he said, "Son, you're getting near time for you to be looking for a job." Well, I'd never thought about that. After I got to be a senior, boys began to write letters around applying for a job, and I decided I'd do so.

So I got me a job teaching. And I was teaching biology and algebra. I was going to work at 8:30 and I was off at 12:00 o'clock. I was just teaching three classes a day, you see, making $20 a month. The average salary was about $60 a month then for teaching. And I was making $20. I was selling insurance for the National Benefits Company. The National Benefits Company went out of business.

And then my next year, I got a job as principal of a high school in Greensboro, Georgia, making $80 a month for nine months. Didn't get paid during the summertime. Then the Depression started coming on. They started cutting salary. They cut me down $10 every year, cut me down. I worked one year for $70, then one year for $60, and one year for $50. Then President Roosevelt started the NRA, see, and he set that minimum salary. Now, here I've got my A.B. degree, and some of these fellows around there that just had their elementary school education, they were making $12.50 a week. And I was making $12.50 a week. They were working the year round. I'm working nine months,

$12.50 a week. And, boy, that thing was disgusting. I said, "I'm going to get me a job doing something else."

My mother got my wife a job here teaching. My wife said, "Well, I'm going to leave you down here. I'm going to leave you down here. I'm going to Atlanta and take the job that Mrs. Idlett got me." So a fellow named Roy, who was the district manager for the Afro-American Insurance Company, he came down there, and I asked him about a job. He said, "Yeah, I'll give you a job when school closes." When school closed I turned in my resignation. Instead of me waiting till the job and send my resignation, I sent my resignation before I got the job. I came to Atlanta and asked old Roy about the job. Old Roy told me the job didn't come through. And then I got a job with the Pilgrim Life Insurance Company. Well, I fell out with the Pilgrim Life Insurance Company, and I got a job working for a wholesale drug company.

President Roosevelt had set up all these NYA, CCC, all that stuff getting people off the streets, started people to work, putting money back in circulation. And we had a recreation program around Atlanta. Me being the athlete, I tried to get in that recreation program, but in order to get in, you had to be on welfare. I couldn't get on welfare because I was working. Then the post office had exams. I took the post office exam, and they called me to work for the post office. And my first paycheck with the post office for two weeks' work was $60. That was as much as I was making a month on the other job. Man, I was rich. That was 1941. So I went on and stayed on at the post office, and I worked thirty-one years at the post office. Then I retired.

Clearly, there were many distinctions between life at Atlanta's black colleges and the city's major white colleges: Emory University for men, Agnes Scott College for women—both church-affiliated schools—and all-male Georgia Tech. Yet there were important parallels as well. Stepping onto a college campus was often a novel, confusing and difficult experience. "I was bewildered by the campus," relates Emory graduate Earl Brewer. "It was so much larger than the junior college I'd been to. The buildings were out of stucco and marble finish, and were very beautiful. I was enchanted by the beauty of those buildings."

Unlike the black colleges where most students came from modest means and all students worked, many of the students at Agnes Scott and Emory in particular came from wealthy backgrounds. For those who did have to work, like Emory graduate Glenn Rainey, combining student life with a job was often difficult: "I got up between 3:30 and 4:00 every morning and delivered a huge Atlanta *Constitution* paper route. I had done pretty much a half day's work before breakfast. So then I would come home and bathe and go on to Emory. And a large part of the time I could hardly keep awake. Then of course I had to do my homework and library work at Emory, and I was active in student activities."

Working was not the only obstacle to study, as Georgia Tech sports star D. I. "Red" Barron relates: "I wanted to be an engineer but I wasn't prepared to enter Tech to study engineering. Well, about two months after I entered Tech, I saw that I couldn't possibly stay in football and baseball and keep up my studies. So I just made the trip to see Mr. Nowell and told him my feelings. And he said, 'Well, you go see Dr. Emerson to get advice.' So I finally got up courage enough to go see him, I was afraid of Dr. Emerson. And instead of telling me that I'd just better give up football, thinking that that would be the number one thing in his mind, 'What's football compared to a course,' instead of that, he said, 'Well, you can't stop playing football, we've got to change you. Now, we'll just change you to the commercial department.' That was the crowning of my first year at Tech, was him giving in so easy when I just knew he was going to say, 'To Hades with football.'"

"You were almost on a close friendship basis with all your professors," states Emory graduate Hunter Bell, repeating a common memory among graduates of all of Atlanta's colleges. "It was before the days of research and publication and grants and that sort of thing," adds Glenn Rainey. "You had an awful lot of sort of wise, nice, leisurely professors who were interested in you, you see, who didn't have to get a grant from something or another and get something published. They wanted to help you and they had time to do it." "And it wasn't unusual," echoes B. R. Brazeal, "for the faculty members to consider some of the students among their best friends and vice versa."

At times, students at both the black and white colleges were exposed to material and ideas that challenged long-standing personal beliefs or community standards. "On my first time in coming to Emory after I had registered," recalls Earl Brewer, "I rode on the streetcar out to the campus with a fellow who had been to school before so he knew his way around, and I latched onto him. We got out to the campus and discovered we were there one day before the dormitories were opened, and they were all locked. So he said, 'Well, why don't we go back downtown and spend the night at the YMCA?' I agreed to do this and we went down and in the meantime we got to talking and I found out that he was a Jew from New York. This was the first time in my memory that I'd ever talked to a Jew. I'd inherited the sort of KKK notion of Jews and Catholics—we didn't have them where I grew up—that all Jews and Catholics were bad.

"But here I was, getting ready to spend the night with a Jew. And I never will forget how scared I was that he going to do me in in some way. I didn't have much money in my pocketbook but I put it under my pillow that night because I was afraid he was going to swipe it. The next day we went back to campus and got registered and got rooms and all that. Later on, after I got to know him better, I told him this story and we both had a big laugh over it. That experience was the beginning of the expansion of my horizons in relationship to the Jewish people."

"We believed in freedom of speech," declares Morehouse dean Brazeal. "We were put under the hammer a number of times by virtue of what some people said over on the campus that the community didn't necessarily agree with. Take the matter of teaching sex. It wasn't popular in those days and it still isn't popular in some places, but [sociologist Walter] Chivers had on his desk some books by Havelock Ellis. The biology people, beginning with some chaps that came from the North, taught what they thought was the truth, regardless of what the community thought finally."

"I had some very disturbing but rewarding intellectual experiences," recounts Glenn Rainey. "I had been a very religious person. I had come up at Grace Methodist Church at the time when we had an old-fashioned pulpit-thumping evangelist sort of person. You might have thought that biology would have, but to me chemistry and psychology were the things that really knocked me out of the magnolias. The world just took on a more complicated aspect. And I was very much disturbed."

On occasion, white students like Earl Brewer even had their values and practices pertaining to race called into question: "The head of the sociology department at Emory challenged me to think about some of the stereotypes that I had grown up with. I wrote a paper on the history of my own racial attitudes. This was the beginning of my thinking critically about growing up in the South and being acculturated into the sorts of racial attitudes characteristic of the South."

Perhaps the white college faculty member of the period who most challenged existing racial mores was sociologist Arthur Raper. Author of seminal works on lynching and sharecropping, and research director for the Atlanta-based Commission on Interracial Cooperation, Raper taught part-time at Agnes Scott from 1926 to 1939. "Dr. Raper was—is—one of those persons who leaves his mark on the lives of all people whom he touches," states Agnes Scott graduate Eliza Paschall. "He exposed us to a lot of things that otherwise we never would have known." "He would take students to biracial meetings and take them into the black community," adds John Griffin, who worked as an intern for Raper one summer. "And of course this was not always well thought of by the parents of Agnes Scott girls. And so there were some problems about this. You see, a faculty person in the thirties who dared to be identified with a position of wanting to do something about the black community, for example, was subject to all kinds of criticism."

Arthur Raper once had to appear before a DeKalb County Grand Jury after taking students on an overnight trip to Tuskegee Institute, and was the target of letter-writing campaigns calling for his dismissal from Agnes Scott. One of his principal accusers was Mrs. J. E. Andrews, head of the Association of Women for the Preservation of the White Race and a thorn in the side of Atlanta's liberals. "She was saying," recalls Raper, "that I was over there pretending to teach but really making white women available for nigger men. She wanted so badly one night to make me hit her. We were somewhere at a meeting and she was there, and she called me all the things you can think of and just kept walking up against me until I was backed up almost out of the door. Well, I wasn't going to hit her, she couldn't make me hit her, because that's what she wanted.

"Dr. [James] McCain, president at Agnes Scott, wanted to know why I didn't sue. He was a very conservative Presbyterian, very conservative. But at the same time he wanted me to teach there, and his daughter was in the sociology class, race relations. I said, 'No, no, no. I don't want to bring any suit against Mrs. Andrews.' And I didn't."

Encouraged by such faculty members as Raper, Brazeal and Hope, a very few college students, often affiliated with campus religious organizations, began meeting on an interracial basis in the 1920s. "We had a little group," relates Glenn Rainey, "a half dozen or twelve of us, who, I guess rather timidly but also very bravely, would meet. You could meet anywhere out at Atlanta University. And it was a long time before we could even be permitted to meet on the Emory or the Agnes Scott campuses."

Such encounters were marked by awkwardness and apprehension. "I was a little surprised," remembers Dean Brazeal. "I didn't know we would find many people—whites—who would take a stand in behalf of Negroes." "At my first experience [at an interracial meeting]," relates John Griffin, "I can remember feeling uncomfortable and cautious because it was out of the ordinary, it was the kind of taboo, you see. Folks who grew up in the time that I grew up never had the experience of sharing a meal in their home with black friends. It just wasn't done. Very few middle-class [white] youths saw black people who were their peers. They came in touch with black people who were cast in menial roles, working in the house or the yard or some menial job in the community.

"So it was really a very unusual experience for a white kid in a Southern college to get acquainted with a black kid who was just as smart as he was, and knew just as much as he did, and maybe had an even better education than he had. And so, these were pretty important experiences, for both sides, I think." "The time spent together by this limited but dedicated and forward-looking group of young people was well spent," echoes E. A. Jones, "primarily for the whites because they were the ones who needed this kind of exposure more than the blacks did. Each one of these persons when they got out of college was important in laying the foundation for building more liberal attitudes between the races."

Other student activities were far more typical, as John Griffin recalls: "Social life for an Emory student was pretty much built around, for those who could afford it, membership in college fraternities. There must have been about fifteen or eighteen fraternities on the campus, and many of these had large, comfortable fraternity houses in which students lived, instead of in a dormitory. There was a great sense of loyalty to your fraternity and great rivalry between fraternities and great activity of trying to rush certain students who were thought of as good material.

"It was sort of a snobbish thing. A man was thought of as a good candidate to join a fraternity because his brother had been in, or maybe his father, or in some cases because of his grandfather. They frequently were boys who came from somewhat more affluent circles. But there were also a lot of poor boys like me that were in college fraternities. And for many kids who had come from small communities or maybe from disadvantaged circumstances, they were important socializing experiences."

"I never dreamed of making any of these social clubs because of my lack of money," recalls Red Barron. "But I tell you, I hadn't been to Tech more than ten days when [football coach John] Heisman made some complimentary remark about me. One of the papers had a picture of me on the field in uniform, and that came out in the Sunday paper. Well, you can't imagine what that picture and that article quoting Heisman did to build up my social standing. Here they came. I got five bids after that. My advisor, you know what he told me? He said, 'Don't pledge yet. Go out and eat everything you can eat. Go out and have the biggest time in the world, but don't pledge anything because if they come after you once, they'll come back.' So I followed that instruction, but I got sick of going out. I just finally said my mind was set on SAE."

Although the black colleges did not have fraternity houses, fraternities also were an important part of black college life, as Arthur Idlett relates: "After you pledged to a fraternity and you got your frat pin, you had to wear your frat pin over your heart. And, man, when you'd go off to visit young ladies, you had your pocket so they could see your frat pin, so they'd see you were a frat man. So the majority of the fellows back at that time would go into a fraternity. It's altogether different now, they're not as fraternity-minded."

Social life on all college campuses was considerably more restricted and regulated than it is today. "It wasn't like it is now," states Red Barron. "No fraternity was allowed to have any alcohol drink in the world. The fraternity houses never had alcohol in them." "It was so strict," adds Hunter Bell, "that the fraternities were not allowed to have dances. The only way in which our fraternity could give a dance was for the alumni to have one and invite us. But that was about the only social activity connected with college life. I never had a date with a girl while I was at Emory because there were no automobiles on the campus, and I didn't know any Atlanta girls since I came from south Georgia. Having no transportation, it would have been rather difficult anyhow —they wouldn't want to ride the streetcar. But some of the boys did have them out for fraternity get-togethers and little social receptions. You could invite them for a little party and drink Coca-Cola. Life there was somewhat dull."

"Unless you had an excuse to be out," relates Arthur Idlett, "you had to be in your room at ten o'clock at night. If you were out without an excuse, you were subject to being campus-bound up to thirty days." "One time," recounts Professor Jones of a curfew violation in the early 1920s, "Dean [Samuel] Archer, tipped off that a certain Morehouse student was out, came in his room and stretched out on the student's bed. The student on returning sneaked up the fire escape, raised the window, tiptoed down the hall, eased his key into the keyhole, opened his door, walked in and flicked on the light. When the light was turned on, he could see Dean Archer stretched out on his bed. And the dean just replied, 'Oh, I'm just keeping your bed warm for you, son. Come on in.'"

Rules and restrictions were particularly tight for the women of Agnes Scott and Spelman. "When you went to see a girl at Agnes Scott in those days," recalls Hunter Bell, "you sat in a parlor with some teacher to supervise her. And they had what I call 'going and coming' chairs—the man sits this way and the girl sits this [other] way. There were bright lights all the time anyhow. I don't think I ever went to see but one at Agnes Scott. It was too much trouble."

"We had to be in at night," recalls Agnes Scott graduate Marie Townsend. "We were not supposed to smoke or drink anywhere in Atlanta. We had to be chaperoned at parties or anything like that. We didn't even realize they were rules and regulations, really.

"We wore stockings and clothes to school, the girls wore *clothes*. And of course the boarding students at Agnes Scott had to wear evening gowns one night a week for dinner, and you were expected to show your very best manners. There was a certain amount of desire in the girls that finished there to know the graces of living as well as academic excellence. They were supposed to act off-campus the way they acted on-campus, and not be conspicuous.

"Miss Hopkins, who was the dean of women when I was out there, used to have a little ditty:

The surest sign of women's birth,
The truest test of women's worth
Is modesty.

And that didn't include wearing tight-fitting clothes and blue jeans."

"They were stricter then," echoes Arthur Idlett, recalling his college days at Morehouse. "They would send you home for playing cards, they would send you home for gambling, they would send you home for several other infractions of the rules." "Students [at Emory] were expected to be there in class," adds John Griffin, "and if a student was absent more than a few times he was severely penalized. Chapel was compulsory. We had a weekly chapel service and an assigned seat, and we were supposed to be there once a week. Those programs were often quite good programs. They were not strictly religious. They frequently brought in speakers of rather general interest and had a devotional program, too."

If anything, chapel played an even more prominent role on the black campuses. "You had to attend chapel every day," says Idlett. "When you went to chapel, you'd have singing, you'd have Scriptures. The chapel served as the job placement at that time, because speakers would come to chapel and tell the students about available jobs.

"You had what we called rhetoricals, a compulsory program in the chapel once a month. You had to go. At Morehouse each student in the English class had to write an oration and recite it in chapel. You would have student declamations, you would have glee club concerts, and you would have Shakespearean plays, all performed by students."

In addition to chapel, a variety of campus activities marked student life at all the area's colleges. Agnes Scott, for instance, sponsored the Blackfriars theater group, a well-known writers series, and an annual May Day celebration. Marie Townsend recalls: "Robert Frost came to Agnes Scott for years and years, every year. And we had Edna St. Vincent Millay and Vachel Lindsay and a good many others. We had good programs.

"Everybody had to take one semester of May Day. We had the Maypole and all, May dances, and interpreted some general theme every year. And what you did was practice for your part in it. I know the year that I took that I was representing Late Afternoon Sunlight—in cheesecloth. I had a flowing cheesecloth dress that had yellow at the top and went down into dark blues and greens at the bottom, in the sleeves. We also made the costumes. And it was quite entertaining."

"The clubs used to play an important part [in campus life]," recalls Morehouse graduate Idlett. "The fellows from Birmingham had a Birmingham Club, the fellows from the state of Florida had a Florida Club, fellows from South Carolina had a South Carolina Club. These clubs would have parties. They would go rent somebody's house and have a party. The piano player would charge you about a dollar to play from eight to one o'clock. You had to be off the streets at twelve o'clock.

"Then you had various clubs throughout the city. Now, in my area, I came from the Pittsburgh area, we had a club called the Ethura Club. Ethura was one of the angels in Milton's *Paradise Regained*. So we named it after Ethura because we had to read all—you don't do all that now—read Milton's poems."

"The college campus in the South," states Julia Coles, "has always been the cultural center for black people, because they had no other place to go. We had an orchestra and we had very good choirs, and we used to give plays." "In the summertime," adds Dean Brazeal, "we would have better theater out here on the Spelman campus than you would have anywhere else. *The Emperor Jones* was presented, *Mr. Pym Passes By, Lady Windermere's Fan,* and a number of other things."

The black colleges also sponsored football and other sports which kindled tremendous rivalry among the various schools. "We say," states Julia Coles, "that if Morris Brown doesn't win a game all season and beats Clark on Thanksgiving, then we've had a successful season, and Clark feels the same way." "By and large during football and basketball seasons," echoes B. R. Brazeal, "the A.U. people didn't like the Morehouse folks, and there you are."

Nowhere was football frenzy more intense than at Georgia Tech, where the Ramblin' Wrecks rose to major football prominence under Coach Heisman, winning a national title in 1917. "Oh, the spirit there, you can't explain it," recalls Red Barron, who held many of Tech's rushing records for decades. "Never a week passed that we didn't have a bonfire, practice yells and this, that and the other. Each player had a blanket, a gold blanket with a big white *T* in the middle with white trimmings. We'd run out single file on the field, each one of us with those blankets over our shoulders.

"It's sad to know my most memorable game, because I lost the game. That's Notre Dame in 1922, Knute Rockne, the Four Horsemen. My two fumbles cost us that ball game. I returned one punt thirty-eight or forty yards, and boy, then I was smashed. That ball went out and a Notre Dame guy caught it. Well, that killed it.

"Then if you think people let me forget it. . . . During the war I worked for the government and my office was in the Candler Building. Right across the street was a place to eat, where office people could run in and you could stand up if you couldn't get a seat. So I went in there one day, and I noticed that the guy on my left kept looking at me, kept looking at me. Of course, you get to wondering, you know, what in the world the man's eyeing you about. Now, in the modern day, I'd probably think he wasn't on Anita Bryant's side. But then finally he said, 'If I'm wrong, pardon me, but aren't you Red Barron?' I said, 'Yes, sir. I'm Red.' 'Lord, have mercy. My name is so-and-so. I never will forget you, never will forget you. I was on my honeymoon when Tech played Notre Dame. I never heard as much talk about a football game in my life. And I had to pay fifty dollars for my two tickets to go in. I was on my honeymoon, now, with my wife, fifty dollars. Then I got busy and put up the rest of my spending money betting on Tech, and my God, you fumbled.' That was twenty years later, 1922 to 1942. I never will get over that."

Whether it was athletics, studies, campus activities or social life, as a rule college meant a great deal to those who were able to attend during the period. "You went to class, and you generally had a good time being in college," sums up Hunter Bell. "I faced outward. You walked out with new confidence. College meant to me the opening of a new world."

Chapter Six

Underside

Despite periodic crackdowns and anti-vice campaigns, bootlegging, gambling and prostitution flourished in Atlanta throughout the period between the world wars. "Well, gambling has always been a problem. Prostitution has always been a problem," admits Herbert Jenkins, who became police chief in 1947. "There was always whiskey available, even though they made Prohibition an amendment to the Constitution, which gave the federal government the responsibility and the authority to enforce it. And, of course, as the records show, it never was very effectively enforced. It was a major problem, that was one of the great problems."

In the early twentieth century, Atlanta had one of the highest arrest rates for drunkenness of any major city in the United States. Local newspapers and preachers denounced the alleged depravity of the city's saloons and dives, and the public intoxication of Atlanta Mayor James G. Woodward became a major political issue. Racial and class tensions of that era, among other factors, helped bring on a wave of temperance sentiment across the state, and in 1908 Georgia passed a prohibition statute, fourteen years before national Prohibition went into effect, although Atlantans still were permitted low-alcohol beer. Jeweler Irwin Shields recalls a ditty from that 1908 temperance campaign:

"In gentle Georgia, my dear old state,
There will be no whiskey in 1908.
There'll be no whiskey, there'll be no beer
In dear old Georgia in many a year."

The temperance supporters who sang that song were guilty of some wishful thinking. Georgia's moonshining industry, which went back well into the nineteenth century, boomed during the Prohibition years. And Atlanta became the white lightning capital. "You could go out and buy a pint of corn liquor in most every alley, especially where the colored people lived," remembers policeman M. Y. Rutherford. "There was always somebody in that alley that could sell you a pint of corn liquor if you wanted it. That was practically all over town."

And not only in the black sections of Atlanta, as country musician Marion Brown recounts: "Oh, there was white ones, too, a lot of white ones around Cabbagetown. Yeah, there was half a dozen right around in that neighborhood because when all them mill people got out, man they headed for a bootlegger. They sure did. They wanted to get them a drink when they got out of that dusty cotton mill."

Middle-class Atlantans also partook of illegal alcohol, as E. B. Baynes relates: "I've seen out at the football games when—all this during Prohibition —that whiskey flowed like water. I mean, everybody had a bottle at that game. And that was out at Grant Field." Forrest Turner, one of Georgia's most famous moonshine haulers of the period, echoes: "One man, occasionally he'd get me to bring some stuff in town, and believe it or not, his clientele was mostly professional men, like doctors, lawyers, the dentists, and he got a good price for it."

While most manufacturing of moonshine took place in the mountains of north Georgia, there were some stills that actually operated within the city limits. Police officer J. T. Bowen remembers: "You had to get in a building somewhere so you wouldn't have your fumes coming out for people to smell. And you could wash your mash and stuff through the sewers. We had one notorious operator, he put one up in a building on Garnett Street between Pryor and Central next door to the Commercial High School."

"My husband was working there at Commercial High School at that time," adds country musician Rosa Lee Carson, "and right next door my husband kept on seeing trucks come in and they kept on smelling a peculiar odor. And so one day while he was up there and everybody was going home, the maid came and told him that there were two teachers up there [who] said they wasn't ready to go. Wayne said, 'Well, I'll just have to see about that.' So he goes up and they told him who they were and they was the FBI men. They found out there was a liquor still right under their noses and they caught it, raided at one o'clock the next day. And they said it was pure alcohol, said it sure was."

Yet most of the moonshine came from the hard-pressed counties north of Atlanta. Professional hauler Forrest Turner first made his bootlegging contacts while working in the Civilian Conservation Corps during the 1930s. He explains the centrality of illegal alcohol to many mountain communities: "Back then it was the only occupation in certain parts of the mountains except farming. It was a way of survival, really. In the economic condition the country was in then, it was actually just hard for anybody to make a living. No one really looked at bootlegging as a crime. It was just a way of making a living.

"I hauled enough to float a battleship into Atlanta back in those old days. We would make a trip maybe three times a week into some of the north Georgia counties like Dawson County. That's about the only occupation they had in that county until they started raising a lot of chickens up in that part of the country [in the 1940s]. Then they started putting the whiskey stills in some of the chicken houses.

Turner recalls how the moonshiners would bring the 'shine' in and stack it in the barns. "The barns usually had a long hallway in them with the little corn-cribs on each side. And each one would be stacked with so many gallons of whiskey. Usually it was in gallon cans. They called them the 'shiny cans.' And some of the old law-enforcement people would say, 'You haul those shiny cans, you're gonna eat out of those county pans.' Back then everybody on the road gangs ate out of a county pan, which was just a tin pan which had just about the same shine as the cans had.

"I usually would haul it in Ford automobiles because back then they were the best. They were the best balanced and you could hop them up. Along in '32, I think, was the first V-8 Ford, which was just a bootlegger's dream. But I think the car that probably hauled more whiskey than any other car on the American market was the '40 Ford. A lot of times we made what we called tankers out of them. You could lower the pan in the back and build kind of a chute where you could take it right on up under the front seat. You could stack it to the windows and all the way on the driver's side, if you stacked it just right. And if you didn't mind taking out the seat on the right, you could bring in seventy-five or a hundred gallons.

"We would take these old bug sprays, you know, like they spray a garden with. We'd take those things and adapt them to the exhaust system and put burnt motor oil in it, which would throw up a smoke screen. We'd get roofing nails, like a keg of roofing nails. And if they were chasing you, somebody would climb in the back and just dump all those roofing nails in front of them. Then we'd take boards and drive a lot of spikes in them and cut them into sections, and you'd put a hinge on them so you could lay them across the road. Usually if a car hit those spikes it would put them out.

"The main thing you'd have to look out for was if your car had been spotted or anything. You know, you could disguise a car or change the appearance of it. I usually kept a pretty good line of accessories that you could snap on and off.

We'd do little things like switch fog lights on them or license plates or different hubcaps. I had unissued license plates, made at the state prison and smuggled out. We always kept a set of red blinker lights."

Turner recalls that there were four or five officers around Atlanta that they really dreaded. "We used to have a real tough detective that was known as a man that would shoot you and kill you, and I remember him jumping me down around Myrtle and Ponce de Leon one night. They had set up this roadblock. I ran into it. I was coming into it, and I whipped on the red blinker lights that I had, and I had a siren on the car and was blowing it. And he backed up and let me pass. As I went past him, I had to get up on the sidewalk. When I got on the sidewalk, he realized what he had done, and he started shooting at me. The steering wheels were made out of rubber, and it knocked a plug out of that rubber and burned my hand real bad where it hit.

"And later I got caught. He was telling me, he said, 'I was really pegging at those tires.' I said, 'Tires, hell.' I said, 'Them damn tires weren't around my neck'—because he was shooting at my head.

"But your main object," says Forrest Turner, "was to get that load off the car as quick as you could. Most of us would haul for somebody in Atlanta who was pretty prominent, that ran maybe a big garage or some sort of a warehouse. Some of them were rather prominent businessmen.

"It was usually some secluded place. And a lot of times it was just a warehouse or something you could drive into, like all those old buildings on Peters Street around where the old Terminal Station used to be. Or I've seen them drive down under the railroad where the Omni is now, pull in among those trestles or pillars and throw it from one car to another and go. You'd set it off and get your money. Then the set-off men would distribute it to the alley bootleggers and the street bootleggers all over the city. They'd rebottle it and sell it by the pints or the quarts."

"Magnolia Street was a little street out through town there," recalls streetcar man A. J. Shupe. "It was just a colored section. And you could see they'd bring carloads of that stuff over there. There'd be one colored man here and one way over yonder and they'd be watching for police. And they'd take a gallon can and set it down in the water meter, to hide it. And then they'd sell it out of there."

"That water meter out there in the street, that's been a hiding place for bootleggers," echoes baseball player Arthur Idlett. "He'd take the top off and hide that whiskey down there or hide it in vacant fields, as long as he didn't have it on *his* property. He'd put it on *your* property and hide it, you see. You've got a vacant field out here, well he always stays where he can watch it, and usually nobody would bother the whiskey."

"They'd have an old automobile stashed out somewhere," adds fireman Hugh McDonald, recalling another hiding place, "and have it in that, old cars that wasn't worth much. And if anybody would go there and want some, they'd tell him to go around here and wait, and they'd go and get it and bring it to him. All out Pryor Street there were bootleggers, and on down Trinity Avenue there was bootleggers all around. Good gracious, a lot of places."

"You could walk down the street in the summertime," relates E. B. Baynes, "and colored people would be standing around on the corner. And he would say, 'Do you want something? Do you need a pint? Do you need a half-pint?' You didn't have to ask him, he would solicit you for his business.

"They called it a pint, but it was a short pint. It lacked two or three ounces of being a pint. And it usually cost a dollar and it was just white corn whiskey. They called it corn whiskey, but it was made mainly, I think, with sugar and had a little corn meal, corn malt in it to give it a little slight corn taste.

"That stuff—oooh, that was mean," relates Marion Brown. "Sometimes they'd call it 'block and tackle.' You'd take a drink of it, walk a block and tackle a tiger. Then they had another brand of that white lightning they called 'chicken liquor.' You'd take a drink and lay anywhere—on a curbstone, on a sidewalk. But I used to know a Jewish fellow, he used to sell peanuts up and down there on Decatur Street. And under them peanuts he had some schnapps and had a little glass. And he'd go in them pawnshops and sell all them Jewish people— you know, that run them pawnshops?—he'd sell them a drink. He had imported whiskey that we would buy."

"You could go into some colored sections of town," says Baynes, "and just walk in most any house and a lot of them were just as clean and nice as they could be, and the people that sold the whiskey, the purveyors, most of them were polite and friendly. You'd go in and you'd buy usually a fifteen-cent drink, which was a peanut butter glass. I imagine it held about three or four ounces. You could get a drink and drink it right there and chase it with a little tap water, or if you wanted to buy a Co'-Cola, most of the places had Co'-Cola."

"All the neighborhoods were spotted with so-called liquor houses," adds nurse Ruby Baker.[1] "And you'd know those houses, but people'd tolerate them because they weren't rowdy or anything. They were just workingmen mostly, bricklayers and laborers and all. When they'd get off from work they would go there, a quarter a shot, and then go home. But it was just an accepted fact, because most people were just trying to live."

Both blacks and whites supplemented their regular income by peddling moonshine on the side. Textile worker Effie Gray describes one such vendor in her neighborhood near the Fulton Bag and Cotton Mill: "There was a man come in here selling milk and he'd swap me up for bread scraps. He'd have that milk in the front, but in the back he'd have them big old five-gallon jars and it had a spout on it, and he'd sell that liquor, gallons at a time."

"If you were having a party," recalls E. B. Baynes, "if you wanted any whiskey to amount to anything, you could pick up the telephone and call up any bootlegger that you happened to know and get him to bring you a gallon. And in less than ten or fifteen minutes that gallon of whiskey would be there at your door. The man would deliver it to you in a brown paper bag and in a gallon tin can. And that whiskey was fairly palatable, too. It wasn't a bad beverage at all. A dollar and a half a gallon."

Atlanta's bootleggers often set up their own private house parties, sometimes with a musician present as a drawing card, to unload their goods and make money. Kate McTell, widow of blues musician Blind Willie McTell, recalls: "Willie said, 'Baby doll, I'm trying to help you get through school, I'm trying to make a living.' Willie's uncle, he run a big whiskey still at that time, and he'd give us all the whiskey we wanted. And we'd carry it back on the train, come down with a great big suitcase and load it up, carry it back.

"I would tell several of my friends, 'I'm giving a party tonight, having a fish fry or a chili supper.' And I'd invite so many people in, you know. We'd always close the kitchen off with chairs. Willie said, 'Now, I'm going to play. You sell the sandwiches and plates and things, and the drink. We sold scrap iron. And, of course, that's where you made your money, selling scrap iron liquor. Sold 'Bell Street Whiskey, make you sleep all in your clothes.'

"A lot of people, they's superstitious, they would tell me, 'You taste it, I don't want nobody's scrap iron liquor unless they taste it.' I said, 'I don't drink.' Willie'd say, 'I'll taste it. Ain't no poison in it.' He'd turn it up and he'd say, 'Now you pay her for that one, and buy you another one.' And you were making money.

"They caught us one time. They said, 'Where you got your whiskey at?' I said, 'Who told you we had any?' They said, 'We got the word, we see the crowd hanging around.' I said, 'Well, if you got the word, you can look for it. It ain't my place to tell you where it's at, if you think we got any in here.' And they just found a small little glass, that Willie had left just a little in, not in a bottle or anything.

"They said, 'Willie, we're going to have to carry you down.' He said, 'I'm going, baby doll, because they can't make me work. I'm blind. I can sit out my ten days.' I said, 'No, I'm going, and they're going to turn me loose.' So I went, and they did turn me loose. The judge told them they didn't have nothing on us, because they didn't catch us with the whiskey and didn't catch us selling it. And they couldn't press no charges against me for selling it. And that was it, they let me go."

The relationship between Atlanta's police department and the bootleg trade was a complicated one. Some officers, such as one described by policeman Stewart Peeples, certainly were strict in enforcing the liquor laws: "Wooster —have you ever heard talk of him?—Wooster locked up more people than anybody in the city of Atlanta. They would say he'd lock his own brother up. Boy, he locked up his share. He worked over there in Summerhill for years and years and years. He'd start out, be twelve o'clock at night. He saw somebody on the street, he stopped. 'Let me smell your breath, boy.' Smelled his breath, and if he had liquor on it, he's locked up. Lock him up for drunk.

"You could have kept a jailhouse full, locking up people like that. It done just as much good to take their whiskey from them and pour it out. If I caught them drinking from the bottle, I'd tell them, 'You're not supposed to have whiskey. Now, if you want me to, I'll lock you up. If you don't, I'll pour it out.'

"I caught lots of them with their whiskey and I poured it out. One of them turned around and called the station house and reported that the policeman up there on the beat was taking their whiskey from them and drinking it up. The lieutenant come up there to check on it, and he rolled up and I stuck my head in the window. He said, 'Well, I can see you haven't been drinking, but we got a report that you was up here taking people's liquor away from them and drinking it up.' I was just pouring it out."

Many police officers, like M. Y. "Pete" Rutherford, would wink at street bootlegging, using small-scale dealers as informers to catch other suspected criminals: "You had to have some guy. Maybe he was selling a little corn liquor on the side. You'd catch him, and he'd get to begging off to keep from getting locked up maybe with a pint of corn liquor. Well, that wasn't no hanging crime, you know, but you would sort of hold the hot rag to him, say, 'Well, if you help me, I'll help you.' He'd say, 'Anything you want. What is it?'

"So something could happen, say, at Glenn and McDaniel Street. You go up there and those colored people wouldn't tell you nothing, didn't nobody know anything. They all knew about it but they wouldn't tell no police. But, if you couldn't find out what happened, you've got to see this man. He owes you a favor about letting him bootlegging. You'd say, 'How about going up there and seeing what you can find out? We'll be back after a while.' He'd say 'All right.' Go back, and he'd tell you the whole story.

"Back in those days the policemen drank a whole lot, nearly all of them did. Half of them did. Nobody thought anything about it. I'll tell you, I've worked with a few down there, quick as he'd go to work, first thing he'd do is he'd go get him a drink of liquor. But I'm telling you the truth, he'd do more policing drunk than a lot of these do now sober."

"I used to know one old policeman way back there that carried it around with him while he was in uniform while he was a-working, and peddled it out," says streetcar man Lloyd Adair. "I've seen him peddle it on the street. A little bitty old flat bottle he had would hold probably a couple of drinks. He'd keep it in his uniform pocket somewhere, keep it around. He'd have it for you if you wanted. I've seen streetcar men go to him and get it. Shoot, there was more liquor runners and the police was mixed up in it."

"The policemen would raid a place over here and take it to another person to sell," asserts Arthur Idlett. "He wouldn't lock up anybody, he'd just raid and take the whiskey, and then take it to another bootlegger to sell.

"The police were mixed up with it. We had a fellow down on Auburn named Nat. Nat was a bootlegger and he was paying a policeman named Payne and Payne was looking out for him. Then for some reason he squealed on Payne. Payne lost his job and Nat never was no more." "Nat told everybody," adds barber Horace Sinclair, "the chief of police, the sergeants and everybody else that he was paying them off to sell this corn liquor. He just tore up the police force. Yeah, he really shook it up. He had to go to the chain gang and them people lost their jobs, the polices."

A 1937 investigation, instigated by Mayor William B. Hartsfield, revealed that some 40 percent of the Atlanta and Fulton County police departments were involved in profit-sharing arrangements with local bootleggers. Police who accepted bribes were dismissed or prosecuted. Street bootleggers—especially black ones—were occasionally arrested and jailed. But, as Officer Rutherford relates, the kingpins of the Atlanta liquor trade usually went scot-free: "The big bootlegger, he'd hardly ever fool with it himself. He'd never touch it. He's the man who'd furnish the money, furnish the automobile, furnish the men. He'd send the men up in the mountains, get a load of liquor and bring it back in. He was plumb clear of that because he wasn't nowhere around that liquor ever.

"They'd get in big chases sometimes with those bootleggers, but they couldn't catch all that corn liquor, though. They'd get some of it, but there was a lot of it got in, yeah a lot of it."

Such problems and abuses associated with Prohibition led some prominent Atlantans to advocate repeal of the Eighteenth Amendment. Atlanta *Journal* reporter John Ottley recalls: "I don't think too many people were in favor of Prohibition. And one of the stories I got that was carried on the front pages of most papers in the United States concerned that situation. One day I was in the office of federal Judge Samuel H. Sibley, who was the finest judge I've ever known. He was a man that I think liked to drink, but during Prohibition would never take one in his home or anywhere else. But we were talking about the minimum sentence, which then for anyone convicted was a year and a day in the federal penitentiary. That was the minimum, even if they got caught with a quart of moonshine whiskey. So he says, 'John, I think Prohibition is doing more harm than good.' And said, 'The finest citizens in Atlanta are drinking bootleg whiskey in the clubs and homes and so on, and yet I've got to give these poor people that are starving to death up in the mountains of north Georgia a year and a day.'

So I said, 'Well, Judge Sibley, could I quote you on that?' He thought a while and said, 'Yes, you could, because I believe that.' So that hit the front page of most of the papers in the United States, a federal judge thought Prohibition was doing more harm than good."

Another Atlantan who made national headlines when he opposed Prohibition was Mayor James L. Key. Herbert Jenkins, then Key's chauffeur, recalls: "About 1931 the French government invited some forty mayors to be their guests, and while they were in Paris, Mr. Key made a public statement that there were many things the American people could learn from the French and one of them was the control and regulation of alcoholic beverages. Then he said that the Eighteenth Amendment had been a miserable failure and should be repealed."

"He was the first person in public office [in the United States] to make that statement," asserts Mayor Key's daughter, Mrs. E. Graham McDonald, who accompanied her father on the Paris trip. "And by the time we went back to New York, we were met by this boatload of reporters and it was all over everywhere."

"When he returned home," adds Herbert Jenkins, "the prohibitionists and some of the others had a recall election in 1932 and attempted to put the mayor out. There was several other things got involved, but Mr. Key's liberal stand on legalization of alcohol was the main issue. But the mayor won. James L. Key stayed in office and served five more years after that."

Although victorious in the recall election, Mayor Key was forced to resign

Bar scene, 1940s. (J. Neal Montgomery Collection, Atlanta-Fulton Public Library)

from Grace Methodist Church. "The presiding elder of the church," remembers Mrs. McDonald, "told him that he would not be allowed to continue teaching Sunday school if he did not promise never to mention his stand against Prohibition. He said, 'I would have thought that he knew that I had better taste than to bring that up in Sunday school,' and so he said, 'No, I'm not going to promise,' and he quit."

The next year, federal Prohibition was repealed. In Fulton County, however, only "near beer" with a low alcoholic content was permitted until 1938. And the bootleg trade continued, as E. B. Baynes recounts: "We still had Prohibition in Georgia when in other parts of the States liquor was legalized. There were places in Atlanta where you could drive up in your car, drive-ins that sold sandwiches and hot dogs and things like that. But their main business was whiskey. And when you'd drive in, a curb boy would come say, 'Yes sir, boss.' And you'd say, 'Give me a pint of 10 High' or 'Give me a pint of Old Quaker' or 'Give me a pint of such-and-such,' depending on what you wanted. And that boy would run in and bring it back out and you'd pay him, just like he had a permit. But it was illegal."

Moonshine whiskey continued to pour into Atlanta, too. In 1951 local bootlegger Fat Hardy mixed a bad batch of alcohol that killed and blinded dozens of Atlantans. Only after that incident did the torrent slow down to a relative trickle, although Atlanta still maintained its reputation as a white lightning center into the 1970s.

"Atlanta never was a wide-open town like New Orleans," says E. B. Baynes. "But I recall at one time they had the old Embassy Club out on the Buford Highway. They had dice tables and a setup for blackjack. You'd come in the front of the place where the drinking and dining area was—beer had been legalized then—and you'd go back into another room where the game room was. And that place ran wide open and it catered to wealthy people—doctors and lawyers, professional people, and entertainers. I happened to know one of the fellows that was employed there, and he was telling me about some of those big well-known entertainers that would come out, and they always invariably lost. I wouldn't say that the game was crooked, but they were fleeced well. But that was about the only one."

"And there was flimflam, of course," adds Herbert Jenkins, referring to the Floyd Woodward "bunko gang" that operated in Atlanta during the early twenties. "Atlanta had quite a well-known case for a few years with some confidence people, had a lot of publicity on that. There were certain confidence games to where the gamblers would get certain people in various games of chance, and then strip them. A guy would wind up . . . he was maybe visiting Atlanta and lost a lot of money. It was that kind of operation. But then the solicitor general and the district attorney finally identified the people and brought them to trial, and they were convicted."

However, the great majority of gambling operations in Atlanta were not so organized or so big-time. Rather, poker, "Georgia skin," craps, and other individual games of chance abounded throughout the city. "Oh, that was plentiful," recalls blues musician Roy Dunn. "You didn't even hear nothing about nobody running no gambling houses, nothing like that, because I know you could just walk out on the corner anywhere and say, 'Where's the gambling at tonight?' Such and such a place, so and so's house, and all like that all over town. People were shooting craps and gambling. They'd just get in an attic somewhere, get on a porch somewhere and gamble. You could easily find them all over town, four and five places right in the same block."

"A lot of them done that on the street corner," remembers Officer Rutherford, "just get in a skin game or a crap game. They'd have four or five of them get down on a sidewalk shooting crap. They'd have one that wouldn't get in the game. He was the lookout man, he'd watch for them police cars. At that time, we just had a plain car, it wasn't no red light or blue light or nothing on it, it was just a plain automobile. But I don't know, there was something about them police cars that them blacks could tell you three blocks away whether it was a police car. I think they could smell them, seemed like it."

"We used to have a lot of fun catching crap games, you know," reminisces Sanders Ivey. "They would shoot crap on the corner—they'd call themselves smart—where they could see everybody. We'd slip up on them, shoot a gun, run them off of the money. We'd take it in to the station captain's office, and if they'd called for it, we'd have locked them up, you see, and they knew that. Then, didn't anybody call for it, they'd give it to us."

"The way it was," says policeman Peeples, "anything that you could hear or see from the street, you had a right to bust in on them. I don't think they've got that now, I think they've done away with that. Usually we'd get a call they're having some gambling there, and then we'd get out of the car and go around the house, and we'd listen. And if you heard them in there slapping the chips and 'I'll raise you this, that and the other,' that was enough to go in. But I think now you have to have a warrant for most of this stuff.

"Lots of times they were white people, a lot of times they were white people playing poker. Their wife would call up because their husband was down there losing their money. And she'd find out where their card game was, and she wanted to stop it, and so she called up. And lots of times a man would lose money, see, and then he'd go and get sore and call the police in.

"But some of your biggest gambling back in them days was done with bridge, and they was never bothered, hardly, because it was a different class of people. Man, there's people that lost a pile of money playing bridge, old ladies. But that wasn't the type that caused you trouble."

"Most of the gambling they'd have back then," says Pete Rutherford, "they'd have a poker game or a crap game, something like that. That was the majority of your gambling back in those days. You very seldom heard of anybody betting on all these horses and baseball games, football games, things like that."

While, unlike today, there existed little or no gambling on the outcome of professional or collegiate sporting events, many Atlantans did bet out in the bleachers of Ponce de Leon Park, where the Crackers and Black Crackers played baseball. According to E. B. Baynes, the bleachers were a haven for gamblers because "at that time they had some kind of law in Georgia that you couldn't convict a man for gambling unless he was in a gambling house, and the house had to have a roof. And those bleachers did not have a roof over them."

The bets were on each individual batter. "They had bookies out there," relates streetcar man Adair. "They'd pay four to one on a fly ball, eight to one on a double, and twenty to one on a home run. A batter would come up and the fellows would say, 'All right! All right! Who wants him?' Held their hand full of money, those bookies would, right wide open. A fellow would say, 'I'll take him for a fly ball.' If he flew, why he had to pay him that dollar and four more. And you could go out there and lose all your money quick sometimes, and sometimes you'd get a pocketful back."

"Oh, it was a lot of fun," recalls postal employee Waldo Roescher. "I remember one game—I played fifty cents across the board on a guy that was up, and he hit a long fly ball to left field to Sheriff Harris, and Harris got a glove on the ball, but couldn't hold it. So the bookie said, 'Well, that was an error.' I said, 'No, it was a hit.' Well, he said, 'You look in the paper in the morning and if they give him a hit, next time you're out here I'll pay you.' So sure enough, he got a triple out of it. And the next time I went out there the guy saw me coming and he met me with my money.

"At that time the police didn't pay any attention to it. Eventually, they broke it up. It got too big, I guess, and no doubt some wives complained that their husbands went to the ball park and lost their food money, which no doubt they did. So, they put plainclothes policemen out there and starting hauling them off. There's none of it now, that I know of."

More widespread than betting at the ball park was the numbers lottery, known then and now as the "bug." Organized numbers operations entered the city around 1930, and reached deeply into both the black and white communities. "You could gamble anything from a penny up," explains E. B. Baynes. "They'd take penny bets, lots and lots of bets of two or three cents and five and six cents and things like that. You selected three numbers that you bet your penny on. And it was determined on the returns from the stock market in New York. When the returns was in, it was always three numbers, and the middle three numbers was the winner. And if you happened to pay a nickel on, we'll say, 246, and that number hit 246, well, they were supposed to pay you five hundred to one. Now, the chance of that thing hitting 246 is one thousand to one, but they paid off at five hundred to one. But that was big business in Atlanta. They had a number of companies that had writers all over town, and they was busy writing those numbers up until a few minutes before the thing was determined, what the number would be."

Especially during the Depression years, playing the numbers was enticing for both poor and middle-class Atlantans of all races. "Well, everybody wrote the bug," says Pete Rutherford. "There was a lot of white people wrote that bug, and nearly all the blacks did. You didn't run up on a black very often that didn't write the bug. And there were a lot of white people, a *lot* of white people played that bug."

"Everybody was playing numbers then," recalls Roy Dunn. "School children, old folks couldn't hardly walk, old ladies. I used to go and sell them milk bottles, two and three cents apiece, to get my grandmama them pennies to play the number. Yeah, Lord."

As Dunn relates, people had different ways of "predicting" the winning number: "Called themself dreaming numbers. They was even selling dream books. Just about every store you go to along in there, tell you what the number is." "There was a number writer in practically every block in black neighborhoods," adds Ruby Baker. "And they would come by and say, 'I'm collecting dreams.' The numbers did more to break the Depression among black folks than anything else."

Of course, the allure of the numbers lay in the fact that practically everybody who played personally knew someone who had hit the bug. Musician Buddy Moss remembers one winner: "I know a woman over on Dodge Street. A joker came over and just gave her a quarter. He said, 'Here, you put this on such-and-such,' I forget the number now. But anyway, she hit the number and she had a hundred and twenty-two dollars and fifty cents. (The quarter would have brought her a hundred and twenty-five dollars, but the writer got his cut.)

Policeman finding hidden lottery tickets, 1948. (Atlanta
Journal-Constitution*)*

Man, you talk about somebody falling out and having a hemorrhage almost, that chick you could hear hollering from here to Statesboro when the guy come shelling out that money."

"They would take the numbers to a central location," recalls Ruby Baker. "Maybe a dry cleaner or a grocery store, you know. And then the pickup man would come and pick up the collection of numbers from a central place —the numbers runner. Walt Cutcliff was one that was famous at that time. And people used to stand out, especially on Hunter and Mitchell Street, to watch him come through, because he'd come through flying. Sometimes the cops would be right behind him, but they couldn't catch him. He was known for his fast driving. There was another one over there, the one called Wild Bill."[2]

"If the police'd see a man cutting it on a motorcycle by hisself, they figured he was a numbers man," remembers Kate McTell. "And they would get him. But if they saw a woman on the motorcycle with the man, they didn't bother, because they didn't figure he had numbers. I had a girlfriend, her husband was named Frank. He would pick up numbers. So, she was afraid to ride the motorcycle with Frank, but I wasn't. And Willie would always say, 'Go on, go on and ride that motorcycle with Frank, carry the numbers in.'"

Occasionally, there would be crackdowns on the lottery, as E. B. Baynes recalls: "One of the newspapers decided they were going to launch a campaign and stop that gambling, that too many people were getting wealthy off of poor people, people that couldn't afford to gamble. And they got the police to where they was arresting them. That was in around 1933 or '34.

"Of course, ordinarily they was ignoring them. They managed to be elsewhere and seeing something else. They'd arrest somebody once in a while. But some of those companies seemed like they just ran with immunity, and some of those police became pretty affluent. Nice big automobiles and homes and various different things. Salaries of those policemen didn't warrant that."

In the 1930s, 1950s and 1960s, scandals emerged concerning the involvement of local police with the lottery. Even though the Police Department may have been cleaned up and playing the numbers is not as common as a half century ago, as Chief Jenkins states, "The bug is still in operation. That's one of our major problems even today. It's still one of the major problems."

At least since the Civil War, when hundreds of camp followers accompanied the troops, prostitution has also been a major part of Atlanta's underside, despite periodic public cleanup drives. In 1912, Police Chief James Beavers, assisted by liberal reformers in the Men and Religion Forward Movement, launched a series of raids on the downtown red-light district. "There was several streets where there was houses of prostitution established and regulated," recounts Chief Jenkins. "There was several streets near the center of town and near the Terminal Station. Madison Avenue, I think, was one street—all this was before my day—and Collins Street was where the houses was.[3] But that was the locations. And eventually Chief Beavers won and closed them."

"I understand that the ministers of the city held marches in downtown Atlanta to arouse public sentiment on the question," states J. McDowell Richards, president of Columbia Theological Seminary. "A concerted effort was made to abolish the red-light district and to help in the rehabilitation of prostitutes. And apparently the program was very effective for a time."

In conjunction with the closing of the red-light district, hundreds of prostitutes were offered jobs, while many others left the city. But prostitution soon returned, as Officer M. Y. Rutherford relates: "Later on, when that was broke up, I reckon the main part was Central Avenue, you know, Central Avenue and Formwalt Street and Pryor, down in there. But Central Avenue was the main drag. That's where most of them were back in those times. When I first went on the police force, why you could drive down Central Avenue and every house you'd come to on both sides of the street nearly there'd be three or four women sitting out on the porch motioning you to come in. Yeah, motioning anybody, anybody went down Central Avenue. Yes, sir."

"I'd say 80 percent of the houses down the whole street were either engaged in prostitution or whiskey and beer and wine, illegal," recalls policeman J. T. Bowen. "And of course all the holdup men and the burglars, they holed up in there, too. It was just a situation when you would drive down the street and you'd see somebody soliciting to ask them to come in, or they beat on the window as people passed by. Some of them would have red lights burning in the windows.

"Bankhead and Marietta was similar, except it wasn't as large an area. It was about a two-block business district for the people in northwest Atlanta that congregated around the beer joints. But it didn't have a widespread area like they did on Washington and Capitol and Pulliam and Central and Pryor and Formwalt and Cooper Street and Georgia Avenue."

There were houses of prostitution in various black neighborhoods as well, including a fancy establishment on the west side of town, described by one Atlantan: "They had Blue Heaven on Simpson Road. That was a beautiful place, they had beautiful girls. This fellow, he was a friend of the family's, he carried us up there, my sister and myself. We were teenagers and we didn't know where we were going, because we weren't even supposed to be going out or anything. And they brought out the liquor on the tray, and beautiful girls. And there was a sun porch, and they had goldfish in there. Oh, it was fabulous. We had never seen anything like it. I realized that we weren't supposed to be there, I had that much sense. But my sister came in. 'Mama, guess where we've been!' I was a little more sophisticated than my sister and I knew what it was, because I'd been reading cheap novels a long time before."

Blues musician Roy Dunn had occasion to know many of Atlanta's black prostitutes: "Big Peck was known to be one of the best and had more women prostituting for her than anyone I've ever known, Big Peck. You know the proper name for them people is lesbians, but they called them 'bull daggers.' She was a big bull dagger, called her Peck on the west side. And all them girls used to be her specials, right there on Mitchell Street.

"Decatur Street, that's where all the prostitutes was. Big Millie was a big one. And then the next one was Joanna, and there was Black Rose from South Carolina, cut a woman's head off with a razor. You might have heard them talking about another woman used to run up and down Decatur Street and was a prostitute. They called her Mae West and the other one Jew Baby. And the next one, they even made a song about her, and they called her Chilly Wind. Chilly was poisoned to death in Pennsylvania."

"Chilly Wind," recalls Horace Sinclair. "She was a nice-looking dark girl, too much avoirdupois, you know, a big woman, but she was loose. She'd show you a good time, you'd go over to her house, she'd wine, dine and dance you, you follow me?"

As Officer Bowen relates, often women in the different houses of prostitution would snitch on each other to the police: "The ones that were in the other houses, they'd call you and tell you, say, 'Well, you locked them up this afternoon,' and say, 'They were bragging you'll never catch them again.'

"So one particular night, one that lived three doors from the other one, she called me and said that they were bragging that we couldn't catch them again. So I drove over there and parked in a vacant lot, walked across the street, went down the hall in the house next door, went out of the house next door, and walked on the back porch. And I knew which one the date room was. And when I heard them on the porch asking people to come in, I just slipped in the room and stood behind the bed—had a closet with a curtain over it. And I stood behind the bed until they brought the date in. So when she come to open the door, I had them handcuffed. Took them on and locked them up. And they quit, they went out of business.

"And then certain times, the captain would tell us to go way out to Bankhead and Marietta and change the beats. And so the girls hanging around the joints would look up and say, 'Well, it's 3:30, time for them to go in and Bowen and Wooster to come on.' So they'd get out of there. Then some days we'd change our pattern and go to work at 2:00 and surprise them. You tried to keep them on the run all the time."

"They had what they call a sundown law with women, you know, a known prostitute," states Stewart Peeples. "Better not get caught out after dark. Lock them up. You know, if they got caught in a restaurant or something after dark. Old Wooster used it a lot. Boy, he locked them up. He locked up women he didn't [any] more know that was prostitutes or nothing. I don't see how he got by with it, but he got by with it.

"He'd stop at a restaurant and, boy, if there was women in there by theirself, if they couldn't give a good reason, they'd go down to the station house. Well, you know, a woman hanging around by herself at night is not good for anything but trouble in a place like that.

"Lots of times we'd come there on Mitchell Street to get a cup of coffee, and the girls that was up there in that district, after they got through working, they'd come down there and get them something to eat. I've seen them there lots of times, used to talk with them. There was an all-night restaurant, Smith's Restaurant, up there on Mitchell Street, right down from the Terminal Station. That was a nightlife district, too. There were some small hotels in there."

"I've known them to go up to these little old ten-cent hotels during the Depression," relates Buddy Moss, "and get them a room, jokers that were working on the WPA. Joker would bring his own dear wife down there, and the Negro'd line up like he's going to the cotton field, fifteen or twenty-five cents. And the Negro was stupid enough to think he was getting somewhere, just because it was a white woman. He thought that was a great thing, because he'd always been told that you can look but don't touch. This is no damn lie."

Prostitutes operated out of both the cheap and the better hotels downtown, clustered in what is now the Fairlie-Poplar area, as Officer Peeples recalls: "You had a bunch of hotels in there, the Ansley, the Atlantan, Robert Fulton, Winecoff, the Ritz and several little hotels up there. There was just a hotel district there. These was all call girls. They'd get a call, you know, and come up to a hotel. Maybe the bellhops might have called most of them, might not have been many pimps involved.

"But it wasn't too bad, it wasn't nothing like it is now. Boy, they wouldn't have put up with that. And finally they cleaned most of those out. There wasn't hardly any of them for a while. I think when the Army come in, they cleaned out most of them, the known girls, that they could. They got rid of them."

During the World War II years, prostitution laws were stiffened and offenders required to take a medical exam, as a venereal disease epidemic hit the city, infecting many of the soldiers passing through Atlanta. "The law at that particular time," remembers J. T. Bowen, "the ordinance said being in the same room with a man or woman, if they weren't married. And it didn't necessarily —[they] just [had to] be in the same room with the door closed. There was lots of arrests made in those days, because the V.D. rate was escalating so fast.

"It never wiped out prostitution, it just scattered them out all over town. They went on out Boulevard to Georgia Baptist Hospital, and out Courtland by St. Joseph's, and of course Williams Street on the west side was loaded with joints and houses." Adds Stewart Peeples, "They'd get rid of this crowd and another one would come in, you know." And even though sexual attitudes and mores have changed since the period between the world wars, prostitution has continued to flourish in Atlanta.

M. Y. "Pete" Rutherford

Pete Rutherford came to Atlanta in 1918. A streetcar operator, he joined the Atlanta Police Department in 1928, coming on full-time in 1931. For thirteen years he had the morning beat in Pittsburgh, a black neighborhood near the present Atlanta-Fulton Stadium.

I was living out here in West End. I thought I'd have to go see some of these councilmen, talk to them, get my friends to talk to them. I talked to somebody, I forgot who it was. He said, "No, you don't." Said, "I'll tell you what to do. You want to get on the police force?" I says, "Yeah." He says, "Well, you haven't got to see but one man. You go out yonder on Inman Street and see

Ozburn and tell him you want on the police force and I sent you there." Said, "That will be all you'll have to do." Ozburn was the councilman from this ward. And so I went out there and I talked to him. He said, "You know what? I'll put you on." I says, "You think I ought to see anybody else, Mr. Ozburn?" He says, "No, that won't be necessary. [I] said I'll put you on." Sure enough, about two weeks later than that he put me on, old Ozburn did.

On the police force back in 1928, when I went on, it would take you about two or three years to get to be a regular patrolman. They had what they called a supernumerary list. There was so many on that supernumerary list that you'd just have to answer all the roll calls. The captain rotated them, assigned the men out. If a man was off, why, he'd call the next man up to take his place. Sometimes you'd go down there and answer three roll calls a day and maybe work two or three days a week—all you'd catch out. I got permission from Chief Beavers to stay on my job with the power company till I went regular. I stayed with the power company three years after I went on the police force.

They'd give you the badge, the gun, and they sent you up there to work. They didn't tell you much. It was very little that they told you. When I first went on the force I walked a beat for about three months on Plaza Way, uptown, up near the railroad. Run from Forsyth—I believe it did—to either Whitehall or Pryor. It was just a big sidewalk and the railroad tracks was down below there. They was bad there. There was burglars going in there at night and throwing bricks through the big plate-glass windows, maybe get nothing but a pair of women's hose.

I'd been on, I reckon, two or three years before I even shot at anyone. One Sunday morning about three o'clock I was walking Whitehall Street. I was standing in the doorway at Silver's store down on Whitehall. I looked down the street, and the young policeman with me that morning, fellow by the name of Hill—it was his first night to work. A load of blacks came up there with an old car. It had a rumble seat in it. There was a furniture store on the corner. They had a nice big radio in that show window. That was all that was in there, a nice big one. They threw a brick through that glass and two of them got out of that car and tried to get that. Well, they did get the radio. We went down there and we got to shooting at them. Well, one of us shot one of them through the calf of the leg. But they got in that car and got away.

I went on and made the report when I got off at eight o'clock in the morning. Meantime, over on West Fair Street they called in that there was a fellow over there shot in the leg. The detectives went over there and got him and got the radio and everything back. That's the only fellow that I've ever shot, I just shot one in the leg.

It's better on you to work on a certain beat, stay there for a while, than it is to stay over here a few months at this beat and then move over to another beat, because when you stay in a place for, you know, ten or twelve years, you just about know every pig trail on it, know where all the streets are. You get on a strange beat, you don't know that, and it takes you longer to answer a call and everything. When I was down there [in Pittsburgh], they'd give us a call, certain number on a certain street, I could tell you about the block that that number was in on that street. That would help you a whole lot.

Part of it was pretty nice and part of it was run-down. There was a lot of those—some of those black people down there kept the house just as nice, the yard cut, no garbage, no trash around, and everything. Maybe down the street a block or two it would be a regular dump, just old garbage strewn everywhere, you know. And then they'd complain about the rats and things. Well, you know what caused them rats is nastiness. You go throwing that garbage all over the place and you're going to have some rats.

There was one little old boy, he was black. He lived down there in Pittsburgh, and, boy, he worked them all over. He had a nickname, and I forgot just what it was. But, boy, he left a lot of scars in Pittsburgh when he left. He left here and went to Chicago and he was up there about a year, and he killed a fellow. He killed another fellow up there, and they electrocuted him.

They had another one, a great big black fellow. I forgot his name, but his nickname was "Blue." The fellow was kind of a bully because of his size. He'd see somebody come along that he didn't like, why, he'd holler, "Stop!" and go over there. And he had a little penknife. The whole thing wasn't much over two inches long. He didn't carry no big knife. But that little penknife had a blade about an inch and a half long, and it was sharp as a razor. He'd call them over and say, "What are you doing here?" They'd tell him. He'd say, "I don't like your looks. I don't want you over here."

He got hold of the wrong little fellow one night. There was some nice-looking little boy come from Auburn Avenue. He rode over there to see his aunt, and he rode a McDaniel car down there. Got over and walked up, and this Blue was standing there. He said, "Hey, boy, you live over here?" "No, I don't." He says, "Where do you live?" Says, "Over at Auburn Avenue, Fourth Ward." "Where you going?" "I'm going down here to see my aunt." "When you leave down there, don't you come back this-a-way, because I don't want you back here." He says, "Well, I don't think you've got anything to do with that. It's a free country. I'm going to come back. Got to come back and catch my trolley." "You better walk on down to Pryor Street and catch one. Don't let me catch you back over here."

So the little boy come back. He was ready for Blue. So Blue got up and walked over to him, got him around the neck with his left hand, opened that little pen blade knife. He'd usually hold them that way. So that night, this little boy, he had a switchblade knife up his sleeve, and had it open. He wasn't but seventeen years old, nice dressed little black boy. And he hit [Blue] in the side with that knife and come plumb around with it.

They called us. When we got there, Blue was laying down in the gutter. This is an old cobblestoned pavement, and dust was about an inch thick. His whole entrails, a bushel of them, laying out there in that dust. We called an ambulance and sent him to the hospital, but he died just as he got in the hospital.

We tried to find out who done it. Nobody seen anything. Said, "I don't know nothing." We was about ready to give it up and go to see someone else to find out for us. We had people that we'd go to to find out what happened. So this old boy walked up to me and he said, "Officer, all these people's lying to you, they all know who cut him." I said, "They do?" "Yes." "Who cut him?" He says, "I did." I says, "How come you didn't run?" He says, "Well, I'll get in trouble if I run." I said, "I'm going to have to lock you up." "Yes, I know that."

We put him in the car and took him to Grady Hospital to see how Blue was, so we'd know what to charge him with. We got down there, and Blue was dead. So we explained to him we was going to have to charge him with murder. He said that'd be all right.

So the trial came up, I believe it was the next afternoon, before Judge Calloway. He come up there and told what happened. So the judge dismissed the case against him, turned him loose. But he done a good deed, you know. He saved us a lot of trouble, because old Blue would give us a lot of trouble. When he got killed, why, that saved us all those calls up there, and saved not only that but them other people from getting cut, because he'd cut anybody that come through there. He'd cut you if he didn't like your looks.

The biggest robberies that we had back in those days was these safecrackers, you know, which you hardly ever hear of them now. You hardly ever hear of a safecracker blowing safes in these places of business. But, boy, they used to blow the dickens out of those safes, get into these grocery stores and filling stations and places like Rich's and Davison's and places like that. Back in those days, they didn't have watchmen like they do now. They'd get in there at night, these safecrackers.

They wasn't local people, they traveled. Two or three or four of them, they'd get together and go to Birmingham, work there a few weeks, a month or two, and then they'd leave there and maybe come to Atlanta. They'd get around, blow a few safes here, and then they'd go on to Chattanooga, somewhere like that. They didn't stay in the same place all the time.

One time I was working morning watch, me and Roy Wall. We came out one morning [at] Stewart Avenue and Dill Avenue, and there was a Rogers store. Wall was driving. We drove down in back of this store. They had a basement, a full basement under that store. Well, there was that door open. And Wall says, "Uh-oh," says, "Burglars in this place, partner." So he just cut the car off and out he went to the door there, and I run back up the alley to the front of the store. And just as I come out of the alley, why, boy, there was a big plate-glass window come a-flying out, and a white fellow came out that window and he run. He went up Dill Avenue about two blocks, and I caught him and brought him back.

Roy Wall went on in the basement, and they'd went in this store—it was where they bored the hole through the floor. They had a big auger, and they just kept boring holes, just bored a hole about this big square out of the floor. And the floor was just high enough where the other fellow—he was sort of heavier than the one I caught—he was trying to come up through that hole, and he got his head through and his arms through. Well, he got there and he couldn't get his body through. He was standing there with that floor right under his arms. He couldn't get back out, and he couldn't get in. So we took that one, called the wagon and locked him up, and then we had to take that auger and bore some more of that floor out to get this other guy out of there.

Went down there and they bound them over. Two or three weeks later I got a subpoena to go to state court on them. I went over there and told the judge what happened. So the solicitor come around after they convicted them and found them guilty. The solicitor said, "They got a record?" Said, "Yes, Your Honor, they done been in three times before for burglary." And the judge says, "Well, they look like pretty good boys. I'm going to put them on six months' probation." That's what he give those two burglars, now—caught them in the place—six months' probation. Now, that's a good sentence, isn't it? That's what kind of disgusted the police. You go down there and do all that work and all that, and you might just as well have turned them a-loose.

The police used to put them off the street. You better not touch one of them now, because do and you're in trouble. But back then when it come midnight, they went to bed. You didn't go down to Pittsburgh or Auburn Avenue after twelve o'clock at night and see no blacks. They was gone. You let them walk the street, why, they'd tote them grocery stores and things off. If you let them stay out there, then they'd still burglarize, just like they do now. But you can't do nothing now.

Chapter Seven

Depression and New Deal

W hile the city's economic base expanded during the 1920s, the Great Depression still hit Atlanta hard. "Everything was at its lowest ebb," remembers barber Dan Stephens. "People were walking the streets begging for a nickel to buy a cup of coffee. You could buy a pound of bacon for ten cents, but where were you going to get the ten cents? Now you see just how bad it was."

"Nearly everybody were affected," remembers policeman Sanders Ivey. "I don't suppose there was any rich people, but I mean all the common people were affected. If a person like me had a job, he always had others in his family that he had to take care of, maybe had a son-in-law or son with two or three children, and he didn't have a job."

The Depression in fact touched people from all walks of life. "I know a lot of boys," relates banker Baxter Maddox, "that graduated at Georgia Tech with a degree, couldn't get a job. They'd walk the streets." "I had that little jewelry repair shop and I just had to close it out," adds Irwin Shields, echoing the experience of many small-business people after the Crash. "Just wasn't getting any business and couldn't make a living, and I just had to close it out."

"That is when my daddy stopped working altogether," recalls Ruby Baker, a bricklayer's daughter. "Just all of a sudden there was no work. Building just halted. And he couldn't find anything, he couldn't find anything to do. And that's when he was going around patching up people's steps and roofs and chimneys and things of that sort, and when Mama took that job for five dollars a week out here in an apartment on Ponce de Leon."

"If you didn't have a friend," says police officer Stewart Peeples, "you couldn't get a job for ten dollars a week. That's the only way that you could get a job, if you had a good contact." And Atlantans resorted to all sorts of strategies just to stay afloat. "Men were going and begging for jobs," recounts Irwin Shields, "and on Monday morning they'd go down to the courthouse, begging, 'Do you need an extra juror?' to get a place on the jury."

Street scene, 1928. (Special Collections, Georgia State University)

"I'd go from place to place trying to get a job," remembers Nesbitt Spinks, laid off during a lengthy power linemen's strike in the early thirties, "and once in a while I'd pick up a few days' work. There was an automobile place right close to where I lived and every once in a while one of the truck drivers, he'd give me a few days' work. We hustled and then we got to where we peddled a little, go to the produce row and buy oranges and things like that, you know, and get out and sell them on the street, and make a few dollars that-a-way once in a while. We managed to keep something together, something to eat. We never did go hungry."

There were different ways in which Atlantans managed to keep food in their bellies. "Miss Dolly, she would give me rice and grits for my children," recounts maid Mary Morton. "My daddy could bring so many things out from where he worked, Kelly Brothers Wholesale Grocery, like peas and butter beans and salmon sometimes, things that wouldn't hold up too good, you see. We had a cow, and a lot of people had hogs and chickens. So we got along pretty good, but a lot of people suffered, a lot of them."

"You heard a lot about the stretching of meals in those days," relates teacher Estelle Clemmons. "You used your meat [judiciously] and maybe you put in a lot of potatoes and a lot of onions." Or, as textile worker Calvin Freeman puts it, "People just—I don't know, seems like they knew how to eat soup and beans. Sort of like the old fellow said, one morning he had bread and gravy, and the other morning gravy and bread."

Others were driven to more desperate measures for lack of food and fuel. "I lived next door to some people," relates Cabbagetown resident Ardell Henry, "that ate corn meal for breakfast, just plain corn meal, that's all they had. They didn't get nothing else."

"And it was common," adds Ruby Baker, "to see kids in garbage cans, getting food. I remember when they would tear down a house at night, for firewood, to keep warm. If you didn't have money to buy wood and coal, then you'd tear down the house. There were some cases where, if people moved out of a house on Friday, on Saturday morning that house would be gone. They were shotgun, raggedy houses anyway, so you didn't need nothing but an axe. Two or three men would get together, tear down the house. They didn't sell the wood, they'd use it. And the owners couldn't find out who it was because so many people participated."

Individuals, charitable organizations and government agencies adopted various measures to try and relieve the plight of the city's destitute. "The firemen had a relief store out there at Number 4's [located at 125 Ellis Street]," recalls fire fighter Hugh McDonald. "They chipped in, each man so much, and buy up this stuff—coal and groceries—and give it to these unfortunate people. Did the same thing over at Number 5's at Spring and Trinity.

"This lady came over there with a little girl, and she was talking about her husband being out of work, and they made up money to give her. Next payday, she was back there the same way. I said, 'Uh-oh, that's a racket. She knows when we get paid off.' But they went ahead and made up the money anyhow and ordered groceries. I guess it was two, three years later, she came back. Disappeared and came back. And her husband had struck it lucky. She was dressed in mink. Boy, I'm talking about they had hit it, and she wanted to come back, wanted to pay it all back. We wouldn't take it."

The Salvation Army, the Traveler's Aid Society, local churches and other organizations all attempted to alleviate conditions as the Depression deepened, to little avail. Long lines gathered at the City Relief Center, headquartered at the Municipal Auditorium. "That was a sad time when there was a soup line," recalls Atlanta University School of Social Work graduate Nell Black-shear. "Men, women and children would come and go through the soup line once a day—it was bad. They had a black soup line, of course. There was no such thing as just people hungry. Even on relief you had to remember that you were black and they were white. They would have hot soup and sometimes just coffee, and bread that was donated from some of the bakeries. I remember the Colonial people and the Atlanta Baking Company giving this bread to go with the soup."

"I knew what was in the food because I was interested to know," relates attorney Mildred Kingloff. "Potatoes, large chunks of meat, onions, celery, carrots in a thick, very nourishing soup. And they would give you your dinner in a tin bucket. You'd bring your own tin bucket, maybe seven inches tall and six inches across, and they'd fill that up and give you a half a loaf of what was a nickel loaf of bread. And I have literally seen lawyers in that line, in the soup line. And when I recognized the person, I would—this occurred maybe two or three times—I would deliberately shield my face so that he would not know that I had seen."

Local and state welfare offices were ill-equipped to meet the pressing demand. "The welfare and the Red Cross," remembers Arthur Raper, "they tried to get their agencies geared up to do something about this. They tried. What could they do, except give these folks a little food, if they could?" "I worked for Family Service, which gave financial aid at that time," recounts Agnes Scott graduate Augusta Dunbar. "I volunteered at first and then they paid me. There was one city worker, one woman looking after the poor in the city of Atlanta, giving financial aid out without visits and without investigation. It was a small amount, I am sure."

Under Mayor James L. Key, the city legalized Sunday baseball and theater, with the revenues going to relief efforts. As Atlanta almost went bankrupt, Mayor Key took austerity measures that affected municipal workers. Police officer Herbert Jenkins recalls: "He favored a program that really reduced the number of employees, and reduced the pay. The city was broke and they didn't have the money to meet the payroll, and they had been borrowing it from the banks until the taxes come in in the fall. Well, there was great disagreement between the banks and the mayor, and the banks would not make a loan. So, the mayor just ordered this scrip to be printed, and on the first of the month, instead of getting a paycheck, we received scrip, which looked very much like a bond, about the size of a paper dollar. And supposedly, you used that for money."

Ostensibly, the scrip could be used like cash, and then redeemed when the city became financially solvent again. But many local merchants refused to take scrip. "You couldn't get scrip cashed anywhere," recalls policeman M. Y. Rutherford. "Like, if you wanted to buy a ton of coal or pay your utility bill or anything, they'd say, 'We don't want that scrip.' You'd say, 'Well, that's all I've got.' He'd say, 'Forget it. Wait until you get paid.' Nobody wanted the scrip."

Other merchants demanded a markup for accepting scrip. "They'd charge 10 percent discount just for cashing it," relates Herbert Jenkins, "and sometimes as high as 25 percent. And that created real problems. But again, there was a demonstration of public officials coming to the city's rescue. Rich's department store, Dick Rich, said to the city employees, 'Bring your scrip to us, we'll cash it at face value.' And that relieved the situation greatly."

"You could go to Rich's," states teacher E. T. Lewis, "and just put the scrip up on the counter and say, 'I'd like to get this scrip cashed.' You didn't have to spend anything. Because of that attitude Rich's became the most patronized store in this city, because if you went to Rich's and got your scrip cashed, something in your conscience would tell you to buy something." "And the teachers all through the years haven't forgotten it," adds H. Reid Hunter, former associate school superintendent for the Atlanta Public Schools. "They used to say more teachers had a charge account at Rich's than anywhere else in Atlanta."

Of course, hard times were nothing new to many black Atlantans. "The Negro had always been in a depression," notes Lewis. "For example, when I was a kid, most of the Negro men were not able to get a job, and they worked for a dollar and a half a day. That was the top wages. And most of the time they didn't have very much to eat. So when the Depression came along in the thirties, it didn't affect me. I heard them talking about the banks closing. I didn't have any money in the bank. What difference did it make to me?"

Still, as the Depression deepened, blacks were affected at least as much as whites. "If I remember correctly," states Wilma Van Dusseldorp, a staff member of the Georgia Department of Public Welfare, "in the black districts unemployment was 70 and 75 percent in some areas, across the city perhaps 25 to 30 percent." "And in some instances," adds Estelle Clemmons, "where there was danger of whites and blacks losing jobs in certain companies and businesses, the black person would be bumped by the white person for his job, and if there was no other job for the black person, he was let go."

Even in the best of times, job competition between black and white workers in Atlanta was often fierce—in the building trades, on the railroads, and elsewhere. Depression conditions greatly increased such tensions. Widespread unemployment spawned a new organization in 1930, the American Order of Fascisti, known as the "Black Shirts," one of a number of white-supremacist organizations that surfaced in Atlanta throughout the period. "Well, the Black Shirts—and I saw them pretty close up," relates Arthur Raper, "they simply took a campaign to get the whites into the Negroes' jobs in the hotels and the barbershops and all around there. They just went out to do it. And they put real pressure on a fellow if he was employing blacks. 'The white man's hungry. You have an obligation to him over and beyond what you have to the black man.' "

"They would intimidate workers," echoes Ruby Baker. "You see, there was a time where in construction practically all bricklayers were black. And they would come around on jobs where blacks were working, at times when they were being hired, and intimidate especially the person doing the hiring."

"And in some places," adds Raper, "they simply shifted from blacks to whites right now. It simply was a shift from black low wages to white low wages. They did it right now in the hotels in Atlanta—the bellboys." "I came back here," remembers Dan Stephens, "and I couldn't get a job around the hotels. The whites were bellhopping and whatnot. They'd taken over the jobs and blacks had to do otherwise. So I decided I would go into barbering."

However, there were some white employers who, for whatever reasons, held their ground against the Black Shirts. "The Biltmore Hotel, Miss Hanson," recalls Ruby Baker. "She was Miss Candler at that time. She refused to be intimidated. She said she was going to keep her black bellmen. As long as the Biltmore stood, she would have black bellmen, porters and doormen. The

A white bellhop at the Henry Grady Hotel, 1939. (Photograph by Marion Post Wolcott. Courtesy Library of Congress)

Henry Grady, the Ansley, the Piedmont, all of those hotels got rid of all their black bellmen. But the Biltmore stood fast."

"You see," explains Arthur Raper, "a man's pretty stubborn when he's hired somebody and he likes the job they're doing, and he isn't going to fire him. 'No, I'm not going to fire him.' But he gives them [the Black Shirts] an out, and the out is that, 'You know, people are always retiring, people are always dying. I just won't hire any more blacks. So, what you are asking me to do today we will have done, in time. I see what you're talking about, but you see what my position is. You be reasonable with me, this will work out all right.' Now, that happened over and over and over."

Fanned by the winds of frustration, membership in the Black Shirts spread like wildfire during 1930. "I went to one of their first meetings down at the City Auditorium," relates Georgia Tech professor Glenn Rainey, who monitored the group for the Interracial Commission. "There were about five or six hundred there. And it was one of the most explosive and intense experiences I've ever had. These utterly inflammatory speeches went on and on and on and on. And then they started a kind of cheerleading business or something. Said, 'Everybody who believes so-and-so, stand up.'

"So I sat there. And pretty soon this guy said, 'What's the matter with you? Can't you stand up?' And I said, 'I don't want to stand up.' It wasn't too long after that the meeting came to a close, and I started out. And this crowd, a small group of toughs, came up to me and said, 'What was the matter with you in there? Why didn't you stand up?' And I said, 'I didn't want to stand up.' Then they started, 'Why, you believe so-and-so?' Then of course I began talking while they began talking, and once they let me get started talking, why they sort of lost their impulse to beat the hell out of me. And so I went out.

"Then later they arose to have scores of thousands of people involved, one way or another, whether they were dues-paying members or not. I went down one time and counted about four or five thousand of these people in black shirts marching four abreast right through Five Points, with the streets just packed and jammed with their supporters. They carried signs like this: 'Why Are So Many White Men Unemployed? Ask the Chamber of Commerce!'; 'Back to the Farm, Nigger!' The thing continued to grow. They had meetings in the parks in Atlanta which had 20,000 or so people, you see. This was simply a Southern phenomenon, that the unrest, the unemployment, the bitterness and so on could so easily be exploited by racial demagogues."

Despite the meteoric rise of the Black Shirts, the organization had major internal weaknesses which contributed to its downfall. There was no developed organizational structure, no newspaper, no program beyond the single demand of white employment. "It was a ragtag type of organization," states Ruby Baker, "and not too well organized." "I don't think the Black Shirts were anywhere as sophisticated as the Ku Klux Klan," adds Arthur Raper, "and the Black Shirts came up more very much like a flash in the pan."

External factors also contributed to the decline of the Black Shirts. The organization drew opposition from Atlanta's white housewives and other employers afraid of losing cheap black labor, as well as from the city's newspapers, who criticized the group's tactics and program, though not its white supremacism. And, as Arthur Raper notes, when the economy began to improve later on in the thirties, many employers went back to business as usual: "Georgia Tech had boys that wanted jobs. They would provide short-delivery boys, you know, at these pickup lunch stands. But presently the economic system changed and the Georgia Tech boys went to other work, and the fellows had to come back again to their black boys. With a smaller economic base choice, they had more dependable workers with the blacks than with the whites. So, although they made the shift one time in response to this pressure, the economics of their business forced them back to the other again."

Depression conditions also helped foster the presence of a small group of Communists in the city. In Atlanta and elsewhere, the Communists organized Unemployed Councils, drew attention to the problems of hunger and relief, and made a point of organizing both black and white workers. One of those who joined the Communist Party was textile worker Nanny Washburn, who became interested after a famous Communist-led textile strike in 1929. She explains: "Ella Mae Wiggins, she was shot down going to a union meeting up in Gastonia, North Carolina. That was really an eye-opener for me, because I was the mother of five children and Ella Mae Wiggins, I think she had had about nine. I had two cousins that was in the Communist Party up in North Carolina, and they come in and brought the literature and all that kind of stuff to tell us about it. And it put my studying cap on.

"Somebody sold my brother the *Daily Worker,* the Communist Party paper, and so that commenced different Communists coming to our home. And so we learned a lot. I'll give them credit for teaching me how to read, and understand this society, how it works and who's the head of it. We joined the Communist Party, some of my family. We would meet, and the most of the places we had to meet would be at the black people's house, in the slummy section. We had to sit by lamplight, people poor and all."

"We went to Communist meetings," recalls Clarence Bacote, who attended with an Atlanta University colleague. "This was in 1932. We weren't thinking about being Communists, we just wanted to learn. We were the only blacks there, the rest were whites. And they were showing a movie—it was a very poor production—of Russia's Five Year Plan. We went again, and I told Bill, 'I saw a warning or something where they had been hearing of Communist activities here, and I think we'd better stay away from there.' Sure enough, they raided that place about a week or two later."

The Communists' program and interracial orientation—all set within the overall ferment of the Depression—aroused the concern of local officials. Between 1930 and 1936, police raided numerous gatherings of Communists, pacifists and others meeting on an interracial basis, leading the American Civil Liberties Union in 1937 to label Atlanta one of the nation's ten worst centers of repression.[1]

Most of the people arrested were charged under Georgia's anti-insurrection statute, a law that had its roots in the aftermath of the Nat Turner rebellion of the 1830s. Among those apprehended was Angelo Herndon, a nineteen-year-old black Communist who had come to Atlanta from Birmingham to organize the unemployed. Herndon's case reached the United States Supreme Court, and became an international *cause célèbre* and a symbol of Southern injustice.

In June of 1932, the Fulton County commissioners slashed relief appropriations by one-third to offset a projected deficit, and Atlanta's emergency relief center teetered on the brink of closing down for lack of funds. In the ensuing debate about what to do, Fulton County Commissioner Walter C. Hendrix alleged that community leaders had "been misled about the huge army of gaunt, suffering people in our city," and suggested that anyone with evidence of widespread hunger bring it forward.[2]

Hendrix's words provided a challenge to local Communists. "That was the big cry," recalls Nanny Washburn. "'Come to the commissioners' office.' Angelo immediately put out leaflets and they was distributed in College Park, East Point, Hapeville and all around, everywhere in Atlanta. And we all went."

On the morning of June 30, close to a thousand people gathered outside the courthouse in what was purportedly the largest biracial demonstration in the South in decades.[3] "It was a great day for me," relates Washburn. "Thousands of people come up there to show them they was hungry and had nothing. There was little children there without any shoes. There was many black people. They finally let some of them go in to see the commissioners, they let some of the whites. They wouldn't let no black people go in. They didn't want to give anything to nobody, but they did gain that day, won a victory of receiving relief."

The following day the county commissioners awarded an additional $6,000 in emergency relief. The size and integrated nature of the demonstration alarmed militantly anti-Communist local authorities, who stepped up their persecution of suspected Reds, staking out the post office box listed on the leaflets. "When he [Herndon] got in there to the mailbox," remembers Nanny Washburn, "well, they grabbed him and arrested him. They got him for insurrection, trying to overthrow the government, when the case was tried."

Herndon went on trial before a packed courthouse. "I went to the trial," recalls Clarence Bacote. "The situation was very tense. Herndon's lawyer was Benjamin Davis, Jr. Benjamin Davis, Sr., was the most prominent black Republican in the state. His son, on the other hand, finished Morehouse and Harvard Law School, had come back here to practice. Well, of course, the case was stacked against Herndon from the beginning, but I'll always admire the way that Ben Davis, Jr., handled the case.

"The assistant prosecutor was named [John] Hudson. Sometimes he was a preacher. And in the course of his remarks he referred to Ben as 'Young Ben.' All right, when Ben got up, he referred to the assistant prosecutor as 'Preacher Hudson.' Well, you know, that didn't exactly lighten the tension." "That blowed up almost the courthouse," echoes Nanny Washburn.

The jury found Herndon guilty and recommended a sentence of eighteen to twenty years. The Communist Party, the International Labor Defense, and the Provisional Committee for the Defense of Angelo Herndon, a fragile alliance of Communists, white civil libertarians and black community leaders, drew attention to the case. In April 1937, the United States Supreme Court finally declared the Georgia anti-insurrection law unconstitutional on the grounds that it was overly vague, and Herndon and the others arrested were eventually freed.[4] Yet Atlanta's Red Scare had its intended effect. By the end of the thirties, Communist and radical activities in Atlanta were essentially nonexistent.

Most significant in blunting the impact of groups on both the left and the right during the Depression was the New Deal of President Franklin D. Roosevelt. "I think Roosevelt prevented a revolution," states social worker Augusta Dunbar. "I'm not sure it would have been a Communist revolution, but there would have been some sort of revolution because you cannot let that many people go hungry very long without a good deal of violence. He came in just in time to stop that."

One day after his inauguration in March 1933, Roosevelt took the first of many steps to combat Depression conditions, closing down the nation's banks. Shortly afterwards, Congress passed the Emergency Banking Bill, established the Federal Deposit Insurance Corporation (FDIC), and approved other banking reforms. By mid-May, most of the nation's banks had reopened, including all those in Atlanta.[5]

The Roosevelt administration went on to establish the Federal Emergency Relief Administration (FERA) in May. Providing both direct aid and work relief, the FERA brought enormous changes in both the nature and extent of local relief efforts. Under the leadership of Gay B. Shepperson, director of the Georgia Relief Commission, which administered federal funds, and one of the very few women state administrators in the country, the FERA in Georgia quickly set up a county structure of relief.

"In September 1933, I became relief administrator of the Fulton County Relief Administration," recounts Wilma Van Dusseldorp. "It was the last county in our state to be reorganized under the Roosevelt administration because it was going to be the hardest; we had the fewest resources. I learned about it the last week in August. While I was cleaning my desk getting ready to go to the University of Chicago, I got a message from the administrator to please come to her office promptly. When I got there, I found the whole state commission was in session there. As I entered the room and looked around, there were somber faces, and they were talking about the terrible conditions that existed in the Fulton County relief. Lines down the alley for our black people were two and three blocks long, waiting to place their application for relief. At the front door, they were equally long for the whites. Miss Shepperson said she was really disturbed about conditions in Fulton County. She had asked Louisa —Louisa Fitzsimmons, her first assistant—to go for a two-week period with me to Fulton County. I should carry the Fulton County reorganization until we could make a better disposition of it. I think that was Friday afternoon, and on Monday morning Louisa and I went over.

"We quickly moved as fast as we could. In early September we took a rough case count. There were only eight or nine thousand families on relief at that time, only 1,800 of which were black. Within three and a half months we had 29,000 families on relief, over half of them black, which showed the difference in the standards of eligibility the New Deal introduced."

Augusta Dunbar describes the hectic scene at the Fulton County relief office, located at 23 Pryor Street: "When they opened it up—and I was there when they opened it up—we had a line around the block waiting to get in. There were just ten of us. The case load, the number of families you have, was in the thousands. Then they brought in people from other states to help supervise the Georgia program, and people from private agencies who had had a lot of experience in social work were brought in to help with the public. We had our case load come down to about two hundred—happily.

"They first visited the office and applied. They had to give the name of their last employer and give evidence that they had no other resources. Then they had to have a home visit. Most of them qualified. They did not usually apply unless they were in need. Another thing, there simply were no jobs open, so there was no trouble proving that you tried to get a job.

"Some of the people who came in had had very good jobs, very substantial jobs, but had neither savings nor relatives who could help them. I remember one man who was middle-aged came into the office. The workers were all right out of college. I don't know why they hired so many young people but they did. And, after he talked with me, he said, 'This office seems to be run by children. Here I am a middle-aged man, I've worked hard all my life, I've saved my money, and I got fired. And I'd like to talk to someone who is at least old enough to know what I'm talking about.' So I did the only thing I could do, I referred him to my immediate supervisor, who was exactly the same age. He said, 'Nothing but children,' and went storming out. He did finally get some relief in spite of that.

"In our country, if you're not working you are almost nobody. So people felt diminished, less valuable, less a whole person. They showed it in their attitude. Some of them were angry, some were humiliated, and some just unhappy. Others showed their resentment that we got a salary. They never walked out without their relief money, but they often walked out angry.

"There's always a little humor in every job. I had a funny incident happen. They used to bring our case records in to us. The waiting room was jammed like the New York subway. People would come up to the desk and get a number, and then a clerk would pull a file and pile it on the caseworker's desk. A lot of these files had a note: 'This man is deaf and dumb. When he comes in, please see me'—his former caseworker—'and I will point him out to you.' So, I called her and she walked out to the waiting room with me and walked up to him, and gestured that I was the person to see, and I gestured for him to follow. I got out a long yellow tablet and asked him questions, and passed it over to him and he answered. And that went on for some time until we had finished the investigation. Then I got up and walked out to the waiting room to call the next person, and as I did I noticed he walked over to a friend who said,

'Jim, what goes on here?' He replied, 'I don't know, but every time I come I draw a deaf-mute for a caseworker!'"

"The staff," recalls Wilma Van Dusseldorp, "was very much at the mercy of the politicians as long as we were under local auspices." And, while Atlanta officials embraced the New Deal, Georgia Governor Eugene Talmadge was a highly vocal critic of Roosevelt and his programs, claiming that most of those on relief were welfare chiselers, and resenting the amount of federal aid that went to urban areas and to black Georgians.[6] Faced with an extensive patronage system, inexperienced personnel, an attitude suspicious of relief efforts and a woman administrator, the personal interference of the governor, and other political problems associated with the Talmadge administration, by January 1934 the federal government removed any significant state involvement with FERA and ran the program directly from Washington.

As a result, Atlanta became one of the first American cities to have a fully federalized relief effort. "When we became a federal program," recalls Van Dusseldorp, "our policies changed. We had to adopt the federal standards for family budgets. Grace Hartley with the Atlanta *Journal* became our consultant for setting up food budgets. We took the standards of food needs for health and found that the minimum food needed for a family of two, three, or four—and we went up to eight or ten children—sometimes was a great deal more than what the people were able to earn, when they were earning.

"One of the things that happened was that a lot of people who had jobs gave them up because the relief standard for just minimum food budget allowance was greater than what they had been earning up and down Peachtree Road— maids and yard helpers. A prominent judge called one morning and said he had heard we were going to adopt a federal standard of relief, and he had heard that an enormous amount of money was going to be given in cash, more than they could earn up and down Peachtree. He wanted to verify that we were going to pay them in cash. He said, 'Well, you know what you are going to do. They're all going to go out and buy booze and the courts are going to be crowded with them next Monday morning.' I said, 'Well, that would be a very interesting thing to find out, Judge. Let's give it a chance.' So, I called a news reporter with whom we had very cooperative relations, and he agreed to be in court Monday morning. I found out later that week that there were fewer in court that morning charged with drunkenness than there had been for several weeks previous. So, that satisfied us. I didn't talk to the judge after that; I thought he probably made his own determination."

"We would only be able to give them a percentage of the family budget," acknowledges Augusta Dunbar. "One of the clients came to me one day and said, 'I know where the rest of that money goes—you all gets it. You've got it there in the back stacked up and I want to go back there and get some of mine. If I don't get but two-thirds, I want to know who gets the other third.' And I tried to explain it and said, 'Well, it's like this. If the doctor said your child needed a quart of milk a day but you could only afford a pint, nobody got the other pint.' He said, 'Yeah, I understand that. I just want to know who gets the other third of my budget.'

"I remember they had a direct aid program called 'surplus commodities,' produce that the government thought was surplus, or left over. And some of them called it 'circus commodities' because they were not used to the word 'surplus.' Some of the food they gave them they were not used to. I remember one of the things was grapefruit, and they told me they found it awfully tough when they'd bite into it. They also gave out flour and anything in surplus."

"I had to buy milk for the families," relates Nell Blackshear. "Even had to buy clothes. We would take the mothers to the stores on Edgewood Avenue. That's where we really worked out a deal with those Jewish merchants on Edgewood. There were all kinds of benefits if we would buy from them for the families. We would buy the clothing, then order and pay for the coal, twenty-five-cent bags of coal.

"I remember the rear of 210 Butler Street. This was a long tenement house. I would have to go get some groceries in the house, or take coal to give to them to make a fire in those little rooms. Sometimes seven or eight people would live in one room. They had a communal toilet outside. It was a deplorable sort of thing. And that's where our clients lived, this is the kind of relief and work with families that I started off doing."

In addition to offering direct aid, the FERA oversaw the Atlanta Transient Bureau, sponsored worker education classes at Atlanta University and elsewhere, supplied medical aid and public health services, and initiated numerous work-relief projects. Other jobs were provided by the Civil Works Administration (CWA), the Civilian Conservation Corps (CCC), the National Youth Administration (NYA), and the Public Works Administration (PWA), which constructed the nation's first housing projects, Techwood and University Homes, as well as school facilities, a new city jail, and part of Atlanta's new sewer system.[7]

The PWA was created in June 1933 by the National Industrial Recovery Act (NIRA), a sweeping piece of legislation which also established the National Recovery Administration, or the NRA. The law provided for the creation of industry-wide codes whereby businesses could control competition and the terms of production. The NRA attempted to stimulate the economy by limiting hours and spreading around employment while maintaining production and boosting wages and prices. The act also gave workers the right to organize and bargain collectively.

Until the industry codes were worked out, compliance with the NRA standards was on a voluntary basis. Those businesses that signed the President's Reemployment Agreement were entitled to display a Blue Eagle emblem in their windows and on their products. The federal government launched a major sign-up campaign to get firms to display the Blue Eagle. In Atlanta, the drive was spearheaded by the Junior Chamber of Commerce, under the leadership of businessman Duncan Peek.

He recalls: "We began our campaign by going to all the businesses in Atlanta and asking them to give us workers to work on the campaign. And we organized I think it was something like 2,000 workers, and these 2,000 workers were to go out and call on every industry, business in the city, and ask them to do one of several things in order help bring about recovery. We were asking everyone to share the work—in other words, have people working every other day or working half a day and so forth, asking everyone that possibly could to create new jobs, to expand the plant, create new jobs and so forth. And it was a vast thing. We called on every firm, even the little grocery store on the corner. It was over a period of possibly maybe ten days, two weeks, something like that. It was really concentrated."

The Jaycees' canvass [actually lasting only five days] resulted in some 500 new companies signing up with the NRA. Other local measures were taken to encourage business participation and compliance. An estimated 50,000 people participated in an Atlanta NRA march on October 4, sponsored by the Atlanta *Georgian,* the *Constitution* and the *Journal.* The city proclaimed October 17 Blue Eagle Day as downtown stores displayed Blue Eagle banners and sponsored sales.[8]

Despite such enthusiasm, opposition to the NRA came from a number of quarters. Organized labor maintained that the codes tended to favor unskilled workers over skilled employees. Some firms, especially smaller ones, found it difficult to comply with the NRA's higher wage standards, and sought ways to get around the codes. In Atlanta, the construction industry and the retail food and grocery trade received the most complaints about alleged code violations.[9]

Many employers resented the NRA's stipulation that black and white workers receive the same wages for the same work. "Whites had been heard to call

The Blue Eagle outside a Marietta Street restaurant. (Atlanta
Journal-Constitution)

the NRA the Negro Relief Act and even No Roosevelt Again," relates Arthur Raper, who in 1934 compiled studies on the NRA in Atlanta and elsewhere. "There were not differentials by race per se, and this was a tremendous strain on the Southern white man, because he was not accustomed to that.

"They tended, a lot of them, to just not hire any more Negroes and hire a white man when the time came, under the Southern ethic that if you're going to pay a white man's wage you'd just as well have a white man. The upshot in Atlanta was that the bigger the outfit was, broadly speaking, the more likely they were to retain their Negro laborers, and the smaller the outfit was, the more likely they were *not* to retain them. If they did retain them, they wouldn't retain them at the expected salary.

"They would have all sorts of ways of getting around it. They'd put them [the black workers] in business for themselves. In other words, they'd let them take tips. Or they would fix it so that, whereas before they weren't paying anything for their uniforms or their food or something else that had just been a part of the job before, why, now they just put a price on that.

"And then, some of the Negroes in these small establishments collaborated in this deception, because they knew enough about the business to know that the man wasn't making but a little bit of money anyhow. And in some instances they cut them down from three workers to one and made the one do the work of three. And he did it all right and got the regular pay the white man had got, and he liked it all right. But the difference was there was two fellows didn't have any work at all.

"The NRA was very much restricted in the areas that it covered. It didn't deal with the largest occupational groups among the Southern Negroes. Agriculture and domestic service didn't even come under the NRA code. There were other types of work not under the codes which involved a considerable number of Negroes: curb service and delivery boys at drugstores and retail establishments working on commissions or solely for tips, yard tenders and family laundresses, outside workers and janitors at cotton textile factories, restaurant curb waiters remunerated solely through tips from patrons, and the like. So it was less than 10 percent of the Negroes in the South came under the NRA codes.

"And then there was a maze of differentials, and some Negroes thought that was primarily to get them. There were differentials, for example, for different occupations. Laundry people got the least, and the Negroes made up the highest proportion of the laundry workers. NRA, some of the Negroes said, meant Negro Removal Act or Negro Rarely Allowed."

Numerous complaints that employers were violating the NRA industry code with regularity and impunity, along with the impetus provided by Section 7(A) of the NIRA, enabling workers to organize collectively, helped bring on a national textile strike in September 1934. Hundreds of thousands of workers, most of them Southern, took part in one of the largest strikes in American history. The strikers included workers at the two cotton mills within the Atlanta city limits: Fulton Bag and Cotton Mill, on Boulevard across from Oakland Cemetery, and the Exposition Cotton Mill, located northwest of downtown between Marietta and Ashby streets.

Textiles were the South's dominant industry.[10] While boosters pointed to the mills as a symbol of an industrial New South, critics pointed to their fierce anti-unionism, low wages and harsh working conditions. Through the first third of the twentieth century, many entered the mills at an early age, and worked for long hours. "I was born in 1903 and I went to work in the last of 1913," relates Clifford Lovins, who first entered a mill in Douglasville, Georgia. "And I saw some in there younger than me. They wasn't doing no hard work, but they was pushing two brooms down the walks, thirty-five cents a day. Well, that was big money then. I come up over here at the Exposition here in Atlanta in 1920, and got a job the twenty-eighth of March. And I went to work for twelve hours and fifteen minutes a night for ten long years. I worked twenty-four years up there and didn't even know what a vacation was, not a day."

"It's really something for someone who's never been in a cotton mill to see it, and to know what they were all about," exclaims Exposition Mill worker Katie Lovins. There were dozens of different jobs within the mills, all performed by whites except for a few menial and especially hot and dirty jobs. Textile workers first cleaned the raw cotton, using carding machines that tore apart the cotton and removed twigs and dirt. "I worked up there in the card room," relates Clifford Lovins, "where they're carding that cotton, all that dust and lint. And, mister, you walked out of there and hit the fresh air and took a puff off of a cigarette, just like a dog a-running a rabbit. Why, you couldn't hardly tell who a fellow was, I'd say from here to the street."

After cleaning, the cotton fibers were combined into a single strand through drawing frames. "It was so funny with my children," recalls Katie Lovins. "They called the frames I worked drawing frames. Well, the children couldn't understand that. 'Well, Mother, what do you do? Do you just go in there and draw?'" The yarn was then twisted and spun further before finally being woven into cloth.

Despite the long hours and cotton dust, work in the early twentieth-century mills was often marked by a relaxed pace and comparatively informal labor-management relations, as Fulton Bag worker Effie Gray relates: "It was an easy time. You'd go in there and work all day long, because you didn't have more than you had to do. It was old frames and sides and you knew how to do it and all, and you could sit down, well, I'd say twenty minutes out of an hour. I used to crochet a lot and I'd take my crocheting up there, and I'd sit down and crochet and then get up and go around to my sides."

"When I started work," states weaver Frank Hicks, who worked at both Atlanta mills, "they didn't have no rules. Any way you could get it done, you'd do it, as long as you didn't get hurt. The fact of the business was, all they wanted you to do is work." "And, brother, if you didn't run your job," adds Clifford Lovins, "they'd tell you there was a peg-legged man out there waiting for your job."

The twenties and early thirties brought a more impersonal style of textile supervision. "They got to where they'd have a few rules," recalls Frank Hicks. "You had to do this and you had to do that. They was wanting to tell you you couldn't go to the rest room but at a certain time. And if you was off a day, you'd have to stay out two days if you didn't have a doctor's certificate showing you was sick."

Textile firms also began to employ new scientific management methods to increase production. "They came in there and wanted people to do more work," states Katie Lovins. "I didn't know what it was all about, but I knew that if you run your machines and kept them going, then they'd give you some more, see. And so, if you worked hard and kept that work going, then you got a little more added on to you till you almost got to the place where you had more than you could do."

Along with the speedups and stretchouts, the introduction of the eight-hour day under the NRA actually put further pressure on textile workers. "After they went on eight hours," relates Effie Gray, "see, we didn't have no lunch time. And I worked many, many, many a day and didn't even have time to eat my lunch, or even time to go to the bathroom." Adds Calvin Freeman, "You just had to eat on the fly."

The companies' influence extended beyond the workplace to the surrounding mill village. The mills supplied housing, sponsored ball teams and other activities, and provided additional services for workers. "They had a nursery down there," recalls Katie Lovins of the Exposition mill. "For years there they kept children for the mothers to work in the mill. And the clinic was there. The mill had doctors [for workers]. And they had a company store. They had just about everything, clothes and groceries."

"The mill would give you a little book of these coupons," remembers Calvin Freeman, describing the system at Fulton Bag, "which people called it 'doo-lolly.' You ordered your doo-lolly from the mill, and they taken it out of your paycheck. You'd get five dollars worth of doo-lolly, buy five dollars worth of groceries, last you a week. And they sold you the coal that went in your fireplace. So actually, you owed the company your whole life, that's what I'll say."

"Well, there was a lot of people that worked there I know," echoes Clifford Lovins, "that never drawed a dime in money for ten years. The store got it all."

Given the paternalistic and low wage structure of the industry, not surprisingly the textile firms were staunchly anti-union. "They would not recognize a union," declares Frank Hicks. "You take Fulton Bag, I heard Norman Elsas, he was the head man, say, 'I'll tear it down a brick at a time before I'll ever recognize a union.'" "The boss come up to me one morning," recounts Clifford Lovins, "like an old setting hen come off the nest. He hit me on the back, he says, 'Cliff, I want you to tell me which one has got the most power, the union or the Congress of the United States.' I says, 'Any dumbskulled fellow'd know that the Congress of the United States got more power than the union.' He says, 'You're fired.' 'Fired?' 'Yeah, because you belong to the union.' I says, 'Ever who says I belong to the union lies by the city clock, 'cause I don't belong to it. And that ain't all, I'm not going to join it.'

"They laid me off, I was off six weeks. But I got laid off for somebody's lie, see. The trouble in them textile plants, the reason why nary one of them never was organized, the people wouldn't stick together. They'd tell you they would, but when it come to a showdown, they wouldn't do it—'Afraid I'll lose my job, and then I can't get one.'"

Despite such resistance by mill management, there had been sporadic strikes and unionizing attempts in Atlanta's cotton mills. In the 1880s, Fulton Bag operatives formed a chapter of the Knights of Labor. In 1897, white workers at Fulton Bag walked off their jobs when the company brought in twenty black spinners. During the World War I era, highly publicized organizing drives at both mills were met with employer intransigence and resourcefulness.

While Southern textile organizing efforts had almost always ended in failure, the changes in the industry along with the overall foment of the thirties prompted the 1934 general strike. In Atlanta and elsewhere the strike was hastily organized and beset by violence. Workers at the Exposition mill were the first in the city to walk off their jobs. Nesbitt Spinks, who had just caught on at the mill shortly before the strike, recalls: "The Exposition Cotton Mill, a union hadn't been messing with them very much up until then. But they got them in there and they got them on strike. Of course, they were striking all over the country.

"The majority of them was out. I don't think they had a lot of people still in there, but they had enough, I guess, to carry on some of the work. They told us all we had to stay out there on the picket line. We'd stay and talk to people as they come and went, and try to turn people back. You know, a lot of people would go in there and go to work, looking for a job. We'd do most of our picketing in the afternoon, when they was changing shifts. Then at certain times there would be big crowds gathered there. So, there was quite a big stir there.

"I guess this freight train coming in there was the biggest stir that I remember. The railroad was trying to get in there to pull some stuff out, and leave some stuff. And they said the railroad was scabbing agin them, you know. We all got up on the track there. There was a crowd of people out there, men and women and, the best I remember, there might have been a lot of children out there. And the train pulled right up there pretty close, and stopped. But of course they wouldn't run over us. The polices come out and ordered us off, and we still didn't go. And they brought tear gas out there and shot tear gas into us. And seemed like the train did go in after that. Of course, they made it rough on the people at the cotton mill, any way they could, that come out on strike."

"I worked at the Exposition Cotton Mill," relates radical Nanny Washburn, who first entered the mills when she was eight years old. "And my sister, she worked there, and she belonged to the union [United Textile Workers of America]. I wasn't on the picket line but just a short time. The day I went is the night I got arrested. We was grabbed by the law, carried to the police station, as two Red agents. And they got us for insurrection, trying to overthrow the government. We didn't even have a gun, just had a *Daily Worker*."

Nesbitt Spinks also was arrested on the Exposition picket line: "There was a squabble at the gate. There was somebody who was trying to push their way in, and they was forcing their way in. Of course, they got a squabble started, and two or three got cut in the time of it. I got this scar and twenty-seven stitches across the back of my neck back there. The company fired me during that time, see."

Fulton Bag was the last mill in the Atlanta area to close down during the strike. Frank Hicks relates: "I was working at Fulton Bag. Fulton Bag hadn't shut down, Exposition had done shut down. And there was a bunch, oh I guess twenty-five or thirty, from the Exposition come over to my house. Some of them come and said, 'What are you going to do?' I said, 'I'm going to work, I've got to get my money.' It was payday that day. 'Well, what's the mill going to do?' I said, 'Well, I'll tell you, I believe they're going to shut down.'

"They come around and told us, 'Now, if the lights flash twice, just top everything off, we'll go out and no trouble.' Well, they flashed once. In a few minutes they flashed again. They all went out at that time."

Then a teenager, Calvin Freeman describes the scene outside the mill, with both strikers and nonstrikers intermingling: "It was pretty rough. People going in, some of them just went on in. They wanted to work, which you couldn't blame them. Actually, I wouldn't have blamed my father if he'd have went back to work, because actually we didn't know what we were striking for. Didn't nobody know halfway what they were doing.

"We all stood outside the gates and picketed. We had about three or four gates, and they were just filled with people. They'd just be milling around. Some guy had a guitar, and he'd play and sing songs. That's what happened when my father got killed. Guy had a harmonica and was up there playing music, and we was all sitting on a curb. And the street dead-ended right where this gate was. And this woman, she comes down the street, rolling down the street. She was supposed to make a right-hand turn there. Instead of turning, she went slam into the curb."

The car killed Calvin Freeman's father. There were many other casualties of the strike, too. "The management was very much opposed to unionizing the mill," recalls social worker Augusta Dunbar, whose district included the Fulton Bag community, "so everybody who joined the union was fired. Not only were they fired, but they were evicted, given notice of eviction from the mill houses." Although Georgia Governor Talmadge went back on his campaign promise and declared martial law during the strike, the New Deal social workers did provide relief to strikers, as Augusta Dunbar relates: "At that time the FERA wanted to feed people who were striking. The businessmen said they should not be fed for they were not unemployed, they were voluntarily unemployed. Well, word finally came down to us that we could feed the strikers and help them, but should not get mixed up in any way with the union. We did give them grocery orders during that time, little slips of paper which they could take to the store and get groceries."

At least one local grocer suffered reprisals for his position during the short-lived strike, as Effie Gray recalls: "They didn't know when the mill would start back up. And a lot of people with big families was short. And Mr. Bradford that run the store up there, he just taken care of a whole lot of them. He had to close his doors when the mill started up, because they said that anybody that traded with him, they'd fire."

"A lot of them were fired," states country musician and Fulton Bag worker Marion Brown. "They culled them out of there, one by one," says Clifford Lovins, "because it wouldn't do for them to fire them on account of the union. The company could be handled for that. But they'd find something wrong with your work. Didn't have a chance. Then, when you went to another mill, 'Well, how come you had to leave the Exposition?' 'Oh no, I just got laid off.' Well, they'd notify them. And there was a lot of them fellers worked in cotton mills for years that couldn't get another job."

Even some workers, like Frank Hicks, who were only *suspected* of union activity were discharged once the unsuccessful strike ended in late September: "I went to go back to work, but my boss man told me I was helping organize because all them people was at my house. Well, I couldn't tell them peoples to go out. Some of them was my kinfolks and some wasn't, but they come over there to see what was going to take place, to see if they shut down. So, they didn't let me go back to work."

The labor shortage that followed the strike further sped up production, as Clifford Lovins relates: "We got an extra machine to run, and only got pay for running the two. They cut out every third hand in that mill. And all over it, brother, not just in one department." And poor working conditions, low wages and a hostile anti-union climate persisted in the Southern mills.

Clifford Lovins

Born in 1903, Clifford Lovins first entered a textile mill at the age of ten. He later worked at the Exposition Cotton Mill in Atlanta, and retired from the City of Atlanta Parks Department.

I went to work in a textile plant in 1913, in Douglasville, Georgia. When I went in this mill up there, my old man was a finishing carpenter, him and his brothers and his dad. I didn't have to work in that thing. I didn't go to school enough to learn my ABC's, going in that place. They told me this, "Well, wasn't no law to make you go to school. Now, if that's what you want, go ahead."

A kid like I was, couldn't even read, couldn't write, anything like that, but I was very easy to learn, you see. Had a little old job pushing two brooms to start off with, what they called sweeper then, thirty-five cents a day. Went on and on and on and I learned how to spin. Then went from that, I learned how to doff. I got all of that I wanted in the spinning room, then my dad got me to come down where my mother's brother was a loom fixer. He learned me to weave, you know.

It was too hot down there for me, and I never could get on the outside like I did in the spinning room—us doffers would generally have an hour's rest. We'd go on outside, fight and wrestle, and then go back in there and work just like nothing ever happened. So I went to the superintendent one morning. I told him, "I sure would like to get a transfer down to the card room." "I'll see if I can't arrange it Monday morning." Put me down there in the card room and I was working there, and that's where I got hurt, got crippled.

I got tangled up in some gear laying out in the walkway. Somebody cut the lights out one Friday night, and I got tangled up in them gears, and this foot went on a rod about, oh, I guess about four or five inches high, and I just twisted it. And I laid there I don't know how long. They carried me out to the stairway and laid me down in the stairway, and I crawled over there and got me a broom and cut the handle off. It took me two hours to get home. And when I got to the house, I couldn't get in the house and I had to call my dad and he come out there. He got his brother, carried me in the house, and I just laid there. It was Monday before this little old doctor come out there. He didn't know nothing about bone break, you know, and I laid there and suffered it out. Laid for nine weeks flat on my back, my bone's busted six inches and my hip wrung out of joint, bone broke there in that collar, shoulder out of joint. And them doctors said I would not be able to work.

I didn't like nobody to tell me nothing. I left home when I was seventeen years old and went on my own. I went to Exposition and got a job, looked like an old country boy right out between the plow-hands. The man looked me up and down and he walked around. He said, "What can you do in the mill?" I told him what I could do. He smoked his cigarette, scratched his head. "I'll tell you what I'll do." He said, "What's that?" I said, "If you'll give me a job, the opportunity to run all three jobs that I tell you I can run, four jobs, if you're not satisfied with my work, all you've got to do is pay me and I'll try to get a job somewheres else."

Well, I went on and I run them jobs. Mister, I was glad the next morning when quitting time come, because it just about separated this old boy from the men. So I went to him, I asked him, I said, "You satisfied with my job?" He said, "Go on out there and get your rest and come in here Monday night." He said, "You'll have a job here as long as I stay here." Well, I stayed there longer than he did.

I didn't have no education and I did love the work, after I got used to it and learned. I was overhauling the machinery and you don't pick that up overnight. And a friend at the Exposition sent [this fellow] through [Georgia] Tech over here, paid his fees. He wanted to learn to be superintendent in the mill, see. He got up one night, nice boy, and he got to watching me. He said, "How do you do that so fast?" I said, "Well, if you stay at it as long as I have, you'll learn." Well, he said, "You know, I know everything about that machine there." I said, "You do?" He said, "Yeah." I said, "How about the drawing frames down there?" He says, "Oh, why I've got a book shows it all. I know it. I sure can." "Well, you stay here," I said. "When any end breaks on that there, push that ladle and stop it. Let me go down here to that drawing machine just a minute." I went down there and I fixed it in just a second. I said, "Go down there and see if you can start that thing up."

Now, I wasn't smart, I just wanted to show him that he had to have a little self-experience. He went down there and he fooled around there about a half a day, and come back there—"I know I got a book here, I know it." And he put his hands on that object, you know what I'd fooled with, I don't know how many times, but he didn't know it, see. So I went down there finally and showed him. He said, "You mean to tell me that you worked to run them things and you know all about that machine?" I said, "Yeah, that's right."

I worked up there twenty-four years. And I enjoyed it, up till they just got to putting so much on you. Whenever they overhauled, they just kept adding more and then more. One morning a little old boss comes up there, says, "Come on and go with me." Well, all he'd ever done, you know, never done nothing but doff in the spinning room. Set him up as foreman till they could get one, the spinning room boss.

He says, "I've got something I want you to do. We ain't got nobody else can do it, and we know you can do it." I said, "All right." Caught the elevator, got down there on the second floor. He says, "We want you to change travelers on them new warp frames." I think it was thirty-five. I had to put the running gears and the builders and all that stuff, I had to put all that together myself. Anyway, he says, "Won't you change travelers down here, until we can get somebody who can learn them?" I said, "You want me to do what?" He said it again. I say, "How much does this job pay?" He says, "Thirty-nine dollars a week." I said, "You know what? I've got news for you. If you think I'd give up an overhauling job to take that for you for thirty-nine dollars a week"—when I was making a whole lot more money than that—"I now quit. If you want them travelers changed, you get at it, boy. I've forgotten more about cotton milling, and not bragging, than you'll ever learn. You ain't never knowed nothing but just to doff. And as quick as they get a boss," I says, "you'll be gone. Never will I change anything for that money." I said, "I'm through." "Oh," he said, "you're froze to the job, boy." "Well," I said, "I got some news. I'm right now defrosting. If you don't believe it, watch me."

Yeah, I said, "Watch me walk out this gate," and I started down. I said, "I'm through. No more cotton mill. I've had it." I went out the gate. Now, if this guy had followed me on to the gate, he'd have got it if he stepped on the outside, but I'm glad he didn't. I'm glad I didn't have no trouble with nobody down there, and I ain't had none since.

Working all them years, twenty-four years, I got two things out of it to show for it today, three counting my Social Security. I got a little old pen for fifteen years, you know, with a bolt of cotton, gold pen. And when I got to twenty-four years, they gave me a pin for twenty-four years. Oh man, we thought we had something, didn't we? The companies, now, they made good money off of them people. Yeah, they certainly did. When they sold this plant out down there at the Exposition, do you know how much money they got out of that thing? Eighteen million dollars. Eighteen million dollars. Who made that money for them? The people that lived there.

Sparked by Section (7)A and by the emergence of the Committee for Industrial Organization (CIO), some Atlanta workers *did* win union recognition and job improvements during the late thirties and early forties. In November 1936, auto workers at the Lakewood General Motors and Fisher Body plants staged the first sitdown in the industry, while local garment, steel and packinghouse workers also made gains during the period.[11]

Yet, for many Atlantans, just finding work continued to be difficult. In recognition of persistent high unemployment and the preference of many New Dealers for work projects rather than the dole, the Roosevelt administration in

1935 instituted a new work relief program under the Works Progress Administration—the famous WPA.

With direct relief waning, the WPA quickly tried to get people working. Margaret MacDougall's husband Robert, a civil engineer, was second in command
in the Georgia WPA, in charge of construction projects. "They had to put hundreds of people to work just overnight," she recalls. "And it was like a war.
Your husband never got home until twelve o'clock at night. And sometimes
they'd work all night long.

"People would call up Bob over the phone, trying to get jobs. And they would
talk on and on and on and on. And he told me that I should listen as long as
people wanted to talk, those people were starving. And I remember, too, that
he couldn't sleep at night. I've heard him scream out in a nightmare, 'I'm so
sorry! I'm so sorry!' And I'd wake him up, and he would have been talking to
starving people."

"What the social worker did in WPA," recalls Augusta Dunbar, "was to certify the family as being in need. There was not any problems in proving that
you tried hard to get a job if you lost your job in the mill and you tried to
get another one in another mill, and that mill was laying people off. So there
wasn't much chance of getting another job. After the social worker certified the
family, usually the man in the family was given a job by one of the men, usually
engineers or construction workers and so forth who were in charge of WPA
projects. The purpose was to give them work to do to keep up their morale.
While they tried to get as meaningful work as they could, some of it was sort
of secondary work, such as cleaning up a park and that sort of thing."

"We just didn't have a whole lot of jobs to send them on," adds Nell Blackshear. "Especially black men. They either had to be laborers or cut grass if
they were not skilled men or craftsmen. So we would just have to almost create
jobs to offer these men."

"There wasn't no jobs. I mean that was all there was," echoes musician
Marion Brown. "And there was all kinds of people on the WPA in Atlanta. I was
foreman on the WPA, and I had a crew. Do you know where Longwood Drive
is? I cut that, cut all the woods out, and we dug that whole street from Northside Drive to Howell Mill Road. I didn't know nothing about digging roads, but
I could tell when a road was smooth and level, see. You had to get it down level
and finish it off so they could pave it.

"The boys seemed like they was worried out there, so I wrote a little song
to try and cheer them up. I'd see them shoveling and picking, and they seemed

Atlanta WPA workers. (Courtesy Atlanta Historical Society)

down. But seemed like when I'd sing this song for them at dinner time or lunch hour, they could work better:

> Now, married life is all right
> If you don't drink liquor and stay out at night.
> Work hard all the week and give your wife the pay
> Keep the good works a-going till judgment day.
> Marry young
> Raise children
> And die slappy—I mean happy.
>
> I was shooting craps the other day
> Making them points every which-a-way.
> Kept shooting around till I caught a four
> Up stepped a cop, said, 'Don't shoot no more.'
> They got scared
> I was hunting Little Joe
> But I got thirty days.
>
> Now listen, boys, if you want to get rich
> Get a pick and shovel and dig you a ditch.
> You'll learn the art in a couple of days
> Then get you a job on the WPA.
> Push buggies
> Move mountains
> Die happy.
>
> Now, the other night I went to bed
> Pulled the cover up over my head.
> I woke up with a mighty pain
> I was lying on the baby's toy train.
> The baby was bawling
> Wife howling
> Home Sweet Home.

"Talking about moving mountains, we actually moved a mountain. There was a mountain out there at Lakewood Park—pretty good-sized little mountain— and we got in there and blowed that thing up, rocks and all, and rolled the whole mountain off with wheelbarrows. Some would be a-digging at the mountain, some loading, some taking it to fills, you know. So, we did move mountains."

Atlanta sanitary sewer project, WPA. (Courtesy Atlanta Historical Society)

Atlanta sanitary sewer project. (Courtesy Atlanta Historical Society)

"They cleaned up parks," adds Augusta Dunbar, "they planted plants along highways, they built buildings, they restored old buildings, they did a great deal of work. In Atlanta, they worked on the Cyclorama, the foreground, not the painting itself." Other local WPA projects included work on Grady Hospital, airport construction, library programs and completion of the city's sewer system.[12] "They used to build outside toilets," states factory worker Ardell Henry, recalling yet another WPA project. "And, man, after they started building them things—they put a cement stool on them and all, and a thing that went like you used in a regular bathroom, the lid and all—that was uptown. They thought they had something real good. But it wouldn't flush or anything like that, it was just outside."

Although the great majority of WPA work in Atlanta was done by men, the agency did set up a Women's Work Division, administering various service projects, "what's generally considered women's work," in the words of Augusta Dunbar. "They kind of made up jobs," remembers social worker Nell Blackshear, "like having workers going into families and showing them how to budget their relief monies. And then they started a nursing service, working with the Metropolitan Nurses Association where we would get the services of these nurses to go in for relief families, because they couldn't all be housed in Grady Hospital." Women also took part in sewing, recreation, cooking and clerical projects sponsored by the WPA.

Like the NRA, the WPA was criticized from different viewpoints. Some workers claimed favoritism on the part of WPA social workers. Atlanta labor leaders attacked the local WPA wage rates, which, compared to the cost of living, ranked among the lowest in the country. On the other hand, housewives and other employers complained that the WPA was pulling away their labor. Still others charged the agency with meddling in state politics.[13]

Yet the most common criticism of the WPA—known in some circles as We Poke Along—was that the agency just provided make-work requiring little skill. "Of course, the politicians," remembers attorney Mildred Kingloff, "commented about the fact that they swept the leaves from this side of the street to that side." "Mayor Key said he had seen the leaves raked from right to left and left to right until the leaves were worn out," recalls teacher Evelyn Witherspoon. "It was almost the same joke over and over," agrees Augusta Dunbar, implying that the criticism was about as worn-out as those leaves witnessed by the mayor, "that they raked leaves and leaned on the rake when they were supposed to rake leaves. Like most jokes, it probably had some foundation.

WPA literacy class, Mount Zion Baptist Church. (Courtesy Atlanta Historical Society)

I'm sure there were people who were either lazy or ill or not very competent workers."

Even the New Dealers told such jokes, including one passed along in various forms among the Georgia staff and associates like Margaret MacDougall: "There was a man named Willy, and his whole family was on relief. But Willy —every time the social workers would ask one of his sisters about Willy, the sister would say, 'Well, Willy, he just ain't found a job a-fitting his talents.' So finally one day the social worker asked about Willy and the sister said, 'Oh, Willy is so happy. At last he's found a job a-fitting his talents.' And [the social worker] said, 'Well, what does he do?' She said, 'He poses as a dead soldier in the Battle of Atlanta at the Cyclorama.'"[14]

"They had all these wonderful engineers out there in the field in charge over the work. And they didn't let them poke along. At the time of the WPA, [Bob] could get qualified people for all the supervisory jobs, because nobody had any work. Just nobody had any work. So, you could hire good people. And my husband said after he went into private industry, that people working for the government worked twice as hard as those in private industry, that you saw more leaning on shovels in private industry than you did in government work."

The WPA sponsored cultural activities as well, including an Atlanta branch of the Federal Theater Project, which produced thirty-six plays, giving 329 performances to about 100,000 Georgians, many of whom had "never seen a legitimate play."[15] As nurse Durise Hanson notes, the agency also helped put in motion some permanent changes in the structure of state and local government: "The WPA stimulated a lot of these standing agencies like the Health Department and the Hospital Services, and sort of coordinated them more."

Through the improvement of roads, water and sewer systems, and the airport, the New Deal helped Atlanta emerge from the Depression with the best infrastructure of any Southern city. It also upgraded school, health care and recreational facilities, developed public housing, and otherwise improved living conditions.[16] Yet, as Augusta Dunbar notes, it was only with the outbreak of World War II that prosperity came back, although blacks and women continued to lag far behind: "As soon as we began to mobilize, the Depression began to fade out. They began to spend money as they had never spent it during the Depression. They were willing to spend money on the Army and for soldiers and their families in billions instead of millions. That reduced the county welfare program to almost zero. And we had instead a boom."

Chapter Eight

Health and Religion

H ealth conditions and medical care in Atlanta have changed dramatically since the World War I years. Sulfa drugs and vaccinations were unknown before the 1920s. City and county officials employed wagons to pick up "night soil" from outdoor privies, and worried about the disposal of dead animals. And both black and white Atlantans ultimately suffered from the effect of a segregated health-care system. "Oh, yes, it was entirely different," states Dr. Leila Denmark, one of the city's first women physicians. "Medicine has really gone a long ways.

"When I moved to Atlanta [in 1926], by ten o'clock you had a mustache. They all burned soft coal, all the heat they had was soft coal. There was so much smoke that you'd inhale it and your upper lip would be black. And we used lots of ultraviolet light in our office on little children because they got no sunshine. It was so smogged-in with smoke because everybody burned soft coal. All the factories burned soft coal. The trains puffed in—a terrific amount. We burned leaves when I moved here, we'd pile them up and set them on fire. You couldn't see across the street. We talk about environmental contamination, you could smell the sulphur all over the place. It was really bad.

"And you'd see an autopsy at Grady Hospital,[1] or any place you'd see the autopsy, if the person was a pretty good age, the lungs were striped. It looked like a zebra! They'd inhaled so much carbon that the lung was black, had black streaks in it."

In addition to contributing to air pollution, fireplaces and coal stoves also created fire hazards, resulting in numerous burn cases. Nurse Durise Hanson trained at Grady Hospital during the World War I years: "I can just see those lines, those long lines of burn patients in the wintertime. Just burned all over. And we had to put on that tannic acid. Just line them up—they didn't have any clothes on—and have tannic acid sprayed all over their body. And they were screaming and hollering. Changing those dressings was just so terrible."

Cramped housing for many of Atlanta's poor helped bring on fire-related injuries. Poor living conditions also helped spread malaria, diphtheria, small-pox, tuberculosis, influenza and other common contagious diseases which often reached epidemic proportions. "It was terrible," recalls Dr. Denmark. "We had hookworm and roundworm. People would go in the yard a lot, instead of going to the privy. People didn't have any form of indoor bathing, they didn't have anything like that. Very few of them had electricity. They would congregate into areas where they could get cheap housing and that's all they could afford. And I've seen them where there'd be maybe three families, four families, living in maybe three rooms. That was all over Atlanta."

"The living conditions were miserable," echoes Dr. Homer Nash, a graduate of Meharry Medical School who opened his practice on Auburn Avenue in 1910. "Most of these little shotgun houses were little dilapidated things. Didn't even have the indoor toilets like you do today. They had the outdoor privies there, and all that stuff eventually reached the water. And they were drinking that water. It carried typhoid germs. Those were the days when typhoid fever was rampant, every which way."

"They used to teach us in medical school," states Dr. James Anderson,[2] a white pediatrician who graduated from Emory in 1919, "that typhoid fever is spread by the three *F*'s: fingers, food and flies. The mosquitoes or flies would get in the excreta and get contaminated and then get in the food—the windows were not too well screened in those days—and then people would get typhoid. And the most of it was in the colored sections of the city because hygienic conditions were bad in those areas. They wouldn't keep things clean, and the garbage would stay out days at a time. They wouldn't bother with it, just throw it out the window, all that sort of thing. And then one of them would get sick and go get in a group of people and contaminate the rest of them through immediate contact."

"There was nothing we could do about it," recalls Leila Denmark. "We had no medicine. You tried to keep them well nourished, and tried to keep the fever down and all that. But we had no medicine in those days, all we had was just nursing care. When you think about practicing medicine with the world like that, it was really something."

"We didn't have any treatment," rejoins Dr. Anderson. "You didn't have any-thing to treat pneumonia, for instance. If they got pneumonia, if they didn't develop enough immunity to cure themselves, they'd die. Wasn't anything you could do about it.

"When I first went on service at Grady Hospital in the summer of 1923, there were so many typhoid patients that we had difficulty getting children in the hospital. The ward was full of typhoid patients. And we started giving vaccine. It was several years after that that the [Fulton County] Health Department got interested in immunizing people. They didn't have enough personnel in the Health Department so they would hire the doctors to go to certain places and conduct a clinic at certain definite times. And there was a good deal of typhoid, oh for eight or ten years after that, before they ever got enough people to take it to quiet the thing down. People just didn't want to take any kind of shot."

"People were kind of skeptical and they didn't want any of that," adds Leila Denmark. "When I started practicing medicine we had just started a little bit of immunization with typhoid fever. And then we got the vaccine, and after the vaccine, just like it was with diphtheria and whooping cough, we don't see it anymore."

Despite the introduction of vaccinations, as late as 1940 there were still thousands of cases of typhoid a year in Fulton County, and numerous annual incidents of smallpox, diphtheria, polio and other infectious diseases. In addition, many Atlantans suffered from a variety of nutritional maladies, often stemming from poor diet and inexperience with urban ways. Dr. Denmark explains: "People moved in from the country and didn't know how to live in the city and didn't have anything to live on. They didn't have their gardens, they didn't have their chickens and the cows and hogs and things to feed the children. It wasn't like going out in the garden and gathering up stuff like they'd been used to, they had to figure that money out. Then when they got to the city there were so many temptations for junk, all the bottled drinks and cookies and junk that they could buy that they'd never had in the country. Well, some of them had no idea how to spend that little money to make it count. If they'd just bought black-eyed peas and cornbread, they could have fed their children fairly well.

"Many people didn't have the money to buy food, they couldn't buy the things that are absolutely necessary. A person has got to have protein three times a day—eggs, meat, soybeans or black-eyed peas. They've got to have protein. And these people didn't make that kind of money. A lot of people just lived on white bread and syrup, things like that. And then they got all kinds of deficiency diseases, scurvy and rickets and pellagra. Pellagra was a vitamin B deficiency disease. We saw children with horrible nutritional deficiencies, and terrific diarrhea. Diarrhea was a killer. A lot of children died of diarrhea."

"More children died from lack of proper amounts of fluids than they did from any other one thing," adds Dr. Anderson. "While they had pneumonia, for instance, they just wouldn't take it. And the people didn't know how to give it to them. If you told a mother to give a baby eight ounces of water, next time she came back [you would ask], 'Did you give your baby the water?' 'No, she wouldn't take it.'

"Things like that, you can get fluid in them by letting them put something in it that was perfectly harmless—to get it in. You tell them to give a child eight ounces of catnip tea, that's medicine they'll pour down. And there's nothing in catnip tea, as far as the catnip tea is concerned. Catnip tea was a favorite thing to give a baby for all kinds of things, for fever or sore mouth or vomiting or diarrhea, anything."

Catnip tea was just one of a wide range of home remedies used by a cross section of Atlantans. "People didn't run to doctors like they do now," recalls textile worker Effie Gray. "If they had a boil or something, they didn't pick up and run to the doctor. They'd put something on there that'd draw it to a head. They'd give their kids different kinds of remedy medicine."

"They called the doctor to me once," says teacher Kathleen Adams. "I had whooping cough and got strangled, and my mother got excited and they sent for the doctor. And by the time he got there, of course, I was all right. I did go into a doctor's office when I was in high school. There was a smallpox scare and Atlanta University asked all of us to bring in a certificate of vaccination. So I did go to the doctor for that. And that was all that I had.

"My grandmother used to line us up in the spring, and I can see the thing out in the yard now. I think she called it tread salve, it's a little weed. And she would have us to break that off. She'd bring it in and she would stew it, put sugar and brown sugar and some molasses with it, and sift in some sulphur and beat it up until it foamed. Then she would say, 'Open your mouths,' and a tablespoon of that went down your throat every spring. They said that was to clear your bloodstream."

"There was several different kinds of things that they'd use," remembers herbal doctor and faith healer Ardell Henry. "I don't know all of them, but I know there was some butterfly root and black gum and elderberry and sassafras. When we got nauseated or had a sick stomach my mother used to boil some peach tree leaves, make tea out of it. And we'd drink that and it would settle our stomach right away. Now that red oak bark, they used to take that and make what they'd call a poultice. They'd put that and vinegar and all that kind of stuff together and then wrap it on a sprained ankle. They'd put it on there and draw the swelling and soreness out."

"My grandmother was a Cherokee Indian and she taught my father all these old remedies," says textile worker Calvin Freeman. "We still use a lot of the old-time remedies around home now. Well, say, for hives on a baby, I take a big red onion, I bore me a hole in it, stuff it full of sulphur, and bake it in the oven. Then when it gets done, I take it and squeeze the juice out of it and sweeten it and give it to the baby. And it scared my wife to death when we give our daughter the first dose of that, but she slept all night long, and the next day you couldn't even put a pin where the hives broke out on her."

Dr. Denmark had a different sort of experience with a red onion-related home remedy: "We went in there and they had a flour sack filled with red onions. They'd cooked them just a little bit and filled a flour sack and had it on the little baby's chest. Little baby's chest was all covered with mucous and it was cold and it was a cold winter day. And I said to the mother, 'Let's take this off and let Mrs. Nolan—she was a nurse—give this little baby a bath and I'll mop its throat, clean its nose and give it some aspirin and see what we can do.' And I said, 'Now, we'll leave this poultice off . . .' That baby was just covered with that old onion poultice. '. . . and we'll see how the baby feels.' And when she saw how much better the baby was after we got it all cleaned up and wrapped up in a blanket, she didn't put the poultice back.

"I thought, 'That baby was cold, freezing, with that mess on his chest.' But I didn't tell her that she was doing that. If I had taken the poultice off and said, 'This is killing the baby,' and the child did die after that, then she would say I killed the baby."

"The people that don't know what to get, they get it mixed up and get the wrong stuff," warns Ardell Henry. "Now, I know vermifuge, the stuff they call vermifuge, and it's good for stomach worms, pinworms and all that. My mother and them used to make it up in sorghum syrup and stuff like that and give it to you. But there was a lady onetime went out and got some for her kid, and she got the wrong stuff, she got jimsonweed. And she made up some and give it to her child and it killed him. She didn't know what she was doing."

"I don't play down-home remedies," counters Kathleen Adams, "because the home remedies moved from these people who from generation to generation had learned what was good for certain things. Some of these things they know are probably good. You didn't have much heart trouble or heart failure a long time ago because the medicine man or the person on the plantation that was interested in the health program there knew that digitalis when they saw it and used it in some type of compound. So I don't suppose you play down the root doctor. Now, if you mean the root doctor that grinds up a little bag of something for you to hang around your neck that's going to keep you from all evil, or that's going to bring evil to someone if you take it and throw it over in their front yard, I think that's silly."

"They were here, too," recalls Dr. Nash. "The root doctor, he was around, too. They didn't have an office—people that used them, they'd find them in this hole and that place. And a lot of people believed in him, even until today. And, of course, you know they live on the emotions of people. People think they're getting something for nothing, but they're not.

"I knew one or two come in this office, ragged as a jaybird at whistling time, you could look at him and see need written all over him, and tell me, 'Doctor, I go out in the woods and get certain roots that can cure cancer.' I said, 'Man, if you can cure cancer, oooh my goodness you need a *tremendous* place to put your money. They can't build a house big enough to hold your money. Rich and poor, black and white, dying with it. They're not dying because they want to die, they're dying because we don't have a cure for it.' 'Well, I can cure it.'"

When people *did* see a doctor, it was often at home rather than in an office. "Oh, everybody made house calls," recalls Dr. Denmark. "Lots of people didn't have cars. My first office was on the trolley line, and a good many people would come on the trolley. But if they lived away from the car line, they had no way to get there except walk. And we did have to make a lot of house calls. And that kept up for a long time.

"One day, after people began to get cars, it dawned on me. I'd made three home calls and I'd driven fifty miles. I'd seen three children that wasn't very sick and there was a car parked at each one of those houses. And I got back to my office and there was a baby there with a temperature of 106. And I thought, 'Now, I've made this person wait all these hours, when I could have been here.' So I began to question them. And if they had a way to bring their baby, I always said, 'If he's not too sick to go in a car to a hospital, he's not too sick to come in a car to my office.'"

"We used to see maybe a half dozen or a dozen patients in the office a day and make twenty-five house calls," remembers James Anderson. "I've left home on Sunday afternoon with as many as twenty, twenty-five house calls on my list that I had to make before I came home. Used to make house calls as far out as Brookhaven and as far south as College Park or Hapeville. I used to wear an automobile completely out in three years, not just sell it because the models changed, completely worn out. I would drive an automobile in three years sometimes sixty . . . eighty thousand miles.

"The man that I was associated with used to accuse me of carrying enough things in my bag that I could connect up to the city waterworks if necessary.

I had to carry all the examining and diagnostic equipment with me, and I had to carry needles and syringes to where I could give intravenous, subcutaneous fluids and all that kind of thing. I had a special emergency bag that I kept in my car, you couldn't carry it around with you. I could do practically anything we do in the hospital now in the home. I've given blood transfusions in the home."

"There wasn't no certain hours," recollects Dr. Nash. "The doctor was called all day and all night. And if you were that doctor, you'd get up and go. Spent all Sunday morning driving around to different houses, didn't get but a dollar and a half a call. You'd be driving around, this one owes you five dollars, this one owes you three, this one owes you more or less. Sometimes you got a little, sometimes you didn't. But there's no need in getting mad with them because they didn't pay you, because they didn't have it. But you went to see them. That's what all the doctors did."

Home births were often part of a doctor's duty. "Until I'd finished medical school," states Dr. Denmark, "I'd never seen a baby delivered in the hospital. They were all delivered at home. Some of the rich ladies, I'm sure, were being delivered in the hospital then. But the biggest portion surely were being born at home."

"I remember very well in those early days," adds Homer Nash, "we had to deliver our pregnant women in the hovels, in the back alleys. All the children that I delivered was in the alley and in these little homes around in different places, in most unsanitary conditions. Woman would call you, she'd tell you she wanted you to deliver her. And we got the handsome fee of fifteen dollars for delivering, and didn't get that. That's right. And we had to do it, and make our best. Go in there and scrub and get sheets and try to make it as sanitary as you could in those poor homes."

"My oldest brother was born at Grady Hospital," recalls Calvin Freeman. "The rest of my brothers and sisters was born at home. Who delivered the babies around here was a midwife, Granny Chambers. She delivered a bunch of babies in Cabbagetown. She probably delivered half of Cabbagetown. She was good at it."

Although midwives existed in the Atlanta area throughout the period, midwife-assisted births were rarer in the city than in Georgia as a whole, where 42 percent of the babies were delivered by midwives in 1936, a figure that had declined to 26 percent by 1946.

In the mid-1920s, the state instituted a midwife certification program. It upgraded the training which midwives received, yet it also led to a large decrease in the number of Georgia lay midwives. Born in 1873, the daughter of former

Dormitory for white Grady nursing students, 1940. (Atlanta
Journal-Constitution*)*

slaves, Mattie Varner was one of the earliest graduates of the program. "All us midwives had to take classes," she remembers. "We had a building up in Decatur that all we midwives went to. That's where we went once a month before the doctor, to see how you treat these little babies when they was born, what you done for them and everything. And all of them that did those things, they got a diploma for it, because they understood what needed to be done. I had to renew my papers every year.

"When the time come, I'd go in there and get my hot water, my towels and everything ready, and examine her and see if she's all right. And if she was all right, I'd get all right. I'd deliver the baby. A lot of times I didn't have to call no doctor because I knowed what I was supposed to know and didn't have a bit of trouble.

"Sometimes the babies didn't come out right. All of them didn't come head-first, some of them came feet foremost. If I couldn't breech the case like it ought to have been, if I saw I couldn't get it moved, I'd call me a doctor. Everything would be all right."

Black midwives were widely accepted in both the black and white communities. Black nurses, on the other hand, had a hard time maintaining a foothold in Atlanta. Despite hundreds of annual applications of admission to the Grady School of Nursing, the Urban League only reported 111 black registered nurses in Atlanta in 1947. Unlike black doctors, black nurses were able to train and work at Grady. Some even made it to mid-level supervisory positions, but both training and staff were segregated. Grady trainee Ruby Baker describes how black nurses were circumscribed in their professional choices and development, from nursing school on: "All black nurses was on one side of the street and all white on the other. And the white trainees wore blue dresses with a different type white bib, which are really professional nursing colors—blue and white. But the black girls wore pink and white.

"I was an undergraduate. Had I been a graduate nurse the only opportunity open would be at Grady Hospital or if you were fortunate enough to be hired by Metropolitan Insurance. They had visiting nurses going around for what few black policyholders Metropolitan had. And really, unless a registered nurse worked in a doctor's office or at Grady Hospital, there was not much open in that field.

"In 1933 I went to work at Battle Hill Sanitorium.[3] And I worked there until it closed and moved to Rome, Georgia. They had a black ward and a white ward. The white ward was in front with the beautiful lawn. The black ward was down by the boiler room in the back. At Battle Hill, I taught the white girls how to

Black nursing graduates, Grady Hospital. (Courtesy Atlanta Historical Society)

boss me. I was really the only one there with any general hospital training, because they were just tubercular patients and received mainly routine care. And these girls would come out from up in the north Georgia mountains who would have a friend already working there. That's the way they were hired, you know. So when they would send down a new supervisor fresh out of Appalachia or somewhere up there, I would have to teach her how to chart, how to take temperatures and pulse, respiration. She would be green, never been in a hospital or a sanitarium or anything before. And then I would have to call her 'Miss' and she'd call me 'Ruby,' and when we would be sitting in the office and she'd come in, we'd have to stand because she was white. But I worked under those conditions because I needed a job so badly."

Black doctors also suffered the indignities of a segregated setting, even within the black community, as Dr. Nash notes: "I was called once to see a lady's little boy who had eaten too much. There wasn't anything wrong with him, just a little gastritis where he'd eaten too much candy. Children—ain't no end to them when it comes to sweets, even now. So, I gave him something which I knew would clear him up. The next day his stomach cramps weren't much better, and his mother called me up and told me, 'Don't you think you better call a white doctor and let him see what he thinks? Then he'll tell you what's wrong with him.' I told her, 'No, you don't need two doctors, you can't pay one. If you want the white doctor, you just get him.' I didn't blame her so much, I understood her condition better than she did her own. She'd been brainwashed into believing white was right. If a white person said it, that's right. If a black person said it, that's wrong." Echoes James Anderson, "I've had any number of them tell me, 'I don't fool with any nigger doctor.'"

"The white doctor had a segregated office," recalls Dr. Nash. "He had two reception rooms, blacks over here and the whites over there. He'd wait on all these white folks and then he'd get to the black folks. That's the way it was."

"There were those who would treat blacks," recalls Ruby Baker. "But you couldn't sit in the waiting room, you would have to wait in the examining room. You couldn't sit down and read a magazine. They would usher you down the halls to the back room as if to, you know, make sure you avoided contact with the white patients."

"I've seen patients in consultation with colored physicians, a lot of them good doctors," relates Dr. Anderson. "Colored physicians have been just as nice as the white physicians. They'd call you and ask if you'd see a patient. If he wants me to examine a patient and give me an opinion, I'll do it that way. If he wants me to take the patient and keep him as a patient, I'll do it that way, too. They frequently wanted you to take a patient off their hands."

"You'd contact him," states Dr. Nash. "He'd come over, look him over and agree with your diagnosis. Then *he'd* put him into Grady Hospital and operate on him. That's the way it worked. You couldn't do it, your face was black. I couldn't put anybody in there—because of segregation. I couldn't even visit there as a doctor, I went in as a visitor that visited somebody. If I went in Grady Hospital, I didn't go in as Dr. Nash, I went in as a visitor. You lost your patient at the front door. When the patient got there he belonged to somebody else. The thing has just been that tight."

Throughout the period between the world wars, there were no black physicians on the staff of Grady Hospital or at any other general hospital in Atlanta. In addition, black doctors could not serve as interns at Grady or obtain other postgraduate training in the city. There were no black physicians in any official public health position until the 1940s. And black doctors could not join the state and county medical societies, and so were shut out of the American Medical Association.

Such obstacles limited professional growth for Atlanta's black physicians and deterred other black doctors from practicing in the city, thus contributing to health problems in the black community. In 1947 an Urban League report stated that black infant mortality and overall death rates were twice those of the white community, despite health improvements brought on in part by the development of the public health sector in Atlanta.

Poor Atlantans of both races went to Grady Hospital. The city ran Grady until 1945, when administration was transferred to the Fulton-DeKalb Hospital Authority. Affiliated with Emory University Medical School, Grady provided comprehensive services, although in frequently overcrowded quarters. Durise Hanson recalls: "We didn't have but very few private rooms for the very ill. And the wards were . . . it wasn't too bad but it meant that we had to have about ten or fifteen patients assigned to us. And of course right across from Hirsch Hall, the nurses' home, was the old pesthouse, for communicable disease."

"The old building was a good building," adds Dr. Anderson, "it just didn't have enough space. The rooms were all all right and the wards were all right, it just wasn't big enough." As an example of the often crowded conditions at Grady, before new facilities were built in 1937 the hospital had but a single one-room maternity ward, twenty feet square, containing eight beds and twelve cots.

Grady Hospital provided separate health care for blacks and whites. "We had a white hospital and a colored hospital," recalls Dr. Denmark. "We had a white clinic and a colored clinic. It was divided until the government made a change." And to this day older Atlantans refer to the once-segregated facility as "the Gradys." Although by and large black patients at Grady received reasonable treatment, they experienced severely overcrowded conditions and long waiting lists throughout the "colored" unit of the hospital.

However, as one woman puts it, "There was no place for us to go to the hospital except Grady." Until 1966, when local health facilities had to comply with the Civil Rights Act of 1964 to get approved for Medicare, most Atlanta hospitals barred black patients as well as black doctors. As late as 1963 only 360 of Atlanta's 2,424 hospital beds were available to black Atlantans. Crawford Long, Emory, Egleston, Fulton, Piedmont, and Scottish Rite were among the hospitals that did not admit blacks on any basis whatsoever.

A few very small privately owned hospitals served the black community, but the number of beds they provided was a minuscule fraction of the total number of beds in the city. "You had a little bitty hospital out here on Hunter Street," remembers Dr. Nash, "Harris Memorial, built by one family. And the rooms were too little for anything, but they were better than nothing. I guess they took in about thirty-five. You take Dwelle's Infirmary, I imagine she could take in about twenty patients. They had a house converted to a little hospital on Boulevard and there was one on Yonge Street, they could take in about thirty. But when you got past that, you had nothing."

The situation was made worse by the fact that, according to the Urban League report, by the end of World War II over half of Atlanta's black population had incomes high enough to disqualify them for treatment at Grady. "I remember saying to a black woman who by that time had become a friend of mine," recalls white liberal Eliza Paschall, "I said, 'What do you do when you get sick? What do you do? Where do you go?' And she laughed and said, 'Oh, we just make it a point not to get sick unless we're in Rochester or Baltimore. We only go to Johns Hopkins or Mayo's.' And I said, 'Well, maybe that's better than the ones I go to.' But I said, 'When your children are sick, what do you do?' And I still wonder, what *did* she do? I don't think I can conceive of having lived and reared children in a situation where you knew that those things were not available to you."

Bolstered by studies like the Urban League report, black community leaders, aided by some whites, sought to obtain additional health facilities for black Atlantans where black physicians could also practice. Arthur Raper, research

Black waiting room, Grady Hospital. (Courtesy Atlanta Historical Society)

director of the Commission on Interracial Cooperation, explains one rationale for whites to get involved: "There was the assumption that if you didn't have more opportunities for people to have access to health facilities, equitable health facilities, why you were building up problems for yourself. This one was told with great relish at one of the annual meetings, about the Negro maid who was in the home of her employer, and she says, 'Why, that child there is coming down with diphtheria just like *my* children have had for a couple weeks.' Okay, you can see that, you can respond to it, you can get a public health facility understood and financed."

In 1952 the Hughes Spalding Pavilion opened—for blacks only. It was the first general hospital in the city where middle-class black Atlantans could be admitted and where black physicians could practice. "From the time I came here in 1910, we wanted to get in Grady," recalls Dr. Nash. "We asked for integration. We tried, tried, tried to get in Grady. We couldn't get in there, so we got the next best thing. We got Hughes Spalding up there on the Grady grounds. It's been operating ever since.

"But today at Grady there are fifty-sixty Negroes specialized in every field of medicine. I belong on the staff of Georgia Baptist [Hospital] now. White or black, it does not matter, today you wait on sick folks, that's all. What a change has come about, a tremendous change! And the change is not stopping now, it's still moving."

Atlantans sought healing of the soul as well. Religion played a major part in the lives of most residents. Like other Southern communities, Atlanta was overwhelmingly Protestant, and much of the city's religious life centered around individual salvation. Many Atlantans, black and white, had intense personal religious experiences in local churches, as well as at tent meetings and other frequently held revivals. "There were a lot of revivals back in those days," recalls police officer Sanders Ivey. "People turned to the Lord. [The preachers] would invite you to come and read from the Scripture or sometimes quote the Scripture. They'd just try to warn you of the danger of going without knowing God, saying that you should be born again. People, they more or less take God when they need Him most, and when they can get along without Him they don't bother Him."

Faith healer Ardell Henry was one troubled individual who found religious salvation: "I don't know what happened to me, but I guess I just got as mean as the Devil himself. I was mean. So I was roofing them houses, and something happened to me. I got to thinking about dying. And I'd always been to these country churches, and I'd heard people talk about Hell, and I didn't want to go there. So I got into such a mess I couldn't work. I couldn't sleep. I couldn't do nothing. I went out one day, trying to go to work, and I couldn't even work. I went on back home, and on the way home I was drinking a little bit. I stopped in a little ten-cent store out in Decatur—I never will forget it—and bought me a Bible and took it home with me.

"So it rocked on. I went to Drewry's Chapel Baptist Church, up here above Marietta, and I went there on Sunday. I walked into that place, and when I knelt down to pray I guess I prayed for an hour. You know, I don't remember too much, actually, that happened. But I was completely—they can call it hysterical or whatever they want to, but it wasn't, because I had cried and cried and prayed to God to save me. I didn't want to go to Hell. And the Lord completely knocked out in the spirit, completely knocked me out. And, man, that was the peacefulest, best feeling I've ever had in my life. It was all over me. I felt like I'd just been washed in super suds or something. I mean, I felt just as clean and pure. I felt that if I died right then I'd been standing right with Jesus."

Tent meetings and revivals were often held at Ponce de Leon Park, Lakewood Fairgrounds and other spacious sites, attracting hundreds upon hundreds of people. "Sometimes eight or ten of us would get together and get the streetcar and ride out to Lakewood to service, to the tent meeting," relates domestic worker Alice Adams. "And we enjoyed it. They would sing and shout. They'd have such good singing and praying."

"August was usually the month for the revivals," recalls Kathleen Adams. "Every summer they would put a tent out in what we called the old showground, bounded by Jackson, Irwin, Auburn and Boulevard. It used to be used for Ringling Brothers Circus and any other circus that came to town. They'd put up this huge tent out there and they'd be out there for about three weeks, probably all the month, of August with their tent revival.

"Oh, they would preach. Of course, you know, they would carry you down and then try to bring you up into the skies. They'd preach all that hellfire and all that kind of stuff, and had a sawdust trail—open the doors and you'd come down and give them your hand. And, oh, people could carry on."

Streetcar man I. H. Mehaffey also remembers a revival at the showground, featuring one of America's best-known revivalists: "It was a great outing, I thought, when Billy Sunday come to Atlanta. That was in the early teens. It was something that I had never seen, that large a crowd under one big tent that went there to hear Billy Sunday. It was a great inspiration to me."

"The greatest meeting that I ever attended anywhere in my whole life," recalls Sanders Ivey, "was at the Baptist Tabernacle at 152 Luckie Street in Atlanta, Georgia. I went down to hear Gypsy Smith that night. And I was in a lot of trouble. You wouldn't have known it. Nobody else would have known it. But God was dealing with my heart that evening.

"When I got there I had to go up on about the second or third landing. He told us a few things that I . . . it certainly went home to me. He asked us, asked everybody there if our children knew where we prayed, and I knew that mine didn't, because I didn't pray. And then he said, 'There's one thing that I want to request of you, and that is to go home and read the third chapter of the Book of St. John, from the first through the thirty-sixth verse.' And I did that. I really was not familiar with the Bible, but my daughter, she looked it up for me. But I was under such conviction that when I read through I bowed my head and closed my eyes and asked the Lord to take out of my life whatever it was that was in it that was not pleasing to Him. And He did it before I could get the words said. And the tears dropped on the leaves of that Bible. Ever since then, it's been so sweet, to walk with Jesus. He's been so good to me."

The churches' emphasis on personal salvation did not preclude social action. In the teens, for instance, the Men and Religion Forward Movement launched a crusade against Atlanta's red-light district and sought arbitration for labor disputes. In the twenties, the Christian Council, an interdenominational group of white ministers, took stands on a variety of issues. And during the Depression, the churches helped provide aid for Atlanta's needy. "We had a pastor that came, and he knew I had a salary," recalls Sanders Ivey. "And he got me to pledge 25 cents a week. Oh yeah, I pledged the 25 cents a week. That was pretty good then."

The thirties saw an increase in church involvement with social concerns. In 1935, Columbia Theological Seminary president J. McDowell Richards joined the Presbyterian Church's Committee on Social and Moral Welfare. "This was a committee," he says, "which was an outgrowth of what you might call the social gospel, a recognition of the church's responsibility in social and moral matters. The committee was charged with studying some of the problems which confronted the church in society and preparing reports and recommendations for the General Assembly of our church. And we each year would select some subject for discussion and the paper. We dealt with such issues as gambling, organized gambling, organized crime. And one—probably more than one—of our papers in the thirties dealt with the race question."

Dealing with "the race question" was quite rare, though, at a time when the churches were strictly segregated, and even talking about racial matters could bring sanctions and criticism. "The churches were more segregated then than they are now, and they are completely segregated now," states Methodist minister Earl Brewer. "It would almost never happen that a black would attend a white service. The bases on which blacks would be attending white churches would be two or three. One, if they were invited to sing, which was occasionally, not often. The other, if they were maids or employees in a white family, they would go sit with the family on special occasions of some sort.

"The much rarer occasion, but it did happen, was when a black minister was asked to speak in a white church. They would have an Interracial Sunday or some other kind of special occasion. [Interracial Sunday] was a Sunday that was nearest Lincoln's birth. It was the day when the churches were supposed to lift up the issues of racial justice. It was observed much more outside the South than it was in the South. And in many cases, just to have a program in a white church was a very daring thing to do, and pastors often got in trouble just using this occasion to highlight the issues and the problems. If a pastor would preach a liberal sermon, he would have people quit coming, they would be turned off by it."

"In my first year at the seminary," recalls J. McDowell Richards, "each student had to preach a sermon before the faculty and the student body, and my roommate and I preached on the same day. I preached on the question of war and peace, and he preached on the race problem. That was perhaps a little unusual. It aroused some excitement. Some of his fellow students got right angry about it. They thought he went entirely too far in calling for racial equality, which was hardly much agitated. The question was hardly much agitated in the South at that time."

Yet the churches did provide an opportunity for some white Atlantans to reevaluate their racial assumptions. After his experience at Gypsy Smith's revival, Sanders Ivey was one who changed: "I went back to the meeting. There was a great big black man. I think he was a preacher. But he came and said, 'I want to shake hands with you.' I said, 'That's fine. I want to shake hands with you.' I said, 'I'll have to be honest and tell the truth. This is the first time I've ever done a thing like this, but I'm glad to be able to do it.' And that came from my heart. Of course, he was delighted to hear me say it."

Christianity influenced many of Atlanta's white liberals who got involved in interracial activities. Playing a particularly large role in such work were churchwomen, especially from the more affluent congregations. "Some of the most liberal voices in this field were women," states Earl Brewer. "The Methodist women in this state were the most important single voice of Methodists in the field of racial justice. They were very strongly focused on the antilynching efforts. They just agitated for a reduction of discrimination in employment and giving blacks a better chance economically. Education was another one. They clamored about the many inequities in black education. You would hardly think that they were the wives of some of the conservative business leaders in the city, but they were."

"One thing, women are one step removed from the economic [arena]," explains liberal Margaret MacDougall. "See, we had the time during the day to go to these meetings that the men didn't have time for. For instance, we went to these church meetings, and our church programs would have a lot . . . they were pretty far-out. But I was great on feeling you could influence your husband."

The Association of Southern Women for the Prevention of Lynching, United Church Women, the YWCA and other organizations reflected the prominence of white churchwomen in liberal affairs. One of Atlanta's foremost interracial activists was Methodist Dorothy Tilley. Mrs. Tilley was active in antilynching work, helped organize a regional group of women called the Fellowship of the Concerned, and served on the Fair Employment Practices Committee shortly after World War II. "She was a fine Christian lady," recalls Reverend Sam Laird, "and was always a strong advocate among the women's groups in our church. And she was so disarming as a person. She would never go about it by being spiteful or vindictive, trying to ram something down your throat. She'd just love you to death, or love you to her way of thinking."

"Miss Tilley had a story," recounts Josephine Heyman, another local liberal. "She would be telephoned, as a lot of these people were, with harassing conversations over the telephone. And she said, 'Wait just a minute.' And she had a recording of the Lord's Prayer, and she would hold that up to the receiver. She said, 'Just a minute. I want you to hear something.' And she would turn on the Victrola with the Lord's Prayer coming out. That's the way she would answer these scurrilous calls."

Most members of Atlanta's white liberal community tended to be considerably more cautious than Dorothy Tilley. Just sitting down with black people was an act that often tested deep-rooted racial taboos. "For many white people the first experience of sitting on a basis of social equality was an almost traumatic experience," relates Georgia Tech professor Glenn Rainey. "I remember somebody telling me about a very fine woman who went to some tea that the churchwomen put on, where there were black women and white women sitting there together. And her hand was just shaking."

"I became very much interested in interdenominational work and was for a time president of the Atlanta Council of Church Women, and also of the Georgia Council of Church Women," recounts Methodist Beulah Mackay, "and I had an interesting experience there. We had become interested in the Negroes, and friendly with them, but we had never invited them to any services where we ate. And so, I raised the question with the ladies and I said, 'It seems to me time that we were really practicing what we preach and inviting them to come to our May Fellowship luncheon.' And to my great pleasure, by far the large majority of them voted 'Yes.' And so we did invite them."

After that gathering, Beulah Mackay received a letter from Sadie G. Mays, wife of Morehouse College president Benjamin Mays:

> I am thanking God for you today. You caused me to have an experience that made me closer to Him today. While I speak only for myself, many other people moved in the right direction. I know it is not the end of fear and problems, but a step so long as that is worth a great deal, more than I can express.
>
> "I have always seen the Council of Church Women in the light of its possibilities . . . I have always wanted to be a part of it, but I could never be a second class member in anything connected with God's church. I hope I was right when I felt today that there were enough members of the Atlanta Council there in the lead to ensure that the possibilities of real Christian fellowship [exist] in the local Council. I enjoyed every minute that I spent in your church. It was easy to forget everything to forget everything but a Christian fellowship which left me free to grow the strength and the faith and the prayer that may develop into action. . . .

Despite such experiences, black community leaders often felt that Atlanta's white liberals moved too slowly on racial issues. "Many blacks felt that the whites were a little too cautious and a little too timid," states Arthur Raper, research director of the Commission on Interracial Cooperation. "Dr. John Hope especially would make the point. And the Atlanta Christian Council, which was very much more conservative than the Interracial Commission was, just took the position that 'You can't satisfy John Hope. If you do this for him, well, he'll ask for that.' Well, of course to goodness he will. That's the reason you ask for this, you hope you can get that, too."

In contrast, the city's black ministers were in the forefront of efforts for racial justice during the period. Black ministers led voter registration drives, spearheaded the campaign to get black policemen, sparked boycotts of local merchants, and took an active role in other struggles. Reverend William Holmes Borders, who assumed the pastorate of Wheat Street Baptist Church in 1937, recalls: "The preachers would announce, the preachers would encourage, the preachers would tell the masses how much good it would do their children. The preachers marched, the preachers would go to City Hall, the preachers would attend the Board of Education meetings. The preachers were physically and bodily evident wherever the problem was most acute."

Wheat Street, Big Bethel A.M.E., First Congregational, Ebenezer Baptist and other churches were at the center of black life in Atlanta. In the words of church worker Phoebe Hart, they provided "the social fervor of the community, the outlook and promotion of ideals and ideas and achievements, as far as blacks in the community." Offering a refuge from a hostile social environment, the churches maintained educational programs, sponsored cultural activities, supplied space for political meetings, and promoted the economic well-being of their congregants.

Many of the city's black ministers combined spiritual uplift with worldly messages. One of the leading pastors of the period was the Reverend Martin Luther King, Sr., who succeeded his father-in-law as the pastor of Ebenezer Baptist Church in 1931. "I've heard him say many a Sunday," recounts Phoebe Hart, " 'You want to know who belongs to a certain church? Well, I've got news for you. I've got them in this church from *Morehouse* to *no house*. And I've got more from *no house*.'

"I've seen him many a Sunday, 'All right, how many in here got insurance on your houses, raise your hands.' He'd look around and, 'Good God Almighty, you're living in a house and you mean to tell me you got no insurance. Stand up over there, Alexander. Stand up over there, Callaway. You see those two [insurance] men? I don't have to say no more. Get out on Monday morning, go get some insurance.' Now, what is he doing? Yes, he's boosting black business. He's in business but not only for his church. So, when you hear these people talk about 'Daddy King,' they have got a right, because he really has been like a daddy to them."

Atlanta's Jews sometimes felt uneasy in such a heavily Protestant environment. "To the average person living here in Atlanta," maintains stained glass artist Sol Beton, "the Jew was more or less considered unique, unusual, and perhaps an outsider." "The South at that period of time having narrow viewpoints and the Ku Klux Klan being fairly active, I suppose there was a certain amount of anti-Semitism that the Jewish people could observe and feel," adds attorney Louis Geffen. "We had to learn to get along as best we could."

On the other hand, many Jews, like attorney Mildred Kingloff, claim not to have been especially affected by anti-Semitism: "Oh, you'd have a fuss or quarrel. You know children can be unkind. I may have been called 'Jew baby' or 'Christ killer'—you know, that was sort of par for the course—but not much. And I did not feel it." Adds Sol Beton, "It wasn't too harsh. It wasn't too bad. We had a cross section of Jews here in Atlanta that had various backgrounds. It was such a variety that it was hard to single out one and say which one represents the Atlanta Jew."

Jews of German origin had been in the city since before the Civil War. They had pioneered such important local businesses as Rich's department store and the Fulton Bag and Cotton Mill, and had helped develop the public school system, Grady Hospital and grand opera. "It was the German Jewish element that had their best foot forward," states Sol Beton. "They were influential in politics and the city. They knew all the important people. They themselves were important. They were very prosperous, they took a part in civic life." The German Jews were thoroughly "Americanized," conducting their Reform services in English rather than in Hebrew.

In 1913, Leo Frank, a prominent member of the German Jewish community, was accused of murdering a young girl who worked in his pencil factory. Despite an outcry from Jewish organizations, Frank was found guilty, then, in 1915, taken from his jail cell and lynched. The Frank case and its attendant anti-Semitism shocked many Atlanta Jews, perhaps especially the well-established German Jewish community. "We knew Leo Frank," recalls salesman Clarence Feibelman. "We knew his wife and her family very well. Of course, the charges were ridiculous, as far as I was concerned. He couldn't be guilty of such a thing.

"I happened to be at Five Points the morning after Frank was lynched. There must have been five or six of these men, they would be called red-necks, drove into Five Points. And they displayed a piece of the rope with which they had lynched Frank. They were pretty well received by the folks at Five Points. You can imagine how I felt. They were hazardous times. They were frightening times. We were all frightened."

The Frank case led many Jews to close their businesses or to leave town. Yet others, like Mildred Kingloff's family who moved to Atlanta in 1917, had a different experience: "My father established his law practice and we moved into what should have been, expected to be real anti-Semitism. I did not feel it. It may be because we were shielded."

Beginning in the late nineteenth century new waves of Jews from eastern Europe migrated to Atlanta. Like the German Jews, they settled south of downtown, near where the stadium is today. Unlike the Germans, they tended to be Orthodox in their religion, with customs that were alien to many Atlantans. "Many of them spoke the English language with an accent. Most of them spoke Yiddish fluently," relates Louis Geffen, whose father Tobias became rabbi of the Shearith Israel synagogue in 1911. "When my father would walk down the street sometimes, since he was a man with a beard, which was unusual in those days, and he also wore the type of long coat that the rabbis of the old country would wear, he would sometimes hear insinuating remarks, 'Say, there goes that Jew,' and smirks and jeers, or something of that nature.

"Some of them did have good skills. For instance, if you were a tailor those people really were able in a short time, after they picked up the language, to get jobs, especially if they were willing to forego the observation of the *shabbat,* which they were reluctant to do, but . . . There were some which had secondhand clothing stores over on Decatur Street, which was the street where this sort of business flourished.

"And many gave credit to the people and of course this was quite an advantage to the black people who lived in the neighborhoods there. They could get their groceries on credit; especially when many of them were out of work they still gave them the credit. And they developed a very close relationship. Now, there were some who took advantage of the situation, but from what I recall, most of the people were not of that nature." Adds Josephine Heyman, "I think the Jewish people were just like everybody else in Atlanta. Some were more prejudiced and some were not."

Beginning in 1911 a third group of Jews came to Atlanta, Sephardic Jews from Turkey and the island of Rhodes. The Sephardics had originally been driven from Spain and Portugal after the Inquisition. The sixty-five Sephardic families who came to Atlanta before immigration laws tightened up in 1924 spoke Ladino rather than Yiddish, and had a different cultural heritage than the Ashkenazi [European Jews] already in Atlanta. "Their customs were different, their speech was different, their rituals were different, the songs that they sang in the synagogue had a different tune," explains Sephardic Sol Beton. "A lot of them owned pawnshops. Some had delicatessens. There were a few shoe repairmen among them."

All segments of the Jewish community were excluded from Atlanta's prestigious white social clubs. "Jewish people were never taken into the strictly Christian clubs," relates Josephine Heyman, "the Piedmont Driving Club, the Capital City Club, East Lake Country Club. Then of course the Jews formed their own clubs. The Standard Club was the oldest one and they were the people who came first, the German Jewish group."

"They would not even allow an eastern European Jew to step into their Standard Club," states Sol Beton. "And, as far as the Sephardic Jew was concerned, he had no club whatsoever, except the home of his neighbor. That was his club." "The ones who came here first," explains Josephine Heyman, "and became Americanized first and made money first resented the arrival of hordes of others who they thought would jeopardize their position."

The barriers between Atlanta's diverse Jewish elements began to break down with World War II and the creation of the state of Israel. "There's no longer a line of demarcation," says Heyman. The arrival of many newcomers from other parts of the country after the war has further transformed the Jewish community. "And," says Sol Beton, "you see a new way of life with the new generations coming in."

Louis Geffen

Attorney Louis Geffen moved to Atlanta in 1911 when his father Tobias became rabbi at the Orthodox Shearith Israel synagogue, then south of downtown near the present stadium site. An Emory graduate, he was also a member of the Board of Education.

What [my father] wanted to do in this congregation was promote classes in the study of the Talmud. These classes were usually connected with the daily religious services that were held. And then on the sabbath, when the people had more time, he would have an hour or two of this type of study. He would continue these studies in a manner that was never-ending, you might say. And when he first started there were people who were immigrants, who had come over and had studied this type of learning in the *yeshivas* in their hometown, wherever they came from. So they were very happy and very receptive to get this type of teaching.

Most of these people still were very observant of the dietary laws in their homes. And this was another part of Rabbi Geffen's activities. He was extremely interested in supervising the kosher products and seeing to it that the kosher slaughterers [were] able to have enough kosher meat to supply the people who desired to have kosher meat. In those day there were no freezers and you couldn't buy frozen meat, and there was a slaughtering house that was used by the non-Jews for the slaughtering of their animals. And there was some kind of agreement worked out whereby the kosher butchers of Atlanta were permitted the use of a part of that slaughtering house for the purpose of having kosher meat. And Rabbi Geffen would check on the methods that were used to see that it conformed to the Jewish dietary laws.

From the viewpoint of anti-Semitism personally, we had very little of it in our family. As youngsters, we frequently played with them [Gentiles], and I don't believe that the parents were that worried or concerned about the relationship that we had with them. We all lived in a very small neighborhood, because everyone in those days wanted to live near the synagogue so they could walk to the services during the holidays and on the sabbath. And for that reason, most of us went to a certain elementary school that was right there in the neighborhood. Naturally, the great majority of the students were non-Jewish and we just had to learn to get along with them as best we could.

All my sisters, we have four sisters, all went to Girls' High School. That was considered *the* high school of Atlanta. And all the boys, the four brothers, went to Boys' High School, because my father wanted that type of training or education for his children. He wanted them to have the basic classical training. My brother was going to follow his father's profession of being a rabbi, so he went off to New York to study at a *yeshiva* which is now Yeshiva University. He stayed there for a year but he returned because at that time Emory University moved into Atlanta from Oxford, Georgia. And my father wanted my brother to have a regular college degree in addition to his Judaic studies.

And it was necessary to make certain contacts in order to be able to attend Emory University, because at that time Emory University had classes on Saturday, and being Orthodox, we do not write on Saturday. And also, where we were living at that time, Emory University was about six miles distance and we don't ride on the sabbath, so it was a problem. At that time Bishop [Warren] Candler was the chancellor of Emory University, so Rabbi Geffen had a conference with Bishop Candler and he told him what his problem was. Bishop Candler said, "Rabbi, we'd like to have your son attend Emory University. And I can tell you this, that he will not have to violate any of his religious precepts.

But he will have to attend because the laws of Georgia require a certain number of days or hours of attendance that we have to certify that a student has attended before we can grant him his degree."

So my father said, "Will he have to do any writing?" He said, "No." [My father] said, "Will he be required to take examinations or tests on the sabbath or on religious holidays?" He said, "No, they will be given an opportunity to take it at some other time." And so they worked out something, and we had to walk the six miles on Saturday and on other religious holidays, which we did. We didn't have to do it but we wanted to do it, and we did it.

Chapel service was also compulsory. We attended chapel service. Of course, we didn't sing the hymns. However, you know, it's a strange thing that I can still sing some of those. I know the words of those hymns even though I didn't sing them. But some of them . . . the music was very beautiful and the wording was very meaningful and significant.

When I went to Emory I don't believe there was a Jewish member of the faculty. Also, I would say even to get a position teaching in the school system for a Jew was not easy. It was very hard to get a position if you were Jewish. I had [a] sister, she had a college degree, had courses in education, and she was qualified to be a teacher in the Atlanta school system. So she applied for a position and they told her they didn't have any vacancies—this was before I was on the Board of Education. We knew that it was the fact that she was Jewish.

At that time the president of the Board of Education was a man by the name of Gaines. My father went to see him and talked to him. Well, this man Gaines was a fairly liberal individual, but of course he was a product of that culture at that time. However, he was very, very cordial to Rabbi Geffen. And my father explained to him that this was the only thing she could do to earn a livelihood or to help—she was living at home then. And so Mr. Gaines said, well, he'd look into the matter and see what the problem was, because she was turned down. And she was very well qualified, because in those days there weren't too many that had college degrees for elementary positions. And also, there was an attorney that was in the office where I was who was a member of Council and he had a lot of influence, too. And I discussed the matter with him, and he said he would see what he could do. In other words, you had to use pressure.

They wouldn't come out and say it was because she was Jewish, they weren't that stupid, but it was a well-known fact that Jewish girls who applied, women —they weren't—all they said was, "There's no vacancy." And in those days it could be a valid excuse, because they had more applicants than they had vacancies, so that could have occurred. But they were taking the young non-Jewish girls who'd just got out of normal school and giving them assignments right away.

In 1935, Louis Geffen was elected to the school board, serving through 1938.

Like every young lawyer, you think that one of the ways to get yourself known is to—you know you're full of vitality and desire to do something for the community. I felt that I would like to serve in the capacity of helping the educational activities of the community. And there was a certain amount of desire to promote my own career and start at the bottom. They said being on the Board of Education was usually the lowest rung of the ladder.

The outstanding problem that the schoolteachers and all the employees of the school system were concerned about was the fact that their pay was so low that they just couldn't make a decent living. The school system of course was having a lot of difficulty then. And we on the Board of Education were trying to do what we could to see that salaries be increased, at least a certain sum of us were. I won't say that all of them were trying to do that, because we had some individuals on the Board of Education who never should have been members of the Board of Education. They wanted to cut salaries, they wanted to cut expenses, and they wanted to cut out many of the important activities that had been developed.

There was man by the name of Sutton who had been a principal of one of the high schools here who had become the superintendent of the school system in Atlanta, and he was a very capable man. He was a progressive individual, too, and he introduced a lot of new ideas and developments into the system. His ideas of textbooks were not as narrow, didn't have such a narrow viewpoint with the Southern touch to it, you might say. I think he was very much interested in introducing the idea of kindergartens, as I recall. And also we had developed the beginning of a very good cafeteria system. And why I was selected chairman of the cafeteria committee I never could understand, but that was one of my committees that I was in charge of, and as a result I began to become interested in it. I helped develop the cafeteria system, a great part of which was to see to it that they had nutritious lunches served for the students at a very minimal price. Because in those days those were hard times then. And there were many unemployed people and people who were working low salaries, so that there were many children in certain areas of the city that they would come to school, they hadn't even had breakfast.

And there was one particular school which I would like to mention. I mentioned Boys' High School, which was the classical [school] for those who were going to college. In the early days [the immigrants] weren't going to college. But there was also a school called Commercial High School. Many of our contemporaries and many of the children of Jewish immigrant families went to this Commercial High School. And they were able at this school to get business training, shorthand, typing, some accounting. They had other courses, too, of course, but these were the specialties for them. And as a result, they developed a knack for business and for commercial enterprise, many of them. And then they broadened on top of that. They developed their commercial acumen, and built up very fine businesses in the community here.

Chapter Nine

Leisure

*I*t was the era of vaudeville shows, fiddlers conventions and grand opera; of the brand-new "talking pictures," big and small bands and old-time radio; of house parties and juke joints; of segregated professional baseball; of golfing great Bobby Jones and the world premiere of *Gone With the Wind*. These were the recreational pursuits of Atlantans during the period between the world wars, often reflecting deep racial, class and cultural divisions within the city's population.

It was a time when young people often assembled at local soda fountains and ice cream shops. "That's when the boys and girls would gather at the drugstore, [of] Mr. Yates and Mr. Milton," recalls barber Dan Stephens, "and the boys would set the girls up to a banana split and a chocolate ice cream and all those things." "There used to be a Nunnally's near where we transferred when I was going to Girls' High," adds systems analyst Marie Townsend, "and we congregated there and ate ice cream and sodas and things. Somebody would have a car and after that we would sometimes go out to the Varsity and sometimes go home."

Many Atlantans only rarely engaged in organized recreation, if at all. The rules and customs of a segregated society meant that many public spots were off limits for black citizens. "Until these places opened up, we've gone around in homes," recalls college professor Anne Scarlett Cochran. "Entertainment was in the home."

Some people, like Willie Rakestraw, the wife of a steelworker, didn't go out because of strong family or religious considerations: "We didn't do nothing. I've been a Christian all my life and I never did want to go to dances or things like that. I just stayed at home with my children." "We were churchgoing folks," adds meat delivery truck driver James Ross. "I never have much participated in any—all through the years I've been very strict about my activities. Only time I was at the Auditorium was when my kids graduated or something like that."

Long working hours and low pay also limited the time or inclination many

Welcome home for Bobby Jones, 1930. (Atlanta Journal-Constitution*)*

Radios on sale. (Courtesy Atlanta Historical Society)

Atlantans had for recreation. "During the week," relates postal worker Waldo Roescher, "you came home from work and you had your supper and you sat down and listened to the radio, and went to bed early and got up early and went to work. Our weekend get-togethers were about the extent of our recreation."

Many people sought leisure activity which required little money or preparation. "We'd get out and sit around and gossip, what I call it, gossip," remembers textile worker Effie Gray. "The men would get out and stand around, sit around and gossip, and the women would. And sometimes on Saturday night we'd have dances or a cakewalk or a supper or something like that. And, well, everybody had a ball team. That was Saturday's business." And, indeed, baseball was by far and away the big game in town, for blacks and whites alike. Atlantans played and followed baseball at all levels, from the professional clubs that drew large crowds at Ponce de Leon Park, to industrial leagues and sandlot teams, to groups of boys who played at playgrounds and vacant lots around the city.

"Football didn't have the popularity of baseball at that time," recalls Arthur Idlett, who grew up in the Pittsburgh neighborhood. "Baseball was the popular sport. They would play when the businesses closed down. Georgia Power Company, Atlanta Gas Light Company, Atlantic Steel, Elsas and May's cotton factory [Fulton Bag and Cotton Mill], and everybody had teams. And people . . . you could put some kids out there playing baseball, and before you knew a thing, you got a crowd out there, watching kids play.

"After school was out, we played baseball from then till dark. And on Saturdays, we played baseball all day, a group of boys playing baseball. We didn't have any good fields. Up there at the school ground, the boys got together with the janitor and tried to grade off a field, but it wasn't much of a field. But yet it satisfied us because that was the best we could do at that particular time.

"Now, the equipment we had, the larger boys played with a regular baseball, but we small boys thought the ball was too hard. We made our own balls. We'd take a golf ball, and if we didn't have golf balls you could take a piece of newspaper, wet it and ball it up and squeeze it real tight, and then wrap it with kite cord. The newspaper wouldn't go as far as the golf ball center. And sometimes we would get a baseball that had been torn up by the older boys, and use that rubber and make our balls."

At the other end of the baseball world reigned the Atlanta Crackers, longtime champions of the Southern League. The Crackers were local heroes, receiving extensive coverage in the newspapers and playing before large, enthusiastic crowds at Spiller's Field. Later known as Ponce de Leon Park, the ball park was part of an early twentieth-century recreation area on Ponce de Leon Ave-

*Watching a sandlot game, 1939. (Photograph by Marion Post Wolcott.
Courtesy Library of Congress)*

nue near the present Sears Building. "Ponce de Leon Springs Amusement Park," recalls jeweler Irwin Shields, "had a Ferris wheel, a merry-go-round and skating rink and all that stuff, and across the street, where the shopping center now is, was a lake. And they filled that lake up and built some wooden stands in 1917, and the Atlanta Crackers played there. In 1923, '24, the wooden stands burned down, and in 1924 they had concrete stands [built]. I saw the first game in the frame stands and in 1924 saw the first game played in the concrete stands."

"I saw some mighty good ballplaying out there," recalls streetcar motorman Lloyd Adair. "I used to see them every time I got a . . . in fact, I lost a lot of time going to see them. I used to lose my run to get to run a car to the ball park. It didn't have too many hours, but you could go in and see the game and stay till the seventh inning. As soon as the seventh inning was over, you had to get out and get on your streetcar and get ready to load up a bunch of passengers going back. And one time I went to a game out there and seven innings was over and we got out. They played twenty-one innings. We was just sitting out there, couldn't see a bit of it. The Crackers played good ball most all the time."

Indeed, the franchise was highly successful, winning seventeen pennants over the years, reputedly more than any other minor league team ever. Strong financial backing, even during the heart of the Depression, contributed to the Crackers' success. D. I. "Red" Barron, who at times both played for and managed the team, recalls: "A bunch of millionaires took the club over, to save the thing someway. L. W. "Chip" Robert was one, and Bobby Jones was another. Now, these millionaires I don't think put a dime in the club. But they, in a business way, they took it over and managed it. The Coca-Cola Company then came in and kept it together. I was offered the job in '33 if I wanted to manage. And they said this, they'd give me $100,000 to buy new players with, but I'd have to be in fourth place or higher July the fourth, or resign. But I just told the two top directors, "My mama never, never reared or taught us to ever resign from anything, so I'm not going to resign regardless. I'm not going to take a contract under those circumstances.'"

Sharing Ponce de Leon Park with the Crackers from time to time were the Atlanta *Black* Crackers, also a championship team. "One time they had [two] pennant winners in Atlanta," remembers Black Cracker player-manager James "Gabby" Kemp, "the Atlanta Crackers and the Atlanta Black Crackers, also. And the Atlanta Black Crackers were given the title of Negro national champs in 1938." Despite their success, many white Atlantans, including even Red Barron, remained largely oblivious to the feats of the Black Crackers: "There was a Black Cracker team, but I never did see them. I never did see them play."

In many ways, the Black Crackers mirrored life in a segregated society. Finances were often shaky, scheduling and transportation uncertain, pay low, accommodations poor, and equipment inferior to that of white professional teams. Black ballplayers frequently faced discrimination at home and on the road. Yet in spite of the hardships and humiliations, the Black Crackers loved the game they played so well. "We weren't making any money," exclaims Black Cracker third baseman Arthur Idlett. "We were having fun playing baseball."

"As to how the Black Crackers franchise came into being," relates Gabby Kemp, "long years ago, way back there in the early twenties, there was a ball club here called the Atlanta Deppens. From that, they organized into the Black Crackers because they wanted to be a team like the white Crackers had then. The white Crackers, Frankie Zoella and those people like that, were the idols of these players, so they just named the team the Atlanta Black Crackers."

The early Black Cracker teams were composed largely of college students who played whenever and wherever they could, without the resources of white teams. Arthur Idlett was one of them: "We got the best players from Morehouse, Morris Brown and Clark, and organized the Black Crackers team. Then school closed [for the summer] and we started barnstorming. Most of the time we was on trains. We went down to New Orleans; Hattiesburg, Meridian, Mississippi; Birmingham, Montgomery, Alabama; Columbus, Augusta, Gainesville.

"The visiting team furnished two balls and the home team furnished two balls. That was four balls. Okay, we've stopped many a game until they found the balls. The Atlanta white Crackers would let us have their old uniforms. They would buy uniforms every year and they'd give the Black Crackers the old uniforms.

"You had to do what you could do, you couldn't carry a big team. We didn't carry but twelve players because of the economics. Pitchers had to play outfield and the catchers had to alternate at first base. Most teams carried about three pitchers. Well, that pitcher could play every third day. We didn't know about tired and all that kind of stuff. They would get sore arms and each one would rub the other down with mustard roll, and we made a concoction of alcohol and black pepper, rubbed him down.

"We didn't have a permanent place. When the white Crackers were out of

A Crackers game at Ponce de Leon Park. (Courtesy Atlanta Historical Society)

town, we would play out at Ponce de Leon. But sometimes, because of the cost of the park, it was more economical to play at Morehouse or Morris Brown, to cut down expenses."

Barnstorming teams played for a percentage of the gate, after the home owner deducted for expenses. "The home team would pay the travel expense of the visiting team," explains Arthur Idlett, "but he deducted it from the gate receipts. See, he's going to deduct the travel expense, baseballs, umpires. Sometimes they had to rent the park—deductions, and we nicknamed it 'de ducks.' And we used to say, 'All them ducks got the money.' So if there were anything left over, then you would divide it equally among the players. Sometimes they got fifty cents, seventy-five cents, or a dollar or something like that.

"We didn't get any money to amount to anything. We certainly got money, but we were really not professionals then, maybe semipro. Then we organized a league, called the Southern Black League. And they wanted to play eighty games, I believe. Well, we never managed to play eighty games because teams couldn't show up. Every time they organized, on account of finances some team would cease playing, so we didn't have a full schedule. It was just economics."

One way the black teams did make money up through the 1940s was by playing independent teams, whose skill and showmanship resembled the Harlem Globetrotters of basketball. "They were a drawing card when they came to your town or when you went barnstorming with them," recalls Gabby Kemp, "and they drew so many people that the ballplayers got paid handsomely.

"The best were the [Indianapolis] Clowns, the Zulu Giants and the House of David.[1] The Clowns had a fellow catching that sat in a rocking chair and, believe me, caught the balls that were being pitched by some hard bullet-throwing pitchers from the mound—Pepper Bassett, the rocking chair catcher. The House of David team was composed of Negroes and Cubans and they grew whiskers and looked like—well, maybe those biblical photographs or those biblical people you see in the Bible.

"The Zulu Giants were from Florida. They wore grass skirts, and underneath these skirts they had short pants with sliding pads and other protectors. They wore wigs and made up like cannibals or had paint all over their faces, yet they had some of the best baseball players on this team, the Zulu Giants, in America."

"They would put on an act," relates Black Cracker first baseman James "Red" Moore of the independent teams. "I can't explain it in a word because you had to see it to believe it, it was just that fantastic. They would do so many tricks with the ball and you couldn't hardly follow that ball, you wouldn't hardly know who had the ball in the way they were handling it out there.

"Shadowball—they don't have the ball then, they're going through the motions. See, you have a batter, he goes up as though he's hitting the ball, and you have your third baseman, he's like he's fielding the ball, he throws it to first base and he fields the ball and throws it to the catcher. And you saw them throw it, it seems as if you're seeing the ball, you know. It's just down to perfection. I mean, it's really thrilling to watch. Everybody just loved to see them perform."

Another top drawing card was the legendary Satchel Paige, star pitcher for the Kansas City Monarchs of the Negro National League. "When we played the Kansas City Monarchs," remembers Gabby Kemp, "we made money. We played them in Macon, we made money. We played them in Waycross, we made money. 'Satchel Paige is coming to town!'

"One of my greatest thrills in baseball was I hit a home run three hundred and forty feet in the left field bleachers off of Leroy Satchel Paige, right out there at Ponce de Leon Park. And Satchel Paige pointed his finger at me, saying, 'I will never trust a turkey any more.' So in that game I came up again. I was the fourth man up, two men out. He walked the bases loaded, and he called his outfielders about six yards from the infield. 'Come on.'

"The first pitch he threw me was a sidearm fastball about as fast as a rifle bullet on the outside corner. [Umpire] B. T. Harvey said, 'Strike One!' I got out of the box, I said, 'Umpire, you need some glasses,' I said, 'You're a bandit.' Get back in there.' So he threw me a ball outside, ball outside, three balls and one strike.

"My classmates at Morris Brown, those I knew at Morehouse and all the people on Auburn and throughout Atlanta were saying, 'Come on, come on, baby, slap one!' And I'm up there, and Satchel's looking at me like a tiger stalking a little lamb. Satchel had an unorthodox type of delivery that came sidearm, which we call crossfire, stepping toward third base. And he stepped toward third base and fired that ball, and the ball was hitting the outside corner. That was strike two. And he told the outfield to sit down.

"So I'm up there, waving my bat, digging in. I'm looking for the ball, and the ball was on its way up there and he was walking on towards the dugout, and Mr. Harvey said, 'Strike three!' And the crowd broke down in havoc. Boy, they applauded Satchel Paige and gave him a standing ovation. And they gave me the boos. Just two innings before, I was a hero. Now he struck me out. Who hadn't he struck out? He'd struck out everybody in the world."

Despite such attractions, the Black Crackers nearly went under during the Depression, at a time when the white Crackers were backed by millionaires and Coca-Cola. The club's fortunes revived in the late thirties when Auburn Avenue filling station owner John Harden and his wife Billie took over the team. "They wanted a real baseball team," recalls Billie Harden. "That's what we wanted to give them. We bought the uniforms, and of course we bought all the baseballs, bats and other headgear and all that stuff.

"My husband bought a bus. Mr. Baker, who owned the team, would use cars in getting the players around. When you had an engagement to go play somewhere, one car would break down, and half the team would get there and the other half wouldn't. So we thought it would be better to get a bus so we could all at least try to get there at the same time." "Now our bus was one of the best busses that money could buy," exclaims Gabby Kemp. "Our bus broke down very seldom, because our bus was serviced while we were in Atlanta. That bus was in triple A number one shape when we left there."

In addition to the bus, the team's roster increased and the pay improved under the Hardens. Yet many of the hardships of life on the road during the era of segregation remained. "Now in some towns," relates Gabby Kemp, "they had white ball parks, and frequently Negro baseball teams weren't allowed to play in those parks. So, we had to get some place that the man had roped off, and play. In those days we called them cow pastures, that's what we called them, cow pastures. Then too, there were some towns in which we had to dress before we got to the ball park because we weren't allowed to go into the white dressing rooms there.

"In those days, the hotels owned and operated by Negroes were few, and you had to maybe ask the manager of the hotel for two or three rooms and the ballplayers would go in, as many as they could, and just lie across the bed and go to sleep." "Well, they called it a hotel," scoffs Arthur Idlett. "Oh, it was nothing like the modern hotels. You would probably have one bathroom way down the hall. Man, we have been in some of them that had chinches that would eat you up, you couldn't sleep, had to get up."

"In some places," adds Billie Harden, "they didn't have hotels, so we'd have to find just people to take them in, in their homes. And the traveling was not to be desired, because you'd go to filling stations and they didn't want you to use the rest rooms and what-have-you. And you couldn't always find a place to eat that you would want to eat in."

"We had to go into places where there was no restaurants," says catcher James "Pig" Greene. "Most of the time, we'd eat out of grocery stores." "Then,

Member of the Atlanta Black Crackers at Ponce de Leon Park.
(Courtesy Billie Harden)

when we did get to a restaurant," relates Gabby Kemp, "we had to line up at the back door or at the back window and wait to get whatever they had there that they would serve us, back in the back. Then we'd park our bus around on the side of the place to eat." "You know, you'd walk into a man's place," remembers Pig Greene, "and tell him you'd want a cup of coffee, doughnut, he'd tell you, 'We don't serve niggers in here. Get out of my place.'"

Segregation also existed at home in Atlanta, where seating arrangements at Ponce de Leon Park differed depending on which team was playing. "When the other teams were playing the white Crackers," recalls Billie Harden, "we didn't go in the front door, we had a side entrance. They called it the bleachers. That's where all the blacks sat then." "We used to call it the buzzard roost," relates Gabby Kemp. "You had to go underneath the white stands to go all the way out to left field to sit out there. But at our ball games, they'd just come in and sit down, both white and colored fans, they'd just come in and sit down [anywhere]."

The segregated seating arrangements when the white Crackers played led some black Atlantans, like Pig Greene, to refrain from going in: "Because I was discriminated against, I didn't go to a ball game. I wouldn't spend my money, I wouldn't take my money down there and buy a ticket. No, I didn't go to no ball game. I'd go over there on the railroad and look at it."

"After the white Crackers made their schedule," remembers Harden, "then we could make ours. Most of my dealings were with Mr. [Earl] Mann, who was president of the white Crackers, and I have never met a finer man. He was always very considerate, and whenever I'd go to his office he gave me due respect."

Earl Mann once even encouraged first baseman Red Moore to break the color line and join his ball club, via a circuitous route: "Mr. Mann said I ought to go to Cuba and learn how to speak a little Spanish, you know, and probably I could be . . . change my nationality, you understand, from black to some other. I said, 'No, it wouldn't do for me to do nothing like that, people in Atlanta know me.'"

"That Ponce de Leon ball park used to be just overflowing," exclaims Billie Harden. "The enthusiasm was great! They just would pour out there to see them play the other teams coming here, because they were winning. And everybody likes a winner."

Everything came together for the Black Crackers in 1938, when the team joined the Negro American League for the first and only time. "This was one of the best baseball teams with the best talent, man for man, that I believe has been put together in Atlanta, Georgia, up until the present day," enthuses player-manager Kemp. "And I remember we won nineteen straight, nineteen pure straight. The Black Crackers were in the play-off with the Homestead Grays for the Negro national championship. We beat the Homestead Grays two ball games, and they were supposed to play us the third game in Birmingham, and the other ball games were to be played at Ponce de Leon Park here in Atlanta. But the owner of the ball club refused to come to Atlanta to play us. Therefore, the Homestead Grays were disqualified, and the Atlanta Black Crackers won the Negro national championship."

Despite their championship season, the Black Crackers did not join the Negro major leagues the following year, in part because of the high costs of travel outside the South. While big crowds continued through the war years, the end of black professional baseball was not far away, after Jackie Robinson integrated the major leagues in 1947. "When Jackie was admitted into the majors," relates Billie Harden, "the demand for Negro baseball began to dwindle. Everybody was happy to see the boys get a chance in the majors, they wanted to see it.

"Well, when the teams were first integrated, the owners of the teams in the major leagues, they thought, 'Well, we don't have to pay these [black] owners anything. These fellows, they're so happy to get in, we'll just walk all over the owners.' And the owners of the black teams received little or no compensation for their players who went into the majors. We went on for a while," says Billie Harden, "but we soon decided, all of us, that it would be better to let the boys go on and do better for themselves, where they could really make a name for themselves.

"I enjoyed every bit of it, it was a beautiful experience, but we have to look forward to another era."

"When I first started out back in 1935," relates Negro American League all-star Red Moore, "I believe I was making a hundred and twenty-five dollars a month. And I had gotten up to six hundred dollars a month in 1940–41. My dad was working for the railroad and that was one of the best-paying jobs there was. I think he was making, at that particular time, around twenty, twenty-five, thirty dollars a week." Black ballplayers made considerably more money than the average black Atlantan, though generally less than their white counterparts.

The same was true for Atlanta's black musicians. Blues artists like Peg Leg Howell, Curley Weaver and many others left farms throughout the Piedmont region and sought to make a living in the city by playing wherever they could.[2]

"They called my brother 'Barbecue Bob' because he worked in a barbecue place," relates Willie Mae Jackson, sister of one of Atlanta's best-known bluesmen, "Barbecue Bob" Robert Hicks. "It was a drive-in place, Tidwell's, out in Buckhead. The people'd come out, they'd come by at night for sandwiches, and my brother would go to the cars when they were eating and start playing different songs for them that they liked and enjoyed. And they would tip him, it wasn't a salary, it was tips."

Another popular drive-in and barbecue where blues musicians played was the Pig 'n Whistle, on Ponce de Leon Avenue. "The stadium used to be out there," remembers Kate McTell, wife and fellow singer of blues great Blind Willie McTell. "It would be people going to the ball games or cars passing by, you know, that would stop in to get something to eat. They would all be white, me and him would be the only blacks there. He would go every night through the week, and Saturday after three o'clock, he'd go. And he would play blues, classical, spirituals, hymns, anything you could name, he'd hit it."

"You had to learn the songs if you're going to entertain," relates renowned bluesman Buddy Moss. "We played quite a few hillbilly songs, some sentimental and all." "For years I used to not play nothing but bluegrass music, for years," adds Frank Edwards, another veteran of Atlanta's blues scene. "Played for nothing but whites. They used to pay more money, you know, be more tips than black folks."

"I'd go in Buckhead," remembers Roy Dunn, who came to town in the late 1930s, "I'd go in Morningside, I'd get my old guitar and start walking down the street kind of slow. Somebody's going to look out the door and see you— 'Hey, buddy, can you play that guitar? Come here and play me a piece.' And after a while, I've got a corner full of people and they're giving me nickels and dimes and things like that. And every time I would see a pint liquor bottle or anything like that, that meant money in my pocket. All I had to [do] was just hit that bottle upside the curbstone, just kind of smooth it off, and then stick it there on my finger and go to work. You've done made yourself a few nickels right there."

Playing before white audiences could be humiliating, though, as Frank Edwards recounts: "Oh yeah, you'd run into a bunch sometimes, might pick at you. A heap of times they just liked to have fun off you, what they called fun, you know, and you'd just go right along with them. Some of them, you know, they—which they never did me like that—I've seen them throw whiskey on a boy's head and all that kind of stuff. When he'd do that, he'd give him two or three dollars. That was their fun."

Things were quite a bit different when blues musicians played on the streets in black neighborhoods and at local black juke joints and house parties. "We'd walk down Auburn Avenue around eleven o'clock," recalls Kate McTell. "That's when they're falling out of the joints. Come on down at Yates' Drugstore, go in there, they'd say, 'Willie, play me a piece.' 'Okay, I'll play you one little piece. Come on, Yates, you're making plenty of money, give me a couple of dollars.' So, he'd play for a few minutes, come on out, keep on down to Fort Street, to Houston, cross Irwin Street, go up by the barbecue grill. They're really breaking it down there.

"He 'd say, 'I'm going to take you home now and let you go to sleep. And I'm coming back here and make some money.' And I'd hear him the next morning, just about the break of day, singing,

> Wake up, Mama, don't you sleep so sound.
> Wake up, Mama, don't you sleep so sound.
> These old blues walking all over your yard.
>
> Blues grabbed me at midnight, didn't turn me loose today.
> Blues grabbed me at midnight, didn't turn me loose today.
> I didn't have no mama to drive these blues away.

"And I'd hear him, and I'd get up and open the door."

"Every Friday and Saturday night," adds Roy Dunn, "somebody in a different place had what you call an open house. They'd give some kind of party, a barbecue or something, in order to give people somewhere to go. Cause there wasn't nowhere until on Sunday, and that was church. Somebody's going to give a barbecue or have a fish fry Saturday night, and tell them old Roy Dunn or old Buddy Moss or somebody from Atlanta's going to be there. 'I'm going to try and hear him! I'm going to try and go! I've heard that he could play!' And you'd have so many people there, and then a person gets there and gets to enjoying your music, then that's where you made your most money at. And if you were a person that drank, every time you'd turn around, somebody was setting another half a pint or pint in front of you."

"You'd be the kingpin," seconds Buddy Moss. "You'd just go to these juke joints. Anywhere there was a juke joint, we'd go. Just like, maybe we'd go stop in Covington, a guy'd want us there maybe five or six hours or something, three or four hours, we'd do a thing there and then come on back here. We were never sitting around much of the time, we'd always kind of have a little something to do."

Making a living through music was an alternative to many of the hard, low-paying jobs open to black Atlantans at the time. On the other hand, the numerous hillbilly and country musicians who poured into Atlanta from the north Georgia mountains and nearby farms often worked a regular job in addition to playing music. "Everybody—all musicians—worked somewhere," recalls Marion A. "Peanut" Brown from Cabbagetown, "and we'd just play during our spare time at night, or days that we might be off. No, you couldn't make a living [playing music], not during the Depression. You had to have a lot of irons in the fire."

Even the best-known country musicians rarely made it on their music alone. "My daddy carried on two operations," relates Gordon Tanner, whose father led one of the most famous Georgia fiddle bands of the 1920s, Gid Tanner and the Skillet Lickers. "In other words, he never moved into Atlanta fully dependent on his music. He always kept his two mules. You see, he was a farmer, a row cropper, you know, planting corn and cotton and had his vegetables. And what time he didn't farm was out with his music.

"He would use Saturdays maybe to go to Atlanta and play, played on the streets some, and he was very much in demand. He would start down the street and some of the merchants that knew him would have him stop and take out his fiddle and start playing, and that would draw the people to the front of the store. I was only six or seven years old, somewheres along that line, and my act was to sing and do a buck-and-wing dance as he played 'Turkey in the Straw.' And I recall an incident or two that we were in Atlanta and he was playing on the street, and the crowd had just packed in and would block the traffic. Even the streetcars had to stop. And then the policemens would come pushing through the crowd with their big nightsticks, and had him to quit playing because he had blocked the traffic."

"We've played in trucks out on the street, at an auction," recalls Rosa Lee Carson, who performed under the name of "Moonshine Kate" with *her* father, the celebrated country musician 'Fiddlin' John' Carson.[3] "They would be auctioning off land in Lawrenceville and right out from Atlanta at other places, and they'd have a big old truck for Dad and myself to sit in to make music while they were auctioning off the land. Dad played at Rich's and the piano store. And then we'd go up there at the Kimball House a lot and sit down in the lobby and make music.[4] Wherever you'd see Fiddlin' John, you'd see his fiddle."

Politicians often employed country musicians to attract crowds to rallies. Peanut Brown accompanied Fiddlin' John at many such events: "Along about 1932, there was a fellow run for governor called Eugene Talmadge, I guess you've heard of him. He was going to kick off his campaign in the old Ansley

Hotel, and me and John went up there and played for him. John, he played for him all during his campaign. Boy, Gene would get up and say all kinds of things with one of his rabble-rousing speeches. Ed Rivers, he was another guy that run for governor and was governor, we played for him, too. And all during the legislature, we'd play up there at the Capitol during the day. Then at night, we'd go around and entertain them at the hotels, too, for them parties for the legislators. Boy, they'd get drunk."

Atlanta hillbilly and country musicians also gave more formal shows, both in town and out in the country. "We went everywhere," recalls Rosa Lee Carson, "We'd play for the sheriff or somebody higher up like that in the courthouse, in the courtroom, and then we'd play outside. We played for the PTAs and in all the schools."

"They was all set up for it," remembers guitarist Joe Parr. "The old farmers, they would come to the schools in their wagons and barefooted. They'd have cakewalks—the women in the community would make cakes and bring them to the schoolhouse, and they'd draw a round ring and they would draw a little line or either have some kind of stopping place, and they would walk around and around with your girl until the music stopped, and if you were the couple standing on the stopping place, why, you won the cake."

"I remember back then," relates Peanut Brown, "where the elite class, they wouldn't allow country music played in their house. That's right. They didn't want their children to hear it, either, 'cause that was common. It was too low. It was low-class, they figured. Most of the square dances in the early days we did among poor folks.

"We played for two or three square dances a week, and maybe a show date once a week. On show dates, here's what we had to do. You wasn't guaranteed nothing. You might make fifty cents, a dollar, you might make five. If you're lucky, you might make ten. It was on commission, see, according to how many people turned out."

At such events, Atlanta's hillbilly musicians showed off their considerable showmanship and cornball humor. "My father," relates Gordon Tanner, "he was one of the best natural entertainers that I ever witnessed. What was very outstanding to me and would always bring the crowd down in applause was his imitation of the fox chase on the violin. He could make all kinds of different noises on that violin that would sound like diffcrent voices of dogs, and it'd sound like a big bunch of dogs running and they'd fade away like they was gone over the hill and all like that, then he'd be 'Here they come, they're coming back!' and he'd be talking all along, and they'd finally catch the fox.

"And he had a lot of comedy songs and some jokes, like he'd come out with his stage clothes and say, 'This is my summer suit—some of mine and some of my brother's,' and things like that, funny things, and the people'd just start laughing. He would have on sometimes a clown suit and sometimes it would be normal trousers and maybe one leg tore off below the ankle or somewhere. Or maybe he'd have used boots, rubber boots, and things like that, and maybe knee-length socks with his pants down in those legs. He was a comedian, he sure was."

"John, now, he was a real entertainer," states Peanut Brown of Fiddlin' John. "They would just raise Cain when we'd play and sing. John wrote a lot of funny songs, mother-in-law songs or—he had one called 'Papa's Billy Goat and Mama's Nanny Goat.'" "Oh, there's a song that Dad composed of 'I'm Glad My Wife's in Europe and She Can't Get Back to Me,'" adds Rosa Lee Carson. "He had all sorts of ways to play his fiddle, you know, and then he would shake hands with everybody, he'd go down in the aisles and he'd shake their hands. And then he go back on the stage and he'd sing another song."

Recording was important to blues and country musicians, as well as to jazz and gospel performers, bringing both a little income and recognition. "See, a record goes a thousand miles further than you will," explains Frank Edwards, "goes places that you wouldn't think about going, a record will. Quite naturally, if folks been seeing your name, heard your music, why, if you happen to be somewhere playing, quite naturally more of them going to turn out for you."

In the twenties and thirties, Atlanta was one of the country's leading field recording centers, with national record companies holding a total of twenty-two sessions in town between 1923 and 1934. "The record companies would send down all their equipment," recounts Peanut Brown, "and they used to set up on the third floor of the old Kimball House, and we'd record. Back then, they'd let most anybody record, but the thing of it is you didn't get any money then, see. People would come in from around the South to record in Atlanta."

In 1923, Fiddlin' John Carson—already a WSB radio star—became country music's first major recording artist. Believing that Fiddlin' John could make records that would sell, OKeh records agent and distributor Polk C. Brockman recorded Carson and several other musicians in a vacant downtown building.[5] "When Dad first started recording," relates Rosa Lee Carson, "P. C. Brockman brought him down there and he put on record by himself 'The Little Log Cabin in the Lane,' and it sounded real good. And then 'The Old Hen Cackled.' He made his old fiddle go just like a rooster crowing and the old hen cackled, and it was real good, too."

Despite the skepticism of OKeh recording director Ralph Peer, Fiddlin'

John's first record quickly became a local hit, then sold like hotcakes in other parts of the country. OKeh released new pressings, offered Carson a contract, and invited him to New York for additional solo sessions. "There are several records that just Dad and myself made together," remembers Rosa Lee Carson, "and then the band came in later. After the band got started, why then we all got together and made records including the band. Well, he made over three hundred records.

"When I started making records, we made a record of 'The Liquor Still,' and P. C. Brockman said, 'Well, I'm not going to call you Rosa Lee. I'm going just to call you Moonshine Kate.' And I've been going by that ever since. On the back of our car was our name—'Fiddlin' John Carson and Moonshine Kate, OKeh Record Artists.'"

Seeking their own hillbilly star to compete with Fiddlin' John, Columbia Records soon picked out Gid Tanner, as Gordon Tanner recalls: "This here A & R [artist and repertoire] man finds him there in Atlanta, maybe on the street, and he tells him, 'Gid, I want you to go to New York, make some records.' And, the way I hear it and gathered, my daddy gave him some argument, that he couldn't go that far, you know. He kept talking with him, and he said, 'Would you go if you could find someone to go with you?' And he said, 'Well, I know a blind boy that lives around here,' and that was Riley Puckett. So, later they made the trip to New York and recorded the first recordings of Gid Tanner and Riley Puckett."

In addition to recording country performers, the companies sought blues musicians for their "race record" line—records by black artists marketed to black listeners. In 1926, Columbia recorded Peg Leg Howell, and added Barbecue Bob in 1927. Blind Willie McTell recorded for Columbia, Victor, then Decca, as Kate McTell recalls: "They would just catch Willie and tell him that they wanted to sign a contract with him to record, asked him did he have anything new. And he would tell them what he had. They said, 'Okay, let's put it on wax,' and they would set a certain date that they were going to have so many to come in and record.

"With Decca, this man heard us over there at 81 Theatre. And that's how we got in contact with him. So, he written us a letter and wanted us to come to Chicago. He did pick us up and drove us to Chicago to record, me and Curley and Willie. We went to Chicago to record the first time in 1934. And I sang only spirituals, all but one. And then they didn't put 'Kate McTell' on the blues, they put 'Ruby Glaze' on it. When I sang blues I didn't use the same name as I do on the spirituals—that's 'Kate McTell.' Because you couldn't at that time, you couldn't be a blues singer and a spiritual singer at the same time. You had to be one of the two.

"They wouldn't let you record over, say, a couple hours. So, about so many people, I'd say three or four, would record in that hour. If me and Willie recorded one record, then we didn't record another one right behind it. Curley would record or somebody else, Fred McMullen or Ruth Willis or somebody else, would come in and record, and then when they recorded one we'd double back and record. They'd give us a chance to catch our breath, you know, relax before we recorded the next one."

In addition to recording local artists in New York, Chicago and elsewhere, the companies frequently brought down their equipment for extended recording sessions at the Kimball House, the Polk Furniture Store and other Atlanta sites. These sessions attracted scores of black and white musicians from around the Southeast, "all they could get a hold of," in the words of Kate McTell. "It was just a sight," exclaims Blanche Puckett, widow of Skillet Licker guitarist Riley Puckett. "It was just a sight to see the people that came to Atlanta to record. It was just an enormous bunch of people."

The recording sessions were a far cry from today's highly produced music industry, to say the least. "Our first records was made up there on Whitehall Street, at Polk Furniture Company," recalls Rosa Lee Carson. "It was in a padded room so to where nothing could go out and everything had to stay in. They'd take thick wax on a machine the size of the records, and the music was on that wax. Then they'd take wax to make the other side, and they'd put them both together and melt them down to one record."

"They didn't have any amplification to them at all," adds horn player Jack Cathcart, "[the sound] was just through the wax. They just had a megaphone hooked up to a pickup of some kind, and two or three trumpets had to blow right in that megaphone. And all the saxes stood right in front of one and did the same way. And, as I say, you didn't get any volume out of it." "They didn't have too much equipment," recalls Peanut Brown, "just set you up a microphone out in the middle of the floor there. Now you go in, boy, there are gadgets and machines and things, looks like *Star Wars*."

"And then," relates Rosa Lee Carson, "before they started, we'd go through our routine and we knew what we was going to do when that little red light came on. It was on the machine that they had, and when that red light came on, everybody had to get quiet. And then the little green light would tell us when to start."

"They'd just set you up there and let you go," remembers Peanut Brown.

"However you played it, that's how it come out. No retakes, no stopping, no going over. Now they got where they can mix it and dub it in and pull it out and take it out. Oh, they got it now. But then, it's the old saying of 'What you see is what you get.' Well, what you done is what you got. If you played it bad, it was bad. And a lot of them was bad."

The equipment was not the only unsophisticated part of the early recording industry. Both the record companies and fellow performers often took advantage of poorly educated blues and country musicians. "If you composed a song back then," says Blanche Puckett, "and you hadn't already had a copyright on it, why somebody'd steal it, they'd take it. They sure would, they sure would."

"We was recording over here on Whitehall Street for Bluebird," recounts Peanut Brown. "There was a blind man named Tom Brown come over to record his numbers. He had a couple of beautiful numbers that he had composed himself, and he could sing and play it on his guitar. And there was this fellow here that was playing on WSB. He was from Carolina. He was down here, and he was pretty famous. But he heard that blind man practicing his songs in a room there. And he went in and told this blind man that he would play with him if he wanted to—it would help his song out, see. And he had him play those numbers over and over till he learned them. And then the blind man—they said he couldn't record till the next day, see. But in the meantime this fellow went in that afternoon and recorded that blind man's two numbers. And the next day when he went to record them, they said, 'Sorry, Tom, this fellow recorded them two numbers yesterday, said they was his.' There was all kinds of stealing like that going on."

Billed as "The South's Greatest Blues Singer" by Columbia Records in the late 1930s, Buddy Moss relates how he was shortchanged early in his career: "When Curley and I teamed up with Barbecue Bob we were called the Georgia Cotton Pickers. So then Barbecue Bob got me to do a record with him for Columbia. Then this guy from Columbia, W. R. Callaway, he discovered us when we were out there to the drive-in one night, out in Buckhead, and asked Curley and me did we want to do a little recording. So, he got my address and came back, and he promised me a flat fee. Well, it sounded pretty good.

"Then in New York they'd pay all the expenses and everything, but see, where you was losing at, you didn't know about the royalties, you taking that flat fee. I learned about royalties in about 1936. A guy just happened to tell me about it, a real good musician named Clarence Williams. We were talking, and he just told me, 'Man, you ought to make good royalties off this and that.' 'What's that you're talking about?' Till finally, he just said, 'Well, you keep it on the q.t. You're supposed to get royalties.' So, when I started hollering about royalties, they wanted to know, 'Who told you about royalties?' I said, 'Well, it don't make no difference. I'm supposed to get royalties.' That was the way I got my royalties started."

Toward the end of the period several developments contributed to the decline of the Atlanta recording industry. By the 1930s, Nashville began to replace Atlanta as the leading country music center, with a more modern distinctive sound. "After the Depression, OKeh Records went bankrupt," recalls Rosa Lee Carson, "and that knocked us out of a job. I had to get a job and go to work, and finally I found one with WPA." Other companies moved away from their emphasis on regional musicians and cut back on field recording visits.[6]

"Then World War II came along," relates Frank Edwards, "and they had to stop making records then. All the material went to the war." In support of aircraft production, the federal government placed restrictions on the use of shellac during World War II. In addition, the American Federation of Musicians halted recording from 1942 until 1944, fearing that radio and jukeboxes were cutting into revenue from live performances. When the issues were settled, many country and blues musicians were dropped. The war years also brought the emergence of electrically amplified music, especially in the blues. "When the war stopped," states Frank Edwards, one of those affected, "they never did pick them songs back up." And, despite occasional forays by the record companies, it was only during the 1960s that Atlanta again became a major recording center.

Probably the biggest gatherings for the region's old-time musicians were the annual fiddler's conventions held at the newly built Municipal Auditorium on Courtland Street from 1913 to 1935.[7] Presiding over the festivities most years was a man who went by the name of Professor Aleck Smart. "Now, Aleck Smart was a tall, slim fellow," recalls Gordon Tanner, "and he wore a clawhammer coat, and he would be equipped with a big old cardboard horn that you speak through—no amplifications. And we walked the streets. He'd have all these musicians, he'd gather them together by ringing this cowbell, and he'd lead them to the nearest radio station. All of us marched and he'd be ringing that cowbell, and then whenever he motioned for the convention to start, all the musicians marched down the aisle. And they didn't just congregate back of the stage, there'd be a long row of them. They would start off the first tune, everybody trying to play whatever was announced to play, and you never heard such a fuss, everybody tuned different maybe, and they're trying to go through the first tune. Then they were singled out in their activities."

"He would get up there and then he'd call off different ones to come up and play," recalls Rosa Lee Carson. "And they was standing up, sitting down on the floor, in the chairs—you had to give the womenfolks the chairs. There was just room enough for Professor Smart to stand out there on that little bitty place and introduce the people."

The popular affair included competitions for the best performer on each instrument, as well as for the best band and buck-and-wing dancer—contests that invited raucousness and shenanigans. "Them fiddler's conventions," remembers Peanut Brown, "boy, they'd break out in some fights if the thing didn't go the way they wanted it to. I've seen a lot of fights up there because they give it to one fiddler and another bunch thought the other fiddler got it, and they'd wind up in a big brawl.

"The first time I played at the fiddler's convention [in 1930], we wasn't playing actually. This was just when I had started out, me and a boy named Fred Sanders. We could play a few of them little fiddle numbers pretty good, you know, but it wasn't nothing extra. We carried our guitars out there, out at the City Auditorium. We were waiting at the side and we seen a man coming with a camera. And he come down there and said, 'Hey, fellows, I'm from the Atlanta *Georgian* paper. I hear they're going to have a fiddler's convention over here and I want to get some pictures of some of the champions.'

"We said, 'You're in luck. Here's three of us right here.' We had never won nothing, but we were bold to get in. He said, 'Is that right?' 'Yeah,' I told him. He said, 'What are you?' I said, 'I'm the Southern Dixie Yodeling Champion.' I yodeled a little, but I wasn't anything. 'That boy right there, he's a guitar champion, he's won it. This fellow Bill Willard here, he's won the banjo picking contest a lot of times.' He lined us up there and taken a picture of us and put it on the headline of the paper—said, 'CHAMPIONS MEET.'

"I went home for lunch that evening and my wife had a stack of newspapers that high, and she says, 'People been bringing in newspapers.' She didn't even know where I'd gone, see. And said, 'How come? How'd y'all get on the headline of the paper here that y'all are champions? You can't even play, hardly.' She'd run us out of the house for our playing. And the ladies was asking her, saying, 'I didn't know your husband was a champion musician.' She says, 'I didn't either.' And that was actually the starting of my playing."

The fiddler's conventions usually were held in February. The atmosphere at the Municipal Auditorium was rather different in early May when the Metropolitan Opera came to town. The Met made its first local appearance in 1910, after two hundred prominent citizens and corporations put up $40,000 to bring the company to Atlanta. Amid much fanfare, some 27,000 people attended the five performances, which grossed over $71,000. In 1911 the opera did even better. This success prompted the Met to schedule a yearly visit to Atlanta, the only place outside of New York where the company performed, greatly enhancing the city's cultural reputation.

In classic Atlanta fashion, the Metropolitan Opera's annual stay was at once an opportunity to hear fine music, a gala social occasion, and an economic bonanza for the city. "Oh, grand opera was the biggest event of the year in those days," relates banker Baxter Maddox, whose father, Robert F. Maddox, helped recruit the Met while mayor of Atlanta. "It attracted many, many people to the city of Atlanta that would come in here and spend money, spend a night, and they'd go down to the various stores and places of business. Maybe they'd see the advantages of Atlanta and decide to open an office here or a branch office or move here. Anything we could do to bring people to Atlanta, anything that would bring people to the city."

"It was a great event," exclaims Atlanta *Journal* city editor Hunter Bell of the Met's annual visit, "probably the biggest cultural event that came here. When the opera came, they came on a special train. We met the train, we had the paper full of pictures every day on the front page. The artists were entertained in the homes of Atlanta leaders. They gave them barbecues at the Druid Hills Carriage Club. They would go to the Capital City Club on Monday night and the Piedmont Driving Club on Saturday night, and sing at dinner dances during Opera Week. They loved to come here.

"You'd go to the opera, you could parade between acts and see everybody you knew, sitting up in the boxes. In those days everyone wore tuxes." "People dressed up just in their very best to go to opera," echoes homemaker Ethel Meyers. "They certainly did, they certainly did." "I think a lot of people went to see and be seen," says salesman Clarence Feibelman. "I think Mother was one of those who went to see and be seen. My father went because he loved good music. And of course they had the finest stars here—Caruso, Scotti, Farrar, Gilli."

The many Jewish families who supported opera were excluded from the elaborate receptions for the stars held at the Piedmont Driving Club and other places in Atlanta "where," in the words of Clarence Feibelman, "our folks were *verboten*." Black Atlantans were not welcome to even hear the Met at the Auditorium, as Morehouse College dean B. R. Brazeal relates: "We couldn't go to operas and the like. They weren't segregated in terms of seating, I mean Negroes couldn't go in.

"Mr. Harold [Morehouse music professor Kemper Harold] shrewdly worked out a way to get his students in there by having them serve as ushers. That's the only way you could get in, as an usher. If he had some outstanding singers that he wanted them to hear, he would get them in. But he explained to the students that that was a makeshift kind of thing, that they should be able to get in as people."

In the mid-1920s the Commission on Interracial Cooperation sponsored one classical concert that black Atlantans *could* attend, although still on a segregated basis. Sociologist Arthur Raper relates: "Before I went to Atlanta in 1926, the year before that, I guess, Clark Foreman had had Roland Hayes there to the Auditorium, and he had sung to a mixed audience, with the whites on one side and the blacks on the other side. And [Morehouse president] John Hope said, 'If I'm going to be segregated, I'd just as soon be segregated perpendicular as horizontal.'"

In response to such slights, black Atlantans sponsored their own "high culture" affairs through various community institutions. "The churches would bring in national artists," recalls longtime Auburn Avenue resident Kathleen Adams. "Dr. [Henry Hugh] Proctor, who was pastor of our church, the First Congregational Church, had national and international connections and brought celebrities to the church. Our church used to give a musical festival in August and bring in celebrities from over the United States. And Roland Hayes was presented by our church to the city of Atlanta. Marian Anderson came to Atlanta. I saw her at Big Bethel Church there on Auburn Avenue. And I could go right down the list." "At Morehouse we had an orchestra," adds B. R. Brazeal, "we had an orchestra. So that I didn't have to go to some segregated section, or nobody else. They'd come out here and listen to the Morehouse orchestra."

Marie Townsend, the stepdaughter of a professional musician, describes other outlets for classical music in Atlanta: "The Atlanta Music Club had a concert series. The All-Star Concert Series was a series that brought people to Atlanta. They would bring the Philadelphia Orchestra here, and opera stars like Lily Pons and Martinelli, and the piano players. These were the best available. The All-Star Concert Series used to be at the old Municipal Auditorium, and they liked to sell the boxes to the Agnes Scott girls so they would wear their pretty dresses and come and sit in the boxes. They looked real good.

"We had a symphony orchestra in Atlanta, it was not anything like the symphony orchestra that we have now. They had concerts on Sunday afternoons. We had a band concert in the park every Sunday." But, as Josephine Heyman states, "We got very little good music. We didn't have anything like the cultural advantages we have now. In those days Atlanta was not a cultivated town."

Though Atlanta may not have been the most sophisticated of cities, it certainly possessed its share of elite social clubs. "That was at that time high society," recalls trumpet player Jack Cathcart about the prominent white clubs in town. "Piedmont Driving Club, Brookhaven, East Lake—they were the three big clubs at the time. Capital City Club was one of the big places. It took a lot of money to get in, but a lot of people with money couldn't get in. And if you ever saw a guy go out there with jeans on and a blue shirt, he wouldn't have gotten past the front door. That was when they really dressed."

The prestigious white clubs have remained off limits to blacks and to Jews. "The Capital City Club, no Jews accepted," says Ethel Meyers. "The Driving Club, no Jews are members." "It didn't make any difference to me, I didn't care," relates Josephine Heyman, "but there were a lot of people that were very hurt by it. The expression was, 'Many a business deal is made on the ninth tee,' and of course the Jews were not allowed to play golf in those clubs. Then the Jews formed their own clubs, the Standard Club first and then they had the Mayfair Club and the Progressive Club."

High society customs and clubs also existed in the black community. The private clubs provided a major outlet for Atlanta's dance band musicians. "The basic form of entertainment or nightlife in certain areas," says saxophone player Edwin Driskell, "was your club dances, or your fraternity and sorority dances. You had your tea dances, your Saturday afternoon dances." "Debutante balls, they always had Valentine balls," adds Jack Cathcart. "They always had Christmas week, New Year's parties which run all night. They were good jobs but they were hard to play. And they always had regular nights. Every Saturday night for years I played at Piedmont Driving Club, just a regular fixture."

There were other places, too, where dance bands played for white Atlantans. "The big hotels at that time," recalls businesswoman Mamie Kimball, "the Henry Grady and the Piedmont and the Dinkler, always had floor shows. And then they had dances, nothing like it is now. Everything was on a more dignified plane." "There were a number of dance halls in Atlanta," relates Jack Cathcart. "There was a place called Segadlo's down on Pine Street, halfway between Peachtree and West Peachtree. A Shrine Club usually had several

A can-can at the Piedmont Driving Club, 1941. (Courtesy Atlanta Historical Society)

Piedmont Driving Club, 1941. (Courtesy Atlanta Historical Society)

dances a week out there. And the Shrine also had dances in the Fox Theatre. There was a club, a dance hall opened on Peachtree called Garver Hall. And that was a college dance hall, full of Tech guys, people from Georgia.

"When Arthur Murray opened a dancing school in Atlanta—he went to Georgia Tech, you know, and he opened a dancing school at the Georgian Terrace Hotel—he had an Atlanta girl that assisted him, Margaret Brian. And when he decided to take his school to New York, she didn't go with him, and she opened Margaret Brian's school at the corner of Peachtree and Third. That's where all the high school and college students gathered."

As Cathcart recounts, national bands often came through town: "There have been a lot of them here. I'll tell you, one of the biggest ones that came here and played at the Shrine Mosque was Rudy Vallee's band. He had a good band, big following. Course, the Dorseys have been here several times, [Benny] Goodman's been here. Ozzie Nelson and Harriet used to play all the Tech dances even before they were married. Harriet Hilliard was his singer. They were famous people then, all had on their fur coats, you know. All the musicians here tried to contact them and be with the big names here in town."

In the mid-1930s, Count Basie, Duke Ellington, Cab Calloway and other nationally known black big-band musicians also began coming to Atlanta. "Before bands started coming here," states Edwin Driskell, "you couldn't get a bunch of black musicians to come out of New York and come down here and play. A lot of them came from the South. They knew what the conditions were, and they just wouldn't come.

"The first band to come here and perform was Cab Calloway's band. Neal Montgomery had been trying for years and years to get bands to come here, and in the summer of '33, I believe, we went to New York. He went for the specific purpose of making connections as a booking agent. He made the connection."

Both whites and blacks could hear the black big bands at the Municipal Auditorium, although on a segregated basis. "When a big band came to town, like Cab Calloway, I can see it just like it happened yesterday," says Edwin Driskell. "They sold tickets to the general public. Whites could come but they had to sit in the audience. The whites could not dance. Blacks could dance. There were some who liked to dance, and they were out there in the middle of the floor having a ball. In some instances some of the activities that went on provided almost a show, watching them out on the floor.

"You'd have one class or one element as among blacks or Negroes who would not be caught on the floor dancing. But they would go to hear the bands, be-

Overleaf: Masquerade ball at Piedmont Driving Club. (Courtesy Atlanta Historical Society)

Municipal Auditorium, 1940s. (J. Neal Montgomery Collection, Atlanta-Fulton Public Library)

cause that was the only opportunity you had to hear a band like that in person. That was another outlet, another form of entertainment for the general public."

Black Atlantans also attended dance halls, although such spots were by no means as numerous as in the white community. "There were two principal places that dances were held," remembers Driskell. One of them was the Roof Garden, which was in the old Odd Fellows Building, located on the corner of Auburn and Bell Street. "The Roof Garden was a prime place that dances were held." "It was a small club," recalls promoter B. B. Beamon. "It featured a lot of local talent, like Graham Jackson, Neal Montgomery, Look Up Jones, the Ambassadors. It was lively. Nightlife, open air. Then, it was the place to go."

"There was another place," adds Driskell, "the old Sunset Casino, later known as the Magnolia, which was also an entertainment parlor." Located in the Vine City neighborhood near the Atlanta University Center, the Sunset included a basketball court, rides and other diversions, in addition to a dance hall. "The Sunset was a good place for private dances," states saxophonist and promoter William Coates. "In fact, that's where just about all the big private dances was held. I started Saturday night dances in Atlanta. I went to Clark College, got me two people, Morris Brown, got me two people, Morehouse and got two people, and made a club. And after the football games every Saturday we would promote these dances for the school kids. And that started Saturday night dances in Atlanta. Because before then, Saturday night was a night when you'd take your bath and get your groceries together."

"Students from all over went there," adds Pauline Minniefield, who played piano in a band while in high school and college. "They had Saturday afternoon dances up there, and twenty-five cents was all you had to pay to dance the whole afternoon. And you knew the corner rats wouldn't be there, Mr. Speedy wouldn't let them in.

"One day I went up there and he wanted somebody to play, and they said, 'Pauline can play.' And I was always kind of shy. But I went up there and played the piano. So then I told my band about it, and we got the job. And we played pretty regular up there. We had a good time, and we danced until about six o'clock. We played for a dollar an hour and we would go home some nights with three dollars and a half after playing all that long. And we just thought that . . . oh, shucks, we thought that was something."

"You had a lot of dancing space at the Sunset," says Edwin Driskell. "They had tables on the side, but a big dance floor. But in the wintertime, Sunset Casino was heated by potbellied stoves lined on both sides of the place. There was no steam heat. And then in later years when they got fed up with the

Sunset, which was, I'd say, around between '35 to '39, then you had your clubs coming up—particularly after whiskey was legalized [in 1938]."

In 1938, several black businessmen opened up the city's first black nightclub on Auburn Avenue. "Mr. [L. D.] Milton and Mr. [Clayton] Yates redecorated an old building on Auburn and made it look like something," recalls Driskell. "When the Top Hat opened, it became the place where everybody migrated to have a dance—if you were a member, let's say, of the Masons or some fraternity and your group wanted to give a dance.

"When the Top Hat opened, I was in the house band. The band was known as the Top Hatters. We had three saxophones, two trumpets, drum, piano and bass. They had dances, they had floor shows. A couple of times a night you had the show. Basically what it was, it was the same thing as what you'd have in a place like one of your better nightclubs in New York. Cotton Club format, that's what it boiled down to. The Top Hat was really the first place where you had this club format.

"The Poinciana was another small club that came up during the war years, in a small building just across the street. You had a small house band in there, maybe four or five pieces. It was what you'd kind of call a small cocktail bar. You'd go and sit, talk, drink, a small dance floor. It was the same type of club, only you didn't have the big affairs going."

As Driskell relates, black musicians also played at all-white functions, although not without meeting discrimination: "There was no question about black musicians playing for white audiences. There was no difficulty, no eyebrow raising or anything. Why, I have been in some of the biggest homes in Atlanta. I have played in the best hotels in Atlanta, right straight through.

"The Biltmore Hotel, incidentally, was the only hotel that a black musician could go in through the front door. That was just a matter of policy. Other hotels then where you played for dances or whatever, you used the service entrance and rode the freight elevator. My thinking is that in terms of where blacks were not allowed to use the front door that it was an effort on the hotel's part not to offend the white guests. You see, you didn't have black guests, period.

"I learned early that on some jobs you went in, the kind of treatment that you got as a black musician depended in part upon the way you conducted yourself. If you went in acting like the typical black entertainer—I say 'typical,' this may or may not be the correct word, but not professional—then somewhere during the performance there's always going to be somebody who's maybe had too much to drink or maybe not, [saying,] 'Good, boy,' 'So and so, boy,' or 'Do this.' You were treated like, well, I'd say like a performer on a plantation. But in other instances when you walked in, you were well dressed, did your job, watched your conduct, in other words were just professional, you never were confronted with that treatment.

"In many instances, whites preferred having black bands. I think in part it was due to the fact that they could get a black band cheaper. When we played for blacks and played for three hours, we got three dollars, a dollar an hour per man. When we played for whites, we got five dollars for that same three-hour gig." In contrast, for white musicians "[union] scale for a three-hour dance during the Depression was seven dollars," according to Jack Cathcart. Even after Neal Montgomery helped organize a black branch of the Atlanta Federation of Musicians, causing base rates to go up, "I don't think they were ever higher than the whites," states Edwin Driskell. "I think the attitude then was, if you've got to pay this much, they'll get a white band."

Segregation prevailed in Atlanta's clubs and dance halls, in large part because dancing suggested social equality and physical intimacy. "You had a strictly segregated pattern in terms of places of amusement," recalls Driskell. "Things were real tight in terms of mixing. It was always either black or white." Throughout the period, black Atlantans were barred from attending dances in white establishments. Whites, in contrast, were able to attend the Top Hat on certain nights, although always on a strictly segregated basis.

"I understand some of the society people would go down [to Auburn Avenue] maybe Friday or Saturday nights," relates Jack Cathcart. "Just go in a group, all in their evening gowns and their tails." "The Top Hat was open from Monday through Friday for blacks," adds Edwin Driskell. "Saturday nights was reserved for whites. The same band, the same waiters, the same bartenders. The only difference was that Saturday night was reserved for white patrons. They would be packed in there on Saturday nights at the Top Hat."

White and black dance band musicians seldom crossed paths in Atlanta. For instance, Jack Cathcart only got to hear Cab Calloway play through a surreptitious route: "I'll tell you how I heard Cab Calloway the first time he played at 81 Theatre. That's when he was playing 'Got the World on a String.' And they could really play, now. I wanted to hear him, and I don't guess I could go to 81 Theatre. Well, I guess I could have, but just nobody did, you know. And a banjo player that I worked with was a friend of the projectionist down there. So we went to an afternoon show and set up in the projection room. That's hard to believe now."

During the World War II years, a few musicians began to cross the color line—in the black clubs only, as William Coates relates: "Freddie Deland, who was one of the greatest piano players in the country, was playing up on Peachtree. Every night, after they finished playing Peachtree, they came down to the Poinciana and jammed till six and seven o'clock in the morning. So, by their coming down, the people started to follow them. And we had no trouble whatsoever. We didn't even have trouble with the Police Department."

"I used to go out and play land sales," remembers Jack Cathcart. "I played a land sale once right at the corner of Piedmont and Cheshire Bridge. And it was out in the middle of the woods. Cheshire Bridge Road wasn't even paved. Played a land sale all day. I played the things at the Southeastern Fair out there for years.[8] The Southeastern Fair used to be a big thing. People used to wait all year to go to the fair. They had bands and then they had stage shows across the racetrack from the grandstand."

Dance band musicians, as well as country, blues and classical performers, also played at local movie theaters. In sharp contrast to today, Atlanta's downtown contained a veritable cluster of theaters. Marie Townsend notes: "We had at that time the Howard, Loew's Grand, of course, the Rialto, the Metropolitan. Then there were a flock of little bitty movie houses between Whitehall and Broad, down at the lower end of town. And we also had neighborhood theaters, the Tenth Street Theatre, one at Little Five Points, and others around town. And you know, you really had a real program. You didn't just walk in to see the movie and walk out."

During the silent movie era, practically all the downtown theaters maintained a full-time house band or orchestra. "At the Grand Theatre, which was Loew's, they had a regular crew that stayed there," relates Jack Cathcart, "probably about fifteen or eighteen people. They played there week after week. And at that time there were no shows on Sunday. That was unheard of. But now, next over at the Paramount Theatre, which was originally Howard Theatre, they used a larger band, anywhere from thirty to forty people. And for years that was under the direction of Enrico Leide. Do you remember him? Leide had the Atlanta Symphony for a long time.[9]

"At the time Leide was at the Paramount another conductor named Buel Rossinger had the same size band at the Metropolitan, which was then on the corner of Luckie and Broad streets. And for some reason, right in the middle of that engagement, after several years they swapped jobs. Rossinger went to the Paramount Theatre and Leide went down to the Metropolitan. They were

Orchestra rehearsal at the Fox Theatre, 1929. (Courtesy Atlanta Historical Society)

Paramount Theatre, 1934. (Courtesy Atlanta Historical Society)

both big conductors and they both had full theater bands. And the Fox Theatre, the Capitol Theatre and the Georgia Theatre, which was later the Roxy, they had their regular house bands. Some of the small theaters just had small bands. I can remember a number of them just had piano and drums.

"After talking pictures came in, then came the era of stage presentations. In places like the Fox Theatre, the Howard, they always ran one big feature film with newsreels, cartoons and a stage presentation with a big band, and they would bring some semi-permanent leader here that would stay there for several months. And he'd be advertised for months before he came in. Everybody watched for him to get here for his stage presentation.

"At the Roxy, which was right where the entrance to Davison's store [now Macy's] is, they had a regular vaudeville circuit show there. They were enjoyable shows. A lot of famous people came through, just on the traveling circuit. They were traveling acts and they stayed a week. Five acts on each show. Usually the opening act was a trapeze or acrobat, and then maybe the second act was a comedian, and maybe a short drama thing for the third act. Then the big act and the closing act would be the fifth act, something spectacular. What preceded the vaudeville was a Fox Movietone News and a cartoon of that day. And they had a feature film with the whole program, see."

While the downtown theaters spotlighted national acts and big names along with the movies, they also sponsored amateur shows featuring local entertainers, as did Atlanta's neighborhood theaters. "All of them had amateur shows in the thirties," recalls Peanut Brown. "They had to, to pull the people in, see, to get them last few nickels they had. They'd have Dish Night where they gave away ladies' dishes, and Amateur Night and Ladies' Night. We got in on all the amateur.

"And I played everything. I started playing blackface comedian, rube comedian, anything they wanted, you know. A rube comedian was a whiteface comedian. He was a dumb sort of fellow, but he always seemed to get his way about things. And then the blackface comedian was . . . well, I'll give you one of those little skits we used to have. We had a master of ceremonies would come out. And I was playing blackface comedian, I was in blackface.

"And he'd say, 'Hey, come here. You want a job?'

"I'd say, 'I don't know. What is it? The last job you got me I think I got six months in jail.'

"He'd say, 'No. This job here, it's a good job.'

"I'd say, 'What is it?'

Billboards, 1936. (Photograph by Walker Evans. Courtesy Library of Congress)

"He'd say, 'Well, the circus is coming into town, and I want you to go into the lion's cage.'

"I'd say, 'No. Wait a minute, boy. You ain't talking to me. I ain't going into no lion's cage.'

"He'd say, 'Well, listen. This lion won't bother you. All you got to do is walk into the cage and the lion will come over where you're at.'

" 'No, you're wrong there. He'll come over to where I was.'

"He'd say, 'No, wait a minute, wait a minute. This lion was raised on milk.'

" 'Yeah, I was, too. But I likes meat now.'

"He'd say, 'Wait a minute. This lion will come over and eat off your hand.'

" 'Yeah, arm, leg, or anything.'

" 'Man, they'll make a moving picture of you in that lion's cage.'

"I says, 'If they make any pictures of me in that lion's cage, they sure will be moving.'

"He says, 'Ain't you ever read the Bible?'

" 'Yeah, I read it.'

" 'Ain't you read the Bible where the lion and the lamb lieth down together?'

"I say, 'Yeah, but I never did read where that lamb got up.'

"Skits like that, you know, we'd pull."

Black performers could not play at the Fox, the downtown theaters, or the vast majority of the neighborhood theaters. Essentially the only theatrical outlet for black entertainers throughout the period was the renowned 81 Theatre, located just a few blocks south of Five Points on Decatur Street. "A fellow owned the theater by the name of Tom Bailey," relates B. B. Beamon. "White man. Mr. Bailey was a black theater entrepreneur. He owned all the black theaters in Atlanta. He was friendly with the other white folks that owned the black theaters, and they formed a chain they called the Bayou Chain—they're like clubs. An act'd come out on the road, play a week in Memphis, come on by Nashville, come on to Chattanooga, a week in Atlanta, go on to New Orleans. The show would be on the road.

"Back then, all the acts were coming into the 81 Theatre. Bessie Smith and Ethel Waters and Ma Rainey and them, going to the 81 Theatre. That's where the bands and shows went."

Local musicians also played at the 81 Theatre. "Graham Jackson was director of the pit band at the 81 Theatre in the fall of '31," recalls Edwin Driskell. "I was a member of that band. We got out of school at 2:00 o'clock, the first show at 81 was around 2:30 or 3:00, and we played shows until 11:30 that night." "Buddy Moss and Curley and Fred McMullen, they all would play with

Willie," says Kate McTell. "All these guitars bringed in together. Then we'd all do the Charleston, Black Bottom, Twiggletoe and along in there. It was more socializing with the musicians than it is now. They were charging at the door, which was about twenty-five or fifty cents back in the Depression. It would be packed in there." "They packed it, they packed it," seconds B. B. Beamon. "The theater seated about 1,500 people. If it was a good show, they packed the house."

For some black Atlantans, though, the 81 Theatre represented low-life entertainment, a place never to set foot in. "Decent people were not supposed to go down there," exclaims Pauline Minniefield. "I'm just telling you the way we were brought up. There were certain classes of people who were not supposed to go down to 81." "I don't like to make a distinction between people," adds Edwin Driskell, "but, let's face it, there are some who are better educated, or who have better jobs, this kind of thing, and those are the type of people who wouldn't go to 81. On the other hand, there were other people who wanted to see a show, whether they had been to college or whatever, who had no compunction about going."

The 81 Theatre was essentially the only place for black Atlantans to see a show in a theater without being subject to the humiliations of a segregated society. "When you went to white theaters, you'd have to sit in the gallery," recalls Arthur Idlett. "White people sat on the first floor, and you had to sit way up there on the second floor, in the buzzard roost."

One particular sore spot for black citizens was Atlanta's showcase theater, the Fox. Erected in 1929, the Fox replaced the Auditorium as grand opera's Atlanta home, and housed numerous other cultural events. "When the Fox opened," remembers Marie Townsend, "you had the organ and people singing with the organ, and then you had an orchestra that always played. I had a stepfather who played in the orchestra there, and Enrico Leide was the leader. He led the music here in Atlanta for many years, way back when. Then you had the stage show, and then you finally got around to a movie. The only place you can see anything comparable now is at Radio City in New York."

Yet for black Atlantans, the Fox was considerably less alluring. "My wife and I went to the Fox Theatre once," recounts Butler Street YMCA director Warren Cochrane, "to see a picture that we wanted to see. And we went upstairs. You had to climb an enormous flight of stairs on the outside to get to the black balcony upstairs. We sat down, but we were so uncomfortable we left. We just felt ashamed."

Accordingly, many black residents bypassed the theaters altogether, except for the 81. "Morehouse students were discouraged from going to those seg-regated balconies to look at movies," recalls Professor E. A. Jones. "In fact, I remember Benjamin Mays when he became president in 1940, I heard him say, 'I wouldn't go to a segregated theater to see Jesus Christ himself.' They had a balcony which blacks could use for seeing ordinary movies, but for a big gala affair like a premiere, like a movie premiere, they were excluded from the theater."

Of course, the biggest gala affair of all during the period was the world premiere at the Loew's Grand of *Gone With the Wind,* based on the epic novel by local newspaperwoman Margaret Mitchell. "Electricity was in the air," remembers Ethel Meyers. "We rode to town that night just to get a glimpse of what was going on and to feel the electricity. In the front of the theater, grass—artificial grass, of course—and trees were planted. It looked like going into a lovely colonial home. That's what the place looked like. The town was brilliant. Atlanta was just electrified."

Atlanta *Constitution* writer Yolande Gwin had an unusual brush with fame while covering the *Gone With the Wind* premiere: "There were newspaper people from all over the world here. [David] Selznick, the producer, was giving a cocktail party for the press. So, I went out with Jack Spalding, who was at that time a reporter, to get a story, and also to attend the party. And we got to the Georgian Terrace and went up to where we thought was the party, and I said, 'I think we're at the wrong place. There's nobody up here, no noise or anything.' He said, 'Well, let's just wait around and see.'

"I was just sitting there, and this girl comes in. This girl came dashing in and flopped down beside me, said, 'Hi,' and I said, 'Hi.' And she said, 'Could you lend me your lipstick?' And I said, 'Well, honey, I don't lend my lipstick to anybody. It's just like my toothbrush, I don't lend it.' And she said, 'Well, I've just got to have some on,' said, 'I look horrible.' I said, 'No, you don't.' She said, 'Lend it to me.' I said, 'Well, all right. Here's some Kleenex. Use it and then wipe it off real good, put it in your pocketbook.' So she got all fixed up. She said, 'Thanks very much.'

"So we just sat there and nobody said anything. In a few minutes Selznick comes charging through the door, and he said, 'Vivien, where in the hell have you been? I've been looking all over this hotel for you.' It was Vivien Leigh —Scarlett O'Hara right there by me that I was supposed to interview. But, you see, she just had on a casual dress, she wasn't dressed up—well, she just didn't look like Scarlett O'Hara."

However historically accurate or inaccurate the book and the movie were,

Scarlett, Rhett Butler and the others indelibly linked *Gone With the Wind* and Atlanta in the eyes of the world. The Loew's Grand, however, burned down in the 1970s, and Atlanta's downtown theater district is but a memory. The civil rights movement led to the integration of nightclubs, theaters and the Municipal Auditorium in the 1960s. As both vaudeville and dance halls declined in popularity, local musicians increasingly sought new outlets. "The Atlanta I grew up in," says Marie Townsend, "is not any more. It's a brand-new kettle of fish."

Radio provided another showcase for many Atlanta musicians in the period between the world wars. On March 15, 1922, WSB went on the air as the South's first radio station, leased to the Atlanta *Journal*.[10] The station quickly opened its doors to a variety of performers. "I played on WSB the first week it opened," recalls Jack Cathcart. "They had something like croker sacks hanging around the room, and they built it on top of the old Atlanta *Journal* building on Forsyth Street. I think at that time they thought it would last about six months, and they didn't go to too much trouble to get it started. I played on WSB for years and years after that." In 1925 the station moved to the recently constructed Biltmore Hotel.

Another early guest on WSB was Fiddlin' John Carson. "They called him one night to WSB to put on a program," remembers Peanut Brown. "I think WSB was about eight days old. We was kind of young boys, you know, but we liked the country music and listened to everybody play it. We went to the studios, WSB up there, with Fiddlin' John and his bunch. There was a kind of funny thing happened that night. Just before his program went on, there was a great violinist up there, putting on a concert. After the fellow got through, they introduced John. John told them, 'Now you've heard this great violinist play, but now I'm going to show you what a fiddle's made for.'"

Fiddlin' John quickly became radio's first country music star, and other old-time musicians soon got on WSB as well. Setting the tone for the new station were general manager Lambdin Kay and amusement editor Ernest Rogers, also a writer for the *Journal*. "Everybody knew Lambdin Kay and Ernest Rogers," relates Jack Cathcart. "They always came on singing a theme like 'Mr. Rogers, Mr. Kay.' And at Christmastime, they always did a thing called the UCG, United Cheerful Givers, where they'd take up a collection for the poor, like a telethon. The big personality, the guy that ran the thing, was Lambdin Kay. He did all the announcing, he did the weather, he did everything up there.

He could just ad-lib from then on. Of course, in later years, just like everything else did, it got corny to people, but he did that for a long time. Oh, he was a fine guy."

Kay and Rogers established a liberal programming policy whereby a wide range of local musicians and others could get on the air often by simply coming through the door. Other early stations, like WGST, WATL and WJTL, followed suit. "Back then," says Peanut Brown, "you could just walk in a radio station and they'd set them up and put them on, let them play right then. A little later on, though, we got where we played regular, and they'd feature you in the paper, and you'd play every day. I've had radio programs from four o'clock in the morning, 4:00, 4:30, 5:00, 6:00, 7:00.

"You know, they'd switch you around. Sometimes you'd have a program at, say, 7:00, and they'd say, 'Well, you and your band will come on starting next week at 4:30.' Have to get up, boy, in the cold and go out at 4:30. But we would go, see. We was committed to it. At one time we had one on WJTL, WGST and WSB, all the same day. And WSB found out about it and they made us cut them out—couldn't play on the other stations. Yeah, we was playing on all three of them. We didn't make no money, but we did get famous around. People would know you."

As interest in radio grew, local companies began to sponsor various programs on the air. "I had some regular programs on WSB," relates Jack Cathcart, "had some bread programs that were on, and I was on one program with about a five-piece band. Ernest Rogers was the announcer, and one little girl called Miss Marita. We were on that thing twice a week for about three or four years. Marita Bread program, Marita Bakery. And people would call in, they would play requests way back then."

Atlanta's most famous corporation also sponsored radio shows. Coca-Cola executive Hunter Bell recalls: "We used radio as much as we could without getting into the comedy angle of it. We always felt that it ought to be dignified. If you are going to have a commercial and you have comedy, it's going to overwhelm you. Mrs. Woodruff [wife of Coca-Cola's president] wouldn't take any of those news programs in those days, because she said that news programs include murder, sadness and so forth. But we used to have many cooperative programs with the bottlers on radio. Mrs. Woodruff was responsible for us playing beautiful music with very few commercials on Sunday afternoon."

Saturday afternoons were a different matter, however, when WSB aired its popular live country music show from the Erlanger Theatre beginning in 1940. "It was called the Crossroads Follies Barn Dance," recounts Joe Parr. "You just had to go take an audition, and if you made some kind of an impression, why, they'd probably hire you. You didn't have too much trouble in getting a job. "It was country music, and there wasn't any black men in it at all."

Black musicians also were largely excluded from the local airwaves. While gospel and jazz musicians did get some air play, throughout the period blues musicians seldom received radio exposure, with all its attendant advantages. "There was very little scene for the black man," states Buddy Moss. "I never heard none—blacks coming on radio. I don't remember any back in the thirties, not blacks that was doing no radio."

It was only with the founding in 1947 of WERD, the first black-owned radio station in the country, and the efforts of white station owner Xenas Sears, who created WAOK in 1954, that black music began to be played on the air in any significant volume, and then basically only on records. As the stations moved to fewer live performances and programming became more organized in the late thirties,[11] Atlanta's country musicians also suffered. "Every year on Dad's birthday," relates Rosa Lee Carson, "we celebrated his birthday on WSB, because they gave him that time. At first we had an hour and then it got down to thirty minutes, and then it finally got down to fifteen minutes, and then after that, why, they just cut it out altogether. I don't know what for." The emergence of a new form of entertainment—television—further served to transform the way Atlantans took part in leisure and recreation. As Peanut Brown sums up, "Oh, it was different then."

Marion A. "Peanut" Brown

Born in 1906, Marion Brown grew up in the Cabbagetown neighborhood. He worked in local cotton mills, then at Bell Aircraft and Lockheed, and played music in a variety of settings, sometimes going by the name "Curly" Brown.

The first time that I got interested in music was 1922. At that time Fiddlin' John Carson was blooming out. After that I heard a record by Gid Tanner and the Skillet Lickers, and Riley Puckett played guitar. And he was just about the best there was around then. He'd make some beautiful runs, you know,

WSB Barn Dance. (Special Collections, Georgia State University)

on old numbers like "Sally Good'n." Seemed like he just kept the music going. That inspired me. I said, 'Boy, I got to learn to play that guitar.' And I decided right then and there that I was going to play.

So I worked around, got up, I think, about a dollar and a half, went up to the pawnshop there and got me an old guitar. I brought it back home and I started playing that thing. My brother, he played, and he had a kind of a band, a bluegrass type band, and sang those old numbers, you know. I didn't know how to play, but I'd watch them, see, making the chords. I'd run in the other room and get my old guitar and I'd make that chord. And I'd go back in there, see him make another chord, and I'd run that chord. I kept on till I learned about three or four chords.

Sometimes they'd be practicing. I didn't know how to keep the time too well, and didn't know how to change the chords. But they'd be practicing and I'd go in, start flamming on my guitar. They'd run me out, said, "You're ruining the music." But I kept on playing till I learnt the thing, learned how to play it.

Me and a boy named Cliff Vaughn was playing together. They'd have ama-teur nights around at the theaters and back then we played against . . . WGST had a bunch called the Sunset Club, dancers, girls. They was playing amateur shows, too. And every theater we'd go [to], here comes this Sunset Club, and they brought their crowd with them. And we couldn't seem to win first prize. First prize wasn't but ten dollars, but that was a lot of money then. I mean, that was a *lot* of money. We'd always come out second. You know, you take pretty little girls coming out there dancing, all their mothers and all out there—you'd think we didn't have a chance with them. But we finally played the 10th Street Theatre out there one night, and we beat them. Boy, we was glad. We had finally beat that Sunset Club.

Then we played—there's a theater on Flat Shoals. It's not there anymore, it's a furniture store now. But we played an amateur contest out there, and then the winner was to go on to the Loew's Grand, and then after that to the Fox Theatre—the winner. And that's where we met a fellow by the name of Bill Gayton. He was there. He entered in the contest. And we got together and formed a band called Bill Gayton Jug Band. One reason we let it go in his name was he had the car, see. Whoever had the car in them days, he was the leader.

At that time there was a station opened up out on the campus of Oglethorpe University, WJTL. They dedicated the station to the air one Saturday after-noon, and me and Bill and another bunch of boys from somewhere up in the country, we dedicated the station to the air. And then we come back downtown and got a program on WSB, and the band got pretty well known. One thing about it, it was the only jug band there was around in these parts. I never did hear of another jug band except one. That was down in Louisville, Kentucky, a bunch called the Ballards Jug Band, a bunch of black men formed a singing band down there.

Another outfit we had—like George Burns. You've heard of the different names he went under? We had another outfit called the Musical Maniacs. We had a band once called Pink Lindsey and the Novelty Four. We got with Pink Lindsey and he knows a lot of Sousa's marches, "Double Eagle March," "Stars and Stripes Forever." We recorded that "Twelfth Street Rag." You didn't find no hillbillies hardly could play "Twelfth Street Rag."

We'd play all types of music. It was kind of embarrassing, you know, if somebody requested you to play a number and you don't know it. We played the old hornpipe music from the Appalachian mountains that they brought over from Ireland, and we played some old popular tunes, like "Down by the Old Mill Stream," and old numbers like that. I had about a dozen comedy songs that I'd do, numbers like "Eleven More Months and Ten More Days I'll Be Out of the Calaboose." I had a bunch of those numbers.

Nobody had dates every night like they got now. The way it would happen—say, I'd play a date with Fiddlin' John somewhere, come back the next night, me and Bill Gayton would play somewhere else. You had to move around to make some money, anywhere anybody that was playing needed somebody. Just whatever they needed for the show, well, we was ready to get in there and do it.

We'd advertise a show and stick our little old posters, sale paper they used to call them, on a telephone pole. I remember one time we went down to a little town down here in Alabama, Edwardsville, Alabama. This was right during the Depression, about 1933, somewhere along there. They told us down there that there wasn't much money. Wasn't nobody hardly had no money. So we put on the sale paper, "If you haven't got money bring chickens, eggs, syrup, meal." And believe it or not, that night here they come. A man would say, "Here, I got two chickens here. Will this get me and Kate in?" "Yeah, come on in." Another one would bring maybe a sack of meal. Another one, a jug of syrup would get them in.

And back then—you know, all musicians drank back then. They couldn't get tuned up lessen they had a drink. And there was a drunk tumbled up there and said, "I ain't got no meal or syrup or chickens, but I got some corn liquor." We said, "Come on in, buddy. You got a seat right on the front row."

He had a fruit jar full of old corn whiskey. And one of the boys, the fiddle player's son that played banjo with us, he hit that jug about two or three times. He wasn't used to that corn liquor. Man, he passed out just like that. And Pink

Lindsey, he was the master of ceremonies at that time, he went out, said, "I'm sorry. We don't think we can go on. There's circumstances beyond my control."

The old sheriff was out in the audience. He said, "Wait just a minute." Said, "We're going to have a show here." Said, "We ain't had a show here in years." Said, "Either we have a show or I'm going to lock you all up."

We said, "The show's going on."

That left just three of us. But we got out there and we fiddled, we sang, we doubled back, played rube comedian, blackface, and put them on a two-hour show. And about time it was over, Raymond, the boy who played the banjo, he woke up. But, oh boy, we had some times back then.

[In 1934] me and John and Moonshine Kate, his daughter, and this old boy Bill Willard recorded in Camden, New Jersey. And the first morning the fellow said, "I know you have to have a drink to tune up. We'll get you some." He went out and got a box full of half-a-pints—bonded whiskey, you know, didn't do it down here—and brought it back in there. And sure enough, me and John and old Bill opened us up that half a pint, taken us a drink, got tuned up and started recording. We recorded till noon and broke for lunch. And I told John, I says, "We need a little drink. Can't you ooze over to that box and swipe out one of them half-a-pints and put in your fiddle case?"

He said, "Yeah." It was sitting over there on the table. He laid his fiddle over, fixing like he was fixing his violin, and he throwed in a half-pint. We went on. We drank it. Done pulled one on the guy, you know.

That night he says, "I swiped one at noon. You get one now." So I eased over there, caught him not looking, stuck one in my guitar case. Went back to our hotel. We drank it.

Same thing happened next day at lunch. And then we wound up recording— we recorded two days. Funny thing, boy, we got ready to go and everything and started out, and there was still, oh, I guess there was six or eight pints and half-pints in that box. And we started to go and we told him bye. And he said, "Wait. You forgot something."

He said, "Your liquor over there. You forgot it." Said, "I don't drink it. I got it for y'all."

We were stealing our own liquor.

When you're singing and playing, believe it or not, it's soothing. You can't be mad and you really can't be unhappy to play music. You got to get in a state of soothing and just let it kind of bathe you, you know. Music's got something or another to it. It grabs people. It identifies.

Chapter Ten

Politics

Several interrelated yet distinct themes shaped much of Atlanta politics after World War I. Class tensions and control over municipal finances were recurrent issues, especially during the Depression years. From time to time, reformers attempted to alter the structure of city government, a structure that lent itself to ward politics, political patronage and corruption, within the Police Department and elsewhere. During the twenties in particular, the Ku Klux Klan wielded great influence at the highest levels of local government. Toward the end of the period black Atlantans began to obtain significant political clout, leading to the integration of the police force in 1948. Each of these developments had an impact on Atlanta's political leaders, including the dominant mayors of the interwar era, James L. Key and William B. Hartsfield.

Atlanta's city government consisted of a mayor and a bicameral Council comprised of aldermen and councilmen elected from each of the city's wards. Council members were elected on a ward basis, rather than citywide. In the teens, twenties and again in the thirties, groups like the Chamber of Commerce, the League of Women Voters and the Atlanta Real Estate Board unsuccessfully sought to revise the ward system in favor of a city manager or other forms of municipal government. Margaret MacDougall of the League of Women Voters, who in the 1970s served on the city charter revision commission, describes one reason for opposition to ward politics: "It made it very hard to get any kind of ordinances passed to the good of the whole. The people elected from each ward wouldn't have an interest in the city as a whole, they'd only have an interest in their own ward. You see, that's why Girls' High School got put way over [near Grant Park in 1925] where it was hard to get to for people on this side of town."

On the other hand, organizations like the Atlanta Federation of Trades opposed charter revision, fearing that such a change would dilute the not inconsiderable white working-class influence in municipal politics. According to one account, close to half of Atlanta's registered voters belonged to trade unions during the World War I era, and local workers took an active role in municipal affairs, including politics.[1] Printer James G. Woodward was elected mayor four times between 1900 and 1916, and numerous other workingmen held elected and appointed positions.

While the principal upper-class wards were the Sixth and Eighth, white working-class political strength was concentrated in the First Ward, centered in Grant Park, and the Fifth, located northwest of downtown, called "the Bloody Fifth" for the intensity of its politics at election time. "Yeah, they named that the Bloody Fifth," recalls city employee and textile worker Alec Dennis. "Well, the reason they named it that, every time there'd be an election there'd be three or four fights. It was pretty bad. If you wasn't for that man that the most was for, you'd better keep your mouth shut, because you'd be liable to get in a fight."

As Dennis relates, money often was an important element in Fifth Ward politics: "If I was running for mayor, alderman, councilman or clerk or anything like that, I'd try to pick some men that I felt like had influence, pay them if they was working people, just pay them. Pay them what you felt like would win them. And that went a long ways in carrying a ward, because there was some people that, for the benefit of the community, would work for people. But they got a little money for it, they got paid for their work.

"I know one time there was an election, this old man was going to work for this politician. He had done got up pretty high by that time, he was going to get fifty dollars, I believe, for his day's work. Well, ordinarily he didn't make over seven, eight dollars [a day on his job]. He'd take about ten campaign workers out of Exposition Mill and they'd darn near carry that election, that ward. But one time, this fellow said, 'We've got to get that ward, regardless of cost.' Went and changed this old man around. He got around two hundred dollars that time. Well, that was big money for then. His poll workers got about ten or fifteen dollars apiece, and they carried the election that time. I was sitting in the office when that flip was made and they switched him over. That's right. I seen it."

Atlanta had a comparatively weak mayor form of city government, with the committees of City Council possessing great control over the everyday affairs of municipal life. Particularly powerful, and often controversial, was the Police Committee, which reviewed promotions and other aspects of police operations. "It's hard to get them politics out of that Police Department," says police officer M. Y. Rutherford, echoing a theme that continues to the present. "I don't care who's running it, it's hard to get them politics out. You had to do a little politicking to get them promotions. You had to have some councilman, a guy who's a good friend on the Council, somebody to pull for you."

Chairing the Police Committee for many years was G. Dan Bridges, who ran a grocery store in Grant Park. "He really took over and run the Police Department," remembers Herbert Jenkins, who became police chief in 1947. "He helped select all the police officers, make the promotions, and he was a powerhouse there for a good many years. And nearly all the police that was employed at that time was people that lived—if you lived in Bridges' district and made an application to the Police Department, you were pretty certain to get on, see. They were pure and simple old-time ward-heeling politics."

"All them policemen went to trade with him," adds Officer Rutherford. "He done a good business with that Police Department because, boy, anytime you worked a beat out there, you passed Dan Bridges' store, you'd see anywhere from one to two to three policemen hung around there all the time, day or night. They just hung around Dan, trying to get promotions and such as that." "He was a great man, he was a great man," says policeman Sanders Ivey. "Somebody was just saying to me this morning that he put on more police and firemen and promoted them more than anybody else. He ran the Police Department and there wasn't no misunderstanding about it. Everybody knew who was boss."

The Police Department was connected to local politics in another way, too, through widespread police membership in the Ku Klux Klan, perhaps the most significant force in municipal politics during the period. "Well, I can almost say that at one time most of the members of the Police Department were members of the Ku Klux Klan," states Chief Jenkins, himself once briefly a Klan member, "and there were officers in the Klan that were also officers in the Atlanta Police Department."

Klan membership extended far beyond the Police Department in Atlanta, the Invisible Empire's national headquarters for a decade after the rebirth of the organization in 1915. That year, shortly after the lynching of Atlanta Jew Leo Frank, a small group of largely "solid citizens" stood atop Stone Mountain and revived the order.[2] Particularly after 1920, membership expanded rapidly, both in Atlanta and across the country, as over two million members joined nationally between 1920 and 1926. Tens of thousands of white Atlantans from all walks of life belonged to the Klan in the early twenties.[3]

"Oh, there was lots of them," recalls ex-Klansman Harold Sheats, city attorney for the adjacent community of East Point and later Fulton County attorney. "Buckhead, Oakland City, East Point, Decatur, out at Stone Mountain. There must have been a dozen lodges in the metropolitan area." Yet, even with such a large following, as Chief Jenkins suggests, "their greatest influence was really not in its membership. It was sympathizers, people that give them moral support, didn't object to it. And that kind of support was the most important thing, I think, more so than the membership."

The known Klansmen and Klan sympathizers in Atlanta during the twenties included Walter A. Sims, elected mayor in 1922 and 1924, councilman and state legislator James O. Wood, Superior Court judges Gus H. Howard and Eugene Thomas, solicitor general John A. Boykin, school board member Carl F. Hutcheson, future governor E. D. Rivers, and dozens of minor politicians.[4]

"Everybody in the courthouse belonged to the Klan," says Harold Sheats. "Virtually every judge down there, the prosecuting officers belonged to the Klan. The mayor of East Point did. That's the reason I joined. I became city attorney and, by golly, I wouldn't join the Klan. I was an idealistic young man. I became city attorney and found all the police and the mayor and the councilmen all belonged. 'Why don't you join, Harold?' Okay, I did."

Policeman Ivey, who also belonged to the Klan, relates how membership could be politically beneficial: "You'd have about five men on the Fire Committee [of City Council], and, you see, if three of them were Klansmen and a fellow that was a Klansman was up for nomination against another fellow that wasn't a Klansman, why if they went according to the Klan, the man that was the Klansman would get the place. I know a fellow that got on the Fire Department through the Klan. I know another fellow, he got to be an officer in the Klan, and he got a job in City Hall, in finance."

The Klan also made its presence felt outside of formal politics. Through its Buckhead robe factory and other enterprises, it pumped millions of dollars into the city's economy, attracting such prominent firms as Coca-Cola, Studebaker and the Elgin Watch Company to advertise in its newspaper. Reflecting both its acceptance in the community and its desire to create a favorable public image, the Klan took part in parades, sponsored a drum and bugle corps, and gave to local charities.

"I would say without any contradiction," states Harold Sheats, "that the Klan was the greatest charitable organization in south Fulton County in those days. We made it out of minstrel shows. I was interlocutor. The interlocutor would usually be dressed in tails, and he'd have six end men in blackface. We went all over the state, made thousands of dollars. And at Christmas and Thanksgiving we literally fed the poor of this area."

Ku Klux Klan poster. (Courtesy Atlanta Historical Society)

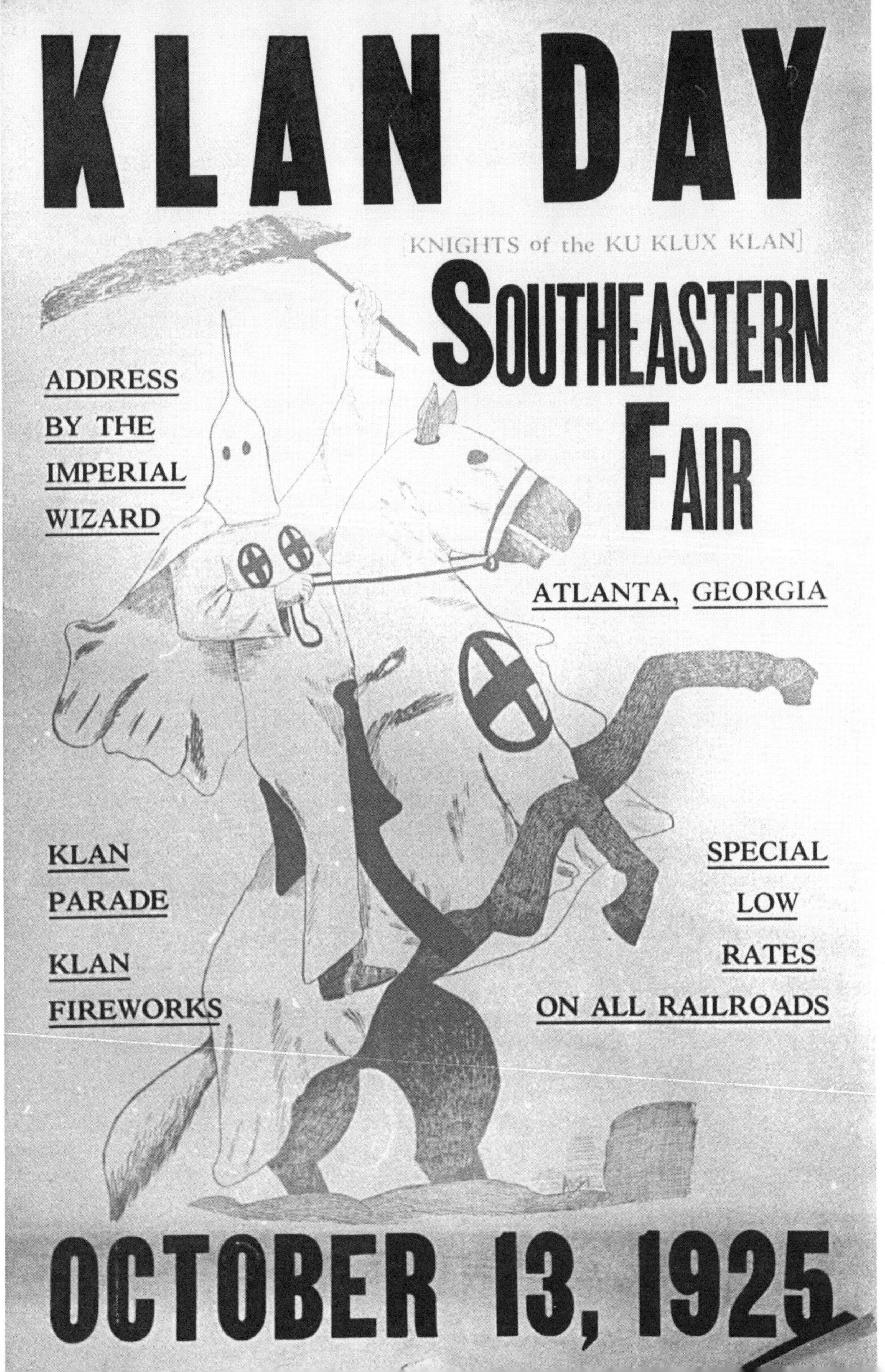
KLAN DAY
[KNIGHTS of the KU KLUX KLAN]
SOUTHEASTERN
FAIR
ADDRESS
BY THE
IMPERIAL
WIZARD
ATLANTA, GEORGIA
KLAN
PARADE
KLAN
FIREWORKS
SPECIAL
LOW
RATES
ON ALL RAILROADS
OCTOBER 13, 1925

"It was a charitable organization—supposed to be—brotherly love and strictly American, you know," recalls Sanders Ivey. "They didn't believe that Jewish or black people ought to be allowed to do business in America or anything of that nature." And, indeed, a far more repressive dimension of the Klan accompanied the charitable and fraternal activities.

The Klan made periodic forays into the black community, especially at times of social stress or rumored intimacy between blacks and whites. "They had a grocery store on the corner of Ashby and Hunter," relates teacher Pauline Minniefield of an incident from the 1920s, "and a colored man went in there to work and they didn't want him in there. And one night Ashby Street was loaded with the Ku Klux Klan marching with the sheets and everything else, just like a whole army. And it kind of frightened some of the colored people, because it was nice colored people."

"I remember on one occasion I had orders from police headquarters to be at Peachtree and Baker Street at eight o'clock that night to lead a Klan parade," states Chief Jenkins. "And there must have been fifty cars in the parade, and of course I knew many of the people in there, the drivers and the others, and they were in uniform. They wanted to parade down Peachtree Street by the Capitol, go down Capitol Avenue to Georgia Avenue, down Georgia Avenue to Fraser Street, which was right in the heart of the black community, and then come back through and disband. And the police escorted them and helped them through. And it was pure and simple an attempt to intimidate black people."

"Then they decided they would go down Auburn," remembers Pauline Minniefield of one of a number of Klan marches in the black commercial district, "because they opened up a nightclub there and the white fellows from Georgia Tech or other schools would go down there and dance or listen to the band. See, the whites loved to go to the Negroes' entertainment. So the Ku Kluxes decided to put fear in Auburn Avenue, which was wrong."

Yet, as barber Horace Sinclair describes another Klan parade down Auburn Avenue in the late 1930s, black Atlantans were not always intimidated by the Klan: "The boy's name I don't remember, but he was crippled, he walked like he had a short leg. He made this expression, 'I reckon I'd do almost anything to get me enough money to go to that dance tonight.' Well, Iron Pete, he heard him, said, 'What'd you say?' 'I'd do anything to get me enough money to go to that dance tonight.' 'Well, if you get me one of them hoods'—they were still passing through—'off one of them Ku Klux, we'll see that you go on up there in grand style.' And everybody laughed, nobody paid the boy any attention, they just thought that it was a statement being made. He toddled over out there and caught a Ku Klux by his hood, it was tied around his neck like a bonnet, and like to pulled him out of that jeep. But he got that hood. And the procession did not stop. He brought that hood back and dropped it on the sidewalk, said, 'Here it is.' And how much money he got I don't know, but I know he got somewhere about ten or fifteen dollars, because boys just kept throwing down half-dollars and dollars. And I didn't want to be in no riot because I was a little kid when the Riot of 1906 was here—I remember it very vividly. I got my hat and coat and caught the streetcar. See, I looked for the Ku Klux to go back and get their reinforcements and tear up Auburn. But nothing didn't happen. But I saw that."

In part because black Atlantans were already subordinated to second-class citizenship through Jim Crow, as enforced by the Police Department, the Klan sought other scapegoats as well, including Roman Catholics, labor organizers and radicals. In 1922, for example, the order used its influence to help prevent the rehiring of a Catholic schoolteacher of some twenty years' standing. In the height of the Depression the Klan rallied against the supporters of black Communist Angelo Herndon. And in 1938, Klansmen beat up a local labor organizer, as Harold Sheats describes: "There was a fellow named Toney, P. S. Toney, who was a CIO agitator for the Scottdale Mills. The members of the Stone Mountain Klan said to the East Point Ku Klux, 'We've got a fellow out here that's a troublemaker. He just stirs up all sorts of trouble. We wish you'd take care of him.' They went by the fellow's house. A Stone Mountain man went with them and pointed him out. And they got him in the car and brought him all the way to Ben Hill, a deserted spot over there, and turned him over a stump and flogged him, carried him back to the car line, gave him carfare, and turned him loose."

Far more common during the period were the Klan's vigilante-like attacks on people suspected of breaking Victorian moral codes. "If some man had a wife and two or three children," states Officer Rutherford, "and he come home drunk, usually some of the neighbors or somebody would see the Ku Klux and get them to straighten him out. They'd give you a whipping. I had a friend, a fellow I used to work with. I used to streetcar and he was my conductor. He had a boy about twenty-two or twenty-three years old, and he stayed drunk all the time, wouldn't work. And his daddy had worked every day. There used to be a beer parlor going toward West End they called The Stump. Well, this boy would go up there at night, and he'd get drunk, fighting around, get locked up. So one night he was up there drunk, and somebody went to his daddy's house

and told his daddy, 'You'd better go over there up yonder and get that son of yours.' So he walked up there. This boy jumped on his daddy and just beat the dickens out of him.

"I was working the beat up there on the evening watch and we got a call out at this boy's house one night. The Ku Klux had come in there that night, three carloads of them, and got this boy and took him off, kept him about an hour or two, and brought him back home. Well, we went in there to get the information, and he didn't want to tell us anything. And I says, 'Well, who was it?' He said, The Ku Klux Klan. 'What'd they do?' They beat the hell out of me. I said, 'For what?' He said, Because I whipped my daddy the other night and wouldn't work and staying drunk.

"I said, 'Where'd they take you?' He said, 'Somewhere in East Point. We went over in the woods they got out there and dug out the dirt and left a big round pile of clay shaped like a barrel. They got me out of the car and took me down to where this place was and told me to get my britches down. I didn't want to do it and wouldn't do it; they caught me and took them down anyway. Four of them held me, two of them held my hands on one side and two with the legs on the other side of that barrel-like piece of clay. This fellow took about a two-inch strap, heavy strap, and he give me ten licks.' And he had them welts from his butt on up to his back, just as red as everything, where they whipped him with that thing. He said, 'They told me, If you don't quit drinking, straighten up, go to work, we're coming back to see you. We ain't whipped you this time, we just give you a little medicine, what you can expect if you don't straighten up.'

"I seen his daddy two or three months after that. He says, 'I'm going to tell you something, but gosh don't never tell my wife or she'll quit me. You know when the Ku Klux Klan come down there and got Walter and whipped him? I had that done.' I says, 'You did? Your own son?' He says, 'I had to, Rutherford, he'd just gone to the dogs. I thought if anyone could straighten him out the Ku Klux Klan could.' "

Klan vigilantism eventually backfired on the organization, however, in March of 1940, when Ike Gaston, a white barber from East Point, died of exposure after being whipped with a long cleated belt. "Gaston was a drunkard and he beat his wife," alleges Harold Sheats. "And his father-in-law wrote a letter to the Klan and said, 'Ike is beating his wife, wish you'd attend to him.' East Point Klan turned the thing over to Oakland City, and an East Point man put the finger on Ike, and they went down there and got him when he closed up his

Ku Klux Klan pickets outside Atlanta Constitution, *1938. (Atlanta* Journal-Constitution*)*

barbershop, one cold night. And they carried him out somewhere on the west side and whipped him. Well, that started the whole thing."

Atlanta's newspapers finally took a strong anti-Klan stand after the Gaston affair, helping mobilize public sentiment against the order, and sparking a series of celebrated flogging trials. "Now, I represented a lot of those fellows," recalls Sheats. "Acquitted most of them, actually acquitted them. There was a man who was chief deputy clerk in the courthouse. He would meet with us over the weekend and give us the names of all of the jurors for the next week who belonged to the Klan. That's one reason we came out as well as we did."

Sheats maintains that the prosecutors in the flogging cases didn't understand the Klan's modus operandi of getting members of a neighboring lodge to do the dirty work: "Almost invariably they got the wrong man. They had the wrong theory. They would go into a community [where a flogging had taken place] and indict some local man. But they never did understand that the local crowd never had anything to do with it. They didn't have anything to do with it, they always turned it over to some foreigners.

"We won a good many of them absolute acquittal. Several of the men went to prison, served a little time. They were paroled as soon as [Eugene] Talmadge was governor. He took advantage of every opportunity to turn them loose, and did.

"And the thing that hurt the Klan in those trials—they burned the records. They burned the records. It is literally true that the rank and file of the Klan took the oath of secrecy seriously. They took it seriously. And when they started investigating the Gaston case they burned their records. If they had kept the records, the minutes of their meetings would have been so embarrassing to public officials that there never would have been anything to it."

One local politician who assuredly did *not* join the Klan was James L. Key, mayor of Atlanta from 1919 to 1923 and again from 1931 to 1937. Born in DeKalb County in 1867, Key graduated in 1888 from Emory College, then located in Oxford, Georgia. An attorney and occasional professor of Greek at Emory University, Key entered city politics in 1902 as an antimonopolist city councilman supporting municipal ownership of public utilities. In 1916 he defended Atlanta's streetcar men who struck against the Georgia Railway and Power Company. Two years later, Key was elected mayor, succeeding Coca-Cola magnate Asa G. Candler, who had taken a leading role in breaking the streetcar strike.

During his first two terms in office, Mayor Key waged a constant battle with the Georgia Railway and Power Company (now Georgia Power), opposing fare

Solicitor Daniel Duke confronting Governor Eugene Talmadge during Klan clemency hearing, 1941. (Atlanta Journal-Constitution*)*

increases, supporting the rival jitney services, and getting bills introduced in the state legislature to authorize the city's acquisition of the company. In addition, he supervised the motorization of the Fire Department in the aftermath of the 1917 fire, and oversaw such public works projects as the building of the Spring Street viaduct, extension of the city's water works and sewers, and the enlargement of Grady Hospital.

Mayor Key also vetoed a Klan-sponsored motion condemning the Knights of Columbus as an un-American order, and prohibited masked parades on city streets. He drew the support of Atlanta's black community for several other actions, helping attain a park and swimming pool for blacks on the west side and a branch library in the Fourth Ward. Dr. Homer Nash relates: "Negroes wasn't welcome in Carnegie Library downtown—they had such a hard time getting books. So he wanted to build a library on Auburn Avenue, which he did. He built a nice one. But he had a time getting that."

During Key's first term, black Atlantans played an important role in voting down two school bond issues. While black people led intensely political lives throughout the period, a cumulative poll tax (which of course also adversely affected poor whites), the Democratic white primary that barred blacks from voting where it counted, Georgia's county unit system which gave disproportionate electoral power to rural counties, widespread election fraud and voter intimidation, and the Disfranchisement Act of 1908—passed in the wake of Atlanta's murderous 1906 race riot—combined to leave only a few hundred black registered voters in Atlanta at the outbreak of World War I.

Although excluded from voting in the Democratic primary, black Atlantans could vote in special elections such as bond referenda, and whenever they had the opportunity did so. After receiving disproportionately small shares of school bond monies in 1902 and 1909, in 1919 Atlanta black citizens registered over 5,000 voters to twice defeat school bond issues. Dr. Nash recalls a mass meeting that he attended: "Bethel Church was the battleground. They came down here to talk to the black folks about this bond issue because the rich folks were not in favor of it, not enough of them to bring it about. And we were in there like sardines, just crowded, because we knew we needed a school. So they got up and told us about the need for schools and what this money would do and all that. We knew what this money could do if you could get it. And then, it came down to milking the coconut. We wanted to know, 'What are we going to get, what are the Negroes going to get?' 'Now, you sit down over there, you're throwing a monkey wrench into the machinery. You pass the bond issue and then we'll talk.' They had their little say and they left to go on to town.

Auburn Avenue branch library. (Atlanta University Collection, Woodruff Library, Atlanta University Center)

But that night they went down the ballot and, to everything on there, 'Smite it, smite it, smite it!' The next day they went out and didn't a thing pass. It was all defeated, everything on the bond issue."

When another school bond issue was proposed in 1921, black Atlantans sought to get city officials to guarantee educational improvements for the black community. Again, Bethel Church was the scene of an eleventh-hour mass meeting, as Dr. Nash recounts: "Of course the Negroes were very excited. To tell you the truth, they were angry because they'd been duped twice. And so they were buzzing in there, crowded and packed in there, and buzzing like a lot of bees. So when James L. Key got up to speak, he said, 'Wait and let us understand one another. If I, James L. Key, mayor of the city of Atlanta, have ever promised the colored people anything and didn't try to deliver it, stand on your feet and say so now.'" With crucial support from the black community the 1921 bond referendum passed, making possible the construction of four black elementary schools and Booker T. Washington High School, the first public high school for blacks in the Southeast.

Key was criticized for his racial stands by Klansman Walter A. Sims, who defeated Key for mayor in 1922 and again in 1924. "Walter Sims defeated him for mayor," claims Mrs. E. Graham McDonald, Key's daughter, "because he called him a nigger lover. The following time [in 1924], when they were both on the same rostrum, he'd speak of Mayor Sims as His Honor and then Sims would come up and say 'nigger lover,' you know. And there are certain types of people who would be affected by that. I just remember my mother coming home so indignant that this Mayor Sims had called him that on the stage, when my father spoke of him as His Honor."

There were other factors, too, that contributed to Key's losing office. He was accused of deficit spending and raising property taxes. In addition, he was hurt by a 1920 investigation of organized crime which uncovered a "bunko ring" with alleged ties to city law enforcement officials. Returning to his legal duties, Key was spared any fallout from a Fulton County Grand Jury investigation in 1929–30 that revealed widespread graft and corruption at City Hall. "There were charges of graft in the purchase of city goods," recalls Atlanta *Journal* city editor Hunter Bell. "I remember it was a Saturday night when the indictments were handed down. I knew the clerk of the court well and I called him up on Sunday. And I said to him, 'We sure would like to get the details on those indictments. It's in the public's convenience.' He said, 'Sure is. I'll go down to the courthouse and bring the indictments out to my home. You bring some fellows out here with typewriters and you can copy them.' And we set up those typewriters and copied the whole text of those indictments, which was the biggest scandal there was while I was in the paper."

In 1930 Key was elected mayor again, as a champion of honest government. The height of the Depression was not an easy time to reenter public office. Offending many of the city's more straitlaced citizens, Mayor Key introduced Sunday theater and baseball to Atlanta, with the proceeds going to municipal relief efforts. "He legalized Sunday baseball," recalls Mrs. McDonald, "and every dime of the profit went to those soup kitchens at the Auditorium and other places around town. He just adored baseball, and he thought it was much better for people to go to a ball game on Sunday afternoon than a lot of other things they could do, and besides help the soup line."

In addition, Key sought to retrench in a number of areas. "There was some work to be done at the airport," relates Herbert Jenkins, "but they didn't have the money to do it. So Mr. Key cancelled those contracts. And he favored a program that really reduced the number of employees and reduced the pay. Police pay at that time was $175 a month, which was good pay. But during the Depression he felt it was necessary to reduce it to $145 a month."

Key also backed a retroactive wage cut in 1932, which harmed city workers. Alec Dennis explains: "He cut some of the city employees from money that they had done drawed and spent. I was a foreman in the construction and I drew my envelope and I think I drawed seven dollars. I know I had two men in my crew still owed the city money. And there was a lot of people really owed the city when they drawed their envelope. And that just burned everybody up and they was going to recall Jim Key."

In addition to his problems with labor, Key got into political hot water shortly after coming into office in 1931. While on a trip to France, he became one of the first American big-city mayors to openly label Prohibition a failure. "Mr. Key got into such a controversy with that," remembers Herbert Jenkins, who served as the mayor's chauffeur from 1933 to 1937. "He was a steward and a Sunday school teacher in the Grace Methodist Church, one of the leading Methodist churches here. But after he came back from France and started advocating the repeal of the Prohibition law, that put him in conflict with the church, and the church made it very clear for him to stop teaching things that was contrary to their doctrine, or get out. Well, he got out, he quit teaching. But then he went downtown and opened up a nondenominational Sunday school in one of the downtown theaters, and he drew great crowds there for a good many years—Key's Sunday school class in downtown Atlanta."

"He got a great many people who were just here from the hotels," adds

Mrs. McDonald, "that he never would have gotten to come hear him at the church. They were just uptown and heard that he had a Bible class at the Roxy Theatre."

Prohibitionists, members of organized labor and others launched a campaign against Mayor Key in 1932, gathering thousands of signatures and forcing a recall election. Because it was a special election, once again black Atlantans were able to take part, and once again took advantage of the opportunity. "Why, down at City Hall, man," states Alec Dennis, "there was lines stretched. People wasn't thinking about that coming, you know, they hadn't been used to it. And that kept Jim Key in there, where if it hadn't been for the colored, they would have recalled him." And, indeed, Key's margin of victory in the recall election was less than the number of black citizens who registered to vote. "We were for him," states Homer Nash. "We went for him, six thousand of us went for him. The recall failed."

As Chief Jenkins relates, the 1932 recall election cemented Key's ties with the black community: "I was working out of the mayor's office as his chauffeur and security guard. Mr. Key was invited out to Friendship Baptist Church on Mitchell Street. Well, white people didn't attend black churches like that, and the mayor under no condition would have gone except under these conditions: he had friends there, and he thought he should go, and he wanted to go, and he went. And I went along with him and carried him. We drove up in front of the church and got out, and there was three or four of them that rushed over and met him like a long-lost brother. He greeted them most cordially and shook hands with them, and turned and introduced them to me. Well, that was the first time in my life that I ever shook hands with a black man. And I wouldn't have then except here I'm a rookie police officer guarding the mayor, and the mayor introduced me. I had no choice."

"For his day," Atlanta University professor Clarence Bacote sums up, "you would consider Key a liberal." And the mayor's courting the black vote during the 1932 recall election aroused antagonism among segments of the white community. "When he went and registered them to keep him from being recalled," remembers Alec Dennis, "that started the ball rolling with them. Well, it just give them a foothold to stay right on his neck from then on out." The mayor also drew opposition from other quarters, as he continued to seek austerity measures, cutting city salaries and the labor force in the process.

These factors helped bring on Key's defeat by former alderman and state legislator William B. Hartsfield in 1936. Hartsfield promised to balance the city budget without raising taxes or reducing salaries. But perhaps the major issue contributing to Key's electoral downfall was his advanced age and poor health, as his daughter recalls: "He was absolutely physically unable to run. But he was just sort of into it so much and didn't want to quit. He just didn't want to quit.

"During the week he went out of office, my husband and I went to New York. And when we came back—we stayed about eight or nine days—I couldn't believe the change in him. He had to be helped up and down the steps. It absolutely wrecked him. And he would not have been able to serve another full term. He went out of office the first of 1937 and he died at seventy-one in 1939."

Key's successor, William Berry Hartsfield, was one of Atlanta's most colorful, controversial and complicated politicians. Born the son of a tinsmith in 1890, Hartsfield lived most of his life in Grant Park, yet in time received the support of the city's northside power structure. Originally a segregationist who introduced Jim Crow legislation as an alderman, he eventually oversaw much of Atlanta's desegregation and coined the phrase "the city too busy to hate." With a brief hiatus at the outset of World War II, Hartsfield presided over Atlanta from 1937 to 1962, at the time longer than any other big-city American mayor.

Hartsfield dropped out of Boys' High School in his senior year to enter the Dixie Business College and become a secretary. Two of his early positions helped pave the way for Hartsfield's later association with Atlanta's business elite. At the Atlanta Ice and Coal Company, he worked for schoolmate Robert W. Woodruff, who took over the presidency of the Coca-Cola Company in 1923. He also served as a clerk in the law firm of former governor John M. Slaton, perhaps best known for his pardon of Leo Frank in 1915. "Hartsfield was pretty close to Slaton," states Harold Sheats, who in his capacity of Fulton County attorney had extensive dealings with the mayor. "He was a protégé of Governor Slaton. That helped him. Governor Slaton had the respect of the business community, Fulton Bag and Cotton Mill, all the insurance companies. He had the money behind him, and of course he was able to help Hartsfield get the support of the upper element of the people in Atlanta."

In 1918 Hartsfield passed the bar and in 1921 he opened his own office. The following year he began his political career, successfully running for the first of two three-year terms as alderman. In 1924 he began his long love affair with airplanes, becoming the chairman of City Council's newly formed Aviation Committee. In that capacity, he helped develop a primitive airport inside an old oval racetrack south of town owned by Coca-Cola founder Asa G. Candler. "At that time the Candler Field—it was called Candler Field—consisted of a dirt runway," recalls Harold Sheats, "a very crude affair with one or two old garages and maybe half a dozen World War I planes. And Hartsfield had the vision of Atlanta being an air center. He was far ahead of his time, he was ahead of nearly everybody in the United States on aviation."

Hartsfield played a key role in bringing the new federal airmail route through Atlanta, rather than Birmingham, Alabama. Taking a hands-on approach to local aviation, he also repaired planes, inspected hangars and landing strips, promoted the barnstormers selling rides out at Candler Field, and took part in an ill-fated venture that was to have been the first commercial flight from Atlanta to New York. Atlanta *Journal* reporter and later airline executive John Ottley recalls: "When Roscoe Turner, who was a noted speed flyer and quite a handsome, swashbuckling fellow, came to Atlanta in this old Sikorsky biplane to deliver as a promotional stunt some very fashionable dresses to Davison-Paxon-Stokes, he stayed around a few days. And I got to interview him, know him, become friendly with him. And due to the fact that he had to fly back to New York anyway with the plane, it occurred to me and other members of the Junior Chamber of Commerce aviation committee that it might just make something out of it that would be worthwhile and helpful to Roscoe Turner, Atlanta and everyone concerned.

"So we got up the idea of the first flight from Atlanta to New York with airmail and passengers. And among the passengers were Hartsfield, myself and several others. So we got the whole thing together and got a check for a million dollars from the Federal Reserve Bank of Atlanta as part of the mail to deliver to the Federal Reserve Bank in New York, and there were many receptions arranged along the way. It was a great publicity stunt.

"But it ended up in a farmer's backyard in Abbeville, South Carolina. We left here at five that morning, just barely got off, dropped a few feet at the end of the runway, but kept going. And water leaked out of the motor in the right engine. So Roscoe Turner circled around a little bit and finally found a place he thought he could get down in in a farmer's backyard. One wing was just barely in the leaves of an apple tree. Naturally, the farmer and his family were scared to death and they were standing in the back door when we got out of the plane. A Fox newsreel cameraman was the first one out and he went over and told the farmer, 'Don't be frightened. We just dropped in to pick a few apples.' And the farmer says, 'Sorry, mister, they ain't ripe yet.' I think the Lord was good to all of us, and particularly that Mayor Hartsfield was one of the passengers who came out of it alive."

Despite such mishaps, Hartsfield continued to make aviation a primary concern throughout his tenure as mayor, strongly supporting the expansion and construction of new municipal airports which opened in 1946 and 1961. And Atlanta's latest airport, finished in 1980 and one of the world's busiest, fittingly bears his name.

In addition to aviation, Hartsfield was closely identified with good government and fiscal responsibility. Also—like James Key—unscathed by the City Hall scandal of 1929–30, Hartsfield called for a cleanup of the Police Department during the 1936 mayoral campaign. Despite Key's budget-cutting measures, when Hartsfield took office the city was some $3 million in debt, nearly bankrupt and still paying its employees in scrip. In December 1936, Robert Woodruff announced that Coca-Cola would absorb that month's city payroll of $730,000. Hartsfield drew upon his ties with other prominent members in Atlanta's business community, too, to help put the city back on a more solid financial footing.

"He pretty much had a kitchen cabinet of businessmen who advised him," recalls Harold Sheats, who unsuccessfully ran against Hartsfield for the state legislature in 1931. "Frank Neeley [the president of Rich's]. A big influence on Hartsfield was Everett Millican. Everett was a mountain boy, was in City Council with Hartsfield, became the top man at Gulf Oil Company. He was one of his prime advisors. Bob Strickland, Trust Company Bank, he was a great builder for Atlanta. Bob Maddox, First National Bank. One of the vice-presidents of the Fulton National Bank was treasurer of the city of Atlanta. They had that type of a setup at one time. They had tremendous influence on Hartsfield."

During Hartsfield's first administration the city's budget system was revised so that the city could not budget more than 99 percent of the receipts of the previous year. Hartsfield also pushed for more efficient management by city department heads; declared that Fulton County should assume more of the burden for streets, hospitals and relief; and called for higher licensing fees for alcohol sales. By 1939 the city's budget was half a million dollars in the black, and its credit rating was high.

In the late forties and fifties, Hartsfield developed something of a reputation as a racial moderate who successfully steered Atlanta over the shoals of racial desegregation. But this was not always the case. In 1926, while alderman, he introduced an ordinance barring black barbers from cutting the hair of white people. In the 1936 mayoral campaign, he was called a tool of segregationist Governor Eugene Talmadge by James L. Key. In the early forties, Hartsfield wrote a letter to Martin Dies, chairman of the House Un-American Activities

Committee, calling for a federal investigation of the National Association for the Advancement of Colored People as a possible Communist front.

Around the same time, while attempting to gain support for the annexation of the then-adjacent community of Buckhead, he wrote a letter to several hundred white businessmen, stating, "The most important thing to remember cannot be published in the press or made the subject of public speeches. Our Negro population is growing by leaps and bounds. They stay right in the city limits and grow by taking more white territory inside Atlanta. Outmigration is good, white, home owning citizens. With the federal government insisting on political recognition of Negroes in local affairs, the time is not far distant when they will become a potent political force in Atlanta if our white citizens are just going to move out and give it to them. This is not intended to stir up race prejudice because all of us want to deal fairly with them, but do you want to hand them political control of Atlanta?"[5]

Hartsfield's letter was a recognition of the emerging political potency of black Atlantans in the 1940s. A variety of restrictive measures essentially disenfranchised blacks for most of the period between the world wars, except for such scattered incidents as the 1921 bond issue and the 1932 recall election. As businessman John Calhoun notes, a cumulative poll tax, in effect in Georgia longer than in any other Southern state, deterred many from entering the voter rolls: "It wasn't but two or three dollars a year, but if you went to register, you'd have to pay for all the years from the time you got to be twenty-one on down to the date. So that made it a burden for Negro voters."

Even if somebody paid the poll tax, the Democratic white primary effectively barred blacks from voting where it counted in an overwhelmingly one-party state like Georgia. Warren Cochrane, director of the Butler Street YMCA, explains: "Under the white primary you didn't have a chance. They claimed that the Democratic Party was like a private club, they could accept only who they wanted to. And therefore only people who were members could vote in the primary. They never accepted blacks. And so, if you can't get in the primary, of course, your vote doesn't mean a thing in the general election. You could vote in the general election, but since the primary was tantamount to election, your vote didn't make any difference. No point in voting."

As a consequence, much of the black political activity that did take place went through the limited channels of the Republican Party, the party of Lincoln. "And the Republican Party," states John Calhoun, "because of slavery and Emancipation and Reconstruction and all like that, didn't have influence in places like Georgia. Republicans didn't have no influence over local governments. You'd never see a Republican mayor or a councilman, or nothing. No, unh-unh."

One of the key black Republicans in the state was Benjamin Davis, Sr. A leader in the International Order of Odd Fellows lodge, Davis was editor of the weekly Atlanta *Independent,* published from 1903 to 1934. At one time Davis served as national G.O.P. committeeman for Georgia, and pushed for black representation on state Republican committees. "Benjamin Davis was a fearless man," says Calhoun. "He would attack anything that looked like discrimination or segregation. He was a fearless man, I never will forget."

Another black newspaper, the Atlanta *Daily World,* sponsored early voter registration efforts, as publisher C. A. Scott recalls: "The *World* is the first black business who had put on its application blanks 'Are you a registered voter?' I have encouraged some people to pay as much as fifty dollars in back poll tax. We were interested in people getting registered to vote."

Another important black Republican was John Wesley Dobbs. "Mr. Dobbs had a very colorful history," states Atlanta University historian Clarence Bacote, himself a key participant in black politics. "He was graduated from Morehouse College and went in the railway mail service, and then he left that to become Grand Master of the Masons. He built up the Masons to be a strong organization. Then he got interested in politics. In the 1930s, he organized the Atlanta Civic and Political League. And this was one of the earliest attempts to get ourselves organized. They would hold mass meetings to get blacks registered.

"Now around 1930–31, Mrs. John Hope, the wife of the president of Atlanta University, had thought of the necessity of starting a citizenship school that would provide our people with information concerning the obligations and duties of citizenship. And out of this grew the citizenship schools that were sponsored by the NAACP. They asked me to be the director, and we held these schools in the Butler Street YMCA. We didn't go into the technicalities of political behavior and so forth. We just wanted to teach them the ABCs of politics, that is, the structure of national, state and local government, the responsibilities of the officers of each, and what we had to do to get registered, explaining the steps in registration. We'd show the power of the Supreme Court and show them how important it was to register in order to vote for the president. It's the president who appoints the judges of the Supreme Court. It's the Supreme Court who tells us what the law of the land is.

"We would insist on them going down and getting registered, and they would show us the receipt. As an added feature, if a person were to attend the citizenship schools four times out of the six meetings, he would get a certificate. And at our commencement, we would have maybe 150 or 200 graduates. That was a great scene. We'd have a graduation ceremony and hand out those certificates. And people would take great pride in those certificates, they'd frame them just like people frame their diplomas."

Despite such efforts, by 1940 there were still no more than a few thousand black registered voters in Atlanta. Registration picked up somewhat during the war years. The war raised in high relief the contradiction between fighting for democracy abroad without democracy for blacks at home, and no doubt spurred some voter registration. More important, the long legal campaign the NAACP had launched to overthrow the white primary began to bear fruit. In March of 1944, the Supreme Court handed down a landmark decision in the Texas case of Smith v. Allright, outlawing the Democratic white primary on the grounds that it was not a private affair but rather a mechanism of the state, and therefore could not be racially exclusionary.

"That was Texas," states Clarence Bacote. "Georgia, on the other hand, said it didn't apply to her. This is the way that Southerners operated; always find a convenient way to circumvent the law. In fact, a few of us tried to vote in the July 4 [1944] primary, thinking that the case of Smith vs. Allright entitled us to that vote. And rumors circulated. Old Gene Talmadge said, 'If blacks attempt to vote, blood will run through the streets of Atlanta.' Well, it did put things in a very tense situation.

"Now on primary day, we had at that time, I suppose, close to 4,000 votes, 3,000 or 4,000. And we couldn't back down at the last minute. Those of us who had been talking loud and saying, 'We've got to vote,' couldn't back down.

"And on the fourth of July—that was a heck of a day to have a primary. You could have someone shooting a firecracker; you'd think they were shooting a gun at you. But we went over to this barbershop over on Bankhead to vote. I remember Colonel [Austin T.] Walden and Mr. E. M. Martin, the vice-president of the Atlanta Life Insurance Company, and a fellow named Hodges, who was the assistant editor of the Atlanta *World,* and I went to vote. Whites lived in this area, they were all lined up on the porches, looking down, seeing these Negroes drive up. *Life* magazine, the press had their photographers there to take a picture of these blacks who were attempting to vote.

"We went in there, and the clerk went through the motions of looking for our names. 'Your name's not on there, Mr. Walden. Your name's not on there,' talking to me, 'Your name's not on there,' talking to Hodges. The crowd by that time had surged all up against the windows. So we walked across the street. We got in my car, and about five minutes later I said, 'Let's drive back to see what has happened.' We drove back, there wasn't a person there. I'm just showing you the excitement created by the efforts on the part of a few blacks to vote."

Ever the practical politician, Mayor Hartsfield also took note of the Smith vs. Allright decision, as Herbert Jenkins remembers: "I was in his office and he picked up the paper. He said, 'Have you read this?' And I looked at it, and it was the case that came out of Texas where the Supreme Court said that the white primary is a practice that's unconstitutional, that you got to let blacks vote where it will count. I said, 'Oh yeah, I glanced at it.' He said, 'Well, you'd better go back and read it two or three times and digest all of it, because what the courts have done is give the black man in Atlanta the ballot. And for your information, the ballot is a front ticket for any-damn-wheres he wants to sit, if he knows how to use it. And Atlanta Negroes know how to use it.'"

Despite questions about the applicability of the Texas decision to Georgia, black voter registration continued to rise into early 1946, when another special election took place. "By this time we had around 7,000 people registered," remembers Clarence Bacote. "On February 12, 1946, we had a special election to succeed Congressman [Robert] Ramspeck [one of the original charter members of the Klan in 1915], and this election involved nineteen candidates. The man who was expected to get Congressman Ramspeck's seat was named [Thomas] Camp. We had extended an invitation for them to come out and talk to us at the YMCA. Of those nineteen candidates, five or six accepted our invitation. But the man who was expected to win, Camp, ignored our invitation.

"The one candidate that impressed us was Helen Mankin. She was a member of the legislature, she was from a very distinguished Georgia family, her attitude on the race question was fair, and she was willing to talk to us. She'd meet us at the YMCA under the cover of darkness. You couldn't afford to come out there in the open, that would have been the kiss of death for a candidate. And in the end we decided to support the woman—she was the only woman in the race.

"We made our announcement in a mass meeting at Wheat Street Baptist Church on February 11. And we made it at 11:15. Why did we make it at 11:15? The news had gone off—we didn't have TV then—the radio news had gone off. Consequently, they wouldn't be able to put it on the air. We didn't want to kill Mrs. Mankin. And right then it spread like wildfire: 'Vote for the woman.'

"For the first time since I don't know when, they had Negro clerks. Colonel Walden was the manager of the precinct at the E. R. Carter School on Ashby

Street, I and Dr. Miles Amos and Prudence Herndon were the clerks. I can always remember the count. There were 1,040 votes cast at that precinct, of which 1,039 were black. There were only 13 that were spoiled. Around eight o'clock—the polls closed at seven—eight that night we heard a banging on the school door, saying 'The election depends on the outcome of 3-B.' They were the reporters. 'Do you have any idea how this precinct voted?' We hadn't even started counting. We were hungry. We were understaffed as far as clerks were concerned. We didn't get through letting them vote until eight. We told them we didn't know any way to make this short.

"When they started counting the votes, in the first 50 ballots Mrs. Mankin had about 46 of the votes. And they immediately rushed to the phone: 'Mrs. Mankin is in,' because Camp came out there with a lead of 156 votes, and he needed to carry that precinct to get his victory. He didn't get it. Mrs. Mankin got 963 votes, and Camp, the man who ignored us, got about 8. At that time the black vote was recognized."

Six weeks later, a federal court ruled in the case of Primus King that the Georgia white primary was unconstitutional, paving the way for a massive black voter registration drive across the state, an effort also kindled by the gubernatorial race between Eugene Talmadge and James V. Carmichael. In Atlanta, black leaders formed a new umbrella organization, the All Citizens Registration Committee, and launched a highly successful campaign.

Campaign chairman Bacote describes the effort: "We put all of these organizations that had been conducting their individual registration campaigns under the auspices of the All Citizens Registration Committee, which was sponsored by the NAACP. The committee was directed largely by the Atlanta Urban League. Under Mrs. Grace Hamilton, the executive secretary, and Mr. Robert Thompson, the industrial secretary, they had the know-how in organizing the community. Bob Thompson discovered there were over 1,000 blocks in which we had blacks living. To make the thing a success you would need 1,000-some-odd block workers. We weren't quite that successful. We did have, at the peak of our effort, around 875 workers who would make weekly reports as to the progress that was being made.

"The YMCA was our headquarters. Everybody was activated. Walden and Dobbs stood out, but the preachers, the schools, the businessmen, Atlanta Life —very important. You'd be surprised at the number of business organizations that made contributions, putting out, paying for handbills. Atlanta Life would give us a lot of free printing and so forth. This was a community effort."

"Going door to door, sending taxicabs, paying for them, getting busses and

Leaders of 1946 voter registration drive, Big Bethel Church. (Courtesy Jacob Henderson Collection, Atlanta-Fulton Public Library)

Black voter registrants, Fulton County Courthouse, 1946. (Courtesy Jacob Henderson Collection, Atlanta-Fulton Public Library)

everything—that's what we had to do to get people registered," adds Butler Street Y director Warren Cochrane. Rejoins Reverend William Holmes Borders, pastor of the Wheat Street Baptist Church, "It was done by committees, by people talking, by preachers encouraging, by knocking on doors, even after dark. I personally hauled Negroes to the courthouse in busses that we had purchased for the use of the church nursery."

"This effort lasted for fifty-one days," states Clarence Bacote. "We were able to increase the registration of blacks in Fulton County from about 7,000 to 24,750. And that's when we were going to be recognized."

Paced by the Atlanta campaign, black voter registration in Georgia grew more than in any other Southern state, although many black voters were later purged from the rolls by the Talmadge organization. In Atlanta, the emergence of blacks as a significant political force had immediate consequences, one of the first being the desegregation of the city police force.

For decades, the police had been a major source of concern within the black community. Black Atlantans deeply resented ongoing police insensitivity, as reflected in one incident that happened to the family of teacher Estelle Clemmons: "I remember one night—we hadn't been living here too long—somebody tried to get in one of the windows on the bedroom side. And my mother and father heard this noise and they turned on the lights and the person ran. My father called the police. And, after a while, the police did come and asked my father didn't he have a gun. He told them, 'Yes.' And they said, 'Well, why didn't you just shoot him? Why would you waste time calling us?' No other kind of interest at all. They just got in their car and went on about their business."

"They didn't want to spend a lot of time on Fraser Street, where everybody was black," adds Herbert Jenkins. "They wouldn't go there except when they were called, and then they had no enthusiasm for what they was doing. They'd rather go patrol on Cherokee, where they were white, see." "Hell, if a Negro give a Negro hell, he'd just get dead anyway, what the hell's the damn difference," comments blues musician Buddy Moss, summing up the cynicism of many blacks toward the police. "It wouldn't have made no damn difference to them if you disturbed the whole neighborhood, just so you didn't bother Mr. Charlie."

"The white policeman wouldn't or couldn't or didn't go in there," declares Georgia Tech professor Glenn Rainey. "I can remember, I believe it was the president of Gammon Theological Seminary, a black man, who at one meeting said, 'The area around us is just hideous. There's no protection at all.'" And, according to publisher C. A. Scott, police indifference led to additional problems in combatting crime in black neighborhoods: "There was about 150 homicides every year, a lot of them blacks shooting blacks. They'd turn them loose, you know why? A lot of our people were so mad with the police they wouldn't cooperate and testify for them. And if you don't get convicting evidence, you can't convict people. The population as a whole was mad at the police, thought they were the enemy."

Police attitudes toward the black community often went beyond indifference. "I can remember," says white moonshine liquor hauler Forrest Turner, "when certain police would ride those districts at night, and maybe turn the corner. Maybe there'd be two blacks on the corner. 'All right, nigger, give me that corner.' And you'd better give it to him, or he'll take you." Echoes hotel worker and entertainment promoter B. B. Beamon, "Down in Vine City at night, police would come down there in a car and say, 'Nigger, give me that corner!' And we got to the place where we knew the police lights. We'd say 'Bright lights!' to let everybody know they were coming. So we'd run and take cover."

Atlanta policemen made use of vague, sweeping laws, like those having to do with idling and loitering, to control blacks and poor whites. As numerous people recall, they also employed an informal curfew, whereby black Atlantans on the street late at night had to present a work pass when stopped by policemen, or risk beating or imprisonment. "Shoot, boy, you'd better get off that street when midnight comes," recalls police officer Pete Rutherford. "It was the police law. Them police didn't allow them to walk the street or nothing after midnight, unless if he worked somewhere, say if he was a janitor in some building uptown and didn't get off until one or two or three o'clock in the morning. Well, where he worked, his boss had to give him a letter stating that he worked late at night. And he'd carry that letter all the time.

"You'd catch him down on the street and say, 'What you doing out?' Says, 'Just got off from work.' 'You got a permit from your boss?' 'Yessir.' He'd hand it to you, and you'd read it. But, if he didn't have nothing to show like that, you'd lock him up. The judges would fine him for it, being out that time of night, would say, 'You ought to be home in bed, you've got no business out,' which he didn't have."

"I was working in an uptown hotel in 1940," recalls B. B. Beamon. "We left out there at eleven o'clock, we had to get a pass from the back door man, verifying that we worked at the Henry Grady Hotel, that we got off at a certain time. You couldn't get a cab, so a lot of us walked home. And when the police stopped you, you had to show them your pass where you were coming from. They would pull upside, throw a light in your face, wonder, 'Where you going, nigger?' And if you stuttered a little bit, he'd be liable to put you in the car, whip your head, and do anything to you." "They knew if they didn't talk right," says policeman Stewart Peeples, "if they didn't act like they was supposed to and tell the truth, that they'd get the devil slapped out of them."

The local chapter of the Commission on Interracial Cooperation tried to monitor incidents of police brutality. In 1933, for instance, the commission reported thirty-one cases of brutality against black Atlanta citizens, twenty-two shot by police and seven severely beaten. The commission also followed the case of Earl Sands, a young black man beaten by the police in August 1940. The two policemen involved were brought to trial, one of the very rare times that happened during the period.

"I got in a little trouble one time," recalls George Robertson, one of the officers. "I got arrested for assault and battery. But the courts saw justice my way and I was exonerated. My partner and I were patrolling about one o'clock in the morning, and we saw this black man walking down the street. And, as was customary in those days, we called for him to come over to the car. And he ran. We didn't know what the boy had done, so we ran after him and caught him right in front of a big apartment house on West Peachtree Street. And he started hollering for somebody, calling for somebody to come out. And the manager of the apartment came and told us to take him away. And we had to scuffle with him, and he grabbed the chain that went around the lawn, the walk, and held onto that, and the chain broke. And we carried him chain and all to the car, and put him in. And I struck him a time or two with my open hand but I never used a blackjack on him.

"We carried the black man to the hospital and he was treated for a cut lip and transferred over to jail. And we tried him the next morning and he was found guilty of disorderly conduct and resisting arrest. And then a lawyer went over to Fulton County court and had a case made against me. I did have this trial before Judge Carpenter, lasted all day long. And in the end, I was exonerated. The judge said that he didn't believe the man had been mistreated, and if he ever had one in his neighborhood prowling around, he hoped the police would get him."

White bookkeeper Marian Doom, who along with her mother was an eyewitness to the same incident, remembers the event rather differently: "There was a little Negro man who was the janitor at the apartment across the street from us. We all knew him, he was just as nice as he could be. He had an apartment in the basement of the apartment. He also had a friend about a block and a half away who lived in one of these servants' houses, and he'd go down and visit him at night. And he'd gone to see this fellow, and these two young policemen saw him and grabbed him. They were just going to have fun with him. And the apartment had metal posts and chains between the posts, with the links about two inches in diameter. Well, they grabbed one chain off and they just beat him unmercifully—for nothing! He had not done a thing.

"And we heard him scream and I called the police before I realized it was the police beating him. They told me they'd get somebody out there sometime. And then I went out and saw it was the police beating him, and I went back in and called them again, and they just laughed at me. They wouldn't listen to me at all. He was badly beaten. And of course they beat him worse when we got over there and tried to help him, and that got to me, I think, worse than anything else.

"Mother had said she was going to court when this came up, and we couldn't even find when the case would come up. And finally she got a lawyer, I believe in the church, to find out for her when it was going to come up. And when she got down there, the two policemen were at the door, watching everybody going in the courtroom. And they told Mother that she'd never have police protection for any reason whatsoever. Mother said, 'We'll see about that,' and she walked in. And she stood up for him.

"After it happened, I called Wright Bryant, editor of the *Journal,* and he let us have it with both barrels, what was going on in the city that the papers couldn't even write about—because it wasn't Mr. Bryant who'd be hurt, it would be his reporters. And he had a responsibility there, so that it never was publicized. And unless we had known the Negroes involved as people, we wouldn't have known what was going on."

Such incidents led black community leaders to make the integration of the police force a top priority, even during the Key administration of the 1930s, as Herbert Jenkins recalls: "On this particular occasion, the mayor told me to be in his office at 2:30, and at 2:30 in come this group of people, about a dozen of them. They was really the black leaders in Atlanta. As I recall, there was only one white preacher in the group, all the balance of them was black. And they came in and requested the mayor of the city of Atlanta to employ Negro police. His reply to them was that their request was very reasonable, but it could not be done at this time, it would create impossible problems. 'Now, before you can do that, the white population as well as the black population must be educated to the point where they are supportive. You go back and educate your people and I'll help you with the white people, and when the time gets right, you come back and I'll authorize the employment of black police.'

"After they left, he said to me, 'I'm getting to be an old man. I'll never live to see Negro police in Atlanta. But unless I miss my guess, you being a young rookie, the day is coming when you're going to have to work with Negro police.' At the time, I thought the old man must be off his rocker, talking about employing black police officers. That was in '34."

With the emergence of black political clout in the forties, agitation for black police stepped up. "I guess it was about 1945 they organized a group on Auburn Avenue to promote the employment of Negro police," recalls Chief Jenkins, "and they marched single file. There must have been a thousand people in it. They come up Auburn Avenue to Courtland Street, right by the state Capitol, circled City Hall, and went back Courtland Street to Auburn Avenue. Just marching, that's all it was. And they carried signs: 'Employment to Negro Police.' That was the first public demonstration in Atlanta that I ever witnessed where they were demanding black police."

Black leaders also approached Mayor Hartsfield around the same time, to little avail at first. "I remember very distinctly," relates Reverend William Holmes Borders, "I, along with Warren Cochrane, John Wesley Dobbs, A. T. Walden, C. A. Scott, and M. L. King, Sr., going to Mayor Hartsfield and asking for black police. And he told us, without the slightest blinking of an eye, that we'd get black police in Atlanta about as soon as we'd get deacons in the First Baptist Church, white." "When we first went to him," adds Warren Cochrane, "he wouldn't even see us half the time. But finally we cornered him, and he said, 'When you get me ten thousand votes, I'll listen to you.'"

In the 1945 mayoral race, most of Atlanta's black voters cast their ballot for Hartsfield's opponent, Police Committee chairman G. Dan Bridges, in a protest over inactivity on the police issue. Accordingly, Hartsfield tended to dismiss the black vote at that time. "He turned around and told Dobbs he didn't owe him anything," says Atlanta University professor Samuel Nabritt. The 1946 voter registration drive changed everything, however. "We went back to Hartsfield," recalls Borders, "and asked him about these black police, and he asked, because of our voting strength, 'How many do you want?'"

Of course, it wasn't quite so simple. "We discussed it at great length," remembers Herbert Jenkins, who became chief in February 1947. "Mayor Hartsfield saw the handwriting, he knew what was happening, and he was in favor of it, but he was moving extremely cautiously. He was not bold about it, but he said, 'We've got to do it.'

"And again, the power structure, as I was reading the power structure—and that's the business people in Atlanta that had really run Atlanta for years—the

March for black police in front of City Hall. (Atlanta
Journal-Constitution)

real power structure was leaning in that direction. Mayor Hartsfield listened to them.

"We discussed it at great length—what could be done, what should be done, what ought to be done, and how it should be done. I would go back and say, 'Well, I need the authority, I don't have the authority.' So he had Alderman Ralph Huie introduce a resolution authorizing the Police Department to employ eight black police officers, and they referred that to the Police Committee. And the Police Committee called for a public hearing.

"That was one of the wildest meetings I think I ever attended, because the Ku Klux Klan and their friends were there, and they had some respectable people, as I recall. Walter Sims, the former mayor of Atlanta, appeared before the committee and made a public statement condemning the whole thing. And the commissioner of agriculture for the state of Georgia, Tom Linder, he appeared. That was two prominent public officials, or former public officials, that appeared on the record opposing and condemning this whole thing."

"I went down there and spoke for the black police," remembers Reverend Martin Luther King, Sr., "and they hissed me, the whites, 'No! Sit him down! No!' I just picked up my voice over it and went on and spoke and said what I had to say. And they say it helped, I don't know. But we got them. I know that."

"There were some members of the Aldermanic Board," states Chief Jenkins, "that said they would not vote on it until they had a positive recommendation from the chief of police. And of course Hartsfield was in the background, coaching everybody all along, guiding the thing politically, until he wanted me to write a letter. And I was very careful in writing the letter.

"I wrote the Board of Alderman, 'At your request, I have studied the proposition of employing Negro police in Atlanta. I've come to the conclusion that there is a very definite place in law enforcement for the Negro police, and to improve police generally in the city I think it is necessary to move in this direction. I therefore indicate my favorable recommendation. I affix my signature to this resolution with the following stipulations: that they not be permitted to exercise police authority except over people of their own race; they not be given permanent civil service status until their success has been proven; that we have a committee in the Police Department to go to Miami and Chicago and study their operations, and from that devise a system. With these stipulations, I recommend it and approve it.'"

There were other steps taken, too, before the first black policemen began work. "We run them though the personnel process," states Chief Jenkins. "I interviewed every one of them personally to see what their attitude was, to make the thing run smoothly. And strangely enough, that was the first group that I ever employed that all of them had had some college training, mostly at Morehouse." In addition, a separate black precinct was set up at the Butler Street YMCA, under the supervision of Warren Cochrane. "I had to cut a door in there," recalls Cochrane. "We wouldn't subject them to the dangers of being mixed down there [at police headquarters]. It would have been impossible in those days, because they would have nothing but fights and everything if they were mixed with the whites."

"We were not welcome at the police station," adds O. R. McKibbons, one of the first black officers. "We not only were not welcome at the police station, we could not wear our uniforms home."

The novelty of blacks on the police force drew many spectators when the first eight black policemen hit the streets in April 1948. "The streets were lined with hundreds or thousands of people everywhere we went," recalls Officer McKibbons. "As we walked along our beats, we had hundreds of people following us, watching our every move to see what we would do in any given situation." "The first time these black police came out on the street in their uniforms from the Butler Y," adds Borders, "Negroes popped out of the ground. Some of them sang, 'Thank God Almighty, I'm free at last.' It was so important to them that they felt that the Kingdom of God had come in this one achievement. Those police did a good job."

The hiring of the first black police helped inaugurate an "Atlanta style" of politics that lasted for a generation. Acutely aware and protective of the city's image, Mayor Hartsfield and his advisors sought to minimize conflict in Atlanta through an approach that was both pragmatic and symbolic in nature, with the mayor personally taking a commanding role in desegregation matters. The recipient of a huge black majority in the 1949 mayoral race, Hartsfield was the first beneficiary of a coalition between blacks and north side whites that ruled the city for years.

While black voters never made up a majority of the city's electorate until the 1970s, especially after the formation of the Atlanta Negro Voters League in 1949, consolidating black Democrats and Republicans, they continued to be a significant force in municipal politics and paved the way for the 1973 election of Atlanta's first black mayor, Maynard H. Jackson, the grandson of former activist John Wesley Dobbs.

"Our job was to keep the rabble-rousers out," sums up Butler Street YMCA director Warren Cochrane. "Well, we played that role and kept this city quiet for twenty years."

John Calhoun

Born in 1900, John Calhoun worked for the Cornelius King realty firm on Auburn Avenue and for the Atlanta Daily World. *A staunch Republican, Calhoun soon became involved in black political activity. He was president of the local* NAACP *in the 1950s and a member of City Council in the 1970s.*

I was born and reared in Greenville, South Carolina. I came to Atlanta in 1934. I finished school at Hampton Institute in Hampton, Virginia, in 1922. And before I got out of school, I got a job at Tuskegee as a male secretary and bookkeeper. I worked there at the school for a year, and had taken an examination at the government hospital, the veterans hospital, and was the only person who passed the examination. And I took a white man's job there, and that got me in trouble. And that was my first experience, my first trouble with civil rights, because I kept the job and the white people in the area objected. The Ku Klux Klan objected to it, but I kept the job anyway.

I worked there from 1923 on up to 1930, when I went to Chicago, stayed there a little over a year. I was very much carried away with the political organization Negroes had in Chicago. They had block leaders, a leader for every block where black folks lived, and precinct leaders for every precinct that Negroes lived in and ward leaders for every ward.

Then I went to Birmingham and stayed a little over a year. And that was when I met W. A. Scott, while I was in Birmingham. He was operating a chain of newspapers, some that he owned and some of them he printed for other people. And the Birmingham *World* was one of the papers he owned, the Birmingham *World,* the Memphis *World,* the Atlanta *World,* and I think the Montgomery *World* for a while he owned. He had a unique way of distributing his papers. He would have these four chain papers, plus some thirty-five other newspapers he used to print for that he would simply bill the editor and the manager for the papers and send them C.O.D. to wherever the paper was located. He wouldn't run up any bills with you. He would send them C.O.D., they'd come by baggage, and you had to pay for them to get them out.

The insurance company who I was working for, National Benefit Life Insurance Company, and had come there from Chicago to work for, went out of business. And I went to work as manager of the Birmingham *World* and worked there for several months, and he finally asked me to come to Atlanta to work with him in the circulation department.

So I came on here to Atlanta to work, just a week before W.A. was killed. And I met him on that Friday, I think it was, before he was killed, and he and I talked. He suggested that I come down with him Tuesday, because he would be tied up Monday, and Monday night he was shot. And he stayed in the hospital nearly a week and he died.

And it was an interesting incident when W.A. and I were talking. I remember we were sitting in the car in front of the *World*. He carried me over to his house and back, and he said he was going out of the newspaper business. And I said, "Oh, W.A., why are you going out of the newspaper business?" He said, "I'm going into the real estate business." I asked him, "Well, who's going to run the newspaper?" He said, "C.A. can run it." Now remember, this was 1934. I said, "You know, we got the Depression on and the real estate market is shot." He said, "It's coming back, it's coming back. Don't worry about it."

He had three contracts. One was to buy lots on Hunter Street, Martin Luther King Drive now, all the way from Washington High School out to Mozley Park, on both sides of the street. He had a second contract to buy all the land between the back of the lots on Mozley Drive over to Simpson Street. And then his third contract was to buy the Odd Fellows Building, that's the block [on Auburn Avenue] where Ben Davis built the Odd Fellows Building. That's the kind of man that W. A. Scott was. And of course his murder knocked all that out.

Negroes weren't in politics, not in politics. They didn't bother too much about politics. They couldn't participate in the Democratic Party, because they had what they called the white primary, you see. And the white primary would not accept Negroes to vote in it. It wasn't until 1945 when a federal judge handed down a decision outlawing the white primary, said it was unconstitutional. So in 1946, registration and voting started, then that was when Negroes began to get active in politics. But before that, it was just a matter of being a Republican and going to vote for the president once every four years. You didn't vote in the local election at all.

J. W. Dobbs, who retired from the postal service somewhere about 1935 or

'36, used to come in our office, Mr. King's office, to pay rent. And he would say, "Mr. Calhoun, there's two things I'm going to do when I retire from the postal service. I'm going to rebuild the Masonic Order"—because he was also the Grand Master of the Masons—"and I'm going organize our people to register and vote." And he came out and did both of these.

He organized the Atlanta Civic and Political League. Ben Davis was one of his cohorts because Ben was a Republican. And Bill Shaw, who was Ben's secretary, was a Republican. They organized the Atlanta Civic and Political League. And one of their first jobs they would do was to get Negroes registered to vote. There weren't but about, oh, something like a thousand Negroes registered all over Fulton County. So, by 1945 they had registered something like 5,000 voters in Fulton County.

Here's the way they did it. There was a man named Johnson, a white man, who was the tax receiver for Fulton County. And down there at the courthouse he had a big desk out in the hall. White folks went inside to rate their tax returns, but Negroes had a big desk as high (you know, where a man could stand up to and work), where old man Johnson had all those books that the Negroes' property was listed in. So he had heard about Mr. Dobbs, and Mr. Dobbs would go down there running his mouth and all. He said, "Dobbs, you talking about [the] poll tax and registering to vote. Say, do you know those books over there, those books have ten thousand Negroes' names in there, who are already paying poll tax? Because when you pay your property tax, you have to pay your poll tax. So their poll tax is already paid." He said, "If you'll send somebody down here, I'll let him copy all those names and addresses."

So Mr. Dobbs got us, I think we paid three hundred dollars to get two lawyers to go down there and copy those names on cards. We got those things back, and we classified those cards according to street addresses, and got ward leaders to go out and organize those blocks where those people lived. That's the way we worked on that thing for about five years, getting those Negroes registered.

In the meantime, we used the type of organization that I had seen in Chicago. During World War II we used that same system to organize wardens, air raid wardens, you see. There were sections and then they'd have block leaders and so forth. And we used the same people who were block leaders and ward sectional leaders in the Civilian Defense program that we used in politics. And that's the way we got Negroes out to register.

So 1945 came around. Mr. Hartsfield was the mayor. There was a man in City Council named Bridges. And police brutality was very rampant in the city of Atlanta and Bridges had promised to do away with it. That appealed to Negroes. So we [said], "We got five thousand Negroes registered." Now that's a good block of votes, at that time. And so, both sides were interested in getting that vote.

We had to decide who we were going to support with our little organization. We had several meetings on it. But I remember the last meeting we had. We passed out ballots. And these were the leaders, you know, doing this. We voted that day by secret ballot and we voted to support Bridges. The thing that caused us to vote for Bridges was that Mr. J. P. Whittaker, who was the secretary of Mutual Federal, had made a loan on a house to [a man] out on the corner of Mozley Drive and Chappell Street, and they were building this house. And Hartsfield gave the Klan a permit to parade by this house. So, when Whittaker told us that, we decided to vote for Bridges, because we were already mad with Hartsfield about his police brutality.

That Monday night we called a meeting at Bethel Church. That's where most of the political meetings were held, in Bethel Church. And in the meantime, one of the aldermen called. He was Hartsfield's campaign manager and he called me, and he said, "Now look, John. Don't you let them endorse either candidate tonight." I said, "Why?" He said, "Because if you endorse Hartsfield, the *Journal* is going to smear it. If you endorse Bridges, the *Constitution* is going to smear it." Anyway, we got in a car and rode all around the neighborhood, four or five of us, discussing on what we could do. So we decided we wouldn't endorse that night, because the election wasn't until Wednesday. [We said,] "We won't endorse tonight. We'll come back tomorrow night, and then they won't have time to smear either one of them." So that's what we did. Mr. Dobbs got up there and asked—the church was packed with people— and asked those people to come back on Tuesday night, which they did. They came back Tuesday night, and they announced that they were going to support Bridges. Okay.

The next morning it rained. People were slow about getting out to vote. About twelve o'clock the sun came out. The *Journal* came out, too. And the *Journal* smeared Bridges. In other words, they wrote that Negroes are going to endorse Bridges. Those crackers turned out there and beat us to death that day. They beat us.

Well, that was kind of a setback to us. But we didn't stop, we kept going. The Primus King decision came down in 1946, so that gave us more impetus to register Negroes to vote. We set up this Atlanta Negro Voters League, and to have both parties represented. Dobbs and [A. T.] Walden were named cochairmen, because Dobbs was a Republican and Walden was a Democrat. Hartsfield heard about it and came down to get our help. So we called the executive committee and we decided we were going to back Hartsfield [for mayor in 1949]. And the League helped elect Hartsfield, and then [Ivan] Allen. And that's the history of it.

Chapter Eleven

World War II

World War II had a considerable impact upon Atlanta. As soldiers poured into the city and Atlantans experienced rationing and blackouts, defense plants boomed and horizons expanded. In many areas, including politics, economic development and race relations, the war years marked a watershed for the city. "It changed a good deal," remarks bookkeeper Marian Doom. "It was just a sleepy little old town, really, before World War II." "The city began to grow," says teacher Evelyn Witherspoon. Adds businessman Duncan Peek, "Well, World War II just carried things to a whole other plane."

The war first really touched Atlanta in 1938, when a small group of Jewish refugees from the Nazis began arriving in the city. "I came to Atlanta in 1939," relates German immigrant Jack Gay. "At the time it was very difficult to come to this country. I was lucky, I had relatives in Quincy, Florida. An uncle of mine had married an American girl and became an American citizen.

"He provided us with the affidavit so that I could come to this country. If you wanted relatives to immigrate into this country, you would provide them with an affidavit of support, which actually means that you, the American, guarantee that this person will not be a burden on the state. After you got your affidavit, you had to wait for a long time to get your immigration visa. Even in spite of the fact that the Jews in Germany were being mistreated and killed, America still did not come forward and permit just anybody to come over here. There was a certain quota. They would only permit a few thousand people to enter this country every year from Germany.

"I went to Bainbridge, Georgia, and I stayed there for a few months, and then I went to Atlanta because it was the nearest larger city. I took a furnished room on Capitol Avenue, and there were other immigrants there. My first job was eleven dollars a week, which was the minimum wage which had just recently begun—twenty-five cents an hour, forty-four hours a week. There was a lot of help available for whoever needed it. There were a number of organizations that helped people with the language, that helped people find jobs, helped people find places to live."

"We had committees," recalls Josephine Heyman, "the Service for the Foreign-Born Committee and the Council of Jewish Women and the Atlanta Federation for Jewish Welfare worked together. We would find apartments, we would get furniture, we would stock the refrigerators. And then my particular interest was in helping them to learn English. We employed a teacher who would meet with them, and a group of us started a modern English class with the ladies. Then we started what we called a Tuesday night discussion group where we got together. I guess there must have been seventy or eighty people that belonged to this group. We had different people who knew about some phase of life in America come and discuss things with us. Then we would have questions and answers. And this group went on for a number of years.

"When the Second World War started, which was early 1942 [late 1941], we had a great problem. See, they were enemy aliens. Now, Hitler was their enemy before he was our enemy. Many of their families had perished in concentration camps. But nevertheless legally, technically, they were enemy aliens. Known enemy aliens could not gather in groups of more than three. Well, here we had fifty of them once a week together. And my husband went up with a couple of other men to see the people in charge here and to explain the whole situation, and we were given special permission to meet.

"And the interesting thing," says Josephine Heyman, "so many of the newcomers could not understand the racial situation in Atlanta. When they got on streetcars and would see the signs, 'Colored people from the back forward,' 'White people from the front backward,' they were so distressed. They said, 'This is like Hitler.' They couldn't understand it. We did say to them, 'Now, look, there's a big difference between sitting in the back of a streetcar and being led to a gas chamber.' And they said, yes, of course they did, but they thought that was the beginning, that was the way things got started. I think gradually they began to understand, but it took quite some doing for them to understand, just as they had to get used to all sorts of foreign things."

After the United States formally entered the war on December 8, 1941, another immigrant group suffered. Sam Laird, then a seminary student at Emory University, recounts: "We had a Japanese student who was in the School of Theology, and he was arrested by the FBI. Being a Christian minister, he was over here getting his Bachelor of Divinity training. He actually was caught here, because of Pearl Harbor, and they wouldn't let him go back home. They just arrested him.

"He was paroled, I suppose you'd call it, to the dean of our School of Theology. He was not permitted to go and come like he wanted to. But he was free to walk the campus, and did so. The dean became responsible for him, because he had recruited him and knew him very well, very intimately, and so knew that he was not violently anti-American and certainly was not a spy. The danger to the community was that everybody thought he might be a spy. If you remember, during World War II we had these Japanese-Americans who were actually dislocated."

"We lost a Jap from here," relates Marian Doom. "He had one of the best lunchrooms, eating places in the city of Atlanta. And because he was Japanese-born he was taken to a camp out in California, and he lost his mind. He'd lived here for forty-odd years, and he'd been an American all that time. People who had eaten with him for years did their best to get him out, and they couldn't. But he just lost his mind over it. I never understood why that was done."

Soon, young men from all walks of life were drafted wholesale into the service. "They was carrying them off," states domestic worker Ruby Owens. "It's the Auditorium where they met at that day, on Courtland Street. They had them in there, lined up to go." "My husband ended up with the 93rd, in the South Pacific," recounts nurse Ruby Baker. "That was an all-black infantry division. They did that to try to keep from integrating too much in the white man's army. Now, you wouldn't believe that, as recently as that was." And indeed, the United States armed forces remained segregated until the Korean War.

"When we went to war," recalls Atlanta *Constitution* society reporter Yolande Gwin, "it was a very lean year for society, because so many men from Atlanta went over, you know. The debutante clubs of that year called off all their large parties because of that." Campus life changed, too. "The student body changed completely," remembers Sam Laird. "We only had a few hundred civilian students at that time. Till the war actually came to an end we had a very small civilian population. Most of our students were involved in the old V-12 program, some Naval Marines. It was a kind of a program to help colleges to train young eighteen-year-olds for a while. You took two or three quarters' work. In addition, you took some naval and marine strategy and history and [they] began to indoctrinate you or educate you in naval affairs."

"I was teaching at Georgia Tech," recalls John Griffin, "and we had on our campus a naval V-12 program. And we also had Marine Corps student units, ASTP, which was an Army unit, Army Specialized Training Program. These students were under military regulations. They lived in the dormitories, and they had to have formations twice a day, and they even marched to class. I remember one group of students who were marching to class there, and they passed the commandant's office and they were singing 'Marching Through Georgia.' The commandant at that time was a Southerner, and he took a dim view of the song they were singing as they marched by his window. These were kids from all over the country."

The military men on campus were by no means the only GI's in town. Due in part to the climate and in part to the influence of Southern congressmen, the South provided much of the nation's military training. And thousands of soldiers passed through Atlanta. "See, this was a transportation center," explains policeman Stewart Peeples, "and they'd just have stopovers on the train and be in hotels and all. It was a good place to spend a leave. Atlanta was a mecca for the soldiers."

To some Atlantans, like businesswoman Mamie Kimball, having soldiers in town from all over the country, speaking in non-Southern accents, was more like the Tower of Babel: "They would come to Atlanta perhaps on a three-day pass over the weekend. And if you went to the old Henry Grady [Hotel] to the Dogwood Room for lunch or for an evening, you would hear utterances and sounds of all types of language, [so] that you didn't even know whether they were saying, 'Hello, we like Atlanta,' or whether they was telling you they didn't like Atlanta. But that was the kind of beginning, I think, of bringing in an international flavor and atmosphere to Atlanta."

"There were a whole lot of them here on the weekends," states Marian Doom. "But except for weekends you didn't see them, because they were in training." "The weekends I'd say were exciting," adds Lucile Scott of the Atlanta *Daily World,* "because these soldiers would come up and they would spend their money and take the ladies to the various clubs and things. And some people trying to live every day to the fullest, because they did not know whether they would get back."

"The town was flooded with soldiers," echoes Ruby Baker, "because of Fort McPherson out there and Fort Benning [in Columbus, Georgia]. Fort McPherson was mostly all-white. Most of the blacks were at Fort Benning. That's where they had the induction center. My brother and my husband's brother were weekday soldiers, five-day-a-week soldiers. They were home every weekend. They worked in that induction center down there. But, now, my brother-in-law said that between here and Columbus they would stop at service stations sometimes to fill the tank, and they would get all kinds of remarks: 'Now, don't you niggers think when this war is over you're going to walk around here in uniforms,' and 'We don't want you killing no white folks while you're in the Army,' all those kinds of things."

Once in Atlanta, the soldiers were greeted with open arms—although on a segregated basis. Nell Blackshear helped open the first U.S.O. for black soldiers: "We had a black entrance and a white entrance there at the Terminal Station, and the whites would go in the white entrance and the black soldiers would come into the black entrance. They would say, 'What can we do? We have about eight or ten hours here.' There were white U.S.O's and black U.S.O.'s, you know. The black soldier did not go in the white U.S.O. Would you believe it? The white worker in the white waiting room directed her soldiers to the white YMCA."

"They had dances at the Georgian Terrace," recalls Yolande Gwin, speaking of the white soldiers, "and so many of the Atlanta girls would go down. And they had a woman that planned the parties, and she had a select group of Atlanta girls that would dance with the soldiers. And those dances were awfully nice.

"There were several canteens around town. There was one out at Buckhead. But I worked mostly at the one downtown, in the building that's across the street from Davison's [now Macy's], upstairs over the S & W Cafeteria. A lot of my friends went down, and we'd go there and have a good time. We served coffee and doughnuts on Sunday nights to the soldiers that would come in. And they had bridge games going and things like that. It was a lot of fun. I enjoyed that. I made some real good friends among those soldiers."

Similar programs went on for the black soldiers in town. "When they came into the Terminal Station," recalls Nell Blackshear, "they would have a black Traveler's Aid worker there. They would say, 'We've got so many hours to see Atlanta.' And we had volunteers who would drive them down to the Butler Street YMCA where we were ready to do something in the line of entertainment. They had all the facilities of playing basketball or swimming in the Y. They could play Ping-Pong. And then we had the ladies come in for dancing. They would allow them to turn the record player on and they could dance in the gym.

"Or we would direct them to other places of entertainment. Auburn Avenue was the hub of things. There was Ma Sutton's restaurant where they could go to eat, or the Segalian Club that they could go up to. That was a nightclub, it later became the Royal Peacock. We would tell them, 'This is Sweet Auburn, where you can find anything you want.'

Playing checkers at the black U.S.O., 1944. (Special Collections, Georgia State University)

"And a lot of the older women invited them to share their services, if they were in town over the weekend, to come to church. Just those little things trying to help those boys who were taken from their home and going to camp to be trained to be soldiers. There were so many volunteer women. It was the most beautiful response that you could ever ask of a city."

As the war effort expanded and Atlanta's reputation as a haven for soldiers grew, the Butler Street facility soon became overburdened. Nell Blackshear recounts: "It was getting so crowded in the YMCA to where the boys it was created for were being pushed out. It got so loaded there with soldiers till we decided we would have to have a U.S.O. unit, and this was set up at Washington High School. It was the gym, and this provided a lot of space for them. And there were more workers, there was space for volunteer workers."

Although the Army was segregated, black and white soldiers sometimes did accompany each other into town. As Blackshear relates, this was typically when they hailed from outside the region: "When they came from the North it was real cute. They traveled together going to a camp. Now, when they got to the camp they went to their area and the black went to his area, but as they were traveling they would come down [together]. I've had many times a black and a white soldier come in. He'd say, 'He was my classmate,' and introduce me. He'd say, 'We want some lunch, Miss Blackshear,' and I sent them up the street to Ma Sutton's. Ma Sutton welcomed the white soldier just like she did the black one. Now, unless the white MP [Military Police] was around or something, the black MP would let him go on in there if he wanted to and eat with his friend. They had black MP's.

"But now by the same token the black soldier could not go with the white soldier downtown and eat in a white place. Fighting for the same country, but being definitely separate."

"That was before this integration stuff come," remarks policeman Peeples, "and they knew their place. If a colored soldier come over here, the most of his time was spent over on Auburn Avenue. They had a good place to go, they had good recreation over there. They had nightclubs and everything over there."

"There was always an MP around those nightclubs," remembers Nell Blackshear. "Now, you know, you cannot say it was a utopia, that there were not drunk soldiers sometimes who got a little out of line, but the MP's kept them pretty well disciplined. You could walk through a group of soldiers without them hitting you or pinching you. No soldiers did that. He was there for an evening of fun and when he got drunk the MP saw to them getting back to wherever they were to be billeted."

Bell Aircraft workers. (Courtesy Atlanta Historical Society)

"I'd have those MP's down with me on Luckie Street," adds Stewart Peeples. "Boy, they'd straighten up when them MP's come by. And I had one particular MP, had a hand as big as a ham. He'd cold-cock a drunk soldier. He'd cold-cock one of them if they gave him any lip. It never was too bad. They could enjoy themselves within reason in Atlanta. They got pretty well the freedom of the city as long as they acted halfway all right. I think the only thing the police and the soldiers had anything about, I think at one time they had to tighten down on the women."

And, indeed, during the war Atlanta experienced a venereal disease problem of near-epidemic proportions. "There were strong charges that venereal disease was really crippling the war program," states Herbert Jenkins, who became police chief in 1947, "because soldiers would go on leave and then come back infected with gonorrhea or syphilis. Then it put him out of commission. And as a result there was a strict enforcement of sexual activities.

"It was unlawful for a man and woman to be in a room together with the door closed that were not married and even have his shirt off, partly undressed. If they were in a room together and were not married and there was a complaint, you had any reason to inquire, then that was sufficient grounds to take them into custody. The regulation was violating more civil rights than would be tolerated today, but under the emergency laws of a country at war they insisted on that. They set up special squads in the Police Department, and they raided place after place."

"You'd go downtown to all the hotels," recalls policeman J. T. Bowen, "and you'd just almost catch the register and tell a fictitious registration. That was Friday night and Saturday night and Sunday night. There was lots of arrests made in those days."

"I learned very quick that all the suffering and casualties were not on the battlefield," says Herbert Jenkins. "I run across some real sad cases, where a young couple was in love and maybe married and maybe wasn't married. And he'd be in training or he was in the Army, he was fixing to go overseas, so forth and so on, and would get a 72-hours pass. He'd call her and tell her to meet him in Atlanta. And they'd have a falling out or there would be some delay, and she'd arrive here and he didn't meet her, for various reasons. But then she was in such a bad state of mind, and under the conditions she was real vulnerable. And she made friends with some soldiers, and they'd go on to the hotel.

"Then we'd get a call from the clerk there. They'd call and tell us that people had just gone in the room. You go up and knock on the door. You find that they were in there, and under the interpretation of the law that was being enforced

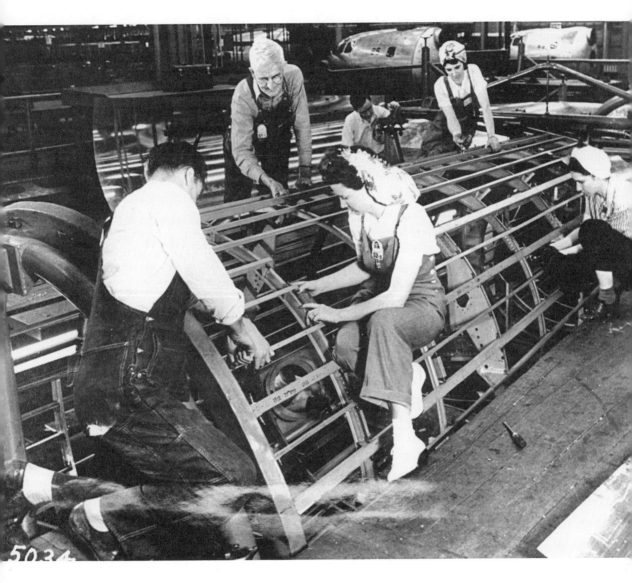

Workers at Bell Aircraft. (Courtesy Atlanta Historical Society)

you had no choice but to put them both in jail. And they couldn't make bond, had to stay until they were tested."

"The bond was eleven hundred dollars," remembers J. T. Bowen. "A thousand dollars for the examination and a hundred dollars for being in the room. When they sent them over to Grady Hospital to have them examined and the test come back, then that thousand dollars would be dropped. Now, if they was infected, they couldn't get out." "Then you had to send them out to be treated," adds Jenkins, "and still couldn't make bond, see. They later modified that a little bit and let them make bond. And if they were infected, that was almost the unpardonable sin. To be infected and date a soldier was real bad business, and the courts was dealing with them harshly."

The crusade extended beyond those actually caught in hotel rooms, as police officer Sanders Ivey relates: "I was assigned to the Health Department, and the nurses would have these contacts, get the information and everything, and try to get these people to come in. If somebody came into the clinic, had a blood test and it was positive, they would ask them who their contacts had been. The nurses would try and get them. And if those people would not come in for this examination, they would turn them over to me.

"I prosecuted people, and some of them had to make time because of their failing to take treatment. And of course it was understood with the judge that he would cooperate with us, and we didn't take just everybody down there that we could, but somebody that we was getting a lot of reports on, you know, and they wouldn't take any treatment. Then we'd take them down there and send them to these treatment centers. They took the old stockade building and began to take the patients down there. And you could go down and stay a week and be cured of syphilis, and a day and a night and you'd be cured of gonorrhea. That was about that time when that penicillin first come out, you know. And the government furnished that stuff for free. Venereal disease was so rampant in Atlanta until they had to do something about it."

The soldiers passing through town brought a great deal of trade to local businesses, including the newly opened dry-cleaning establishment of Louise Chandler: "It became a success immediately because it was at the beginning of the war, and we had plenty of business. I recall they were going to ship out a group from the Army and they had to have clean uniforms. And they'd come up here and say 'How quick can you get these uniforms?' I'd say, 'Park out there. Two hours.' We would wash those soldiers' uniforms, we would press them and load them up and away they would go. And I've had sailors come into town and something would happen to their uniform, and they'd come out here."

Form OPA R-535

UNITED STATES OF AMERICA
OFFICE OF PRICE ADMINISTRATION

APPLICATION FOR
SUPPLEMENTAL GASOLINE RATION BOOKS

(FOR SUCH PASSENGER CARS OR MOTORCYCLES
AS ARE PRESCRIBED IN THE REGULATIONS)

This form is to be used by holders of basic gasoline ration Books "A" or "D" in applying for supplemental gasoline ration. Application for an individual may not be signed by an agent.

The registration card of the motor vehicle must be presented before issuance of the ration book. A separate application must be filled out for each motor vehicle for which such ration is desired.

This application is to be used by persons requiring a supplemental ration for the pursuit of business; gainful employment; a regular and recognized course of study; or other work regularly performed which contributes to the war effort or to the public welfare.

It is *not* to be used for taxis, jitneys, vehicles available for public rental or held for resale, ambulances, hearses, Government-owned or Government-leased vehicles, or for a vehicle which is part of a fleet of four or more of the same type used principally for the business or occupational purposes of the same person or organization.

Name of Applicant (Print)

Tracy W. O'Neah
(First) (Middle initial) (Last)

644 Lexington Ave. S.W.
(R. F. D. or street and number)

Atlanta   Ga   Aug-15-1942
(City or post office)   (State)   (Date)

Ration required for period beginning Aug 15- 1942
(Date)

<table>
<tr><td colspan="4">(NOT TO BE FILLED IN BY APPLICANT)
RECORD OF ACTION OF BOARD</td></tr>
<tr><td colspan="2">Date _____</td><td colspan="2">Board No. _____</td></tr>
<tr><td colspan="2">City _____</td><td colspan="2">State _____</td></tr>
<tr><td colspan="4">REJECTED (Check) ☐ or RATION BOOKS ISSUED AS FOLLOWS:</td></tr>
<tr><td>Class of Book</td><td>Serial No.</td><td>Expiration Date</td><td>Number of Coupons in Book</td></tr>
<tr><td></td><td></td><td></td><td></td></tr>
</table>

(Print plainly or type)

Tracy W. O'Neah
(Name of registered owner)

RESIDENCE ADDRESS 644 Lexington Ave SW
(R. F. D or street and number)

Atlanta   Ga
(City or post office)   (State)

BUSINESS ADDRESS #5- Forsyth St
(R. F. D. or street and number)

Atlanta   Ga
(City or post office)   (State)

33839-E
(Vehicle license number)

Ga-
(State of registration)

1940
(Year model)

Dodge
(Make)

4- Door
(Body type)

APPLICATION IS HEREBY MADE FOR A SUPPLEMENTAL GASOLINE RATION FOR OPERATION OF THE MOTOR VEHICLE DESCRIBED ABOVE

Item 1. Has previous application for a supplemental coupon ration book for this vehicle been made by the applicant? (Yes or no) No   If "Yes," state when and where such application was made and action taken thereon _____

Item 2. Is motor vehicle customarily garaged or stationed within the area which this Board is designated to serve? (Yes or no) yes   If "No," give reason for making application to this Board _____

Item 3. Is gasoline from owner's or applicant's own storage tank placed in the fuel tank of this vehicle? (Yes or no) No

Item 4. What is the principal occupation of the principal user of this vehicle? (For example, bookkeeper, machinist, etc.) Newspaper Photographer + Farming + Poultry

Item 5. By whom is he employed? Atlanta Journal -#5 Forsyth St Atlanta Ga.
(Firm name)   (Street address)   (City)   (State)

Item 6. In what industry, business or profession is he employed? (For example, shipbuilding, wholesale grocery, etc.)
Newspaper Photographer.

Item 7. For what purpose or purposes is the vehicle used in the occupation of the principal user? (For example, driving from home to work, repair calls, sales trips, etc.) Driving to + From Work, Emergency Calls, Hauling Poultry Supplies,

(This form may be reproduced)

16—28963-4

Application for supplemental gas rations, 1942. (Special Collections, Georgia State University)

In other ways, too, the war stimulated Atlanta's economy. "Once we started the war effort," states Duncan Peek, "then of course the jobs and the money and everything was just flowing freely. And that just picked up the economy. There was a tremendous amount going on around Atlanta, military-wise. Fort Mac was enlarged. The General Depot was a tremendous thing down at Conley. It's Fort Gillem now. That's the supply base for the Army for the Southeast. It had a very strong impetus on the growth of the city, no question about it. A lot of war industries came in here."

The largest single such firm that settled in the Atlanta area was Bell Aircraft, the forerunner of Lockheed. "I worked at Bell Aircraft during the war," recalls country musician Marion "Peanut" Brown. "People worked at Bell Aircraft, you know, from Alabama and all over Georgia. There was a lot of pretty well-known musicians there from all over the country. We put on shows. Had a theater out there and people would come down from eleven to one o'clock, and we would entertain them. And we got some write-ups on that, and they made a documentary movie of us playing. And then we would also go and put on shows around at the hospitals, Navy hospital, Army, Fort Mac."

With many of the men off at war, Bell Aircraft also provided jobs for Atlanta's versions of Rosie the Riveter, like Catherine Cohen: "A lot of people used to work over there who couldn't go to war, women and men. They had one I bet you was a hundred years old. I worked over there for two years, [building] the B-29. I used to work with electricity, I used to solder. I used to solder plugs. The money was better."

Government work also opened up for some women at least for the duration of the war, often providing both pay and promotion advantages over the private sector. "I was in the auditing department of the War Department," recalls Marian Doom. "There were women in supervisory jobs in the whole building I was in. And that was fairly new then. They had been assistants, but they hadn't been supervisors. But of course the men were taken into the Army, so they had bigger jobs."

"During the war years the government did not discriminate as much as private businesses did," adds Mamie Kimball, who left Sears to go into government work. "If you could qualify for the job, you had a chance at most of them. But I left Sears a little too soon because after so many of the young men had to go into the service they began to promote girls at Sears, the young ladies, into managerial jobs. Then they began to promote women who had been there a long time."

"The Second World War helped out considerably," echoes Marie Townsend,

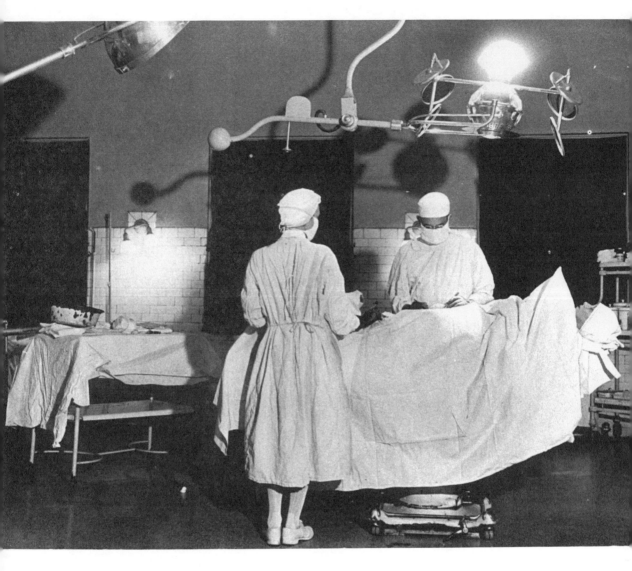

Grady Hospital operating room with special blackout curtains. (Atlanta Journal-Constitution)

a systems analyst for Southern Bell, "because as the men left the women were given their jobs. I really think the war taking place, in the South, was more responsible for women getting better jobs in big companies than anything else. It actually happened to me."

As white women moved into defense work or received promotions, and as black men entered the service, some new opportunities opened up for black women, too. In fact, there existed a widely reported shortage of domestic workers. "I know during the war there was a hard time trying to get help," recalls Yolande Gwin. "It was wartime, and they didn't do domestic work because they got more money otherwise."

"A friend of mine," relates domestic worker Willie Mae Jackson, "her husband went in the Army and he worked at Sears and Roebuck as a tailor. And she went in there and held his job down till he come back out of the Army. And sometime I would do extra work as a waitress at the Biltmore on the weekends, because men were so scarce. And that was very exciting, because so many women were out there doing waitress work because so many waiters had to go away. It was a lot of fun. You made good tips there."

In response to a threatened march on Washington over racism in defense plants and the armed forces, President Roosevelt signed Executive Order 8802 in June 1941, outlawing discrimination in defense contractor and government hiring, and establishing a Fair Employment Practices Committee. Yet, while some black workers did enter defense industries, in Atlanta and elsewhere they remained largely confined to lower paying, more menial positions.[1] "When I worked in Lockheed," recalls Catherine Cohen, "colored people were just to clean up."

Joel Smith, however, was one black citizen who did obtain a better wartime job: "I worked for the aircraft plant during World War II as a counselor. My job was to help apply for gas, tires or whatever they had to have through the Rationing Board. We had a Rationing Board at the plant, and my job as a counselor was to interview those people and see that they got whatever they needed to get on their job every day."

Often depending on the type of work done by the user, both gasoline and tires were rationed in an attempt to conserve rubber for the war effort.[2] "We had gas coupons," remembers Ruby Baker. "And we had to get special certificates to get tires, and retreads at that." "We used to ride around on a bicycle some," relates Coca-Cola executive Hunter Bell. "In fact, we even rode from Peachtree Battle down to go to a movie on our bicycles one night. But there was a medium amount of gas if you had to go to work. We didn't suffer too much."

Celebrating V-J Day. (Atlanta Journal-Constitution*)*

Teacher Evelyn Witherspoon disagrees: "At the beginning of World War II I couldn't get gas. Teaching either was deemed not essential, or they thought I could ride the bus. And in order to get to school on time, I left home at five minutes after 6:00 A.M. I couldn't ride the bus one hour later because it made me five minutes late at school, and that was intolerable."

Meat, sugar, coffee and other foodstuffs were also rationed. As with gasoline, families received coupon books for the amount of these commodities they were supposed to use each month. As with gasoline, these quotas often were lower than a family's actual consumption level. And, as with gasoline, Atlantans could find ways to get around the ration system. "The tickets give out," explains barber Horace Sinclair, "you'd got to go get you some more tickets so you could buy, don't you see. There was a black market all right, even on the gas."

"There was a big black market going on for gas," remembers Ruby Baker, "if you had the money to buy it. There were some service stations that even would sell you gas without coupons. There were people that would apply for cards, that didn't even drive, and sell them."

"I remember an incident during the time of rationing," relates Nell Blackshear. "I went out to buy some meat on Memorial Drive. I had been buying meat there before the rationing thing come along. And this man said, 'Keep that card and go on to another store. I have some excess meat here.' He would let you have it and let you take your rationing card to another to show that you still had your card and hadn't overdone it."

Sugar rationing extended to soft drinks, including Atlanta's best-known product, Coca-Cola. Realizing the potential impact on sales, Coke successfully lobbied to exclude the military from sugar rationing, then obtained the soft drink contract with the armed forces, and literally followed the troops on three continents, thereby greatly expanding its worldwide influence and cementing its hold on American GIs.[3] "Eisenhower sent a telegram back from Algiers," states Hunter Bell. " 'Send eight Coca-Cola bottling plants.' And he moved over to Italy and to Paris. They had a big bottling plant there. They bottled it in England. In the campaign in the Pacific they built some bottling plants. They had bottling plants in Taiwan. They bottled it behind the lines wherever it could be. Before the thing was over we sent two or three hundred bottling plants over the world.

"Our people had a simulated rank. They were not officers but they had a simulated rank of captain or major or something. We sent technicians out to be sure the product was right. We even made what you call portable backpacks you could carry on your back and take right up to the line and serve it to the men, almost in combat.

"Whenever they heard that there was a bottling plant out there, they'd send trucks a hundred miles to get a load of it. It reminded them of home, it was something familiar—'There's a bottle I know at home. Same bottle, same price, same drink.' The military appreciated it. It was still selling for a nickel and it went all over the world."

Back home, the government set up Civilian Defense groups to act in the event of an enemy attack. "There was quite a concern," relates J. McDowell Richards of Columbia Theological Seminary, "as to the possibility that American cities might be subject to bombing. And Atlanta was among the cities which prepared. Some were convinced that as a transportation center of strategic importance in the Southeast, this would be one of the very first targets of the bombers. So, the defense teams were organized to be on guard and be prepared to respond to fires and casualties."

"They had different Red Cross training, for emergencies, in case of bombing," recalls corset shop worker Cassie Dollar. "And I took those courses. We had places we had to go so many nights a week to take training. Blocks were set up by volunteers, and most of them were men in the neighborhood. You had an air raid signal. When that air raid thing come on, they went out on the streets, the men who were in charge, and everybody else was supposed to get inside and turn out all lights everywhere."

"I remember at my house one night," recounts Yolande Gwin, "we heard a car come in the driveway, and Mother peeped out behind the black shade. And somebody banged on the door, and my father said, 'Who is it?' Said, 'It's Civilian Defense.' Said, 'You have lights peeping out from behind the black shades.'"

"Usually these blackouts lasted for several hours," recalls J. McDowell Richards. "People were thus prepared for the day when the Germans would arrive, which fortunately they did not."

"Then the boys started coming back home," says Gwin, "and so many people married their beaus, which had gone to war and everything. Things started picking up. Dancing started again and the other debutante club came up that year. And everything started over, you know, with the parties and everything."

Yet, life in Atlanta was different after the war. "You had what you might call the beginning of the modern Atlanta," states Emory University professor Earl Brewer. "And the boom time was just upcoming." "After the World War started the real boom," seconds Georgia Power Company engineer Roy Harwell. Adds Mamie Kimball, "Then Atlanta began to grow."

"I went in the Navy in 1943," relates Techwood Homes resident Waldo Roescher. "When I got back and went back to the post office my salary was over the limit [for public housing], but they would make us move then, because there wasn't any housing available. See, Atlanta became kind of a boom town during the war and the population rose, and nobody had any money to build houses. Everything went towards the war effort. Weren't any houses being built and you couldn't find a place to buy or even rent hardly."

"During the war years it was definitely hard to find an apartment," echoes Mamie Kimball. "During the Depression there were so many vacancies, you could almost get your pick. But that became history. It was replaced by 'no vacancy' signs."

"There were a lot of people from outside Atlanta who came in," adds Marian Doom. "The activity all around us of the Air Force and the Army and so forth brought a lot of good interesting people into the city. A lot of the boys who were stationed around here liked it in the South, and a great many of them came back to live. I think that's had a lot to do with why the city has changed so and grown so."

As important, perhaps, were the broadening experiences that people from Atlanta and the region had during the war. "I had never known anybody except from the South, you know," relates Eliza Paschall, who served with the Red Cross from 1943 to 1945. "It was all I had known. You met people from Iowa and New Jersey and really weird places that you never in your life thought you were going to meet. New York. Until that time, there was no occasion or way, really, to get out of the South."

"World War II had a profound experience on the whole culture," says John Griffin, "and part of that influence certainly touched on traditional attitudes and values in regard to race. For example, one of the most important of those who headed the Southern Regional Council, Harold Fleming, was a Georgian. He grew up partly in south Georgia and partly in Atlanta. And Harold Fleming, during World War II, was an officer in charge, I believe, of a company of black soldiers in the South Pacific. That experience led Harold Fleming to a new understanding of race relations and the problems of race relations. When he came back to Atlanta and was looking for a job he went to Ralph McGill,[4] told him about his experience and said, 'I want to find some work that's sort of related to this.' Ralph McGill said, 'Go on down there on Auburn Avenue. There's an outfit called the Southern Regional Council. Maybe they've got something for you to do.'"

Founded in 1944, the Atlanta-based Southern Regional Council, a leading lib-

Soldiers celebrating Nazi surrender, May 7, 1945. (Atlanta
Journal-Constitution*)*

News vendor, May 7, 1945. (Atlanta Journal-Constitution*)*

eral organization in the South for decades, was itself a product of the changes taking place in race relations during the war years. Labor leader A. Philip Randolph's March on Washington movement heralded a new level of mass militancy among black Americans. The black press developed the theme of the two-front war—-fighting for democracy at home as well as abroad. And Southern black leaders began to speak out more openly against segregation itself.[5] "The fact that we were fighting as a democratic force against Naziism," explains John Griffin, "the Four Freedoms speech of Roosevelt, for example, and the whole ideological bag that was a part of the rhetoric of the day was inconsistent with practices that had been going on in this part of the country for a long, long time.

"The council came together through a challenge which was put together by the black community in Durham, North Carolina, the so-called Durham Statement. This was kind of a challenge to the leadership of the white South to do something important about the problems of race relations. And this was responded to by an Atlanta Statement, a statement that was drawn up here. And I believe there was a Richmond Statement, too. And these statements and responses produced the initial meeting of a new organization called the Southern Regional Council.

"The council got off to a very good start. It continued an education program and had some people very skilled in writing material. But it didn't tackle head-on the problem of segregation. The council was pushed hard toward taking a position on segregation by several people. A man who pressed the point hard was Al Dent, the president of Dillard University [in New Orleans]. He brought it up at one meeting, two meetings, and no action was taken. He pushed it again and said, 'You know, we've got some unfinished business that we've got to address. We've got to face the business of where do we stand on segregation in this region.' And at that time the council took a position."

"The climate was a little more moderate than it was in the thirties," allows Earl Brewer, who returned to Atlanta in 1946. "There was a little more openness—not a great deal more, but there was a little more openness. And the leadership of some whites and blacks was moving towards a more moderate position, you might say. But segregation and political incorporation of the biracial society was still dominant."

Indeed, despite the changes the war years brought, the segregated society stayed solidly intact for decades. Black Atlantans continued to be sicker and to die earlier than whites, black workers continued to get lower pay. Atlanta's busses remained segregated until the late 1950s, Atlanta's schools until the 1960s. It was not until the modern civil rights movement and subsequent fed-

Overleaf: Celebrating V-J Day. (*Atlanta* Journal-Constitution)

eral legislation that black residents could eat anywhere they wished, that black patients could enter any hospital in the city. "You do not realize how tight that the whole idea of segregation was at that point in history," exclaims Atlanta University professor Frankie Adams. "Even as late as 1961, there were no places downtown where Negro and white people could sit down and have lunch. At that time students and others were boycotting downtown places."

"There was a time when you couldn't eat," remembers Lucile Scott. "Now you can eat anywhere you want to eat, *if* you've got the money. There were times when you had to go to the back door if you wanted to see the New York plays. But you can go in the front door now. I've seen so many changes in Atlanta. Things seem to have gotten better."

The sweeping transformations of the fifties and sixties could not have occurred without developments in both the black and the white communities during the period between the world wars. "All of it came out of that," declares Reverend William Holmes Borders. "You had police, you had better schools, you had desegregation of all the means of travel. You had hotels, you had restaurants, you had eating counters—all of it desegregated, everything. All of the stuff that [Martin Luther] King did had a lot of this as the foundation before he moved. See, we had built a foundation for him to stand on."

The dramatic changes that have taken place in Atlanta since World War II have tended to obliterate the city's segregated past. "Now, you see," remarks Nell Blackshear, "a lot of people don't remember those days, but there were those days." For many, the memories of segregation remain bitter and painful. "It was a terrible thing," states barber Dan Stephens, "and now I don't like to think of it too much, I don't like to remind myself of it. It was a kind of terrible thing." "I remember how I felt then," recalls Ruby Baker. "It just made me sick. I don't care if I am able to go to the top of the Peachtree Plaza now, I can still remember what was done to us."

Appendix:

Living Atlanta Interviewees

Lloyd Adair	streetcar worker
Alice Adams	domestic worker
Frankie Adams	Atlanta University School of Social Work professor
Kathleen Adams	Atlanta University alumna; school teacher
C. R. Adamson	train conductor
Annie Alexander	centenarian; nurse
James Anderson**	physician
Clarence Bacote	Atlanta University professor
Ruby Baker**	nurse
D. I. "Red" Barron	Georgia Tech football star
E. B. Baynes	witness to 1917 Fire
B. B. Beamon	hotel worker; music promoter
Hunter Bell	Atlanta *Journal* editor; Coca-Cola executive
Walter Bell	Atlanta Public Schools historian
Sol Beton	artist; Sephardic community member
Nell Blackshear	social worker; director black USO
Mrs. J. B. Blayton	widow of first black CPA in Georgia
Dorothy Bolden	maid; founder National Domestic Workers Union
J. H. Bond	train conductor
William Holmes Borders	Wheat Street Baptist Church pastor
James T. Bowen	policeman
James P. Brawley	Clark College dean and president
B. R. Brazeal	Morehouse College alumnus and dean
Earl Brewer	Emory alumnus and professor
Hallie Brooks	Atlanta University librarian
Emma Rush Brown	Atlanta University alumna
Marion "Peanut" Brown	country musician; Bell Aircraft worker
John Calhoun	Atlanta *Daily World* staff member; Republican

Jack Cathcart   band musician
Louise Chandler   first woman dry cleaner in Atlanta
Estelle Clemmons   Washington High School teacher
William Coates   band musician
Ann Scarlett Cochran   Clark College alumna
Warren Cochrane   executive director, Butler Street YMCA
Catherine Cohen   refugee from Nazi Germany; Bell Aircraft worker
Julia Fountain Coles   Morris Brown College alumna and professor
Solomon Coles   Morehouse College graduate
James Colvard   train porter
T. R. Couch   streetcar worker
Mattie Culbreath   witness to 1917 Fire
William Culbreath   witness to 1917 Fire
Lula Daugherty   domestic; early resident of Atlanta's public housing
Leila Denmark   pediatrician
Alec Dennis   textile worker; city worker
Cassie Dollar   corset shop worker
Marian Doom   bookkeeper
Pearlie Dove   Washington High School graduate
Edwin Driskell   band musician
Augusta Dunbar   New Deal social worker
Roy Dunn   blues musician
Frank Edwards   blues musician
Fred Ferguson   train fireman
Clarence Fiebelman   businessman
T. J. Flanagan   Atlanta *Daily World* staff member
Edwin Fraport   train porter
Calvin Freeman   textile worker
Opal Futch   New Deal social worker
Jack Gay   refugee from Nazi Germany
Louis Geffen   attorney; school board member
Clara Gibson   early resident of Atlanta's public housing
T. G. Goodrun   train engineer
Dexter Gray   train porter
Effie Gray   textile worker
James Greene   Atlanta Black Crackers baseball player
John Griffin   Emory alumnus; Georgia Tech professor
Yolande Gwin   Atlanta *Journal* society reporter
Durise Hanson   nurse
Billie Harden   Atlanta Black Crackers owner
C. C. Hart   plumber

Phoebe Hart	Clark College dean; church worker
Mrs. B. T. Harvey	Atlanta University alumna; widow of Morehouse College coach
Roy Harwell	civil engineer
Voncele Heggood	early resident of Atlanta's public housing
Edith Henderson	Techwood Homes landscape architect
Ardell Henry	factory worker; faith healer
Josephine Heyman	member of liberal and Jewish organizations
Frank Hicks	textile worker
H. Waldo Hitt	train engineer
Matthew Housch	train porter
H. Reid Hunter	assistant superintendent, Atlanta Public Schools
Arthur Idlett	Morehouse College alumnus; Atlanta Black Crackers baseball player
Sanders Ivey	policeman
Willie Mae Jackson	maid; sister of blues musician Barbecue Bob
H. E. James	streetcar worker
Henry James	train porter
Herbert Jenkins	police chief
Rosa Lee Carson Johnson	country musician "Moonshine Kate"
Edward A. Jones	Morehouse College alumnus; Atlanta University professor
Flossie Jones	Washington High School teacher
Millicent Dobbs Jordan	Spelman alumna and professor
L. D. Keith	chauffeur
Laurie Keith	Summerhill resident
James "Gabby" Kemp	Atlanta Black Crackers player-manager
Adele Kendrick	early resident of Atlanta's west side
Mamie Kimball	businesswoman
Martin Luther King, Sr.	Ebenezer Baptist Church pastor
Mildred Kingloff	attorney
Sam Laird	Emory University chaplain
E. T. Lewis	Washington High School teacher
Clifford Lovins	textile worker
Katie Lovins	textile worker
E. R. Lyon	one of Atlanta's first black police officers
Devereaux McClatchey	attorney; school board member
Mrs. E. Graham McDonald	daughter of Atlanta mayor James L. Key
Hugh McDonald	fireman during 1917 Fire
Margaret MacDougall	liberal; widow of New Dealer Robert MacDougall
O. R. McKibbons	one of Atlanta's first black police officers

Annie McPheeters	Spelman College alumna; librarian
Kate McTell	nurse; widow of Blind Willie McTell
Beulah Mackay	United Church Women member
Baxter Maddox	banker
Ella Martin	beauty shop owner
Benjamin Mays	Morehouse College president
I. H. Mehaffey	streetcar worker
Ethel Meyers	Jewish community member; centenarian
Nina King Miller	witness to 1917 Fire
Eloise Milton	Atlanta University alumna
L. D. Milton	Citizens Trust Bank president; University Homes trustee
Pauline Minniefield	Atlanta University alumna
James "Red" Moore	Atlanta Black Crackers baseball player
James Moore	train porter
J. Y. Moreland	Washington High School graduate; associate school superintendent
Mary Morton	domestic worker
Eugene "Buddy" Moss	blues musician
Samuel Nabritt	Morehouse College alumnus and professor
Homer Nash	physician
A. L. Nelson	streetcar worker
John Ottley	Atlanta *Journal* reporter; airline executive
Ruby Owens	domestic worker
George Palmer	train fireman
Joe Parr	country musician
Eliza Paschall	Agnes Scott alumna; liberal
Walter Payne	storekeeper
Duncan Peek	businessman; Jaycees president
S. G. Peeples	policeman
Ida Prather	Neighborhood Union member
Blanche Puckett	widow of musician Riley Puckett
Mildred Quarterman	Clark College alumna
Glenn Rainey	Emory alumnus; Georgia Tech professor
Willie Rakestraw	early resident of Atlanta's public housing
Arthur Raper	Commission on Interracial Cooperation staff member
Ruth Reese	teacher
J. McDowell Richards	Columbia Theological Seminary president
George Robertson	policeman
Waldo Roescher	early resident of Atlanta's public housing
James Ross	early resident of Atlanta's public housing

M. Y. "Pete" Rutherford	policeman
C. A. Scott	Atlanta *Daily World* publisher
Lucile Scott	widow of Atlanta *Daily World* founder
Harold Sheats	East Point attorney; Ku Klux Klan leader
Irwin Shields	jeweler; worker in coroner's office
A. J. Shupe	streetcar worker
Horace Sinclair	barber
Lester Smallwood	country musician
Joel Smith	Atlanta *Daily World* reporter
Stella Smith	witness to 1917 Fire
Nesbitt Spinks	textile worker; lay preacher
J. R. Spratlin	train fireman and engineer
Dan Stephens	barber
Preston Stevens, Sr.	Techwood Homes architect
Louise Mack Strong	Atlanta University alumna and faculty member
Gordon Tanner	country musician and son of Gid Tanner
Marie Townsend	Agnes Scott alumna; statistician
Forrest Turner	hauler of illegal alcohol
Bazoline Usher	Atlanta University alumna; Washington High School assistant principal
Wilma Van Dusseldorp	New Deal social worker
Mattie Varner	midwife; centenarian
Nanny Washburn	textile worker; radical
Evelyn Witherspoon	school teacher
Samuel Young	railroad executive
**pseudonym	

Not all those individuals interviewed for the Living Atlanta radio series appear in the book.

Notes

Introduction

1. Scott Ellsworth, *Death in the Promised Land* (Baton Rouge: Louisiana State University Press, 1981).

Chapter One: World War I

1. Howard L. Preston, *Automobile Age Atlanta: The Making of a Southern Metropolis* (Athens: University of Georgia Press, 1979), p. 51.
2. For descriptions of deteriorating race relations at the turn of the century, see C. Vann Woodward, *The Strange Career of Jim Crow* (New York: Oxford University Press, 1974); Rayford W. Logan, *The Betrayal of the Negro* (New York: Macmillan, 1970); and Joel Williamson, *The Crucible of Race* (New York: Oxford University Press, 1984).
3. The name used here is a pseudonym.
4. See Bertram W. Doyle, *The Etiquette of Race Relations in the South* (Chicago: University of Chicago Press, 1937), for a general discussion of race-linked behavior in the region during the period.
5. A great deal has been written on this case. See, for instance, Leonard Dinnerstein, *The Leo Frank Case* (New York: Columbia University Press, 1968).
6. See Kenneth T. Jackson, *The Ku Klux Klan in the City* (New York: Oxford University Press, 1967); Robert K. Murray, *The 103rd Ballot* (New York: Harper and Row, 1976).
7. For one account of the fire, see Steve B. Campbell, "The Great Fire of Atlanta, May 21, 1917," *Atlanta Historical Bulletin* 13 (June 1968): 9–48.
8. By this time double sessions were outlawed in the white schools.
9. White Atlanta women had, however, already voted in city elections.

Chapter Two: Neighborhoods

1. Works Progress Administration, *Report of the Real Property, Land Use and Low Income Housing Area Survey of Metropolitan Atlanta* (Atlanta, 1940), p. 53.

2. See *Atlanta Historical Journal* 26 (Summer-Fall 1982), especially Timothy J. Crimmins, "The Atlanta Palimpsest: Stripping Away the Layers of the Past," pp. 13–32, for a good discussion of the diverse influences shaping Atlanta's growth.

3. Crimmins, "The Atlanta Palimpsest," pp. 28–29; Don Klima, "Breaking Out: Streetcars and Suburban Development, 1872–1900," *Atlanta Historical Journal* 26 (Summer-Fall 1982): 67, 72.

4. Crimmins, "The Atlanta Palimpsest," p. 26.

5. Dana F. White, "The Black Sides of Atlanta: A Geography of Expansion and Containment, 1970–1870," *Atlanta Historical Journal* 26 (Summer-Fall 1982): 215–16; Alexa Henderson and Eugene Walker, *Sweet Auburn: The Thriving Hub of Black Atlanta, 1900–1960* (Martin Luther King, Jr., National Historic Site and Preservation District), p. 17.

6. White, "The Black Sides of Atlanta," p. 215.

7. Ibid.

8. Timothy J. Crimmins, "Bungalow Suburbs: East and West," *Atlanta Historical Journal* 26 (Summer-Fall 1982): 90–91.

9. The Ashby Street School had recently shifted from an all-white to an all-black school.

10. White, "The Black Sides of Atlanta," pp. 199, 203, 220–22.

11. Charles F. Palmer, *Adventures of a Slum Fighter* (New York: Van Rees Press, 1955); Florence Fleming Corley, "Atlanta's Techwood and University Homes Projects: The Nation's Laboratory for Public Housing," *Atlanta History* 31 (Winter 1987–88): 17–36.

12. Corley, "Atlanta's Techwood," pp. 17–29.

13. Liquor became fully legalized again in Fulton County in 1938.

Chapter Three: Transportation

1. A. Philip Randolph founded the Brotherhood of Sleeping Car Porters.

2. Sterling D. Spero and Abram L. Harris, *The Black Worker* (New York: Atheneum, 1972), pp. 284, 307.

3. Ibid., pp. 289–99; John Michael Matthews, "The Georgia 'Race Strike' of 1909," *Journal of Southern History* 40 (November 1974): 613–30; William H. Harris, *The Harder We Run: Black Workers Since the Civil War* (New York: Oxford University Press, 1982), p. 71.

4. Harris, *The Harder We Run,* p. 48.
5. Preston, *Automobile Age Atlanta,* p. 49.
6. For years Georgia Railway and Power owned an interest in the Atlanta Crackers baseball club.
7. Preston, *Automobile Age Atlanta,* p. 51.

Chapter Four: Commerce

1. See Preston, *Automobile Age Atlanta,* especially pp. 113–25, 132–34.
2. Henderson and Walker, *Sweet Auburn,* pp. 15–16.
3. Crimmins, "Bungalow Suburbs," pp. 90–91.
4. Julia Kirk Blackwelder, "Quiet Suffering: Atlanta Women in the 1930s," *Georgia Historical Quarterly* 61 (Summer 1977): 116.
5. Ibid., p. 117; Blackwelder, "Mop and Typewriter: Women's Work in Early Twentieth Century Atlanta," *Atlanta Historical Journal* 27 (Fall 1983): 21–30.

Chapter Five: Education

1. Philip Noel Racine, "Atlanta's Schools: A History of the Public School System, 1869–1955" (Ph.D. dissertation, Emory University, 1969), p. 193.
2. Boys' High School was located across from the Municipal Auditorium on Courtland Street until 1924. Girls' High was catty-corner from the Capitol until 1925, when it moved near Grant Park.
3. Henry Reid Hunter, "The Development of the Public Secondary Schools of Atlanta, Georgia, 1845–1937" (Ph.D. dissertation, Columbia University, 1937).
4. Tech High School was on Marietta Street from 1909 to 1924. Commercial High was located on South Pryor Street near Garnett.
5. Hunter, "The Development of the Public Secondary Schools," p. 177.
6. Racine, "Atlanta's Schools," p. 230; Jackson, *The Ku Klux Klan in the City,* pp. 33, 39.
7. Racine, "Atlanta's Schools," pp. 182–83, 247.
8. The Sunset was an amusement park and dance hall at the corner of Sunset and Magnolia streets.
9. Racine, "Atlanta's Schools," pp. 193, 247, 312–13.
10. Ibid., p. 200.
11. Ibid., p. 193.
12. Hunter, "The Development of the Public Secondary Schools," pp. 98–99.
13. Ibid., pp. 92–94.
14. Ibid., p. 95; Racine, "Atlanta's Schools," p. 286.
15. George A. Sewell and Cornelius V. Troup, *Morris Brown College: The*

First Hundred Years (Atlanta, 1981), p. 181.

16. The General Education Board, a Rockefeller-related philanthropy, was the principal financial backer of Southern secondary education.

Chapter Six: Underside

1. As has been noted elsewhere, Ruby Baker is a pseudonym.
2. The man Ruby Baker is recalling was immortalized in Sterling Brown's poem "The Last Ride of Wild Bill," a colorful portrait of numbers running in Atlanta.
3. Madison is now part of Spring Street south of Alabama. Collins Street ran directly under the site of Georgia State University.

Chapter Seven: Depression and New Deal

1. Charles H. Martin, *The Angelo Herndon Case and Southern Justice* (Baton Rouge: Louisiana State University Press, 1978), p. 17.
2. Ibid., pp. 2–4.
3. Ibid., p. 6.
4. Ibid., pp. 83–96, 211 and passim.
5. Douglas L. Fleming, "The New Deal in Atlanta: A Review of the Major Programs," *Atlanta Historical Journal* 30 (Spring 1986): 23–45.
6. Ibid., pp. 25–26; Michael S. Holmes, *The New Deal in Georgia* (Westport, Conn.: Greenwood Press, 1975), pp. 2–3, 10–11, 23, and passim.
7. Holmes, *The New Deal in Georgia*, pp. 44–45, 48–50; Fleming, "The New Deal in Atlanta," pp. 25–31.
8. Holmes, *The New Deal in Georgia*, pp. 185–87.
9. Fleming, "The New Deal in Atlanta," pp. 33–34.
10. This account of textiles and the 1934 strike owes much to Jacquelyn Hall, Robert Korstad, James Leloudis, Mary Murphy, Lu Ann Jones, and Christopher B. Daly, *Like a Family: The Making of a Southern Textile World* (Chapel Hill: University of North Carolina Press, 1987). See also John Allen, "The Governor and the Strike: Eugene Talmadge and the General Strike, 1934" (M.A. thesis, Georgia State University, 1977).
11. Neill Herring and Sue Thrasher, "UAW Sit-down Strike, Atlanta, 1936," *Southern Exposure* 1 (Winter 1974): 63–83.
12. Fleming, "The New Deal in Atlanta," pp. 36–38.
13. Holmes, *The New Deal in Georgia*, pp. 99–103, 110–11.
14. See also Fleming, "The New Deal in Atlanta," p. 28, for another version of the story.
15. Holmes, *The New Deal in Georgia*, p. 159.
16. Fleming, "The New Deal in Atlanta," pp. 40–41.

Chapter Eight: Health and Religion

1. Atlanta's charity hospital, Grady first opened to the public in January 1892.
2. The name used here is a pseudonym.
3. Battle Hill was the city's tuberculosis sanitorium, and one of the few public sites outside Grady Hospital where black patients could be admitted.

Chapter Nine: Leisure

1. The Clowns, also known as the Ethiopian Clowns, were owned by Globetrotters owner Abe Saperstein, a major figure in the booking of black baseball.
2. For a comprehensive treatment of Atlanta's blues scene, see the booklet accompanying the record "Atlanta Blues 1933," JEMF-106, John Edwards Memorial Foundation, Inc., 1979. See also Bruce Bastin, *Red River Blues: The Blues Tradition in the Southeast* (Urbana: University of Illinois Press, 1986).
3. For a good account of Fiddlin' John and the Georgia hillbilly music scene, see Gene Wiggins, *Fiddlin' Georgia Crazy: Fiddlin' John Carson, His Real World and the World of His Songs* (Urbana: University of Illinois Press, 1987). See also John A. Burrison, "Fiddlers in the Alley: Atlanta as an Early Country Music Center," *Atlanta Historical Bulletin* 21 (Summer 1977): 59–87.
4. The Kimball House was a famous hotel on Pryor Street dating back to the nineteenth century.
5. Wiggins, *Fiddlin' Georgia Crazy,* pp. 73–75.
6. Burrison, "Fiddlers in the Alley," pp. 83, 105.
7. Ibid., pp. 46–60.
8. The site of the fair was the present-day Lakewood Fair Grounds in South Atlanta.
9. Leide directed an early version of the Atlanta Symphony, which lasted from 1920 until it went under during the Depression years. Under the auspices of the Atlanta Music Club, the current symphony was reorganized in 1947.
10. For a summary of WSB's history, see *Welcome South, Brother: Fifty Years of Broadcasting at* WSB, *Atlanta, Georgia* (Atlanta: Cox Broadcasting Corporation, 1974).
11. Ibid., p. 26.

Chapter Ten: Politics

1. Mercer Griffin Evans, "A History of the Organized Labor Movement in Georgia" (Ph.D. dissertation, University of Chicago, 1929).

2. Jackson, *The Ku Klux Klan in the City*, p. 5.
3. Ibid., pp. xii, 37, 262n.
4. Ibid., pp. 30, 32, 33, 39, 42.

5. Harold H. Martin, *William Berry Hartsfield* (Athens: University of Georgia Press, 1978), p. 42.

Chapter Eleven: World War II

1. See Harris, *The Harder We Run*, pp. 115–17; and Richard M. Dalfiume, "The 'Forgotten Years' of the Negro Revolution," in Bernard Sternsher, ed., *The Negro in Depression and War* (Chicago: Quadrangle Books, 1969), pp. 305–6.
2. Richard Pollenberg, *War and Society: The United States, 1941–1945* (Philadelphia: J. P. Lippincott, 1972), pp. 14–18.
3. E. J. Kahn, *The Big Drink* (New York: Random House, 1960).
4. McGill was editor, and later publisher, of the Atlanta *Constitution*.
5. Dalfiume, "The 'Forgotten Years,'" pp. 298–316.

Index